ROADS TO NOWHERE

By the same author

Pyrenean High Route: A Ski Mountaineering Odyssey
Wheathampstead, UK: Tiercel Publishing, 2000

ROADS TO NOWHERE

A South Arabian Odyssey
1960–1965

John Harding

Foreword by
The Rt. Hon. The Lord Luce KG GCVO

Arabian Publishing

Roads to Nowhere: A South Arabian Odyssey, 1960–1965

by John Harding

© John Harding, 2009

First published in 2009 by Arabian Publishing Ltd
4 Bloomsbury Place, London WC1A 2QA
Email: arabian.publishing@arabia.uk.com

Editor: William Facey

A catalogue card for this book is available from the British Library

ISBN: 978-0-9558894-2-4

Typesetting and digital artwork by Jamie Crocker, Artista-Design, UK

Printed and bound by ScandBook AB, Sweden

When eventually I made my choice, I did not realise that the road had no signpost and led to nowhere. ... At the start of my journey, I did not know that I was going to nowhere, nor did I know how full of travellers is that broad highway, nor how much of adventure and companionship the traveller can find as he wanders down it. When at last the end of the road is reached and the weary traveller exclaims, "I have got nowhere!" he can count himself richer by the philosophy, learned in a hard school, which allows him to say so with a certain satisfaction.

The Master of Belhaven (Lt.-Col. The Hon. R. A. B. Hamilton),
The Kingdom of Melchior, p. 1

Contents

List of Photographs

All photographs were taken by John Harding, 1960–65, unless indicated otherwise.

Between pp. 96 and 97

1. Aden: Jebel Shamsan and Steamer Point from Al-Ittihad.
2. Aden Port with Little Aden across the harbour. The Secretariat is the whitewashed building on the quayside to the extreme left.
3. A stitched fishing *sanbuq* below Ras Boradli, looking across the water towards Little Aden.
4. The dhow harbour at Ma'alla, Aden.
5. A picnic near Kirsh, Amour, north-west of Lahej. From the left: Kenyon, Pirie-Girdon and Guillet.
6. The "Indian Gate", Mukalla (since demolished).
7. The Residency, Mukalla.
8. Mukalla: Al-Bilad and harbour.
9. Mukalla: the palace of the Qu'aiti Sultan.
10. Mukalla: Sir William Luce's farewell visit.
11. HH Sultan 'Awadh Al-Qu'aiti of Mukalla (left), with the Amir Ghalib.
12. The view from the author's house, Mukalla: the camel park at Therib.
13. Bedouin cameleers from the interior at Therib, Mukalla.
14. Mukalla's Armed Forces assembled at Riyan. Right to left: Qu'aiti Armed Constabulary, Hadhrami Bedouin Legion, Mukalla Regular Army.
15. Residency staff at Mukalla in Col. Boustead's time. Front row, left to right: Abdullah Shawtah, Pat Booker, Jock Snell, Willie Wise, Col. Boustead, Ralph Daly, Cen Jones, George Coles. Second row, centre: Michael Crouch, with 'Isa Musallam to his right. Official Aden Government photograph.
16. Sir Charles Johnston takes the salute outside the Residency, Mukalla.
17. Arthur Watts with John Lanfear.

18. Fisherman up from Fuwwa, near Mukalla.

19. The launch of Mukalla's crayfish industry: Alec White and Ali Maas.

20. Sayun in Wadi Hadhramaut, capital of the Kathiri State.

21. The Kathiri Sultan's palace, Sayun.

22. Well outside Shibam, Wadi Hadhramaut.

23. The main square of Shibam.

24. Husn al-'Abr, in the Northern Deserts.

25. Camels of the Sai'ar at Al-'Abr.

26. An elder of the Sai'ar in the Northern Deserts.

27. At the edge of the Sands, Northern Deserts.

28. The well at Thamud, Northern Deserts.

29. My team for the return journey from Thamud.

30. Salim Baraghan, Desert Guard, my driver back to Sayun from the Northern Deserts

31. A gazelle for the pot in the Northern Deserts. 'Umar Al-Sai'ari stands to the left; Salim Baraghan holds the rifle.

Between pp. 216 and 217

32. The fair at Meshhed, Wadi Hadhramaut.

33. Camel loaded with fodder at the fair at Meshhed.

34. Women and livestock at the fair at Meshhed.

35. Laudar, capital of the 'Audhali State, Western Aden Protectorate.

36. The Dhala' Plateau in the Amiri State, Western Aden Protectorate. The Assistant Adviser's house stands left of centre, with British Army lines to the rear.

37. The summit of Jebel Jihaf, looking over the Qataba plain below.

38. En route to Sha'ib, Dhala': Godfrey Meynell in white shirt; John Malcolm seated.

39. 'Awabil, capital of Sha'ib.

40. A Saladin descending the Khuraiba Pass.

41. Thumair Fort, Radfan: British Ferret and Saladin armour.

42. Qaid Haidar Al-Habili, Federal Guard Commander, during the Wadi Misrah operation, Radfan.

43. Godfrey Meynell goes to war, Wadi Misrah, Radfan.

44. Advance up the Wadi Misrah, Radfan.

45. Sultanic palaces in Lahej.

46. Subaihi: village poverty with backdrop of Yemen mountains.

Abbreviations

AA	Assistant Adviser (aka Political Officer)
AACA	Assistant Adviser Coastal Areas, (EAP)
AAND	Assistant Adviser Northern Deserts (EAP)
AAR	Assistant Adviser, Residency (EAP)
ACS	Assistant Chief Secretary, Aden
ADC	Aide de camp
AIC	Aden Intelligence Centre
AISLC	Aden Internal Security Liaison Committee
APL	Aden Protectorate Levies (subsequently Federal Regular Army)
APT	Aden Port Trust
ARAMCO	Arabian American Oil Company
ATUC	Aden Trades Union Congress
AWOL	Absent Without Leave
BA	British Agent (Head of British advisory cadres in Eastern and Western Protectorates respectively)
BP	British Petroleum
CDC	Commonwealth Development Corporation
CD&W Scheme	Colonial Development and Welfare Scheme. British government funded development projects
CSM	Company Sergeant-Major
DBA	Deputy British Agent
DMS	Deputy Ministerial Secretary, Aden
EAP	Eastern Aden Protectorate
EAS	East African Shillings (Aden's official currency)
EXCO	Aden Colony's Executive Council
FG/FNG	Federal Guard/ Federal National Guard
FIO	Field Intelligence Officer
FLOSY	Front for the Liberation of Occupied South Yemen
FRA	Federal Regular Army
GSO2	General Service Officer
HBL	Hadhrami Bedouin Legion

HE	His Excellency (The Governor of Aden, 1937–63; High Commissioner for Aden, 1963–67)
HMG	Her Majesty's Government
HMOCS	Her Majesty's Overseas Civil Service (formerly Colonial Service)
HPS	Hadhrami Pump Scheme
ISC	The Deputy High Commissioner's Internal Security Committee, Aden
JAA	Junior Assistant Adviser
KSLI	King's Shropshire Light Infantry
LEGCO	Aden Colony's Legislative Council
LIC	Local Intelligence Committee, Aden
MARA	Military Adviser to the Resident Adviser, EAP
MRA	Mukalla Regular Army
NLF	National Liberation Front
PCL	Petroleum Concessions Limited
PDRY	People's Democratic Republic of Yemen
POL	Political Officer (aka Assistant Adviser)
PSP	People's Socialist Party
PWD	Public Works Department
QAC	Qu'aiti Armed Constabulary
QTG	Qutaibi Tribal Guards
RABA (or RA)	Resident Adviser & British Agent, Mukalla (responsible for EAP)
RAF	Royal Air Force
RASC	Royal Army Service Corps
RSM	Regimental Sergeant-Major
R/T	Radio Telecommunications
SA	Senior Adviser
SAA	Senior Assistant Adviser
SAL	South Arabian League
SAS	Special Air Service
SIS	Secret Intelligence Service
SOAS	School of Oriental and African Studies, London University
SQMS	Senior Quarter Master Sergeant
TOP	Temporary Occupation Permit
UNP	United National Party
WAP	Western Aden Protectorate
YAR	Yemen Arab Republic (1962–90)

Foreword

T HE BRITISH EMPIRE is long dead, yet it will always remain a fundamentally important component in the history of our nation. In order to understand the significance of that imperial era, it behoves us to preserve the records of those of us who had the privilege of colonial service during the Empire's closing years, so as to add detail to the bigger picture.

John Harding has given us a trenchant and entertaining account of his own service in Her Majesty's Overseas Civil Service in South Arabia from 1960 to 1965. Having myself served as a District Officer in Kenya at roughly the same time, I came to realize, like him, how fortunate we were as young men to have shared that unforgettable, if transient, experience. I was also enabled to follow closely the last phase of Britain's disengagement from her Arab dependencies. My father, the late Sir William Luce, was Governor of Aden from 1956 to 1960, before becoming Political Resident in the Gulf, and then being recalled from retirement by Lord Home to negotiate Britain's withdrawal from the Gulf in 1971. Subsequently, as a Minister of State, I became involved at first hand in the concluding chapters of Empire.

The comparison between the implementation and aftermath of Britain's withdrawal from South Arabia in 1967, and that from the Gulf only four years later, is striking. Despite strained and protracted negotiations, we pulled out of the Gulf in an orderly fashion, leaving behind a legacy of political stability, the creation of the United Arab Emirates, and the retention of the goodwill and friendship of both its rulers and peoples. By contrast, the collapse of the

South Arabian Federation, hastened by HMG's precipitate and cynical abandonment, was a tragic and ignominious ending to 128 years of British governance, and one which left in its wake a long and unhappy period of instability, impoverishment and repression.

The author's candid and colourful picture of what it was like to serve, at grass-roots level, both in Aden, then at the pinnacle of its prosperity, and in its wilder Protectorate hinterland, will revive vivid memories for those who shared that experience. It also offers insights into why good intentions went awry, and why the Federal project failed so spectacularly. In particular, it pays dutiful tribute to the devotion and ideals of those British colonial officials who strove selflessly to serve those for whom they assumed responsibility, and to the virile peoples of South Arabia who, despite many vicissitudes, have preserved their unique cultural identity.

We are entitled to take whatever view we choose about the merits of Empire, yet we cherish our links with the Arab world, and, whatever the mistakes of the past, these cannot undo or deny the personal friendships, goodwill and mutual affection that have survived testing times, and which stretch across a quarter of the globe.

The Rt. Hon. The Lord Luce KG GCVO

Preface

THE BRITISH PRIME MINISTER'S cap-in-hand mission, in November 2008, to the Gulf States to persuade their rulers to bail out our struggling Western economies, spectacularly illustrated the rub of Aladdin's lamp. Barely fifty years ago, the half dozen or so shaikhdoms of the then Trucial States were only just emerging from a dark age of feuding, slave trading, piracy and privation. Today, these same states, now become the United Arab Emirates, are rich beyond even Aladdin's dreams. Emirates has become almost the world's biggest airline, Abu Dhabi drowns in oil, while Dubai boasts the world's biggest shopping complex, and the Middle East's biggest container port. Dubai has also established an international finance centre set to rival the City of London, and the 1,539-room Atlantis Hotel which offers the ultimate in £25,000-per-night luxury. Mr Brown's £9,000-per-night suite in Abu Dhabi's 7-star Emirates Palace Hotel might have been modest by comparison, but at least his host, Crown Prince Shaikh Mohammed bin Zayed, kindly footed the bill. One wonders whether that Arabian Nights experience gave our Prime Minister cause to reflect on outrageous fortune, or to recall that, until 1971, these same shaikhdoms had effectively been under British protection for the best part of a century and a half.

Whatever his musings on the Gulf States' transformation, Mr Brown is unlikely to have given much thought to the fate of another ancient port, Aden, tucked away in the south-west corner of Arabia a thousand miles away across the Empty Quarter. Aden has all but dropped out of British consciousness. Yet fifty years ago this, the finest natural harbour on the Arabian Peninsula, was enjoying its own spectacular boom as a British Crown Colony. It had grown exponentially since 1839 when it was acquired as Queen Victoria's first imperial possession, and, by the early 1960s, had become one of the world's biggest bunkering ports and a hub of international shipping and airlines, home to BP's most modern oil refinery, and Britain's most important overseas military base. Its multi-racial community enjoyed advanced social services, the rule of law, and a level of economic development that had earned it the sobriquet "The Hong Kong of the Middle East". And then, precipitately and controversially, the British quit Aden in 1967 after a tenure of 128 years, leaving behind disorder, bloodshed, economic collapse, and what was to become the Arab World's only Marxist state.

What was once Aden Colony, along with its Protectorate hinterland twice the size of England and Wales, is now part of the Republic of Yemen. But while the fortunes of the Gulf States have waxed, those of the former British South Arabia have waned. Today, Aden is better known for the brazen attack on the USS *Cole* in 2000. The Gulf of Aden, a vital conduit for Arabian oil, has become a pirate-infested lake. The Yemen itself, a wildly beautiful but impoverished country with an energetic people, is notorious as the former homeland both of Osama bin Laden and of four out of ten of Guantanamo Bay's detainees. Now targeted by al-Qaida as a centre for operations, it bravely struggles to come to terms with the modern world, yet few would regard it a safe tourist destination.

Why should there have been this dramatic reversal of fortunes, and what were the British doing in this remote corner of the Arabian Peninsula in the first place? In the flood tide of Britain's 19th-century imperial expansion, Aden was chosen as one of a string of strategically sited fortresses to safeguard the sea routes to India, and its wild hinterland provided a convenient *cordon sanitaire* against Turkish expansion from the Yemen. For the next hundred years, Aden prospered modestly as a military base and bunkering port, but the hinterland was generally left to its own anarchic devices, under the threatening shadow of a Turkish-occupied Yemen. In 1914, an Anglo-Turkish convention confirmed the alignment of the long-disputed Yemen frontier with the British-protected hinterland states. Yet, notwithstanding British protective treaties, several of these states were invaded and then occupied by Turkish troops during the First World War, and some by Yemen irregulars thereafter. Not until the 1934 Treaty of San'a was a *de facto* Yemen Protectorate frontier grudgingly recognized by the Imam, and not until 1937, when responsibility for the Protectorate was ceded to the Colonial Office, were the first advisory treaties signed with Protectorate rulers.

By the end of the Second World War, Britain was a spent imperial force, and fast losing its role as the predominant Middle East power. In 1947, the decision to quit India, and dramatically changed economic and political circumstances, offered us an opportunity to reappraise our world-wide commitments. However, with Aden, this would be a case of realism deferred, in part due to the memory of past glories, but also because new and inconvenient challenges had to be faced. The 1956 Suez fiasco, the threat posed by Arab nationalism, Gamal Abdul Nasser's territorial designs on Arabia, the 1958 Iraq revolution, successive British military involvements in Jordan, Oman and Kuwait, and the spread of Soviet influence, hardened the belief that Aden must be retained as a key military base to protect Britain's Gulf oil interests, and provide a bastion against Communism. By the early 1960s, Aden had achieved the acme of its commercial prosperity, and the transfer of Middle East Command from Kenya, triggering the construction of a hugely expensive new military complex at Little Aden, seemed to confirm Britain's determination to retain its Arabian toehold at all costs, even though the base was already economically unsustainable, and arguably obsolescent.

In this book, I describe something of the background to the events that led to Britain's inglorious, if inevitable, disengagement from South Arabia in 1967. In my Envoi, I have also summarized the final two years of British rule and its bloody aftermath, to which I was not witness. My justification for writing this personal, and cathartic, account is to add a footnote to an almost forgotten chapter of British imperial history, and to pay tribute to the British and Arabs I met along that rocky road during my five and a half years of colonial service.

The Colonial Office was good at recruiting high-calibre, balanced and committed men to administer the British Empire. Many such exemplars toiled away in Aden. Service in the tribal hinterland demanded other, esoteric qualities. I have tried to paint a picture of both types of officer, generally affectionately, and what motivated them to return to Far Arabia again and again. Some might have been drawn by its romance, others by the prospect of adventure. Most are now dead. All had a sense of vocation to serve their

Queen and Country and to improve the lot of the people they also served. That not all my more distinguished contemporaries feature in my account, is simply explained by the geographical separation of the areas in which we were stationed.

I have drawn heavily on my own diaries, correspondence and papers to recreate those times. I am most grateful to Lord Luce, himself a former member of Her Majesty's Overseas Civil Service, for agreeing to contribute the Foreword. I owe a particular debt of gratitude to John Shipman, a brother officer and outstanding Arabist, for his generous advice and critical textual analysis; also, to my publisher, William Facey, for his encouragement and meticulous scholarship; and, finally, to my wife for her loyal support and forbearance.

John Harding

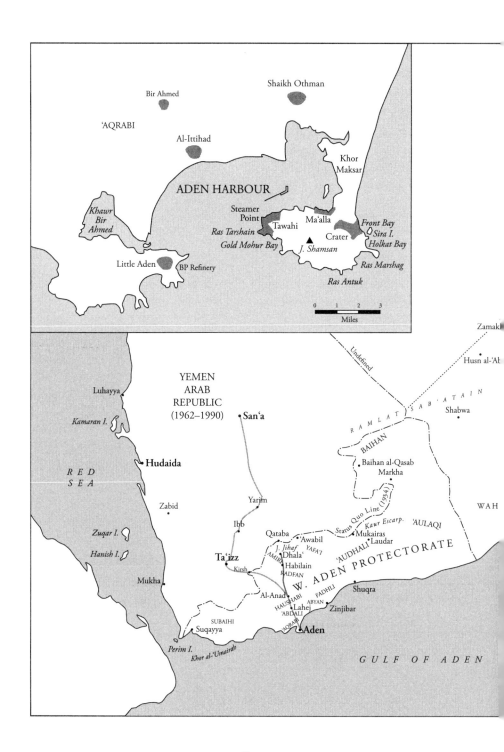

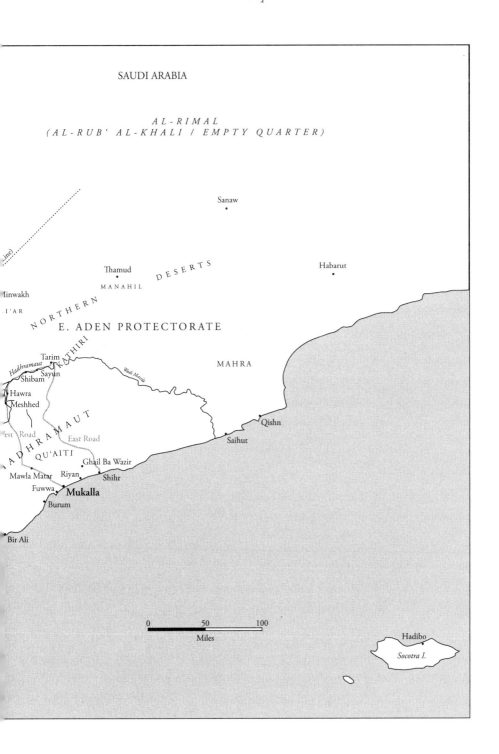

SAUDI ARABIA

AL-RIMAL
(AL-RUB' AL-KHALI / EMPTY QUARTER)

Sanaw

DESERTS

Thamud

MANAHIL

Habarut

Minwakh

I'AR

NORTHERN

E. ADEN PROTECTORATE

KATHIRI

Tarim

Hadhramaut

Sayun

Shibam

Wadi Masila

MAHRA

Hawra

Meshhed

HADHRAMAUT

Qishn

West Road

East Road

Saihut

QU'AITI

Ghail Ba Wazir

Mawla Matar

Riyan

Shihr

Fuwwa

Mukalla

Burum

Bir Ali

0   50   100

Miles

Hadibo

Socotra I.

1

At the Crossroads

WHAT BEGAN AS A TRICKLE had become a spate. It coursed under the lino-covered table to inch past my feet and spread, delta-like, across the mud floor's surface, scummed with dust and dead flies. And then I tumbled. My host, Shaikh Muhammad Al-Kharusi, had already sunk half a bottle of gin in the heat of a South Arabian August before midday. This was injudicious even for a man of his physique and appetites. Yet, for that moment, it was not so much the timing of his incontinence, but the capacity of his bladder that nonplussed me.

We were sitting opposite each other in the bare, lime-washed space that served as the orderly/reception/dining-room, and everything else that passed for civility at Husn al-'Abr. This Beau Geste-style fort, a nodal point for a skein of ancient trade routes traversing the fringes of Arabia's Empty Quarter, had been rebuilt in 1939 by the British pioneer administrator Harold Ingrams to control the wells which sustained all life around. Apart from its strategic importance, Al-'Abr also served as a customs post, levying tolls on traffic between Hadhramaut and Saudi Arabia.

What was I doing in a place like this? As a recently appointed cadet Assistant Adviser in HM Overseas Civil Service, I had been posted here by my boss, Arthur Watts, Her Britannic Majesty's British Agent and Resident Adviser for the Eastern Aden Protectorate. My instructions were to undertake a familiarization tour of the one of the British Empire's remotest corners, a desolation of sand and stone, supporting nothing but a few Bedouin and their camels.

Britain's original objective for maintaining Al-'Abr, along with a string of similar forts built in the early 1950s close by the 1,000 mile border with the Yemen and Saudi Arabia, had been to deter blood feud, cross-border brigandage and hostile incursions. Known as the Violet Line, and clearly delineated as such on British maps, this finger in the sand was unrecognized by the Bedouin, whose nomadic way of life knew no boundaries. In recent years, a new factor had given it significance – the prospect of oil.

I stared at Kharusi wondering how to react to his bravura performance. I had met him only a couple of days earlier when he had been sober and affable. A more experienced Political Officer might have handled the situation with *sang froid.* As a new boy, I was simply bemused. I also felt certain that Watts, a Machiavellian type, would be carefully marking my progress back at headquarters. He would definitely have considered Kharusi's conduct to be unbecoming for the officer responsible for running this politically sensitive area. Furthermore, unlike most of the old-school British South Arabians, Watts was a strict teetotaller who strongly disapproved of Kharusi's drinking: "Not a proper Muslim activity, John. An appalling example."

Kharusi had originally been brought over to serve with the local Qu'aiti State some twenty years before at the instigation of Harold Ingrams. Subsequently, he had transferred to the British Residency staff. As a former heavyweight boxing champion, who had once laid out the British Fleet's champion for twenty-four hours, he was not a man to be crossed. Although theoretically senior in rank, I was still on probation and effectively under Kharusi's command. In terms of local knowledge and experience, I was his inferior in every respect and this was his manor. He returned my incredulous stare unabashed, his mouth drooling and his huge arms hanging loosely across his chest.

The night before, when more or less sober, he had sketched out our itinerary for a month-long tour of the Northern Deserts, stressing that we must make good time on this first day and leave soon after lunch.

"I'd better get my things together, Shaikh Muhammad," I said, stiffly pushing back my chair from the table. "No doubt we'll be leaving shortly."

"Plenty of time for that," he growled, eyeing me balefully. "Anyway, we can't leave now. It's too hot. The engines will blow up."

"As you say," I replied, shrugging my shoulders and backing purposefully out of the room.

And yet, as I retreated to my canvas tent across the white-hot courtyard with the midday sun boring into my head like a gimlet, I knew he was right. It would be crazy to set off in this heat. More worrying was that a relationship which had begun so well should now be going disastrously wrong. The prospect of being stuck with this man for a whole month made me wonder, not for the last time, what had brought me to this barren land that offers little to its own and even less to the stranger.

* * *

My decision to join the Colonial Service had been protracted. After military service and three gilded years at Cambridge, I had reacted against my family's legal tradition and had plumped instead for the thoroughly modern profession of advertising, as a trainee account executive. However, the business of tracking down a drug-benumbed leopard as a gimmick to launch poncy Italian shoes, turned out not to be my style. My next career move, volunteering to work in Antarctica, was aborted by a tubercular hip operation that laid me up for fifteen months. During that time, I tried to write a book about a mountaineering expedition to Iran's Elburz Mountains. After what seemed a lifetime doing research, I had nothing to show for it on my return to normal life save a sheaf of illegible manuscript notes. By now, most of my university contemporaries were gainfully employed. I was offered jobs I didn't want and was rejected for others I did. I turned to the Cambridge University Appointments Board, who suggested the Colonial Service. No cissy stuff here. No sycophantic account executives trying to mollify artwork prima donnas, or squaring slick copywriters. There was a slender family tradition of service in India, but my main source of information about the "Silent Service" was John Synge, a nephew of the Irish playwright, to whom my father had awarded his Cambridge Rugby Blue. John was nostalgic about his Colonial Service days in Nigeria, from which he had retired prematurely in broken health, but was bitterly critical of HMG's shabby treatment of its loyal servants.

Ever since Harold Macmillan's 1957 Imperial Audit, it had been clear that the British Empire had entered its twilight phase. Far-sighted British statesmen had for long realized that our own brand of imperialism, however enlightened and idealistic, was anachronistic, and that general disengagement was inevitable. Yet, when I joined it in 1959, Colonial Service recruitment was continuing unabated, and its establishment of serving officers had reached an all-time peak. Colonial Office publications assured prospective Administrative Branch recruits that there were good career prospects "for many years to come". I recognized this as disingenuous, but was young enough to reckon that the future could look after itself. As a product of National Service, and a public-school regime in which prefect rule, competition and team games ingrained a sense of service, Newbolt's call to "Play up and play the game" still struck a resonant chord. The Colonial Service might be in extra time, but no one had yet blown the final whistle.

Having completed an exhaustive application form, I was "directed by Mr Lennox-Boyd" to attend an interview at the Colonial Office. The Service's recruitment procedure had changed little since Major Sir Ralph Furse had regularized it during the inter-war years. Furse's basic principles were that a man must be fit for the vacancy chosen; that personality and character were of prime importance; and that these qualities could not be adequately tested by written examination. Ergo, selection would be based on expert interviewing, after a thorough examination of the candidate's previous record. The fifth Marquis of Salisbury, Furse's fag at Eton and a former Secretary of State for the Colonies, thoroughly approved of this system "based not so much on brains but personality", though he did concede, "I do not say that brains do not matter". In judging character, Furse attached particular importance to the handshake. Weak ones worried him. After an otherwise satisfactory interview with a candidate applying for a particularly demanding posting, he suddenly seized the man's hand in a vice-like grip. When the applicant's flaccid fist responded by becoming "hard as nails", acceptance was a formality.

At this stage, Arabia was still a far-away country. My peripheral Middle East experiences had centred on Iran and Turkey. Of Britain's colonial territories, Kenya, with its immensely wide horizons and the magnificent twin-peaked mountain whose snows bestrode the Equator and lent the country its name, had been my first choice. On reporting at the Colonial Office, I was disconcerted by the run-down appearance of the place. A shuffling attendant led me through musty corridors to an anonymous office, on whose brown painted door he gave a series of timid taps.

"Come in!" boomed a voice. Obeying, I came face to face with the Director of Colonial Service Recruitment.

Shabbily suited, with a gnarled pipe clenched determinedly between broken and slightly yellowing teeth, the Director wore a world-weary expression and seemed to embody another Furse precept that "a good man is more likely to recognize goodness in others". Working his way unhurriedly through my application form, he had said little save to comment on my "tortured handwriting" until he reached the section on sport. Knowing that the Colonial Service took this seriously, I had recorded meticulously my own unexceptional list of achievements.

"Keen on sport are you, Harding. D'you think team games important?" enquired the Director, glancing up at me quizzically.

"Certainly, Sir. Good for character building and for working as a team player," I gushed shamelessly.

"Really," he said, looking distinctly unimpressed. "You seem to have played most games. What's your favourite?"

"Definitely rugby," I replied, guessing from his battered appearance that he might once have had some acquaintance with the front row.

"Hmmm …," he muttered. "So you ran the rugby at the Guards Training Battalion and captained your college?"

"Yes," I responded brightly.

"But you never got a Blue?"

"Sadly not, Sir," I replied.

"Pity about that," he said dismissively. "What about Football?"

"I played soccer at my prep school," I replied airily, "but don't rate it as good a game as rugger."

At this the Director stopped short and glared at me. "That's what you think, is it? Not such a good game, eh? What d'you think they play in Africa then? Soccer's the game there, Harding – football to you. D'you think you might descend from your lofty pedestal and teach the Africans to play football?"

"Of course I'll teach football if necessary," I blurted back.

But this had evidently touched an old wound. For the first time, the Director removed the pipe from his mouth and began jabbing it at me like an assegai. "And what if the buggers won't learn, Harding?" he spluttered. "Africa's not like the Brigade of Guards or Cambridge, you know. You'd better get that fact of life into your head if you're ever offered a job in this Service."

My interview was at an end. I didn't get the handshake treatment, but left Sanctuary Buildings assuming that I'd blown it. Yet, within the month, I was back again for a final interview before the full Colonial Office Selection Board, seated around an immense semi-circular table, with me in the middle. Questions were fired in rapid succession from left, right and centre, but no one mentioned football of either code. A week later, I got a letter confirming that my application had been successful, subject to a satisfactory medical. There was an immediate vacancy in Northern Rhodesia. Within days, another letter arrived offering me Kenya – in Jan Morris's words, "the most coveted posting of all".

My relief was tempered. It seemed that the Colonial Service might have a recruitment crisis. In that case, I could surely defer Africa a bit longer. I wanted to finish my book and, more to the point, had fallen in love, though had not committed myself to marriage. The Director agreed to my request for a four-month postponement. However, without a job I had no money, so I inserted a small ad in *The Times*: "Cambridge graduate seeks interesting job. Anything legitimate considered." My only reply came from one Geoffrey Handley-Taylor. He suggested that we meet at the raffish Arts Theatre Club. I was wary as to where this might lead, but Geoffrey turned out to be a most affable Yorkshireman, a friend of Vera Brittain and a literary entrepreneur, who promoted an ingenious line in alternative *Who's Who*s, covering anything from music to literature, principally targeted at American academic egos. Geoffrey appointed me as his research assistant to compile a bibliography of the Poet Laureate, John Masefield. When that was finished, he urged me to waste no more time and join the Colonial Service, as having "the right stuff". I remain forever indebted to him for having thrown me that £5-a-week lifeline – and also for his warning that the writer's profession was "vile gloom in the shady streets of literature".

By now I was enjoying London life, riding an emotional roller coaster and beginning to have second thoughts about Africa. I was also so broke that, after applying for, and being granted, "indefinite suspension" by the Director of Recruitment, I turned to male modelling. Having invested the last of my savings in an expensive photographic portfolio, I bluffed my way into Peter Lumley, London's top modelling agency, having survived a terrifying interview with the Agency's Chief Executive, Carole Thompson, a devastating blonde with glacial eyes. Had the Director known of this temporary career change he might not have been so accommodating, as male modelling was not then considered respectable. After a sticky start, the money began rolling in. Yet, it remained my constant worry that, somehow, he might recognize me as the preposterous Sherlock Holmes look-alike, leaning casually against a De Dion 1900 vintage car, under the caption: "Why be antiquated? Go to C & A." I finally cracked when Carole secured me the coveted Gibbs Toothpaste slot. The prospect of my cheesy grin being splashed over the national press prompted my resignation. In any case, as Carole put it over our farewell drink: "You are not the type I would expect to really like the peculiar world of fashion."

By now, I had persuaded the Colonial Office to allow me to switch from Africa to Aden, Britain's last imperial outpost in the Middle East. Apparently, Aden Colony was well-ordered, compact and directly administered by British officials. By contrast, its Protectorate was twice the size of England and Wales and divided into two parts: the Western Aden Protectorate (the WAP) and the Eastern Aden Protectorate (the EAP), comprising some twenty-one disparate states ruled by a collection of sultans, sharifs and shaikhs, to whom we were merely advisers. From Colonial Office literature, the WAP sounded so wild and outlandish that it seemed likely to stay that way indefinitely. Here one might expect visits from tribal delegations at any time of day or night, accompanied by chanting and rifle fire, as a prelude to "fruitless discussion of trivialities, until the real purpose of the meeting comes to light".

The EAP sounded altogether more settled and sophisticated. Here, an Adviser's day might include meetings with state officials, followed by inspections of schools, medical centres and agricultural schemes. That done, both he and his wife might dine quietly with members of the local merchant community. The EAP also had something for pioneer types, whose task was: "the penetration of the desert frontier area, getting in touch with the tribes, building forts … facing extremes of heat and cold, spending endless hours of talk with Bedouin tribes to whom time means nothing."

To bone up on this astonishing place, I read the works of the two outstanding pioneer Political Officers of the 1930s, Harold Ingrams' magisterial *Arabia and the Isles*, and the Master of Belhaven's lyrical *The Kingdom of Melchior*. Ingrams had overseen the pacification of the EAP's Hadhramaut before becoming its first Resident Adviser. Belhaven, formerly R. A. B. Hamilton, was a dashing and unconventional soldier, but had been a less successful peacemaker in the more intractable WAP, and was ambivalent about this "scallywag work". He issued a bleak warning: "To confront the challenges of this extraordinary land, a man needs the power of self-criticism and a deep sense of humanity if he is not to serve his country sick at heart."

While attending a lecture on Arabia at the Royal Central Asian Society given by Sir John Glubb of the Arab Legion, I ran into a former Stowe contemporary, James Nash, an ex-cavalryman with a penchant for hare-brained adventure. When James told me that he was about to be posted to the WAP, we agreed to meet again to hear Colonel Hugh Boustead lecture on the EAP, from which he had just retired as Resident Adviser. Boustead, already a legendary figure, was the only man to have received a free pardon for deserting the Royal Navy as a midshipman in order to see action on the Western Front. He had subsequently fought with the Russian White Army against the Bolsheviks, served with the Gordon Highlanders in Turkey, commanded the Sudan Camel Corps, raised the Sudan Defence Force, and helped Orde Wingate restore Haile Selassie to his throne. Military service had earned him both DSO and MC. He had also boxed for Oxford, represented Great Britain in the Modern Pentathlon at the 1924 Olympics, and reached 25,000 ft on the 1933 British Everest Expedition.

Boustead was boyishly enthusiastic about service in South Arabia, but advised me to keep mountaineering in perspective. After the lecture, James cooked me a gourmet dinner, showed off his newly acquired *Shorter Encyclopedia of Islam,* and impressed upon me that "all the real gents are going to South Arabia".

"How does one manage about girl friends?" I asked him.

"Simple," replied James. "You don't. Best get married."

"But isn't it a bit risky, taking a young bride out to the WAP? Sounds a pretty rough sort of place."

"Yes, dear boy, it is. But Arab women are strictly off bounds, and personally I don't care for camels."

Two days later, I was invited to luncheon at his club by another proper gent, the Hon. Alec Cumming-Bruce, then an Assistant Chief Secretary in Aden. Taut, punctilious and unkindly nicknamed "the Cunning Brute", Alec was actually a kind, civilized man steeped in the traditions of public service. He described Aden as a well-run, bustling modern city with a relatively sophisticated infrastructure and efficient public services.

"What about the Protectorate?" I asked him.

"Which one d'you mean?" he replied sharply. "They're very different, you know."

"I rather fancy the WAP. It sounds very challenging."

"Chaotic, you mean," said Alec sourly. "Interesting enough for an anthropologist doing some socio-political study, but not the place for someone who wants to get stuck into constructive administration. It's a ragbag of quasi-independent states, ruled by a bunch of feudal rulers of very variable quality. Few have achieved even a semblance of governance, and much of this sorry situation is entirely our own fault. That apart, what goes on in the WAP is pure Cowboy-and-Indian stuff. You'd be better off in the EAP."

Before taking up my South Arabian appointment, I was required to undergo a basic Arabic course at the School of Oriental and African Studies. On arrival, the course director suggested that I should look out for Roy Somerset, a serving WAP Political Officer. In a tiny class, in which American ARAMCO lawyers were over-represented, the square-set man with the boxer's jaw could only have been Somerset. Related to Belhaven by marriage, he had made national press headlines the previous year, after being besieged in a fort on Jebel Jihaf, an 8,000-ft massif overlooking the Yemen. The siege had been lifted only after the RAF had strafed the dissidents, and a company of Aden Protectorate Levies, supported by British troops, had stormed the fort. For his part in the action, the Levies' commander, Major Bill Boucher-Myers, was awarded an immediate DSO.

Puzzled why such a distinguished veteran should be attending a basic Arabic course, I introduced myself.

"Good God," said Somerset, looking aghast. "You haven't really signed on for South Arabia have you? You must be raving mad!"

Taken aback, I mumbled something about the romance of Arabia.

"For heaven's sake, get that silly nonsense out of your head," he spluttered. "The whole place is like a loony bin. Where on earth have they decided to send you?"

"I don't know yet," I replied guardedly. "Alec Cumming-Bruce has recommended the EAP."

"Well, he would, wouldn't he," snorted Somerset. "But it couldn't be any worse than the WAP. Of course, you know the form when you reach Mukalla, don't you?" I shook my head. "Draw your rifle damn quick from the stores!" he said, roaring with laughter. "But seriously, I'll give you one piece of advice. If you can stick it, the Colonial Service is a damned good life for the first ten years. After that it's profitless."

Roy had served in the Royal Artillery during the war, and been a District Officer in Nigeria before coming to Aden, an experience he described as "descent from order to chaos". One morning, he said to me, "I'm having lunch with Johnny Johnson today. He's the Deputy British Agent in the EAP, so you'd better come to meet him." In a pub where the din made normal conversation impossible, a large, bluff man with a flushed face had commandeered a corner, in which he was shouting louder than anyone else.

"There's Johnny, follow me," said Roy, pushing his way through the crowd.

If Somerset had seemed a cowboy, Johnson came over as Custer. During the war he had been a "Chindit", a member of General Orde Wingate's elite Long Range Penetration Group in Burma. Afterwards, he had joined the Colonial Service in South Arabia. "Coming to the Protectorate are you?" boomed Johnny. "Tell you one thing. If you come to the EAP, you'd better like football."

I was beginning to get the message, but before I could enter the conversation, the party was joined by another South Arabian, Bob Serjeant, an Arabic scholar, then attached to SOAS. He had done wartime service in the WAP and, when the three of them began swapping yarns, I reckoned I'd be better off drawing a Bren Gun than a rifle.

Neither Somerset nor I distinguished ourselves scholastically at SOAS. Our dimmer paths were lit by the genius of Tom Johnstone, a no-nonsense Glaswegian tutor who spoke several languages, and made Arabic more comprehensible by explaining that both the Greek and Arabic alphabets derived from a common Proto-Sinaitic root. He also insisted that the best way of learning the basic Arabic verbs was by rote, so he had the whole class of mature students conjugating them in unison. My uncertain progress was due partly to the American contingent's insistence that we should always finish the day with "Artillery Punch", a lethal cocktail of claret, whisky, brandy and sherry; and, more particularly, to a tempestuous *affaire* which was occupying more than my waking hours. Surprisingly, when the final examination results were announced, I attained 68% in a ridiculously easy paper, and came only half way down the order.

While at SOAS, I heard Wilfred Thesiger lecture on his two epic crossings of the Empty Quarter. I was captivated by his descriptive genius, but disconcerted by the uncompromising bleakness of his experiences. Of other existing South Arabian paladins, Belhaven was a sick man, but Harold Ingrams was still very much alive. I attended a lecture Ingrams gave to the Overseas Services Club, when he came out strongly against the concept of the newly inaugurated Federation of South Arabian Amirates, comprising six leading WAP states. When I cheekily introduced myself, he promptly invited me to luncheon. Serene in his certainties and exuding authority, Ingrams was a charming host. Once again, he expatiated persuasively on his opposition to a federated South Arabia: "It is my firm belief that only the Arabs can find their true destiny. The worst thing we can do is to try to impose upon them our own creation."

When I politely ventured a clumsy contrary view, his geniality suddenly vanished. Turning the full weight of his powerful personality on me, he summarily dismissed my arguments, and put me very firmly in my place. I met Ingrams once more before I left for Arabia. "I am never tired of talking about Aden," he said kindly. "So you do me a favour by coming." He had the presence and personality of a great man, but I had glimpsed his darker side.

On 1 January 1960, I boarded the train that then ran direct from Swansea through Central Wales to Birkenhead, to catch the boat to Aden. I was leaving Britain with an overwhelming sense of failure. Two and a half years on from Cambridge, I had spent fifteen months hospitalized and convalescent, and had squandered most of the rest on false starts and self-indulgence. Lack of gainful employment had put a strain on my relationship with my parents. I had not finished the book on Iran; I had failed to bring to a happy conclusion a long-lasting love affair; and I was about to start a new career with a very uncertain future. The auspices for the new decade were not particularly good. However, at least I would now be earning £792 a year rising (so the Secretary of State's letter of appointment assured me) by annual increments of £39, with, assuredly, the prospect of adventure.

2

A Taste of Aden

O N 1 JANUARY 1960, the day I was due to sail to Aden on the Bibby Line's SS *Leicestershire,* Britain phased out national service, and also entered the Swinging Sixties, the decade that effectively saw out the British Empire. Liverpool dockers eschewed work on New Year's Day, so departure was delayed by thirty hours. I was not particularly worried. The Government of Aden never quibbled about a few days' extra travelling time at either end. Bibby's was a genteel, old-fashioned line, and the *Leicestershire,* displacing 10,000 tons, a shrimp compared with P&O's leviathans. Its 75 predominantly elderly passengers, mostly bound for Ceylon and Burma, still dressed for dinner, and its meticulously attentive Goanese stewards served meals on time, even though the chef's curry dishes, available at breakfast, lunch and dinner and variously attributed to Bombay, Simla, Bangalore, Singapore, Madras or Calcutta, all tasted identical. Battling down the Irish Sea and across the Bay of Biscay through winter gales, I seldom saw any meals through to completion.

Shipboard life, frustratingly dull at first, developed its own rhythms. A zealous American missionary bound for the Sudan kindly agreed to give me Arabic lessons, until his brattish daughter's interminable interruptions recalled my SOAS mentor Tom Johnstone's maxim that "learning a second time is never so vital". I sought the more congenial company of Jean Gray, a bewitching Sinhalese concert pianist who had studied under Louis Kentner. Jean's *à deux* Chopin recitals revived a spirit parched from the standard ship's fare of tombola, housey-housey and liar dice.

On reaching Port Said, I picked up a letter on blue airmail paper headed *Secretariat, Aden*. It was from Alec Cumming-Bruce, informing me that I was definitely being posted to Mukalla in the Eastern Aden Protectorate after spending three weeks in Aden, "doing what the Americans would probably call 'orientation'. The EAP is much the nicest posting and one of your colleagues recently came to see me, pathetically asking not to be sent on leave as he was enjoying himself so much!" Although I had half-expected this, I felt a pang of disappointment that I was not going to the wilder WAP.

As a Royal Mail carrier, the *Leicestershire* took precedence over all other ships, so led the convoy through the recently reopened Suez Canal at a steady five knots. I was up on deck just after dawn, when it was still chill enough for the *fellahin*, trudging silently to work along its banks, to have wrapped their heads in cotton shawls. Entering the Bitter Lakes, the triangular sails of fishing boats flashed white against the horizon, as scudding flights of pink flamingo swept low across the water. Next morning, still steaming down the Gulf of Suez, what I had first thought to be a bank of white cumulus cloud transformed itself into the bleached mountains of Sinai.

My last full day on board coincided with the finals of the men's deck tennis when I was thrashed 0–6, 0–6 by the steely-wristed, sixty-year-old Major Hoskyns. Afterwards, his wife Lilian implored me to look up "a dear friend now living in Lebanon. A most charming man whom I know you'd like." On a slip of writing paper, she scribbled "H.A.R. Philby, Hotel Normandy, Beirut". At that time, the British security services were already closing in on the traitorous "Kim" Philby, yet another three years were to elapse before he was spirited out of Beirut on board the Russian freighter *Dolmatova* to self-imposed exile.

My shipboard friends had wondered how I would cope with Aden. However, that first sight of the sunlit volcanic hulk of Jebel Shamsan, rising 1,800 ft sheer from out of the Pink Arabian Sea, revised my preconceptions of Kipling's "unlit barrick-stove". I was met ashore by Ted Eyre, a pukka ex-Sudan Political Service officer, immaculate in his pressed white drill shorts and long stockings. He whisked me through the Customs House past a throng of tourists surrounded by touting Arabs, Indians and Somalis offering anything for a consideration. We drove up a winding road to an imposing multi-verandahed house perched on a promontory overlooking the sea. Alec

Cumming-Bruce was waiting in its louvered doorway, beaming a warm welcome.

Originally designed as bachelor pads for Cable & Wireless employees at the turn of the century, Ras Boradli's apartments were strictly the preserve of senior government officials. Their spacious verandahs, facing westwards, gave panoramic views across a wide bay, dotted with sailing boats engaged in a regatta. Beyond its sparkling blue waters, a fleet of tankers stood off shore in the lea of the comb of peaks that marked Little Aden and the BP oil refinery. A hundred feet below us, waves lapped gently against a bulwark of sun-scorched cliffs, stretching away eastwards in a succession of rugged promontories. Save for some unfamiliar sounds and smells, this might have been some Mediterranean shore. Tea, served by a turbaned bearer, and poured from a Georgian silver teapot, had a peculiar brackish taste. After unpacking my things, I joined my host on the verandah where we sipped Campari sodas. Fanned by a cool breeze, we watched the setting sun silhouette the spiky peaks of Little Aden. The view was magnificent. I reckoned I had landed on my feet.

As was customary with many senior government officials, Alec had left his wife and family behind in England. He kindly offered to have me to stay until I moved on to Mukalla. He had two other house guests, Christopher Pirie-Gordon, the British chargé d'affaires in Ta'izz, and Cecil Kenyon, who ran Aden's Lands Office. All three were old friends, having served in Palestine together. Over dinner, they gave me some unexpected insights into the present and future.

Apparently, Britain was retaining Aden, its toehold on the Arabian Peninsula, for reasons of strategy, its air base and the port. Aden Colony's economic viability was underpinned by the BP Refinery. This had been completed in April 1954, after only twenty months, making Aden one of the world's foremost bunkering ports. An unresolved problem was how to yoke a thriving Colony with an impoverished Protectorate. Cumming-Bruce was sceptical that the proposed merger of Aden with the existing federated states would transform the economic and political situation.

"Federation's a sophisticated concept, and there's no certainty that it will be successful here," he explained. "As presently constituted, it's essentially a mutual defence vehicle for both HMG and those Arab rulers with whom we've signed treaties of protection. Some of them are justifiably suspicious of our motives, and the prospect of Aden joining raises a whole new set of problems.

It can only work if the Aden politicians and the federal rulers are prepared to compromise on a range of issues. Aden has enough problems of its own. Its very affluence and the British base threaten its future stability. The thousands of illegal Yemeni immigrants now working here represent a fifth column. They're essential to maintaining Aden's economic momentum, but have been harnessed by the Aden Trades Union Congress which, in turn, has become a front for the People's Socialist Party. It's banked and supported by Egypt and peddles an inflammatory anti-British line, but has caught the mood of the people. Aden's politics are moving faster than we are. Unless we keep abreast, our position will become untenable."

Kenyon, who had had direct experience of working in the WAP, was equally gloomy. "Without massive funding and proper administration, profitable development in the Protectorate is well-nigh impossible. Aden Colony is prosperous because it's directly administered. Like Hong Kong, we've given international commerce its head. But no one's going to make money out of the Protectorate. By the normal standards of British Colonial administration, the place is a shambles."

"Then surely, it must be in everyone's long-term interests that we provide more aid?" I queried.

"Perhaps, but aid without tight supervision doesn't work. HMG's £270,000 loan to set up the Abyan agricultural scheme was put to good use because it was run by a professional board. But much of the £770,000 Protectorate grant, allocated five years ago to build new schools, health units and hospitals, seems to have vanished. There's still not a single tarmac road in the entire WAP. Given Britain's parlous economic state, I don't see HM Treasury stumping up any more British taxpayers' money."

Cumming-Bruce switched the conversation to the Yemen for Pirie-Gordon, a charming Foreign Office man with wide Middle East experience, to join in.

"The Imam doesn't like us and we may not like him," explained Pirie-Gordon. "However, we've got to handle Yemen a lot better than we're doing at present. Imam Ahmed holds a personal grudge against the British for allowing the Free Yemeni movement to maintain a presence in Aden when it was doing its best to get rid of him. Despite that, and all the border troubles of the 1950s, we've managed to maintain diplomatic links. Until a couple of years ago, we and the Italians were the only Western countries allowed to have legations in Ta'izz. Now, the Russians, Chinese and Americans have all moved in offering aid. The Imam is busy playing them off against each other, and at least knows the British as tried old enemies. Naturally, he wants to take over Aden, but he'd prefer to play a long game, and knows we're bound to give it up eventually. Relations were immeasurably improved when the Governor, Sir William Luce, visited him last year. The problems now are more at this end. Trevaskis and the Federal rulers remain obsessed with Yemen as a threat, and will brook no compromise. Unfortunately, the Imam's a sick man and his son and heir, Prince Badr, is a naïve socialist who's been cosying up to Nasser."

These were deep waters, so Cumming-Bruce again changed the subject. "We're all getting a bit gloomy on John's first night," he said brightly.

"Let's talk about your own work, John. First, I'd like you to read the Petrie Report which recommends a different approach to Ingrams' policy of non-interference, and suggests that many of the Protectorate's problems can still be solved by administrative rather than political measures. Then, to put you in the Colony picture, I'll be sending you round some of Aden's better-run government departments. Finance is particularly important: the key to good government and promotion too."

That night, I pondered on the bleak assessments of these three veterans, to whom Aden's future seemed a foregone conclusion. Disengagement, self-government and independence were inevitable in the longer term, but surely not so soon? Over the next few weeks, advice on my post-Colonial Service career was freely on offer. Pirie-Gordon spelled out the Foreign Office career path I should follow, and stressed that I should "beware the Anglo-Saxon society of foreign parts. In choosing your friends, keep to colleagues in Government." A visiting Colonial Office mandarin advised me against "going Arab", while Ian Baillie, the Colony's Deputy Financial Secretary, cautioned that "if you want to be a useful administrative officer with good chances of promotion, don't play Cowboys and Indians in the Protectorate for too long, but get stuck into sound administrative procedure."

Next day, I learned that I would be spending almost a month in Aden before being posted to Mukalla. The Colony was to prove a lot more interesting than its dire reputation as a former punishment station for the Indian Army. Already a thriving incense entrepot during the 1st millennium BC due to its position on the sea routes linking the Indian Ocean to the Red Sea, it became a flourishing commercial centre in the Middle Ages, with fine mosques, colleges and public buildings. Vasco de Gama's 1492 discovery of the Cape route signalled its gradual decline. When Captain Stafford Haines of the Indian Navy captured it in 1839, as Queen Victoria's first imperial possession, its great buildings were in ruins and its population had fallen to a mere 600. Haines transformed an impoverished fishing village into a British fortress that became a key coaling station en route to India. Since then, its growth had been steady. Currently, it was experiencing a period of unmatched prosperity and positively buzzed with activity.

Official government office hours were 8 a.m. to 2 p.m. but, after a brief afternoon break, most senior government officials worked on long into the evening. By lunchtime on my first full day, I felt quite exhausted. In the cool of the evening I trekked up Shamsan to get the feel of the place, and saw the sun sink behind the peaks of Little Aden as eagles wheeled overhead. Alec's conducted tour the following day began at Ras Boradli. Dotted around the promontory were the official residences of Aden's top military brass whose houses, sited according to their seniority, occupied fine vantage points overlooking the bay. We drove down the hill into Steamer Point, originally Tawahi, in whose grubby back streets coolies were still sleeping out on charpoys, wood-framed cord-stringed beds. Here, goats roamed free to urinate, defecate and hoover up rubbish. Nearer the waterfront, Steamer Point's character was pukka British colonial, far removed from Arabia and wearily familiar to Aden's several thousand British government officials, servicemen, oilmen, shippers, traders, businessmen and their families. Mixed in with the banks, warehouses and mercantile and shipping offices, were Armed Services cantonments, barracks, hospitals and messes. Anglicans could chose between Christ Church and the RAF garrison church. Roman Catholics, Presbyterians, Methodists, Baptists and Congregationalists were also catered for. Red-painted "ER" pillar boxes marked street corners. Lost somewhere in the overgrown shrubbery of the Crescent Garden was an enthroned statue of Queen Victoria. Amazingly, it still survives. Here too were the watering holes of Aden's old guard, the Crescent Hotel and the Union Club, where you could gripe about Aden, the parlous state of the "YouKay" and the world in general.

On most days, Steamer Point was awash with day-trippers straight off the great liners of P&O, Union Castle and Shaw Savill which passed to and from Australia, the Far East, India and Africa. Aden had been a free port since 1853. Business had never been better for the scruffy little shops, stuffed with duty-free cameras, binoculars, wirelesses, tape recorders and watches, that lined The Crescent. This colonnaded shopping mall still housed remnants of Aden's original trading caste of Indians, Parsees, Egyptians, Maghribis, and the once-flourishing Jewish community. They preferred to keep a low profile. Ostentation was to be avoided for fear of Arab envy.

Adjacent to the Victorian Customs House, on the Prince of Wales Pier, stood a two-storeyed, oblong edifice built in Indo-Colonial style, its ground floor embellished with arches. It might have gone unnoticed save for the red-turbaned peons, wearing starched, khaki uniforms emblazoned with HMG-inscribed brass buttons, who stood guard at its wooden-latticed entrance doors. The outsize Union Jack, fluttering from its rooftop masthead, proclaimed this as a place of importance. And indeed it was – nothing less than the Secretariat, built in 1868, and still the headquarters of Britain's South Arabian administration.

"I'm now going to introduce you to the men who run Aden," announced Alec, purposefully leading me up a broad flight of stairs to a wide verandah where file-laden peons scuttled from room to room. "We'll kick off with Ken Simmonds, the Chief Secretary."

Aden's Chief Secretary was second only in the chain of civil command to the Governor, Sir William Luce. Twenty years of distinguished service in East Africa had lent him an air of easy authority that might have passed for complacency. As he crossed the room with a friendly smile to shake my hand, I noticed that the whole of the wall space behind his desk was filled with a mounted black-and-white mountain photograph.

"What a magnificent photograph," I gasped. "Isn't that Mount Kenya's North Face?"

"Correct," beamed Simmonds, turning round to trace a line up its sheer rock face with his finger. "I did that route with Arthur Firmin before the war. We only just failed to make the summit."

I was impressed. Firmin had been Kenya's outstanding pre-war mountaineer. Having discovered a common bond, Simmonds reminisced enthusiastically about his climbing days as President of the Cambridge University Mountaineering Club.

"I think we'd better keep John moving on, Ken," Alec interrupted impatiently, as he eased me towards another door marked "Financial Secretary". Its occupant, Tom Oates, third in Aden's civil command structure, was a former Senior Wrangler at Cambridge. He had spent most of the war in minesweepers before joining the Colonial Service. After stints in Nigeria, British Honduras and HM Treasury, he had recently transferred to Aden. Charming and diffident with tousled hair, his donnish manner belied a tough inner core. He ended a distinguished career as Governor of St Helena, and with a knighthood.

Oates's Deputy, Nigel Pusinelli, was a brusque, no-nonsense type who had won an MC with the British Expeditionary Force to France in 1940. He had then survived three gruelling years of jungle warfare in Burma before joining the Colonial Service. Recently promoted to Aden from the Gilbert and Ellice Islands, he made no pretence of being extremely busy. After cursory greetings, Alec moved me on to meet Aden's other Assistant Chief Secretary, Robin Thorne, a charming man who, in years ahead, would become my boss.

Oates, Pusinelli and Thorne, all ex-Oxbridge men with formidable intellects, were to remain pivotal figures in Aden's British administration, and soldiered on almost to its bitter end as Deputy High Commissioners. They typified the best type of Colonial Service officer, serving their country with courage and conviction in both war and peace. Yet not one of them had any previous experience of the Arab World generally, or had ever served in either of the Aden Protectorates. None spoke more than basic Arabic.

Driving eastwards along the coast road past the warehouses, cranes and derricks of Aden's bustling port, we entered a concrete canyon of ugly, high-rise flats. "The Ma'alla Straight," said Alec with a grimace. "One mile long and jerry-built, mainly to house British service families. They're now living hugger-mugger with locals of every sort and condition. Doesn't make the remotest sense to me, but that was a military not a civilian decision. At least it's good for local trade, and the developers have made a killing." Six years on, the Ma'alla Straight would become Aden's "Murder Mile" – a killing ground for terrorist gunmen.

"Beyond those gaps between the flats," he continued, "you can just see the shipyard where Noah built the Ark, and where they're still building ocean-going dhows. To your right is the old Jewish cemetery. Looks a bit unkempt now, but before the 1948 diaspora there were probably over 7,000 Jews living in Aden. Today, there are only a few hundred left."

The road climbed on in a wide sweep, towards a bleak pass which narrowed to a cleft blasted through the rock. Here, Alec stopped the car. "Now take a look below you. Behold, the original Aden." Enclosed on three sides by dirty grey and black cliffs, composed of what looked like clinker, was an unattractive modern town laid out in a grid pattern. Could this really have been the ancient Aden, the Biblical Eden, a Roman emporium in Constantine's reign and, for two thousand years, the most prosperous port in Arabia? "Not much to look at," said Alec, as if reading my thoughts. "But it's humming commercially, and has once again become the 'Eye of the Yemen', as Haines envisaged."

To the British, "Crater" was a fair description for what occupied the bowl of an extinct volcano. It was also disagreeably hot, in both summer and winter. In its narrow streets and suqs, the aromatic scents of spices and coffee mingled with the stench of urine and raw sewage. Scrawny goats, brought in for slaughter from the hinterland, foraged in the shade of broken-down lorries. Deformed beggars crawled along the ground on their hands and knees with plaintive cries of *baksheesh*. Veiled women wove like snakes through jostling crowds. Coolies, staggering under colossal loads, brushed aside filthy urchins playing in the dust. Crater was essentially an Oriental emporium, a place where you could buy almost anything from the cheapest tat to the finest Bakhtiari kilims.

Next day, I began my three weeks of induction, starting with the Immigration Department. Alec had explained that much of my work in Mukalla would involve passports, pilgrim visas and consular functions. "Hadhramis are inveterate travellers. Here, we've got the opposite problem: massive, uncontrolled Yemeni immigration. Seeing how we handle it should give you some insight into what you'll soon have to cope with yourself."

If Paddy Orme, the resolutely relaxed Deputy Head of Aden's Immigration Department, had a massive immigration problem, he didn't show it.

"There's absolutely no way we can stop them coming in," said he, leaning back into a large, comfortable chair behind an empty desk. "Aden's frontiers are completely porous. Anyway, we need their labour. Most Yemenis are good workmen. Once they've made their money, they usually go home. The real problem is housing. We can't build new houses quickly enough, so most immigrants have to live in shanty towns, breeding grounds for disease and discontent."

"What about passports? Alec Cumming-Bruce said I'd be having a lot to do with them in Mukalla."

"Did he, now?" said Orme, grimacing. "Well, as far as we're concerned,

Mukalla's a law unto itself. I've no idea of what goes on there, though they seem to issue passports to any old Ali, Abdu or Muhammad on demand. I can tell you one thing, though. There's damn-all liaison between this department and Mukalla, or with the Secretariat, for that matter. However, if you're interested in passports, see what you can make of this lot."

With that, he shoved across his desk a copy of the *British Nationality Act, 1948*, and a thick binder-leaf file entitled *Foreign Office Passport and Visa Regulations*. Working my way through both for the best part of the morning, I finally gave up, and passed the time more agreeably with Paddy's shapely secretary, who was more than happy to reveal the secrets of her filing system. Paddy's working day tended to be a short one, which usually ended up in the Union Club's bar. Like all good Irishmen, he had little time for the Establishment, and even less for the Secretariat: "Bloody load of pen pushers the lot of them." Yet his general attitude to Aden was one of amiable acquiescence. He solemnly warned me about the dangers of alcohol, overspending and bribery. His boss Jack Sale, more at home at the Crescent Hotel's bar, gave me somewhat similar advice and complained that Aden's potential was being squandered by "ignorance, corruption and greed".

The remainder of my induction had little relevance to what lay ahead. Alec had originally allotted me five days at the Treasury as "essential to give you a proper grounding in finance". When I got there, no one had the slightest idea what to do with me. Eventually, an excitable Indian clerk thrust into my hand a copy of *Colonial Office Accounting and Financial Procedure* to digest. I only lasted another two days, leaving with the indelible memory of £50,000 worth of East African Shilling notes, Aden's official currency, being shredded by a monster perforating machine.

At the Intelligence Department, I was encouraged to browse through secret files that would have made any journalist salivate. At the Electricity Department, I was shown its £1-million generator, tended by a dozen Europeans and 600 locals, which alone kept Aden's lights ablaze. When I put it to Arthur Wiltshire, Aden's Chief of Police, that a single saboteur might bring the whole place to a standstill, he replied: "Don't worry. We've got everything well under control. I rate my Arab policemen higher than any of those I commanded in either East Africa or Somaliland."

The Head of the Public Relations Department, Nigel Watt, was less sanguine. "Quite simply, we're losing the propaganda war. We get so little

HMG funding that it's impossible to compete with Cairo's *Voice of the Arabs*. They're operating a highly sophisticated service which beams anti-British propaganda, twenty-four hours a day, to every Adeni and Protectorate tribesman who owns a transistor radio – that's just about everyone. My budget is so stretched that I can only manage one hour's broadcasting daily."

Virtually every government department in Aden was headed by a British official supported by Indian and Arab staff. One exception was the Aden Municipality, run by locally elected councillors. Its driving force remained its Town Clerk, Bill Gunn, an imperturbable Scot who had built the town's £45,000 swimming pool, meat market, cinema and municipal gardens. The Colony's other experiment in local government was the Shaikh Othman township. This Arab village and sweet-water oasis had originally been acquired from the Sultan of Lahej in 1881, and then rebuilt to house Crater's overspill. Its wells had supplied Aden's drinking water by an elaborate pumping system and a six-mile aqueduct. Some visionary Victorian architect had laid out a 30-acre garden with paths, flower beds, trees and lawns of which remnants were still visible. Unfortunately, with no Bill Gunn to lead, the Shaikh Othman municipality's urine-reeking corridors were filled with a scrum of beggars and petitioners, vainly trying to attract the attention of listless officials who had barricaded themselves behind barred doors. On my first visit, flustered peons and shouting guards were doing their best to control a mini-riot.

Alec urged me to attend a session of Aden's Legislative Council (LEGCO), "to get a broader view of Aden's political development". LEGCOs were the traditional British colonial vehicle for promoting the democratic process that would eventually lead to independence. In Aden's case, Lord Lloyd had warned, in 1956, that Adenis should not "aspire to any aim beyond that of a considerable degree of internal self-government". Events had since overtaken this pronouncement. In 1959, Aden was given its first general election, with a franchise limited to Aden-born males or sons of Aden-born fathers. Representing barely 5 percent of the population, this franchise had become the single most intractable issue faced by successive Aden governments. It had also provided both the ATUC and the anti-British United National Front Party with an excuse to boycott the LEGCO elections. Despite intimidation and violence, LEGCO was now up and running, with a mixture of British-appointed members, and a locally elected majority of nine Arabs, two Somalis and one Indian.

A Christian church had existed in Aden in the 4th century. In 1868 the British had built an Anglican church in Crater in neo-Gothic style. This had recently been deconsecrated to house the LEGCO chamber. High above the Governor's throne, replacing the high altar, a full-length portrait of the Queen surveyed this fledgling Parliament. The Strangers' Gallery was thronged with schoolgirls in purdah, teenage boys from Aden College and a bemused group of Aden Protectorate Levies. The fully-robed Speaker, Arthur Charles, was a distinguished ex-Sudan Political Service officer who maintained strict Westminster-style protocol. LEGCO's parliamentary procedures seemed well-ordered enough, with the Chief Secretary disposing of humdrum business with panache. However, at the equivalent of Question Time, pandemonium broke out. One elected Adeni member after another launched into a barrage of vitriolic questions which were followed by resolutions that opposed virtually every policy initiative recently proposed by the Governor in his "Queen's Speech". Simmonds stood his ground as fists were banged, order papers flung about and personal insults traded.

At dinner that night, I expressed surprise to Alec that debate should be so uninhibited, and that the Adenis were pursuing an agenda so radically opposed to our own.

"Much of that was just inflamed rhetoric for public consumption," he replied. "Aden has always had a free and vigorous press. These newly elected politicians must show their mettle. The last impression that any of them will want to give is that they're British lackeys."

"But if they're so strongly opposed to British rule, why not let them get on with it? If the Aden base is so important, wouldn't it be better for us to become advisers, as we are in the Protectorate, rather than direct rulers?"

"You're racing ahead a bit, John," replied Alec. "Actually, HE has already made somewhat similar proposals to London. However, I can't see them being accepted, altogether too radical. We're here, above all, to defend our strategic interests. Any decision which affects those will be made, not in Aden, but by the Chiefs of Staff in Whitehall."

One evening, Alec showed me the drafts of a new book being written by a Cambridge scholar, R. J. Gavin, to record Aden's early historical and political development. Gavin's magisterial *Aden Under British Rule* was only published fifteen years later, by which time the British had long since abandoned Aden. During his researches, he had scoured the Aden Government's archives, still housed in a Victorian wooden-latticed bungalow, on the hillside above the Secretariat. Next day, I inspected them for myself. Rack upon rack of massive leather-bound folios, riddled with worm, and written in Haines's original copperplate, had been left to rot in the elements.

"Has this unique archive ever been catalogued?" I asked Alec, in dismay. "It's surely irreplaceable. Presumably, the whole lot will eventually be shipped back to England for safe keeping?"

"I'm afraid that's most unlikely. We've long pleaded with the Colonial Office to do just that. They've rejected it on grounds of cost. They also maintain that such records should belong to whatever future indigenous government takes over from us."

I was granted a few precious minutes with the Protectorate Secretary, Horace Phillips. His brief was to keep the Governor informed on Protectorate issues, and their interaction with Aden and foreign powers. Phillips, a career diplomat seconded from the Foreign Office, was coming to the end of his four-year stint. As the grandson of Jewish immigrants from Eastern Europe, his background was very different from that of the Secretariat's Oxbridge elite. From humble beginnings, he had emerged with the rank of major after distinguished wartime service, during which he had discovered an exceptional gift for languages. Joining the Foreign Service as one of the new breed of British diplomats, he had made meteoric progress. Fluent and sharp-edged, his briefing was brusque.

"The first thing to realize, Harding, is that we're not going to be here for ever. While we are, your job is to secure Britain's best interests."

I had never heard my job described quite like this before. First and foremost, my duty was to give patriotic service to Her Majesty the Queen yet, as an employee of the Government of Aden, I was also pledged to serve the interests of the peoples of South Arabia. When I put this to Phillips, he enlarged on Britain's overriding objectives, and hinted at the many balls we were having to juggle. Like Ingrams, he was unguardedly critical of federal expansion policies. I was grateful for his candour, but could understand why he was not universally popular in Aden. At his farewell party, he confided to me that the feeling was mutual. Eight years on, Phillips was nominated to take over as British Ambassador at Jeddah. He was deeply committed to the peoples of the Middle East, but the Saudis rejected him on account of his Jewish faith. Disappointment was softened by his becoming Britain's ambassador to Turkey, with a knighthood.

Thus far, I had never been out of Aden Colony. So, when Christopher Pirie-Gordon suggested that Kenyon and I should accompany him and Amedeo Guillet, the Italian Minister at Ta'izz, to the Yemen border, I leapt at the chance. Alec had scrounged the Secretariat's newest Land Rover, normally reserved for archaeological trips, to make the journey by road. This followed an ancient trade route that had become so important strategically that Government Guards were posted at all principal villages en route. I had no previous experience of driving on the Protectorate's appalling roads, and, once beyond Lahej, this one became an obstacle course of potholes and boulders. Wrestling with the wheel as we ground up the desolate Wadi Aqqan, its flanks hemmed in by blue-glazed mountains, I strained my ears above the din to catch something of Amedeo Guillet's tales of wonder.

Just short of the frontier, near Kirsh, we stopped for a picnic lunch by the roadside, unwittingly disturbing a family of baboons who took to the rocks above screeching in fury. Amedeo produced a couple of bottles of Chianti which he cooled in an icy stream. I never realized, until many years later, how privileged I had been to meet this exceptional man. Guillet, born of an aristocratic Piedmont family, and an intimate of Italian royalty, had been the star of Italy's equestrian team in the 1936 Olympic Games. He had taken part in the Duke of Aosta's conquest of Ethiopia and, during the Italian East African Army's subsequent defeat in 1941, had led a full-scale cavalry charge on a white stallion against the British Army. Although badly wounded, Guillet avoided capture, and became a notorious guerrilla leader with a price on his head. He escaped to the Yemen by boat, was imprisoned in shackles, and was almost at death's door when Imam Yahya granted him an audience. Guillet came to befriend both the Imam and his son, Crown Prince Ahmed. After the war, he entered the Italian Foreign Service and, on his appointment as Italian Minister in the Yemen, became Imam Ahmed's only European confidant.

"What is Imam Ahmed really like?" I asked Amedeo.

"A Napoleon in Elba," he replied. "A man too big for his country."

Amedeo Guillet remained in the Yemen until appointed Italian ambassador to Jordan in July 1962. Subsequently, he became ambassador to Morocco and India. Now, in his centenary year, he divides his time between Rome and Ireland.

Sadly, Christopher Pirie-Gordon's Yemen posting was coming to an end.

For someone who listed his recreations as "dining, wining and talking", a succession of plum European consulships would be just reward for his long Middle East service. As we shook hands in parting, he said: "Always remember, John, the Arab is both the son and the father of the desert."

I greatly missed Christopher, but his earlier advice that I should choose my friends only from amongst government colleagues was not easy to follow, as none of my contemporaries were then stationed in Aden. Social life was cramped, for although over-worked senior officers kindly invited me to sober luncheons and dinners, I was too much a new boy to get many invitations outside the narrow government circle. Ken Simmond's convivial Sunday curry lunches, where government officials, the Armed Services, business, the foreign Consular Corps and prominent Adenis intermixed, were always good value. It was here that the German Consul gave me a hair-raising account of his capture on the Russian Front aged seventeen, followed by five years' incarceration in Siberia.

One afternoon at the Gold Mohur Bathing Club, my preoccupation with bikini-clad sea nymphs was disturbed by a familiar voice.

"How's the Secretariat? Haven't they packed you off to Mukalla yet to draw out your rifle?"

I swung round to face Roy Somerset, wearing flippers with a snorkel mask pushed back over his forehead.

"As a matter of fact, Roy, I'm just about to go there. I've had enough of office desks to last me a while."

"I wouldn't worry about that," grinned Roy. "Plenty of time for fun and games in the WAP, if that's what you really want. You should see what your chum Nash has been getting up to, rampaging around an area half the size of Wales, doing his best to start the next world war. Incidentally, I'm just going out to inspect a coral reef. Care to join me? I've got some spare equipment in the car."

I looked beyond the shark net that enclosed the club's swimming area to the deep blue sea beyond. Aden was still buzzing with the gory tale of the RAF wife who had been taken by a Tiger shark. But *amour-propre* was at stake, so I meekly followed in Somerset's wake, my face glued to my mask. I froze as a shoal of barracuda knifed below us through a multi-coloured coral reef swarming with exotic fish, but never met anything more serious that day than jelly fish. Only when I had clambered round the shark net to safety, did I notice that my legs and arms were covered in their stings.

Roy suggested that I visit him next day at the WAP Office, recently rehoused at Al-Ittihad, the Federation's new capital. This complex of gleaming white government ministries and offices, just off the road to Little Aden, had sprouted like mushrooms from a chunk of desert leased to the Federation by the Aqrabi Shaikhdom. Still resembling a construction site, Secretariat wags had already dubbed it "WAPopolis", or "Palmyra in decay". In fact, when I got to go there, I was impressed by its brisk sense of purpose, and an enthusiasm markedly absent in Aden. The Federation's existence owed much to the forceful personality of Kennedy Trevaskis, the WAP's British Agent for the past six years. Trevaskis was staking his reputation on this hotchpotch of Arab states outlasting the British mandate. For the moment, at least, one vital component was still missing – Aden Colony.

The gulf in attitude and aspiration between Aden and Al-Ittihad was palpable. Trevaskis was as mistrustful of urban Adenis as he was scornful of Aden's British officials. This had created an unseemly friction between the Secretariat's over-stretched administrators, trying desperately to control Aden's spiralling political devolution, and the WAP's Senior Advisers, working equally hard to make the federal machine work. The Secretariat jibbed at the WAP's "Protectorate Cowboys", while WAP men affected to despise the Secretariat's desk-bound "File Wallahs". Few WAP officers had ever served in Aden. Fewer still of the Secretariat's senior administrators had ever served in the WAP.

Somerset introduced me to some senior WAP officers: Arthur Watts, Ralph Daly and Robin Young. Daly, ex-Welsh Guards, and Young, ex-Royal Navy, were both transfers from the elite Sudan Political Service. Watts, on the other hand, had originally been posted to Aden during the war as an RAF sergeant before joining the Colonial Service. Affable and enthusiastic, his exceptional bent for Arabic had furthered his steady promotion. He invited me to lunch with Young, with whom he seemed to have nothing in common, and, later, with a contemporary Assistant Adviser, Godfrey Meynell.

Meynell I had known slightly at Cambridge. He had already completed one tour and, like James Nash, was planning to get married later that year and bring his young bride back to Arabia. Positively pulsating with nervous energy, he suggested that the following day we should drive out together to Zinjibar, the capital of the Fadhli State, where he was about to take over from Young. Early next morning, we picked up an armed escort of Government Guards at

Champion Lines before driving eastwards into the sun along a seemingly endless beach, towards a black bank of cumulus cloud capping a huge inland escarpment. Fish eagles wheeled overhead as Godfrey weaved in and out of a scattering of fishing boats, drawn high up on the sand to avoid the breaking surf.

"I'd better tell you something about the Abyan Delta before we get there," said Godfrey. "It's the showpiece of the WAP, and the pride of the Fadhli Sultanate. Fadhli is the most prosperous state in the WAP after Lahej, but more progressive with much nicer people. I'm enormously looking forward to working there."

As the beach petered out, we entered a wide delta, patterned with cotton plantations, cultivated fields and palm groves. The setting was idyllic, with all but the southern horizon rimmed by imposing mountains. Robin Young was waiting for us at his house in Zinjibar, dressed in open-necked shirt, knee-length khaki shorts and long stockings. Smiling broadly and smoking a pipe, he looking altogether more at ease than when I'd met him at lunch with Arthur Watts.

"Let's show John around the parish," he said to Godfrey, in a hoarse, gravelly voice. Then, turning to me, he murmured *sotto voce*, "Godfrey's about to take over from me. I'll be very sorry to leave."

He proceeded to whisk us round Zinjibar's school, health centre, police station, prison, suq and a brand new children's playground, like some avuncular squire showing off his country estate. Everyone seemed to know him and he knew everyone else.

"Wasn't always like this," said Robin. "Until quite recently, no one did much here except shoot each other. The two local tribes were forever at each other's throats over the ownership of the Wadi Bana's flood waters. Eventually, HMG was persuaded to cough up enough money to establish the Abyan Development Board. The locals then began to see that they could make a better living growing long-staple cotton than feuding and fighting. Since then, Abyan's become an example to other WAP states of what can be done if minds are put to it."

"Then security's not a problem here?" I enquired.

"No. It's not that simple. The Fadhli and Yafa'i tribes still don't like each other, and the Imam's always stirring things up. You'd better come and see what really underpins all development, not only here, but in the WAP generally."

We drove a few miles to the east of Zinjibar, to where a military encampment was strategically sited beneath an impressive mountain cirque. Pointing towards a battery of 3-inch mortars strung out around the camp's periphery, Young explained the set-up. "That company of Aden Protectorate Levies is permanently stationed here for good reason. They're the Federation's principal defence force, trained on Indian Army lines, recruited from the warlike tribes, and officered by British and 'Aulaqi regulars. They're the best guarantee we've got to keep the peace. Without them, there'd be no agricultural development in Abyan. Even so, it's a precarious balance. Peace in South Arabia's a very fragile thing."

Driving back to Aden, the incoming tide left just enough space for our Land Rover to avoid a ducking. Godfrey was singing along in a low, rumbling bass as Jebel Shamsan's silhouette bulked black against the setting sun. Before coming out to South Arabia, I had narrowly missed meeting Trevaskis at an Old Summerfieldian preparatory school reunion. Had I done so, he would most probably have asked me to come to the WAP. If he had, I could not have refused.

3

Mukalla

WHEN I SAID GOODBYE to Alec on the balcony of his flat, he told me that this was going be his last tour. Although only forty-three, he looked much older. He had decided to take early retirement through ill health, from the service in which he had spent the best twenty years of his life. I felt immensely grateful to him for his kindness and support that had verged almost on patronage. But now that he was leaving Aden, I wondered whether the magical scene that unfolded itself every morning, on the narrow strand below his flat where the fishermen unloaded the night's catch, would stay with him as a sweet or bitter memory. Aden was not an easy station. In summer, the humidity was only just tolerable. For married men with young families, long separations were accepted as part of the job.

My Aden induction, illuminated by some disturbing home truths, had generally been enjoyable. However, I had few regrets about boarding the Aden Airways Dakota DC3 on 9 February 1960, bound for Mukalla, capital of the Qu'aiti State. The 350-mile overland route from Aden took a minimum of two very uncomfortable days, but since the French merchant-entrepreneur Anton Besse had opened Aden's first commercial air service in 1937, the flight to Mukalla's "airport" Riyan, one of the RAF's air bases linking Britain to India and the Far East, took only two hours.

Riyan was built on a strip of sand abutting the sea, 20 miles east of Mukalla. The moment I stepped out of the plane, the fresh sea air put a spring into my step. As I walked across the tarmac towards a control tower and a sprawl of

Nissen huts, a tall, imposing figure dressed in a loose khaki jacket and trousers strode out to meet me.

"Harding?" he enquired, grasping my hand. "Wilson – how d'you do. Welcome to Mukalla!"

When I noticed his monocle, I knew at once that this could only be Archie Wilson, aka Lt.-Colonel Archibald Wilson DSO, whom I had heard described by habitués of the Union Club as a "real character". Cumming-Bruce had been less reverential.

"Must be damned thirsty after that flight. Better get you a drink sharpish," said Wilson, steering me into a tin shed marked "RAF Club". The Club's interior resembled the sort of place where white trash might have spun out their lives in a Central American banana republic. Over an introductory can or more of chilled beer, Archie got down to business.

"Glad you're here at last. You know, of course, that you're taking over from me as AAR?"

"What *is* AAR, Colonel Wilson?"

"For God's sake old boy, do call me Archie. You're not in Aden now, so forget the flannel. But surely those Secretariat wallahs gave you a proper briefing?"

"I'm afraid not, though I did get a tour of various government departments."

"Fat lot of good that will do you here," grinned Archie. "And typical of those paper pushers not to put you in the picture. We don't run this show like Aden. But to answer your question, AAR means Assistant Adviser Residency. It's a dogsbody job but somebody's got to keep the place ticking over."

"I was told that I'd have a lot to do with passports."

"Oh that!" exclaimed Archie, dismissively. "I wouldn't worry too much about passports, not just yet at any rate. But I expect you'll be getting a full briefing from the RA tomorrow. You'll be staying with him at the Residency for your first few days. Help you get to know the ropes. Alastair's an excellent man, knows everything there is to know about South Arabia, and goes one hundred percent at everything he does. You'd do well to take on board everything he tells you. There's nothing like hands-on experience for this job."

The RA (pronounced "AHRAY") and Alastair were synonymous. Alastair James McIntosh CMG, OBE was Her Britannic Majesty's Resident Adviser and British Agent for the Eastern Aden Protectorate, and otherwise my boss.

Preliminaries over, Archie didn't encourage any more questions. After downing several more cans in quick succession, he led me across the runway to a battered Bedford pick-up truck. We shot off westwards into the late afternoon sun along a featureless beach, swerving erratically to avoid the incoming tide before being forced inland, and getting completely stuck in the sand.

"Bloody awful road, this," remonstrated Archie. "About time someone did something about it. Must speak to Booker."

He didn't explain who Booker might be. From the tone of his voice, I assumed that he must be one of his minions. Eventually, Archie managed to flag down a passing lorry to pull us out. Two hours later than scheduled, we arrived outside the walled city of Mukalla. Slaloming through an encampment of tethered camels, Archie sped through impressive city gates built in Neo-Gothic Indian style. He then wheeled sharp left into a walled compound, accelerated across it and came to a juddering halt inside the portico of an elegant, three-storeyed building. Walls plastered with white limestone gypsum produced a stucco-like effect, and the four cast-iron cannons facing seawards gave the impression of some exotic baronial hall. As Archie jumped down from the truck, three Arab guards, dressed in white-skirted tunics, belted with red cummerbunds and crossed with ammunition belts, came smartly to attention.

"Here we are then, the British Residency Mukalla," announced Archie. "Once a sultan's palace, architecturally a mess, but basically Indo-Georgian."

He gave the guard a cursory salute, muttering something uncomplimentary about "Bloody Gray's Legion", and then led the way up a flight of steps to a double doorway, surmounted by a faded device reading "British Consular Agency". Beyond this lay an inner hall, and stairs which Archie took two at a time before coming to a halt inside a spacious office overlooking the compound.

"Ah, there you are, Archie. And this must be Harding. Welcome to Mukalla."

The Resident Adviser walked quickly across the room to greet us, seemingly unconcerned that we were more than two hours late. Small and rotund, with darting eyes and a toothbrush moustache, this was not the proconsular figure I had expected to fit the mould of an Ingrams or a Boustead.

"You must be quite whacked," said the RA solicitously. "Luckily, you're just in time for a quick swim to freshen up. Get yourself unpacked. You've brought your bathing costume, of course?"

Within minutes, I was seated alongside the RA in a long-wheel-base Land Rover. We roared out of the compound through the same city gates, startled a few more camels, and then crossed a wide wadi before heading westwards along a seemingly endless beach, sending shoals of land crabs scuttling for cover as we bowled along. The RA's idea of a swim was to wade out waist deep, launch himself onto a breaking wave, and surf inshore like a turtle. It was already dark when we got back to the Residency.

"Get yourself settled in upstairs and then come down for a drink," said the RA. When I rejoined my host in his comfortable, if rather shabby, sitting room he was sunk deep into an armchair.

"Brown or white?" he enquired.

I blinked back, not knowing how to reply.

"Brown or white?" he repeated, a touch irritably, and then pointed to a tray on a side table cluttered with gin and whisky bottles.

"Brown please, with water," I replied.

He got up, poured out half a glass of whisky, added a finger of water and eyed me critically. McIntosh might have lacked the dynamic persona of his predecessors but, as I soon discovered, he was no lightweight, and had few equals in South Arabian experience. An Oxford organ scholar with Firsts in Theology and Hebrew, he had once contemplated holy orders before settling for academe to read Arabic at both Bonn University and the American University, Beirut. After active military service throughout the Second World War, including a spell in Palestine, he had joined the Colonial Service in 1947. For the next eleven years "Toosh", as the Arabs called him, had served as a Political Officer in both Protectorates, undertaking several tough trouble-shooting assignments before succeeding Boustead as the EAP's Resident Adviser in 1958.

Over dinner, Alastair became resolutely uncommunicative. By breakfast next morning, he seemed in a better mood. The Residency was popularly known as "Dysentery Hall", yet my breakfast of pawpaw, bacon and eggs and local honey, was better than anything I had eaten at Ras Boradli. Sensing a more receptive atmosphere, I enquired why the interior walls of the Residency had been painted such a startling sky blue.

"Obvious," replied the RA. "To keep down the glare. Take a walk outside when the sun's up, and you'll soon see what I mean."

Remembering what Archie had told me yesterday, I broached the subject of the AAR's role and responsibilities.

"Surely Archie has already been through all that?" Alastair retorted impatiently. Sensing an emerging pattern, I said nothing but merely shook my head.

"Oh well, if he hasn't already given you the guff, I'd better do so myself. It's a dogsbody job, but important nonetheless for it's essential that this place functions efficiently. The work's not without interest, and should give you a useful introduction to both administrative and advisory work."

"Alec Cumming-Bruce told me that I'd be spending a good bit of time dealing with passports."

"Oh he did, did he?" said Alastair, muttering something under his breath. "Certainly, you'll be involved with passports. Moreover, that whole boiling needs sorting out, so I'd like you to take on full responsibility for all consular functions from now on. Didn't you read law at Cambridge?"

I nodded warily.

"Good. Then don't get the wrong idea. Passports are very important and one of the few areas over which we exercise direct control here. The Hadhramis are compulsive travellers, so they *must* have travel documents to do their business. It's our job to provide them. To make things work smoothly, we bring the local states into the act, so you must get to know your opposite number, 'Isa Musallam, the Qu'aiti passport man. That'll also give you some inkling of how an Arab state department works. Always remember, our influence largely depends on our getting on well with the locals. That's bound to involve some "keeny-meeny" – jiggery-pokery, political manoeuvring. It's a critical ingredient in Arabian life so you'd better get used to it. Incidentally, the *Hajj* is about to begin, the annual pilgrimage to Mecca. Pretty soon this place will be flooded with every sort of Ali or Ahmed from the interior, the Gulf, Pakistan, or whatever, and all howling for Pilgrim Visas. Its damned important that we keep up with demand. Archie will give you a full briefing before he pushes off to the Northern Deserts. Excellent man, Archie, and a very distinguished soldier. Didn't get his DSO for nothing. You'd do well to listen to his advice."

Archie had indeed been a very brave soldier. However, his military career had suffered an irreversible setback after the tank duel he had staged in Beirut's main square with a US Army captain, for which he had been court-martialled.

"When *is* Archie going to the Northern Deserts?" I asked, cautiously.

"In just a few days. Plenty of time for you to get your feet under his desk before he goes. Make a start now, and get down to the Residency office. You'll find Archie's there already, always an early riser."

Bolting down my coffee, I trotted across the dusty Residency compound to a lime-washed block of buildings with tall shuttered windows. Unlike the WAP Office, whose origins went back to the mid-19th century, the British Agency, Mukalla, had come into existence only twenty-three years before when Harold Ingrams had been appointed as the EAP's first Resident Adviser. The Eastern Aden Protectorate comprised four states – Qu'aiti, Kathiri, Wahidi and Mahra. The first two, the "Hadhrami States", had signed advisory treaties with Britain in the late 19th century. As the premier sultanate, the Qu'aiti State's capital, Mukalla, had been the natural choice for the British Residency.

The Residency had grown apace since Ingrams had run it with only his formidable wife Doreen and a brace of Arab clerks. By 1960, the EAP's British Advisory staff had risen to nearly a dozen. They included the RA's Deputy, Johnny Johnson; his Intelligence Officer, Charles Inge; two Senior Advisers, Jock Snell and Pat Booker; and the AAR – all based in Mukalla. Three other British advisers were based in Sayun, the capital of the Kathiri Sultanate. Both the Wahidi Sultanate and the Northern Deserts Area also had one each. Mahra, still largely *terra incognita*, had none. Locally employed staff numbered about forty. The RA also had a Military Adviser, who was supported by the Commandant of the Hadhrami Bedouin Legion (HBL), plus two training officers seconded from British regiments. In McIntosh's time, relations between the civil and military arms enjoyed about the same degree of cordiality as had existed in India, when Curzon was Viceroy and Kitchener the Indian Army's Commander-in-Chief.

In the recesses of the Residency's office complex I ran down Archie.

"Morning to you," Archie greeted me, genially. "Alastair given you the run-down?"

"Not exactly," I replied. "He told me that you'd be giving me a full briefing this morning."

"Did he now? Well, there's not really that much to brief you about," Archie countered amiably. "As I told you yesterday, let experience be your guide. This is the sort of game you can only pick up as you go along. However, you'd better get used to finding your way around the odd file. Take a pew, and have a look at this one."

Selecting a battered cover at random from a small heap cluttering a corner of his desk, he shoved it in my direction. Its contents consisted of some flimsy bits of paper, punched with a hole at the top left hand edge, and held together by a green toggle. I studied them intently, and eventually gave up. They might have been hieroglyphics.

"Sorry, Archie, but I really don't begin understand what this is all about."

"They're Savingrams, old boy," he replied. "This lot will have come in from AA Northern Deserts. He'll write his text in message form. It will then be transmitted by wireless from some HBL fort up there, to HBL HQ down here for transliteration. The whole process is done by *jundies*, Arab soldiers to you, so messages can get a bit garbled. The trick is to pick out the key words. Take a squint at this file, then try your hand at drafting an answer."

I read the file from beginning to end while Archie settled himself down on the other side of the desk, puffing contently at a large curved pipe. Half an hour later, I was little the wiser.

"How you getting on?" asked Archie.

"Not too well, I'm afraid. However, I think this is all about some tribesmen squabbling over the ownership of a well."

"Sounds about right," he smiled, reassuringly. "That's the usual form. But what's your solution?"

"Sorry, Archie, I really haven't a clue."

"Don't worry, old boy", he replied cheerfully. "I doubt that I have either. But you'll soon get the feel of things, and when I get up to the Northern Deserts, I'll send you down a few, just to get your hand in. Don't bother to reply unless it's anything to do with oil. In that case, make sure you take it straight to Alastair, pronto."

Returning to my struggle with Savingrams, and occasionally disturbing Archie's contemplation with questions which he dispatched with impressive economy, I tried another tack. "This business of passport issue, Archie, do we hold copies of the *British Nationality Act* and the *Foreign Office Consular Regulations*?"

"Good God, no!" exclaimed Archie. "Where on earth did you hear about them?"

"At the Aden Immigration Department."

"Oh, that useless lot! We don't bother about FO regulations here. There's probably some bumf floating around the office, but I've never found any use for it myself."

"Alastair told me that I must get to grips with passport issue, and that the *Hajj* was about to start."

"I wouldn't get too fussed about that," said Archie, pleasantly. "As I told you before, there's really not much to it. You've got an excellent passport clerk in Noah Johannes who handles things very capably. Mahra passports can be a bit tricky, but in that case, just refer to Abdullah Mahri. Incidentally, Abdullah's also the Residency's Quartermaster, and as stores are part of your remit you'd better get to know him. Delightful chap, but a bit up in the clouds. Anyway," he added, glancing at his watch, "it's already past elevenses, and we both need a break. Better get down to Johnny's house. Most people will be there already."

"Most people" in Archie-speak meant a very select segment of Mukalla's British community, which had grown appreciably in recent years. It now included a Fisheries Officer, a Co-operative and Marketing Manager, three engineers, four doctors, the Manager of the Eastern Bank and his deputy, plus a selection of wives. Of these, only Sid Morrison, a hard-bitten Scots mechanic, was a member of the charmed circle that met every morning for extended elevenses at Johnny Johnson's house, conveniently situated just inside the gates of the Residency compound.

I had, of course, already met Johnny, otherwise Mr E. R. Johnson OBE, as the soul of SOAS pub life. In his unkempt sitting room were foregathered Alastair, Jock Snell, Charles Inge, Sid Morrison and Jim Allen, the RA's male personal secretary, the female variety being un-Islamic and therefore politically unacceptable. Only one member of the Advisory Staff was missing, Pat Booker, the AA Coastal Areas, a punctilious and committed Scotsman addicted to hard work. Judging from the heap of empty beer cans that littered the floor, Archie had certainly left it a bit late.

"Bit slow off the mark this morning aren't you, Archie?" chided Johnny. "Tut, tut. And introducing John to bad habits already!" He handed me a chilled can. "Doesn't do to get yourself dehydrated in Arabia."

Introductions over, the morning's real business continued unabated. When I noticed that it was already well past noon, I swigged down the remains of my can and mumbled: "I'd better be getting back to the office if you don't mind. I'm finding things a bit confusing at this stage."

"If you must," rumbled Alastair. "But be sure to be back at the Residency at one o'clock sharp with your bathing costume. We're having a picnic this afternoon with Coleridge, the Chief Auditor."

In the colonial scheme of things, government auditors were people of consequence. I duly reported at the appointed time and, an hour later, the rest of the party assembled: Alastair, Coleridge, Johnny, Archie, Charles Inge, his wife Dorothy and seven-year-old daughter "Bint", supported by attendant drivers, guards, cooks and bearers. This entourage took off in two long-wheel-base Land Rovers and, after driving through the now familiar Indian Gate, headed westwards along the beach. As both drivers raced each other, dodging and weaving past the incoming breakers, we gradually closed the gap between ourselves and a distant promontory of blue hills. Now left far behind, the white-washed mosques, palaces and mansions of Mukalla, spread out beneath the pinky-grey hump of Jebel Qarat, looked a distant vision.

Sun-screened by a huge multi-coloured umbrella, the picnic was eaten *à table* off pressed white linen. Surfeited with King Fish cutlets, lamb pancakes served piping hot from thermos flasks, and alcohol, the party sprawled itself out on one of Alastair's fine Persian carpets. Conversation, never more than desultory, then lapsed completely. While most went to sleep, I swam a couple of times to clear my head. Wandering amongst the sand dunes behind the beach, I spotted a hoopoe and several ospreys.

On the way back to Mukalla, Alastair suddenly came back to life.

"When we're home and dry, get yourself ready to meet the Sultan. We're going to his palace this evening with the Chief Minister, Jehan Khan, to introduce you. Smarten up and put a suit on."

Of all the sultans, sharifs, shaikhs and amirs who, by their different lights, ruled the twenty-one separate states of the Aden Protectorates, only two, the 'Abdali Sultan of Lahej and the Qu'aiti Sultan of Shihr and Mukalla, were accorded 11-gun salutes and the dignity of being addressed as "Your Highness". On this criterion, His Highness Sultan 'Awadh bin Salih Al-Qu'aiti, ruler of the Eastern Aden Protectorate's paramount state, was a man of significance. Yet he owed his position more to the ambition and energy of his predecessors than to his own abilities.

The rise of the Qu'aiti dynasty in the 19th century had coincided with Britain's forward policy of controlling the South Arabian coastline in order to safeguard the sea routes to India and suppress the slave trade. Trading and cultural links had long existed between South Arabia's maritime states and the Indian princely state of Hyderabad which, during the latter half of the 18th century, had effectively fallen under the East India Company's control. To maintain his position as a Muslim ruler in the face of Hindu aggression, the Nizam of Hyderabad had recruited his military bodyguard from the co-religionist South Arabian warrior tribe of Yafaʻi. One of these was ʻUmar bin ʻAwadh, founder of the Quʻaiti dynasty. The wealth and property that ʻUmar and his successors accumulated financed the expansion of their power and influence in Hadhramaut, at the expense of their rival tribe, the Kathiri. After a period of protracted Quʻaiti/Kathiri warfare, the Quʻaitis came out on top, thanks to British intervention. Friendly relations, officially established in 1882, led to a formal treaty of British protection in 1888. Under its provisions, the Quʻaiti ruler agreed to be guided by the British in foreign affairs, thus enabling the British to control the coast, without having to get involved with the interior, following the model of the Gulf's Trucial States.

The Anglo-Hyderabad connection also influenced the structure of the Quʻaiti Sultan's administration, the training of his armed forces, and even the style of Mukalla's architecture. Quʻaiti sons were educated in Hyderabad, usually married wealthy Indian women, and brought over officials from the Subcontinent to help govern their South Arabian domains. Such a man was Jehan Khan, a Punjabi of peasant stock who had formerly served in the British Somaliland Customs Service, and had since become the Quʻaiti State's Chief Minister. He picked us up at the Residency, to drive all of one hundred yards to the Sultan's palace, just over the road. At the entrance hall of this multi-turreted Indo-Victorian extravaganza, built on a low cliff overlooking the Indian Ocean, we were met by the Sultan's ten-year-old younger son, ʻUmar, and a Lord Chamberlain, so decrepit that he only just made it to the top of the stairs. In a garishly furnished throne room the Sultan, sallow and sickly-looking, greeted us without enthusiasm. Our audience was little more than a stiff exchange of formalities. After an awkward hiatus, the Sultan rose unsteadily to his feet to signal its conclusion. The speed of the British Resident Adviser's exit was embarrassing.

Back at the Residency, Alastair's humour was partially restored by a rapid succession of browns.

"Complete waste of time having to see that poor man," he grumbled peevishly. "He's not at all well and has become a pale shadow of his father,

Sultan Salih. Thank God, there's an elder boy, Ghalib. He's a good lad who shows promise, but he's only twelve and still at school in England. Let's hope he won't be ruined by harem life, and will rule this place like his grandfather did."

"Who runs Mukalla, then?" I asked.

"Mukalla is run by Jehan Khan, and a merchant oligarchy most of whose members sit on the Sultan's State Council. In the provinces, there are also various state officials, Naibs and Qaims, who run rudimentary administrations. All in all, the system doesn't work too badly and Jehan Khan knows a bit about finance and administration. He's not universally popular with the Qu'aitis, but is canny and capable. Has to be when dealing with the State Council. They're the ones who own Mukalla."

"What about the Sultan's father? Ingrams seems to have admired him."

"A man of many parts, a genuine polymath who spoke several languages and had travelled widely," replied Alastair. "Sultan Salih, I mean. I knew him when I was Boustead's deputy. Unfortunately, he died four years ago. Ingrams might have claimed that he was personally responsible for making everything in this place work. In fact, Salih had already pushed through any number of administrative, educational and agricultural reforms before then, despite strong opposition from the backwoodsmen. Before the last war, the Qu'aiti education budget was twice that of Aden's, and by the mid-1950s Qu'aiti revenues were several times more than those of the entire WAP. Salih got Aden's Director of Agriculture over here to introduce a new strain of tobacco to improve the Ghail ba Wazir crop. He also built the West Road to Wadi Du'an, and introduced electric lighting to Mukalla. Ingrams could not have brought peace to Hadhramaut without the support of Sultan Salih and Sayyid Abu Bakr Al-Kaf. You'd do well to realize that it's not the British who run this place, but the Arabs. They do it pretty well, all things considered."

"Then what *is* our role here?"

"To advise the states as and when required. To provide technical support, encourage the odd development scheme and try to keep everyone's noses clean. This place isn't a bit like the WAP, let alone Aden. The Hadhramis are a proud people with their own civilization. But they're economically and politically backward, and haven't got the money to get off the ground. The key to their future is oil. Its discovery would transform the place. The Hadhramis are convinced that it's around somewhere, but no one's struck lucky yet."

"What about agriculture, health and education? Alec Cumming-Bruce told me that the Protectorate was starved of development funds, but that the Ramage Report might induce HMG to give more financial support."

"He's never worked here, but he's broadly right, though I'm not that confident about Ramage," replied Alastair, sourly. "We're lucky to get £100,000 a year out of HM Treasury, and could use all that just to improve the fishing industry. That hasn't been a success to date under Veevers-Carter, but he'll be going soon. Fisheries is also Booker's responsibility. Ask him to enlighten you on the problems."

"But if there's no money for development, what are the prospects for the future?" I persisted.

"This is getting tiresome," growled Alastair. "Anyway, whose prospects are you talking about? Theirs or yours? Let's get it quite clear. The Hadhramis' long-term prosperity depends on finding oil. Yours on what the British Chiefs of Staff decide to do with Aden. In the meantime, just remember that our job here is to maintain the status quo as long as we can. Don't dream up unrealistic pet schemes expecting the British taxpayer to divvy up. It's up to us to make do with things as we find them. The Hadhramis get by on overseas remittances largely from Saudi Arabia and the Gulf. They're resilient people and inveterate traders. That's why British passports are so vital to them, and that's why yours is an important job. And now I'm damned bored answering your questions, and want something to eat. Archie will show you round Mukalla tomorrow."

Archie's tour of Mukalla was perfunctory, but included a mercurial whisk round the Qu'aiti Secretariat. He didn't seem to know many people there, but at a door marked "Qu'aiti State Passport Office", stopped short.

"Here we are at last," sighed Archie. "Now for the business. I'm going to introduce you to 'Isa. First class chap, plays tennis." 'Isa Musallam, the Qu'aiti Sultanate's Passport Officer, was effusively charming and spoke good English. "You two should have a lot in common," said Archie. "'Isa also issues passports, so you'll be seeing a lot of each other from now on."

"I thought it was my job to issue passports," I said, puzzled.

"Yes it is, but it's his job too. Anyway, now you two have met, we must move on smartly to see if Rahman Khan's still manning his Customs Post. Incidentally, you should know that customs dues are by far the most important source of Qu'aiti revenue. As Mukalla's the only half-decent port in the area, the State's got a stranglehold on trade and levies dues on imports, exports, goods in transit and shipping. Unlike some people round here, Rahman Khan, who runs the show, is a stickler for form and dead straight. So don't get on the wrong side of him."

"Ah ... Hullo, Hullo – here's the man himself! Rahman, I'd like you to meet John Harding, the new AAR. Perhaps you'd kindly show him around your domain as I must be going now. I'll just leave you two to chat about contraband."

Rahman Khan gave Archie a disapproving look. A Punjabi, like the Chief Minister, though a more devout Muslim, he was unsmiling yet courteous. He also spoke good English and gave me a thorough tour of the Qu'aiti Customs Department.

The Customs House was built on the promontary of Al-Bilad, the oldest part of Mukalla. It overlooked the picturesque harbour, now filled with small-fry fishing boats and ocean-going dhows drawn up along a narrow strand undergoing repairs. At the landward end of an elegant colonnade of shops, the spires of the new town's mosques peeked out from between the facades of the multi-storeyed merchant houses that blended Hadhrami and Hyderabadi architectural styles. Dominating the town itself was Jebel Qarat, a 430-metre-high mountain, whose black basalt ridges stretched down towards the sea like skeletal fingers between ochre coloured screes and pinkish limestone cliffs. Mukalla looked the sort of place from which Sindbad might have sailed a thousand years before. In fact, it had been little more than a fishing village until the mid-19th century, and only since had become South Arabia's pre-eminent port after Aden.

From this same Customs House verandah, the artist David Shepherd was about to paint his famous picture, *Mukalla*. His arrival at RAF Riyan coincided with a needle cricket match between the Residency and the RAF, played on the landing strip. Alastair had persuaded Coleridge, a class batsman, to turn out for the Residency. Our nail-bitingly close victory was secured by his two hurricane innings, and prompted Archie's gleeful "There'll never be any trouble with the books in Mukalla after this!" Johnny celebrated the triumph by bending double, in three minutes flat, the 53 empty lager cans that he, Alastair and Archie had accounted for between them, as the game's scoring troika.

Shepherd and I had been at school together. I never had the nerve to ask if I might keep just one of the rough sketches of his painting *Mukalla* that I'd seen him dash off, having been discouraged by his reply to my flip question "Do artists still live in garrets, David?" "Definitely not. Untypical of the modern school." Shepherd later became famous both as a painter and a wildlife conservationist. He regarded the Wadi Hadhramaut as the most memorable place he ever visited. His South Arabia paintings vividly capture the genius of the place.

A sense of unreality overhung my early days in Mukalla, for I still had a new boy's enthusiasm for "getting things done". Aden's Secretariat officials had never seemed to stop working, whereas in Mukalla, the admirable Pat Booker apart, the clock usually stopped at elevenses. Life took on a more serious turn when Archie finally left for the Northern Deserts in a Land Rover stuffed with booze, accompanied by an outsize HBL escort. His parting words – "You'll learn more about this place talking to people like Johnny and Jock over a glass of beer than reading a dozen books" – was the only hand-over I ever got.

The day after his departure, I was wrestling with a batch of Savingrams, when a procession of white uniformed peons, led by the Chief Filing Clerk, wheeled in a train of trolleys piled high with files.

"What's all this about?" I asked him.

"Files for your attention, Sir," he replied, motioning his peons to dump them in tottering heaps around my desk. On the front cover of each was pinned a slip of paper with the instruction: "Bring up for urgent attention 18 February".

"Excuse me, Sir," the Chief Clerk continued. "Colonel Wilson particularly asked me to show you this one as a matter of urgency."

He thrust into my hand a pink file marked "Secret and Very Urgent". It concerned the arrangements that AAR was supposed to have made for the Governor, Sir William Luce's valedictory visit to the Eastern Aden Protectorate. Archie had never mentioned this visit. Apparently, it was to take place in two days' time. With mounting alarm, I read that I was supposed to be attending a meeting to discuss arrangements in the RA's Office at 9 a.m. that very morning. I was already five minutes late, when a breathless peon arrived with a hand written message: "Kindly report to my office at once – RA."

Doubling across the compound, I raced up the stairs to the RA's office to be confronted by a red-faced Alastair, flanked by Johnny Johnson and Alastair's Military Adviser, Lt.-Colonel George Coles.

"You're late!" exploded Alastair. "What on earth happened to you?"

"I'm extremely sorry," I gasped. " I hadn't realized that there was this meeting until I read the file just now. I do apologize."

"Never mind your apologies," snorted Alastair. " Don't you realize that the day after tomorrow, HE plus Lady Luce, his niece and two ADCs will be arriving here? This is HE's last official visit to Mukalla, so we've got to put on a damned good show. Surely Archie told you that you were responsible for making all the necessary arrangements. Have you sorted out the transport yet?"

"Not quite," I replied, lying through my teeth. "But I'm getting on with it."

The men primarily responsible for keeping the Residency's ageing transport fleet on the road were Sid Morrison, the manager of the Qu'aiti workshops, and a mechanical wizard when sober, and his overlord, Gordon "Tubby" Dawson, the HBL's highly efficient Transport Officer. Morrison promised to give the whole fleet a thorough going-over, while I instituted a last-minute regime of early morning inspections for all Residency drivers.

On the appointed day, the Governor's party was met at RAF Riyan by the entire Residency advisory and military team. It was then escorted back to Mukalla in five highly polished Land Rovers, their drivers immaculately turned out in white denim uniforms and red turbans. As the cavalcade drove through the Indian Gate, a breach-loaded cannon of 1786 vintage let off a series of thunderous explosions. These continued intermittently as HE reviewed the massed ranks of the Hadhrami Bedouin Legion, Mukalla Regular Army (MRA) and Qu'aiti Armed Constabulary in the Residency compound.

Military parades were an essential feature of all VIP visits to Mukalla, major festivals and Sultanic whim. They also touched on inherent martial pride. Although this colourful militia might have looked a touch Gilbertian as they marched around in their swishing skirts or shorts, all came from good fighting stock. The HBL was modelled on Glubb Pasha's Jordanian Arab Legion. The MRA, the Sultan's state security force, largely recruited from warrior Yafa'is and slave stock, had formerly been trained by Indian Army officers. The Qu'aiti Armed Constabulary, a paramilitary force responsible for internal security, was also recruited from Yafa'i irregulars and local tribesmen. As HE took the salute, all three arms swept past the dais with their curious, high knee-jerking marching action, in a swirl of red, white and khaki, to the strains of *Colonel Bogey*, bashed out under the baton of the MRA's Punjabi bandmaster,

Jaswandi Khan. He, most resplendent of all, wore a white ceremonial uniform and khaki turban, topped with a rampant cockscomb.

Much the same ritual was repeated that afternoon in the Sultan's palace compound, before Mukalla's commonalty. After the armed forces had marched past, the Bedouin Boys Cadet School, shrimp-sized lads dressed in calf-length, dark blue shirts waisted with red sashes, emulated their elders at Rifle Brigade pace, toting .303 Lee Enfield rifles as tall as themselves. Masters and boys then delivered mega-decibel speeches of welcome, which were followed with poetry recitals, plays depicting Aesop's fables Arabian-style, and such homespun maxims as "Don't see a quack – see a proper doctor". Alarmingly realistic depictions of violent death and epileptic fits were greeted with gales of laughter. The show finished with an astonishing *coup de théatre,* when the entire squad walked the breadth of the parade ground on their hands, in precise military formation. After that, nobody could be bothered with the Bedouin Girls' handicrafts exhibition. HE's departure was the signal for a free-for-all mass exodus through the compound's single-exit gate. As I battled my way through the crowd to the Residency compound, I passed a Land Rover overwhelmed by twenty would-be passengers, sinking slowly to the ground.

Gubernatorial visits represented the highpoint of Mukalla's social calendar. Protocol and precedence were studiously observed because invitations to parties offered glory for the chosen, but chagrin for the rest. Alastair took pains to ensure that no one was overlooked by hosting an all-embracing informal dinner. At this, Jaswandi Khan varied his standard Gilbert-and-Sullivan selection with a livelier Indo-Arab mixture, once as familiar to members of the Raj as it had become to Mukalla's expatriates.

Sir William Luce was a patrician veteran of the Sudan Political Service, with a common touch. He was the most far-sighted and charismatic of the four supremos under whom I served. After dinner, he took me aside and talked easily about Arabia, the Colonial Service and Wilfred Thesiger. By now, Luce had already submitted to London his own blueprint for South Arabia's future. He had recommended that Britain should surrender its sovereignty over Aden and the Protectorate by 1962, after Aden's status had been converted from colony to protectorate. The whole package was to be underwritten by a generous development programme. Luce's imaginative scheme was not accepted by Whitehall. Successive British governments remained obsessed by the mantra of Fortress Aden, but none were prepared to pour British taxpayers' money into the economic wastelands of South Arabia.

One object of Luce's valedictory visit was to persuade the Hadhrami rulers not to jettison the delicate oil exploration negotiations they had been conducting for over the past year with Petroleum Concessions Limited (PCL), a British subsidiary of the Iraq Petroleum Company. British oil companies still exercised significant control over the Gulf's major producers, so were loath to encourage expensive operations in remote, unproven areas such as South Arabia. Backing their instinct, and somewhat flimsy geological evidence, the Hadhramis were more bullish. Before the Second World War, Sultan Salih Al-Qu'aiti had signed an exploration agreement with Imperial Petroleum. In 1946, Major Tony Altounyan made his first exploratory journey into Mahra. In 1947 he returned with the PCL geologist Mike Morton to undertake on camelback a ten-week, surface survey of the area including the Wadi Masila, the seaward extension of the Wadi Hadhramaut. Their findings were inconclusive, but in 1960 PCL remained the front-runner in the search for oil in the Northern Deserts.

By now the quest for Hadhrami oil, and the political and economic consequences of its discovery, had reached a critical stage. Shortly before HE's visit, PCL's Mr Krafer had been closeted for days with the EAP's Sultans in Mukalla. Krafer maintained that his company's explorations had yielded nothing. The Hadhramis didn't believe him. Without Luce's mediation, the talks would have broken down, with the potentially disastrous consequences of Bedouin unrest in the desert and rioting in Mukalla.

Less than a month after Luce's visit, McIntosh was bidden to Aden for further talks to persuade PCL to start fresh EAP exploration. This trip coincided with a second spectacular March flood, which severed the road to Riyan for a week. Instead of flying, the RA was obliged to sail to and from Aden by dhow, a red ensign fluttering at the mast, with Alastair below vomiting continuously both ways. Before departure, his last instructions had been that I requisition a Residency minion's house to accommodate the second Krafer delegation. Just back from Aden the morning Krafer was due, Alastair summoned me to his office, still suffering from his double dhow debacle.

"The talks have now been cancelled," he groaned. "PCL are losing interest in the Middle East, and are now looking to North Africa for new operations. They've decided to move all their equipment out from the Northern Deserts to Muscat. I can scarcely believe it. But maybe this place is destined to remain a backwater, undefiled by the modern world, and most likely all the better for it. If the Chiefs of Staff decide that Aden's isn't worth holding, we'll all be out of here before we know it anyway. God only knows what will then happen to these people we're supposed to be serving. This is a bloody awful note on which to end my time here. At least I've done my best, and can now go on leave with a relatively clear conscience."

That was not quite the end of the oil quest saga. Three weeks after Alastair's departure on leave, Mr Green, of Shell, took over the slippery baton, and complained to me that Mukalla was an impossible place in which to do business.

"The State Council seems to be run by a blind autocrat whose intransigence is breathtaking. We've offered very favourable oil franchises but he simply won't accept our terms."

"Shaikh Bubakr Barahim's an able man who won't be pushed around," I told him.

"In that case, whose side are you British on anyway?" demanded Green. "Are you for us and progress, or are you hooked on supporting these anachronistic rulers and their preposterous administrations?"

"It's not that simple," I replied, self-righteously. "We have to serve two masters. We can only *advise* the rulers, and are most likely to achieve the best results for both sides by doing all we can for the local people."

Nothing significant ever came of British oil exploration in the EAP. However, by 1999, the Hadhramis' hunch had been proved right, when oil and gas were first exploited in commercial quantities by a Norwegian company operating out of the same Wadi Masila that Morton had surveyed fifty-two years before. Oil now represents 70 percent of Yemen's exports, most of it from the Wadi Masila, with Mukalla the principal oil exploration centre.

Four days after Luce's departure, Mukalla was shaken by a salvo of heavy gunfire from out to sea, prompting a summons from Alastair.

"It's that wretched Yankee warship the USS *Duxbury Bay* again," he spluttered. "It's been here before, but this time it's got some bloody admiral on board so we'll have to put on some sort of show. He's asked six of us to luncheon on board today. Tell Morrison to release Boustead's rusting Mercedes out of dock to get us down to the harbour."

"Who should I invite to luncheon?"

"We're bound to ask the Coles," Alastair grimaced. "He's our top military brass, and at least Bridget's a peer's daughter. Better have the Veevers-Carters along too, as Wendy's an American. But definitely not Johnny. He was in Burma, and hasn't cared much for Yanks ever since. You'd better come in his place."

Down at the quayside, two immaculate USS launches awaited our arrival. When one sank under our combined weight, we were speedily transferred to the other, before luncheon in the admiral's air-conditioned cabin. Its walls were filled with enlarged photographs of the aircraft carrier *Forrestal*, and the battleship *Missouri*, on which he had previously served. Inevitably, the *Duxbury Bay* was bone dry, so while my conversation with a serious young naval officer became embarrassingly intense, Alastair lapsed into resolute silence. "Bloody Yanks," he growled, as we drove back to the Residency. "Can't even be trusted with a can of lager."

Inside the Residency compound, I was confronted by a distraught Johnny.

"This visit's turning into a disaster," he groaned. "The Yanks now want to play a football match against Mukalla this evening – to get to know the locals, if you please. I've had to rearrange the fixture list completely. I want you to turn out for the Mukalla team."

"But Johnny," I protested weakly, "I haven't played football since my prep school."

"Nonsense," he replied. "This is an important match politically. We've got to field one white face, and you're the only one available."

I wondered about my gammy hip, and then recalled the Director of Recruitment's interview at the Colonial Office. Duty and football triumphed, for you didn't let Johnny down. He might have handed in his rifle but he hadn't hung up his boots. In his eyes, football was the only way to win Arab hearts and minds, and he rated both tribes and individuals by reference to English Football League rankings. Normally he refereed home matches, but protocol demanded that on this occasion he should host the American admiral on the touchline. His cook, Qassem, was deputed to take his place.

Most of Mukalla's male population had turned up to support their team. When the Americans took the field, it seemed to shrink visibly. Their pumping-iron physiques made the men from Mukalla look like Lowry stickmen. For me, the game should have finished early when I caught the *Duxbury Bay*'s goal-keeper in possession, and floored him with a ferocious shoulder barge. When I had last played the game, this was a perfectly legitimate tactic. No longer. A circle of angry seamen swiftly gathered around me threatening to "Fill you in, Buddy". Qassem quickly intervened with a warning that he'd send me off for any further infringement. The game was never much fun after that. However, although physically challenged, Mukalla proved the more skilful team, so we won comfortably 2–0. On the strength of my *Duxbury Bay* showing, Johnny persuaded me to turn out for the Residency team on a regular basis. Sadly, after I had been cautioned for two further red-card-worthy incidents, he dropped me as a political liability.

Johnny had already laid the foundations of South Arabian football with his Hadhrami Football League. Sir Richard Turnbull, Aden's penultimate High Commissioner, must have had him in mind when he told Denis Healey that Britain's colonial legacy would leave little behind it save the expression "F… off ", and football.

4

Losing the Plot

O NLY AFTER ARCHIE had vanished into the Northern Deserts did I learn what AAR's remit really involved. The Registry's dysfunctional filing system became my particular bugbear. There were no filing cabinets and no filing system so, unless an incoming letter's heading coincided exactly with that of an existing file, a specially appointed "file chaser" might spend hours, or even days, trying to find the file that fitted. This Mad Hatter process had so bemused Archie that he had given up answering most letters. Lack of more creative work forced me to reorganize the Registry, by introducing a system of subject classification, and ordering filing cabinets from Aden.

AAR's other dogsbody jobs included those of Quartermaster, Housing Manager and General Merchant for Mukalla's memsahibs. The last included adjudicating on the allocation of air conditioners and fly swatters, as well as organizing the weekly grocery delivery from Aden. The official Quartermaster was Abdullah bin Ashur Al-Mahri, the most courteous of men, who was happiest when discussing philosophy at his fly-infested house overlooking the fishing harbour. Abdullah was temperamentally unsuited to guard the Aladdin's cave that housed the Residency's stores, and too trusting to rid the place of the two-legged rats that infested it. However, as a distinguished Mahra tribesman, he performed invaluable services in identifying genuine Mahra passport applicants from phoneys, and in as acting as guide/interpreter for any official visit to Socotra or Mahra. His gentle nature masked heroic courage. When the Marxist National Liberation Front took over the Eastern Aden Protectorate in 1967, he was the first to sign a declaration proclaiming Mahra's independence. For this, he was imprisoned and executed, after enduring unspeakable tortures.

As Housing Manager, I won a cheap early victory over the Sweepers Union in a demarcation dispute as to who was responsible for repairing the Residency compound's potholes. I then hit a much harder rock in the shape of Shaikh Hadi Bahayan, an illiterate but cunning State Councillor, who was also Mukalla's Director of Public Works. By custom, Shaikh Hadi had always looked after Residency house maintenance, sub-contracting the manual work to the Subian slave caste for a pittance. When I refused to pay one particularly exhorbitant bill for whitewashing, he stormed out of my office swearing that I had impugned his honour. "For this insult," he raged "I will report you to the RA." I heard nothing more from Alastair, but Johnny gently cautioned: "Direct confrontation with Arabs is seldom productive. Always leave them a way out." As usual, Johnny was right.

AAR's real business was passport and visa issue. Archie's assurance – "Really nothing to it, old boy" – could not have been further off the mark. Shortly after his departure, a noisy crowd gathered in the Residency compound. "What's the problem?" I asked my Passport Clerk, Noah Johannes. "No problem, Sir. These people are pilgrims. They want visas for Mecca. The *Hajj* is about to begin." Soon enough, we were issuing more than a hundred visas a day (180 was my record) from the scruffy whitewashed cubicle that passed as Her Britannic Majesty's Passport Office. This was also the Residency's only shop window to the outside world. Noah was a clever and efficient young Eritrean Christian whom Colonel Boustead had literally picked up off the beach, and then put to work. As a Christian, he was generally despised by the local populace and outlawed from Muslim society. His overriding ambition was to become a British naturalized citizen. His religion and an explosive temperament could create problems. Frustrated visa applicants, unused to queuing, were quite prepared to force their way past the guards, and threaten Noah with sticks, or even spears.

Pilgrimage visas were serious business because every Muslim, provided he has the health and resources to do so, has a sacred obligation to undertake the *Hajj* to Mecca at least once in a lifetime, whatever the trials and expense involved. This offered scope for unscrupulous exploitation. Late on in the *Hajj* season, Jock Snell detailed me to carry out a health and safety inspection of the pilgrim ship *Arafat*, moored in the roads off Mukalla. Forcing my way up a gangway blocked by struggling women and screaming children, I found every inch of space on the upper deck occupied with people standing, sitting, sleeping, squabbling, or brewing up on primus stoves. Below, in a filthy hold awash with swill, bedding had already been laid out to stake claims. I ordered the ship's seventy-year-old Italian captain to produce his Aden manifest. This purported to authorize the carriage of 460 passengers. Minutes later, the ship's doctor, a portly Egyptian, took me aside to whisper that there were already more than 560 on board.

It was too late to delay passage. Only after the ship had sailed for Jeddah did Snell let slip that the *Arafat* had already back-tracked from Aden to Mukalla, to enable the local shipping agent and State Councillor, Ba Sumaid, to squeeze in another hundred, on top of an undisclosed number smuggled aboard before the Qu'aiti Immigration Department had opened that morning. That same evening, sipping iced lemonade in the air-conditioned captain's cabin of a British cargo ship delivering a consignment of Bedford 3-ton lorries to the HBL, I tried to square my conscience.

If pilgrimage visas were a seasonal phenomenon, passport issue was a permanent fixture. Trade and travel remained the lifeblood of Hadhramaut, and every Eastern Aden Protectorate citizen was entitled to a British Protected Person passport. In 1960, I processed over 6,000 travel documents with a skeleton staff consisting of Noah Johannes, a typist and myself. Abdullah Al-Mahri was occasionally brought in to verify Mahra applicants. That I was not the only one issuing passports was something I discovered when 'Isa Musallam arrived in my office with a large bundle, tied with red tape, which he plonked down on my desk.

"What's this, 'Isa? " I asked him.

"They're passports, John. Please sign them for me."

"But where do they come from? I'm holding all British passports here."

"These are Qu'aiti State passports," he countered, airily . "All *you* have to do is to sign them."

I took a closer look. They were identical in shape, size and format to my own but issued in the name of the "Qu'aiti Minister to the Sultanate".

"But these aren't proper British Protected Person passports, 'Isa."

"Oh yes they are. They're supplied by the Crown Agents like yours. I issue them from my office. Just take a look inside."

Sure enough, clearly printed within was the official rubric: "The Resident Adviser and British Agent on behalf of His Excellency the Governor of Aden in the name of Her Britannic Majesty."

"But this is ridiculous! I can't just sign them on your say-so. I haven't the slightest idea whether your Abdullahs, Alis or whoever are entitled to British Protected status."

"Precisely. That's why you have to take my word for it. None of these people have birth certificates but we know who they are as our agents always check out their families and tribes. You can't possibly do that."

"Presumably, you were trained in Aden to do this work, so you must have copies of all the relevant Foreign Office manuals and British nationality statutes?"

"Of course not. I've never seen any such stuff. We rely on you for that."

This bizarre arrangement made a nonsense of Britain's constitutional relationship with the Qu'aiti State. Ever since the 1888 treaty, foreign affairs (including passport issue) had been an exclusively British responsibility. 'Isa's system effectively reversed the roles of protector and protected. Grudgingly at first, I eventually came to live with the Qu'aiti and Kathiri (dealt with in Sayun) passport issue, but I never cracked Mahra.

This wild chunk of country, tucked away in the most easterly corner of the EAP, was inhabited by xenophobic, warlike tribes who spoke a pre-Islamic, unwritten language unrelated to Arabic. It had barely been penetrated by the British. Its titular ruler, 'Isa Al-Afrar, the Sultan of Qishn and Socotra, preferred to live on the island of Socotra, 350 miles to the south in Kipling's "pink Arabian Sea", cut off from the outside world for most of the year by ferocious monsoons winds.

Socotra was itself a miracle, the fabled Abode of Bliss. Here the Phoenix had died in a nest perfumed with cinnamon and frankincense. Its Dragon's Blood trees were reputed to have supplied the resin with which Stradivarius varnished his violins. When Captain Haines first surveyed the South Arabian coast to secure the British sea routes to India, he reckoned that Socotra might make an ideal base. The Sultan refused his offer of 10,000 Maria Theresa dollars for a quick sale, but Haines had already taken the precaution of occupying the island with Indian troops. Their stay was short-lived due to endemic malaria, so Haines plumped for Aden instead. Despite this early fiasco, Britain concluded a treaty of protection with the Socotran Sultan in

1886. From then on, all Socotri and Mahri subjects became effectively British Protected Persons.

Mahra passport issue posed unusual problems as Socotra's isolation made communications extremely difficult, and many mainland Mahra tribes were reluctant to recognize Sultan 'Isa. Colonel Boustead had favoured a mainland sultan, Khalifa bin Abdullah, as "the most likely person to serve our purposes". When Sultan 'Isa persuaded an Aden printer to run off 14,000 Mahra passports for private sale, Boustead confiscated the lot. 'Isa reverted to issuing his own travel documents which were cheap, freely transferable, and accepted by many Arab countries, provided they bore his rubber stamp. His three mainland agents, operating on commission, were in direct competition with Sultan Khalifa, who eventually put 'Isa's main agent, Muhammad bin Shaghrait, out of business by printing thousands of Shaghrait facsimiles offered at a discount to all comers, including ships' captains who bought in bulk. The Saudis freely accepted most forms of Mahra travel document until an influx of prostitutes, looking for business in Bahrain, forced a change of policy. Whatever their allegiance, the Mahri were spoilt for choice. The only significant advantage that my pukka British passport offered was Abdullah Al-Mahri's guaranteeing repatriation expenses, something Sultan 'Isa never rose to. After 1967, the Sultan issued no further travel documents. The Marxist thugs who executed most of his family on Socotra imprisoned him in Aden. He impregnated his wife during his incarceration, but died there in 1977.

One positive that came out of this imbroglio was my getting to know 'Isa Musallam. He had a velvety charm, was a crafty tennis player, a tolerable shot and a generous host at beachside picnics, where freshly slaughtered kids were barbecued on hot stones. His views were liberal and, in his cups, he would yarn about healing rings, ghosts and ghouls, and soliloquize on the wanton ways of Hadhramaut: "You know what I mean by the Arabian Nights – beautiful dancing girls, and ways to enjoy them – I can do all that with my rich friends in the Wadi." 'Isa could be indolent and self-indulgent, and the vendetta he pursued against Jehan Khan and Rahman Khan, the twin Pakistani pillars of the Qu'aiti administration, was petty and vindictive. Yet it was his capacity to bridge two worlds that enabled Mukalla's passport system to function after its own fashion. Before tumbling to its merits, I had bombarded my superiors with tedious reports, spelling out the legal and constitutional absurdities of a system that would have given Petty France apoplexy. There are now some

90,000 British subjects of South Arabian origin living in the United Kingdom, principally in South Shields, the Midlands and Cardiff. Maybe Archie was right all along.

One mystery I never solved was Abdullah Al-Mahri's willingness to underwrite Mahra repatriation expenses. Although highly respected, and a fount of knowledge about Mahra affairs, he was not rich. Defraying repatriation costs could be ruinously expensive. I discovered this when trying to resolve the Ahmed Abu Bakr Basendwah affair. This Egyptian-born Hadhrami had been deported from Egypt to Aden for running a brothel. Legally, he was a British Protected Person. However, neither Aden or Mukalla were willing to accept him as such, still less pay the bill of £12,000 he had run up over the past two years, staying at Aden's India Hotel. Orme was right about Aden and Mukalla's inability to compromise. Neither side would budge so the matter stuck there.

The estate of the late Vincenzo Massimo exposed another murky consular corner. This Italian engineer had been employed by a local entrepreneur, Bin Kuwair, to supervise a fish-canning factory. Deprived of European company, Massimo's penchant for taking out his frustrations on Mukalla's prostitutes had landed him in court. Bin Kuwair persuaded the *qadi*, Shaikh Bamatraf, to keep his employee out of prison, subject to Massimo being banned from entering Mukalla. The previous December, he had been killed outright in a head-on car crash. Five months on, Bamatraf and the Italian Consul in Aden were still arguing about the disposal of his personal effects. When I visited Massimo's miserable hovel near the canning factory, the roof had caved in, the smell inside was overpowering, and the only decorations were faded Egyptian pin-ups stuck to the walls. Massimo's personal effects consisted of some dirty clothes and a stack of girlie magazines stuffed away in a battered suitcase. I wondered what had made life bearable for this wretched man, shunned by both European and Arab society.

Yet neither was Mukalla's British society an entirely happy one. Much had changed since the days when Ingrams had habitually worn Arab dress, frowned on alcohol, and applauded Freya Stark's dictum that the British were always popular until they brought out their wives. This in no way discouraged him from bringing out his own, the much-loved and respected Doreen. But the Ingrams edict that "officers must find interest and entertainment in local society" was not endorsed by Boustead, who strongly discouraged the British community from "going native", and frowned on fraternization with the likes of Massimo, or even the kindly Greek bachelor, Costa Papantrakis, who for years had lived alone with his old mother until he, too, died neglected and unmourned.

Mukalla was no longer a close-knit club of male officers, bonded by common experience. It had split into two mutually antagonistic camps, the Old Guard and the Rest. The Old Guard – McIntosh, Johnson, Wilson, Snell and Inge – had broadly similar backgrounds. Individually, they had served longer in South Arabia than either Ingrams or Boustead. They had been the trouble-shooters of their day, serving Queen and Country in lonely, flea-ridden forts, parlaying endlessly with hare-brained tribesmen, and striving to square the circle of impenetrable tribal politics. Now, as South Arabia's last white tribe, they had reverted to a fatalism that matched that of their parishioners. Yet still they loved this barren land, and could laugh without rancour at the whole ridiculous business of attempting to trammel its fiercely independent people.

The Rest represented most of an expatriate community now grown to more than thirty, including wives and children. Wives with medical qualifications made important contributions to community life. But some memsahibs found the restrictions imposed by Islamic codes frustrating, and others created a disquieting new dimension. The Old Guard were wary of incomers and, as former wartime soldiers, tended to patronize the younger military contingent for their less fluent Arabic and ignorance of tribal politics. In turn, the Rest, and particularly their wives, strongly disapproved of the Old Guard's attitudes and boozy ways. Their principal protagonists were the RA's supremely relaxed military adviser (MARA), Lt.-Colonel George Coles, and Qaid Pat Gray, a blustering South African mercenary who commanded the HBL. Neither was on intellectual terms with McIntosh whose own sensitivities and *amour-propre* became more brittle as his energies and convictions faded. It was also Coles' misfortune to have mounted the stage while his veteran predecessors, Jim Ellis and Jock Snell, were still in the wings. Pat Gray was pompous and short on humour, but a generous host, staunch in adversity and brave to a fault.

The Coles/Gray axis had the unofficial heavyweight support of Mukalla's Senior Assistant Adviser, Pat Booker, a meticulously conscientious Scot, and his unexceptional wife Catherine. Standing on the sidelines were the HBL's two bachelor Training Officers, Major David Eales (murdered five years later by his bodyguard while asleep) and Major Jack Carruth, an upright if uptight Seaforth Highlander, who disapproved of the Old Guard, but generally kept his own counsel. Carruth was shortly to be replaced by an altogether more explosive character, Captain Julian Johnston of the King's Shropshire Light Infantry. During his first EAP tour, Julian Johnston had strayed into Manahil country without a proper escort. Forced to retreat when confronted by hostile tribesmen, Johnny Johnson's rebuke – "Bad loss of face" – was about as damning as he ever uttered. Julian frequently complained that the British administration was "mismanaged, incompetent, and lacking any sort of plan". Once, when his Land Rover broke down, he shot off handwritten notes to both Johnny and me: "I have no intention of cranking it in the sun, surrounded by a lot of jeering Arabs saying, and I quote, 'I expect he's drunk. They all are'. I shall remain in my house until permanent and efficient transport is provided." A keen apiarist, naturalist and pianist, Julian could be charming when the mood took him but, seeing the world only in primary colours, he was incapable of compromise. He was tragically drowned off Jura in July 2008.

I empathized with the Old Guard as fading figures from a heroic past, but Alastair's leadership was not inspiring. Although intelligent, generous and fiercely loyal to his friends, he could be capricious and his drinking was prodigious. When I first stayed with him at the Residency, lunch was usually postponed into late afternoon by browns or whites. Marathon Bridge sessions, garnished with endless reminiscence, could neutralize an entire evening. He observed an erratic social protocol, hosting select parties for those who amused him, yet barely offering even token farewells to the infinitely deserving Bookers or the stalwart Jack Carruth. Once, when I defended Carruth for being a teetotaller, Alastair turned on me with: "So you're just another of those damned prigs, are you? I only hope it's not a matter of you're being over-concerned with your promotion prospects!" After celebrating the end of Ramadan with a three-hour gin binge, he confessed to me the following day: "I've abused my body dreadfully. Don't follow my example." Yet during Lent, when he observed strict abstinence, a stream of terse directives issued from his office. He always saw the big picture, but squandered his considerable talents.

Despite the feuding, social life in Mukalla was generally agreeable, if banal. Ingrams had ordained that his officers: "Must not expect a life of ease and comfort … and must do without the ordinary amenities of life, such as games, clubs, European society and its distractions." Twenty years on, European society was well established, and the Residency's multi-racial local staff had their own social club. The resourceful Michael Crouch, while AAR, had built a tennis court used by expatriates and locals alike. Most people were embarrassingly hospitable and it was difficult to avoid a relentless round of drinks, dinner parties, picnics and gossip. For some, this social merry-go-round provided a lifeline to the world they had left behind. Unusual party frolics became conversational landmarks, as when the first spring flood, or *sayl*, swept down from the hills on the evening of 17 March. It carried with it, and then out to sea, a civilian lorry and much of the camel park. Returning from a staid dinner party, I almost lost a year's salary by way of surcharge when my own Land Rover narrowly escaped the same fate. Jim Allen nearly drowned while attempting a drunken Hellespontic crossing from Sherij to Mukalla while attending an Old Guard party that left other guests marooned overnight. Enterprising fishermen subsequently made a killing with an impromptu shore-to-shore ferry service.

Such distractions failed to dispel my own growing sense of frustration. The dogsbody tag was wearing thin. For better things to do, I was willingly press-ganged into the Residency shooting team, to compete in the Hadhrami Armed Forces' annual shooting competition. Captained by an ex-soldier tribesman orderly, Salim Ba Khuraiba, our team of Gordon Dawson, 'Isa Musallam and myself cut no dash besides the immaculately uniformed Hadhrami States Forces, whose martial banners fluttered in the breeze outside their bunting-adorned mess tents. For four days we trailed bottom but, on the final day, Julian Johnston's jibe about this being "another Residency shambles" raised our game. And so, when Jaswandi Khan's band struck up a bustling Punjabi march, it was the Residency Four who stepped forward smartly to receive prizes from the Sultan for the Snap, Balloon Shooting and the Falling Plate competitions.

Ba Khuraiba was so delighted with our success that he invited me to stalk gazelle with him, before going on to Fuwwa to attend the farewell luncheon party given for the Residency's Senior Accountant, Abdullah Shawtah. At the turn of the century, game was still plentiful in South Arabia. The pioneer Political Officer Wyman Bury, who adopted native dress and the Arab name Abdullah Mansur, recorded bags of greater bustard, ibex, gazelle, baboon, hyrax, hill panther, ostrich, hare, duck, teal and Arabian Oryx (though only when mounted with spears). Most of these animals had since been shot out.

Of my contemporaries, only Michael Crouch still shot for the pot, armed with a 12-bore shotgun, a .375 Holland & Holland Elephant gun, and a .38 Smith & Wesson revolver tucked discreetly under his bush jacket.

I drew my .303 Lee Enfield from the stores and, next day as dawn flushed the inland hills purple, Ba Khuraiba and I pounded down the beach to Fuwwa. A translucent band of night cloud soon evaporated, and it was already hot when Ba Khuraiba, waving an arm towards the interior, issued directions that would have confounded any Highland stalker: "Best if we stalk separately. You go this way, I go that. If we lose contact, just fire off one round, and I'll do the same. We can then meet up."

I didn't question these Delphic instructions, but within half an hour we had completely lost sight of each other. My uncontrolled descent into a steep-sided wadi loosed off an avalanche of boulders that must have alerted every living creature within miles. At the bottom it was like a furnace, with no vestige of cover. Here, I heard a couple of faint shots, so scrambled back up to the top of the ridge. Scanning the horizon I could see nothing of my companion, so set my own course for the interior as the sun approached its zenith. The barrel of my rifle felt red-hot, and its stock squirmed like an eel. Far to the north, I spotted three animals, moving purposefully up a scrubby wadi. Gazelle? Moufflon? Or, maybe, even Ibex? I raced up the rocky streambed stumbling, dodging and crouching to close on my quarry. At two hundred yards, I was in range of a flock of goats.

I collapsed exhausted, and fired off a single shot. Way back, a muffled fusillade replied. It took over an hour to regain the spur overlooking the beach that we had agreed as our fail-safe rendezvous. Here, I squatted on my haunches with my sweat-soaked underpants wrapped round my head, waiting for Ba Khuraiba. Eventually, a Land Rover appeared on the beach below.

"Whatever happened to you?" I asked him testily.

"I might say the same. I've been looking for you all morning."

"But did you shoot anything? I heard a volley of shots."

"Not a thing, though I spotted three gazelle. I thought you might have bagged them."

Chilling off in the garden of the Sultan's decaying palace at Fuwwa, beside a murky green pool overhung by date palms, limes and pawpaws, any hopes of luncheon were dashed by the failure of the British contingent to show up. Late that afternoon, George Coles, Julian Johnston and Jim Allen staggered in, fractious and dehydrated. Their Land Rover had broken down someway back along the beach, so they'd had to hoof it. That evening, the Chief Minister joined a less than animated party. I tried to lighten the mood by recounting our stalking fiasco. He merely rebuked me for not having a shooting licence.

Swimming was my main antidote to Mukalla Blues. Most days, I swam off the magnificent beach that stretched twenty miles to Ras Burum, trying not to think about sharks or sly stingrays lurking in the sand. A professional shark hunter, a nephew of Conan Doyle, once fetched up in a smart yacht to hunt Hammerheads. His bravado evaporated when he saw local fishermen bringing in fearsome Makos single-handed in their tiny *huri*s. It was Mark Veevers-Carter, Mukalla's Fisheries Officer, who reintroduced me to snorkelling. He and his wife Wendy, the daughter of Clarence Day, author of the 1940s bestseller *Life With Father*, lived in some style in a disintegrating Sultanic palace, built on a rocky headland east of Mukalla. One Friday, the three of us, accompanied by Wendy's black Labrador Retriever, flippered out to sea for a "fun hunt". After gliding over coral reefs teeming with stingrays, octopus and shoals of brightly coloured fish, Mark tugged at my arm and excitedly pointed below. A Moray Eel, thick as a man's thigh, was sticking out from a hole in the rock. The hunter dived and scored a hit. But instead of coming quietly, his prey curled itself around the harpoon thrashing and spurting blood. Mark was unable to handle it. When we both surfaced, Wendy's frenzied sign language, "Shark Alert!" saw the three of us frantically striking out for the shore. I almost drowned when the randy Labrador tried to mount me in the water.

Red-bearded, swashbuckling Mark would have better served Captain Henry Morgan on the Spanish Main. Instead, he and Wendy had ransacked Hadhramaut for the rare artifacts, tribal silver and fine Malabar chests that embellished the interior of their rented palace, with its intricately carved latticed doors and window shutters. Mark was amusing and Wendy a generous hostess. Their relaxed hospitality was a tonic, yet their freebooting and non-conformist ways had made enemies. Jack Carruth refused to have anything to do with them. "Mark badly beat one of his boys for running over a pye dog. Yet he makes sport of potting them with his .22, and then leaves them to die a lingering death. The Arabs despise dogs, but they don't understand the attitude of a man who does such things."

Months later, I discovered for myself the chaotic legacy of Mark's four-year stewardship of Mukalla's fishing industry. The circumstances of his departure from Mukalla, to take up his new appointment as Fisheries Officer to the Government of the Seychelles, were disgraceful. On the day, 6 April, when he was scheduled to sail to Mombasa by freighter, I joined a select farewell party on board by rowing boat. By now the Old Guard's anchors were well aweigh, but just as we were about to settle down to a slap-up luncheon in the Captain's saloon, the ship's whistle sounded.

"What the devil's happening, Mark?" demanded Alastair. "Why's that whistle gone off?"

"Sorry, everyone," announced Mark. "That signal's for immediate visitor disembarkation. I'm afraid lunch is off. Ship's got to get moving sharpish. Captain's orders."

Back on the quayside, staring out to sea towards the fast-retreating stern of the freighter, I bumped into an apoplectic Rahman Khan.

"I've been trying to board that ship all morning to arrest that man," he spluttered. "He's stripped the palace of its doors, shutters – everything. That is state property, and that fellow's a rascal. He has cheated us and disgraced the name of you British."

I now knew the intended destination of the stack of crates that I'd seen lined up on the quayside the previous day.

 Mark's posting to the Seychelles was his last. Sacked from his job as Fisheries Officer after the Governor of the Seychelles had been drowned on one of his fishing escapades, he bought a small Seychellois island for retirement. In 1965, he went to Mombasa to have his wisdom teeth removed, but died during the operation. It was weeks before Wendy learned the news. Years later in Tasmania, I bought a recipe book called *Mure's Fish Tales*, written by the chef/owner of Hobart's most famous restaurant. One particular dish, Pomfret in Mango Sauce, an exotic blend of spices, fish and fruit, was dedicated to Mark and Wendy Veevers-Carter: "In memory of happy days spent together on their enchanted tropical island."

The Veevers-Carters' departure heralded a general exodus of the Old Guard. Alastair left only a fortnight later, on 19 April 1960. Two days before, he had conducted the Residency's Easter Day service, while accompanying the hymns on his miniature organ. He then played Kathleen Ferrier's 78-rpm recording of *I Know that My Redeemer Liveth* on an old gramophone, for once drawing Mukalla's warring factions together in worship. After the service, Alastair might have doubled for Trollope's the Reverend Septimus Harding in

Barchester, serving his guests with white wine and chocolates. A series of farewell celebrations had preceded these last rites, including Johnny Johnson's beach picnic, when our host slept throughout; the Residency Club's lemonade-only party; and a sumptuous feast given by Mukalla's merchant community. The Sultan failed to turn up for his own dinner party at the palace, but appeared at the farewell parade in the Residency forecourt, flanked by a phalanx of State Councillors. As the combined armed forces of the Eastern Aden Protectorate swung past the dais in double time, saluting their outgoing Resident Adviser to the strains of *Colonel Bogey*, a purple-faced and heavily perspiring Alastair looked utterly miserable. He might not have been universally popular with the British community, but he was much liked and respected by the Arabs, whom he had served so loyally. When the parade ended, Jehan Khan turned to me and said: "This is a sad day, Mr Harding. Just as we get to know a man as a friend so that he may help us, you take him away."

Two months later, Johnny Johnson also left Mukalla, for ever as it transpired. Few of the *Ahl Ingleez* , the "English Tribe" as he described his countrymen, ever achieved the Arabs' comparable love and respect. Johnny had spent his earliest South Arabian years doing famine relief work in Hadhramaut. As a Political Officer in the WAP, he was given the toughest assignments, and had brought a measure of peace to some of its most ungovernable areas. In the early 1950s, against Johnny's advice, the Governor, Sir Tom Hickinbotham, had ordered the occupation of Rabizi tribal territory. In the fighting that ensued, a woman was accidentally killed during an RAF reprisal raid. Johnny wanted to pay the family blood money himself. Aden forbade it. This breach of tribal custom led to an ambush in which six Aden Protectorate Levies and two British officers were killed. As a result, Rabizi was abandoned with a heavy loss of British prestige.

Johnny, the gentle warrior, never really got over that episode. By the time he returned to the EAP, as Alastair's deputy, he was a spent force. Although he nursed a sneaking sense of injustice that he might have been passed over for promotion by younger ex-Sudan men, this was probably misconceived for he finished his South Arabian career as the WAP's Deputy British Agent. However, by then, his health was in ruins. His two months as the EAP's Acting Resident Adviser were like some Greek tragedy. For years he had suffered stoically from bouts of malaria picked up in the Burmese jungle during the war, exacerbated by heroic drinking. On the morning of the Sultan's Accession

Parade, I had to rouse him from his bed after a night out at RAF Riyan. He took the salute on autopilot. The following day, Aden's Commander-in-Chief, Air Vice Marshal Patch, dropped in without warning. Johnny was unruffled and took that too in his stride. Yet not even his faithful cook, Qassem, could halt the disintegration of the Residency's household management. Alastair's fine Persian carpets were replaced with lino and, at one of many British farewell parties given in his honour, Johnny turned up in an old white shirt, ripped all the way down the front. Two years after leaving Mukalla, this most unaffected and lovable man died from Blackwater Fever. Old men still revere his name.

5

A New Broom

THE MILITARY JUNTA heaved a collective sigh of relief when Johnny Johnson's plane took off from Riyan. His hand-over to Arthur Watts, the new Resident Adviser, had taken less than a week. Watts was no stranger to the EAP, and could claim longer residence in South Arabia than any serving British officer save Charles Inge. Like Johnson, he had been a Hadhramaut Famine Relief Officer under Ingrams, but had since progressed further up the ladder. I had met him most recently at one of Trevaskis's dinner parties in Aden, when the principal guests had been Naib Ahmed Al-Fadhli, the Federal Minister of Agriculture, and his spirited wife. In such company, Watts was in his element – friendly, unstuffy and enthusiastic. His reputation for hard work promised a new sense of direction. For all this, I wondered why Alastair, Johnny and Archie had sniped at him so relentlessly and why, on his arrival, Jock, now promoted his deputy, should have gone into decline, and Charles Inge into hiding.

The day before the new RA arrived in Mukalla, I had asked Johnny what formal arrangements we should make to welcome him. "Nothing special," he grunted. "We don't want any fuss. Just make the whole thing as unobtrusive as possible."

"Shouldn't we stage a reception party for him at Riyan?"

"Not necessary," replied Johnny. "Just get the Residency staff turned out smartly to meet him when he gets here."

On the morning of 9 June 1960, a crescendo of cannon fire from the

Sultan's palace announced the new RA's arrival. The traditional Land Rover cavalcade, with HBL escort, swept into the Residency compound to deposit him inside the Residency portico, where I had lined up all senior staff to welcome their new boss. The man he was taking over from was nowhere to be seen. After I had accompanied Watts round the Residency offices to meet the junior staff, George Coles buttonholed me.

"What the hell happened to the Residency at Riyan?" he growled. "The entire military contingent turned out to greet Arthur, yet not one of you were present! I can tell you he's not best pleased."

Early next day, a Friday and therefore a holiday, I bumped into the RA before breakfast in the Residency compound. "I've just managed to locate the duty driver, but what's happened to the Duty Land Rover?" he demanded, without so much as a greeting. Residency transport was my remit. The RA had his own Land Rover as well as the Mercedes. I had first call on the Duty Land Rover.

"It's parked outside my house," I replied.

"Then please ensure that, in future, both that Land Rover and its driver are always parked outside the Residency, available for my personal use."

A couple of days later he summoned me to his office.

"How are you finding your work here, John?" he asked solicitously. "You've now been in Mukalla for almost six months. I'd like to have your impressions."

Well aware of the blacks I'd already put up, I replied warily. "I've been kept very busy with passports and routine administration, but otherwise I've got into a bit of a rut. I've never yet been outside Mukalla, so would very much like to see something of the Protectorate."

"I can quite understand that," he replied. "You've been stuck here too long. The good news is that Husain Minhali, a bright young Manahil tribesman, has just completed the Colonial Administration Course at Oxford, and will shortly be taking over from you as AAR. Once he's settled in, I'll be sending you off to see Wahidi, Hadhramaut and the Northern Deserts. Does that appeal?"

"Most certainly," I replied, eagerly.

"And another thing," he went on, "I need someone to help me compile an authoritative gazetteer detailing the roads, resources, tribes and customs of the EAP. Would you be interested?"

"Of course, Arthur. I'd be delighted to help."

He invited me to stay on for lunch. No browns or whites in his house.

Instead, a delicious Hadhrami meal *sans* alcohol. Afterwards he suggested we take a walk along the beach. The south-west monsoon was cooling the sea, and his enthusiasm was infectious. "You know, John," he confided, "Mukalla is the most wonderful place in the world." We discovered a common interest in music. He was an accomplished violinist, and we spent a happy evening together following the score of a Bach study played by Millstein.

Life got a further boost when Captain Richard John of the Royal Scots Greys passed through Mukalla with a British Army Psychological Warfare Team. "We're here to win Arab hearts and minds," explained Richard. "Frankly, I'm dead bored with regimental soldiering and this job's great fun. Unfortunately, the only films I've been given are one of Princess Margaret's wedding, and another starring an alcoholic hero. Neither likely to gain us many friends in these parts." Richard and I hatched preposterous plans for joint Arabian adventures. Sadly, none materialized. He went on to serve most of his military career in the Gulf States with distinction.

Spurred by Watts' enthusiasm, I thought I had glimpsed the sunlit uplands. Instead, I found myself on a steep learning curve. Our first serious contretemps again involved the Residency's transport fleet, whose efficient functioning was essential to the effectiveness of the British advisory machine. Vehicle lifespans were alarmingly short because of the EAP's appalling roads. Proper maintenance was therefore of critical importance. The day after our lunch together, the RA summoned me.

"In future, I want you to ensure that both my personal Land Rover and the Duty Land Rover are always maintained in tip-top working order, and available for my use at any time. The replacement Land Rover must be kept on chocks for emergencies."

"I'm sorry, Arthur, but we don't run to a replacement Land Rover."

"I find that difficult to believe. It was never like that in my day. Kindly show me the Transport Audit."

Neither Dawson nor Morrison, on whom the Residency fleet's serviceability depended, had heard of such a thing. Nonetheless, we cobbled together a report detailing the pedigree of every vehicle allocated over the past three years. When I presented this to the RA, he threw it down on his desk, after barely reading the first paragraph.

"This isn't at all what I wanted. I asked you for an audit of the Residency's transport establishment, not a history of its allocation."

"None of us have heard of a vehicle audit," I replied. "I've had to assume that establishment and allocation are the same thing."

"Nonsense," he glowered. "Vehicles can go missing. There *must* be a vehicle establishment. It's your job to find it."

Snell, in attendance at his side, remained mute. I left ruffled and baffled. Later that day, at a meeting to discuss the EAP's Advance Budget Proposals, a standard Colonial Service financial procedure for determining the following year's expenditure, our tiff might never have been. Vehicle audits were never mentioned again.

A couple of days later, the RA called me up again.

"This Passport Report you did for Alastair McIntosh. I simply don't agree with your conclusions."

I didn't have a fraction of Arthur Watts's knowledge of South Arabia, but I had spent hours compiling this report and knew my facts and the law.

"What precisely don't you agree with, Arthur? I've made certain procedural recommendations, but the situation's so complex that I couldn't possibly reach any definite conclusions. My report made that quite clear."

I realized from his expression that he couldn't possibly have read the report properly. When he backed off with bad grace, I left his office wondering what he was trying to prove.

The new regime sent Mukalla's mini-planet spinning into a new orbit. Politically astute, Watts excelled in Arab company with a combination of bonhomie and earthy ribaldry. Reputedly anti-military, he nonetheless established a close working rapport with both Coles and Gray. He could be charming and convivial one to one, but on formal occasions stood on his dignity. The cosy assumptions of the Old Guard's rump – Wilson, Inge and Snell – were swept aside. Archie, now posted to Wahidi, was least affected, and continued to treat the RA with the affable condescension that a Commanding Officer might have extended to a senior Warrant Officer. In a bug-ridden Wahidi fort, as dawn was breaking, the RA's rebuke – "Bit early to be drinking alcohol, Archie?" – was met with Archie's riposte: "My dear Arthur, I don't rate beer as alcohol and anyway this isn't my first of the day." The exchange quickly passed into EAP lore. Archie simply didn't give a damn.

Charle Inge was altogether less robust. A multi-faceted Arabist, and a nephew of William Inge, the "Gloomy Dean" of St Paul's, Charles had dug at Ur under Sir Leonard Woolley. In 1941, he had worked in the Aden Secretariat alongside the brilliant scholar Stewart Perowne, Freya Stark's short-term husband, and later became Aden's Director of Antiquities, a post that combined Registrar of Special Marriages and Inspector of Brothels. He also served under Ingrams and, in 1951, gave valuable support to Wendell Phillips's pioneer American archaeological expedition to the Yemen. Sadly, Charles's active career came to an abrupt end in Dhala', when his close friend Bob Mound was shot in his house before his very eyes. He never recovered from this trauma and, under Watts, effectively became redundant, choosing self-imposed isolation with his heroic wife Dorothy and their seven-year-old daughter Bint in the Subian village of Sharaj. Before going on leave at the same time as Alastair McIntosh, he had made me one request: "Please water my roses once a week while we're away."

Jock Snell had even greater cause to regret Watts's appointment. Although their backgrounds were somewhat similar, the two men were otherwise incompatible. Commissioned from the ranks and proud of it, Jock had originally served as Military Adviser to Boustead's predecessor, Kennedy. Subsequently appointed a Political Officer and the HBL's Commandant, he and Jim Ellis between them had built most of the forts in the Northern Deserts. Unschooled, but of an enquiring mind and prodigious memory, Jock had compiled authoritative lists of the EAP's tribes, and was the only European to have witnessed witch trials in Socotra.

Jock's beetroot complexion betokened a pickled liver and the ravages of typhoid. He also shared the Wilsonian ideal of so organizing his day that nothing remained to be done, even before it had started. Nonetheless, Watts saw Snell as a rival, not in terms of rank but in knowledge and experience, exacerbated by what Belhaven once described as "a common fault with many Europeans who go to Arabia, a desire to be thought unique". The RA lost few opportunities to belittle his deputy, but Snell was his own worst enemy. Once, he asked me to take him through the EAP's Advance Budget proposals, one of his prime responsibilities.

"Paperwork's not my thing," admitted Jock, as he slipped silkily through the various items of revenue and expenditure, pausing occasionally to recall with relish some past budgeting fiasco perpetrated by "that crassly inefficient, misguided and pathetic lot in Aden". And then, tiring of this exacting exercise, he disclaimed any further responsibility, and told me to get on with it myself.

On only one issue did Watts, Snell, Inge, and even Johnny Johnson have common cause – an unseemly aversion to Harold Ingrams. Inge maintained that Ingrams had been responsible for the consequences of the famines which devastated Hadhramaut in 1943 and 1944, parodying him in a scurrilous doggerel, "Hadhrami Harold the Scourge of the South", whose eleven verses were sung to the tune of *Galway Bay*. Watts was even more jaundiced in his view, describing Ingrams as "a sadist, and a bastard to his junior officers, who allowed the famine to go just so far to teach the Kathiris a lesson. Unfortunately, it got out of hand, and eventually that broke Ingrams."

South Arabians could be harsh critics of their own kind, but the substance of these attacks is difficult to credit. Sir Bernard Reilly, Aden's first governor and Ingrams' chief, considered him "a man of vision, power of planning and assiduous application". Ingrams' report of his exploratory journey through Hadhramaut, with his wife Doreen, not only earned them the Royal Geographical Society's most prestigious medals, but also formed the basis of Britain's policy of pacification in the EAP. This was subsequently implemented largely by Ingrams himself, and resulted in the cessation of internal warfare, and the conversion of anarchy into order and progress. The drought-induced famine that afflicted all South Arabia in the mid-1940s was exacerbated in Hadhramaut by the Japanese occupation of South-East Asia, which effectively cut off food imports. Yet it was Ingrams who established Hadhramaut's famine-relief grain distribution centres, and got the RAF to fly in grain. Undoubtedly, his forceful personality and forthright views made him enemies, and he brooked no rival. Yet the "Ingrams' Peace", which he masterminded, remains British South Arabia's most lasting monument. Both his pre- and post-Arabian careers in government service were immensely distinguished, and it remains a mystery why he was never knighted.

As a new broom, Watts was bound to stamp his personality on what had become a demoralized British advisory corps. Shortly after his arrival, he issued to every Assistant Adviser a personally signed Secret Newsletter, "to keep the EAP Advisory team in touch with the problems of the whole area and deal informally with outstanding problems and policy". Our instructions were to discourage political groups from supporting any evolutionary process that might upset the status quo, including any proposal to establish legislative councils and local elections. We were urged to impress upon any member of the Qu'aiti Sultanic Council, who might agitate to scrap HMG's advisory treaties, of "the fatal difficulties that the application of democracy has encountered in the Middle East". To counter any criticism of Aden Airways and the Eastern Bank's monopolies, we were to point to the advantages that such monopolies gave to "backward areas". Whether Watts concocted this combustible stuff himself, or whether it came down from Aden, I never had the inclination to propagate it.

True to his word that I should tour the Protectorate, the RA invited me to attend the annual *ziyara* at Shihr with him and George Coles. "*Ziyara*s are fairs," he explained. "Shihr's is the most important on the coast, and 10,000 people are likely to attend. It celebrates the life of a local divine, Sayyid Salim bin 'Umar Al-'Attas. This will give you a chance to see something of life outside Mukalla and the workings of a local administration."

On a muggy summer's day, I followed the RA's Land Rover at a respectful distance along a barely perceptible coastal track. We drove through scattered fishing settlements until, after thirty-five miles of dust and sand, we reached a wide beach festooned with nets where literally millions of sardines were drying in the sun. The stench was overpowering. "Shihr," spat my driver, making a dismissive gesture towards the disintegrating mud walls of the once-grand merchants' houses that lined the foreshore. Marco Polo mentions Shihr as renowned for fishing and textiles. Up to the mid-19th century, it remained Hadhramaut's main entrepot for the collection and distribution of East African slaves, a profitable trade that was doomed once the British had taken control of Arabia's southern seaboard. When Shihr's Kathiri rulers allied themselves with their Ottoman co-religionists in Yemen against the rival Qu'aiti dynasty, Shihr's prosperity collapsed.

The Rest House overlooked the main square, where a noisy crowd of men and women had already gathered to watch a troupe of tribesmen perform an outlandish dance. After some low-key cavorting, the performance reached its climax with the entire ensemble leaping up into the air simultaneously, clashing long wooden staves above their heads. Watts turned to me with a meaningful wink.

"This is the one *ziyara* when both sexes can meet each other, but clandestinely, of course. Just listen to those women ululating."

"What's all that about?" I asked him, wide-eyed.

"That's the Sultan's harem," he replied, glancing archly at Coles. "They're awaiting the Sultan's return, to enjoy their fleshly pleasures."

For once, Arthur had got it wrong. At dinner that evening, Sultan 'Awadh complained sourly that he had still not slept with a woman for six months.

Next morning, the Residency party did a routine inspection of the Shihr Health Unit, accompanied by its grotesquely fat director, Dr Husain. After a quick flit around an operating theatre, thickly coated in dust, where surgical instruments lay abandoned in rusting heaps, the doctor made an elaborate show of washing his hands in a filthy basin filled with dead flies. Moving on to an empty dispensary, Watts asked him what had happened to his patients. "It is *ziyara* today," the doctor replied. "No one sick today."

Unsurprisingly, the Shihr Boys School was also bereft of pupils, so we wandered unaccompanied around what had once been a grand Sultanic palace. "Someone's going to have to do something about this," said Watts angrily, pointing up at the water-streaked, teak-beamed ceilings and crumbling plasterwork of a once elegant stateroom. "They must have employed hundreds of skilled craftsmen to build this place. Now it's almost beyond repair. I will speak to the Sultan about it."

The Sultan had more immediate priorities that day. His main function at the *ziyara* was to make a personal act of homage at the saint's tomb. Before he performed this rite, we were invited to take tea with his personal assistant, Sayyid Ahmed Al-'Attas, a direct descendant of the saint himself. Al-'Attas invited us to join a circle of silent, solemn guests sitting cross-legged around a smoking incense burner, whose exhalations all present inhaled as it circulated between them. Outside in the square below, the shrill, ululating crescendoes of Shihr's womenfolk, perched crow-like atop its surrounding walls, combined with a booming, monotonous chant from the men that swelled and fell, yet never reached a climax. These unfamiliar sounds lent the ceremony a mesmeric atmosphere until, suddenly, the Sultan rose unsteadily to his feet.

"We must leave at once," whispered Watts. "The Sultan's act of homage is about to begin. As Christians we're not expected to attend."

As the three of us filed out self-consciously from that claustrophobic room, I pondered on our role in an Islamic world in which we would always be outsiders. The dilapidated state of both Shihr's Health Unit and the Boys School had evidently shocked Watts. He was devoted to the Arab cause and, like most of us, had joined the Colonial Service to change things for the better. Yet in South Arabia, change so often seemed beyond our control. I never met Al-'Attas again. Later, he replaced Jehan Khan as the Qu'aiti State's Chief Minister, but in 1967 betrayed his trust by abandoning young Sultan Ghalib when the future of the Sultanate was hanging in the balance, and the revolutionary National Liberation Front was waiting expectantly in the wings to take over.

Shortly after the Shihr trip, Watts gave me my first solo commission to visit Karl Schlatholt, an agricultural officer stationed near Maifa'ah Hajar in the Wahidi Sultanate. Wahidi was a rough sort of state sandwiched between the EAP and the WAP but owing allegiance to neither.

"You should know that Schlatholt served in the German Navy during the early war years, and was lucky to escape capture," explained Watts severely. "He managed to get himself to the Yemen, worked for the Imam and, after the war, was given a job with the Abyan Cotton Board as an engineer. I've just been down to Maifa'ah myself to see what he's been up to. I want you to make your own confidential appreciation of his work, and to deliver this sealed envelope to him personally. Let me know his reaction. I've no idea what sort of reception you're likely to receive, so better take your cook and houseboy, just in case they don't ask you to stay the night."

I knew nothing about engineering, nor what to make of these veiled instructions, but two days later was driving westwards down Mukalla's magnificent beach, Wahidi-bound. At the fishing village of Burum, my driver turned sharply inland, and struck north through a cleft in the headland towards a tumble of spiky peaks, rising tier upon tier to the horizon. Unyielding yet ethereal, this looked the sort of place where a man needed a strong faith to survive. When I located Schlatholt, busy in his workshop, he seemed surprised to see me.

"Ve haf just had the RA visit us. Vy do you come so soon?"

"Didn't the RA signal that I was coming?" He shook his head, and then led me through a Mediterranean-style villa with furniture that was definitely not Crown Agents' issue. Arched porticos led to a stone patio with panoramic views of the surrounding mountains. Karl's attractive wife, Gisella, came across to meet me.

"Welcome to Hajar," she beamed. "This is our *heimat*. Please stay the night."

The Schlatholts were both cast in the German pioneering tradition of Niebuhr, von Wrede and Hirsch. In the wilderness of Hajar, the land of stone, they had created a small corner of Europe.

"What a lovely house and what a marvellous view," I enthused.

"Ve built it ourselves, Gisella and me in three months. No PWD – just us and local labour," said Karl proudly.

After a delicious lunch we sat on the verandah drinking coffee while I tried to explain why I was there.

"And the RA asked me to give you this personally," I said, handing Karl the envelope. He looked at it suspiciously and grimaced.

"Ach – those damned fools in Aden. I think I know vat this is all about. I von't read it now. First, I must show you vat ve do here, and then ve talk about it."

He drove me a little way down the wadi, before stopping by a fine new dam. Below it, an alluvial fan of silted land was laid out with freshly dug irrigation channels.

"We haf only just finished building this dam," explained Karl. "I had to extract £17,500 from those silly buggers in Aden who wouldn't believe that I could build it with only local labour. Maybe it will encourage Aden to give us more funds when they see what can be grown here. All that those idiots, sitting on their bums, can do is to interfere. They know nothing of field conditions. I only ask for their co-operation not their petty jealousy."

That evening we discussed the report. Written by a Colonial Office Inspector who had spent two weeks in Aden, and three hours at Maifa'ah Hajar, it was critical of Karl's work for technical reasons I couldn't fathom. A shower before bed that evening in saline water left my hair set like a cake. I barely slept a wink on account of relentless heat and a sand-laden wind that shrieked and whirled around the house. Before I left next morning, Karl's last words were: "I vill haf to come to Mukalla to discuss this bloody fool report with the RA." I felt uncomfortable. I had brought them bad news, while they had given me unstinting hospitality. I marvelled at what the Schlatholts had achieved, and vowed to write a glowing report for Watts. As we pounded back to Mukalla along the beach, I ran into the RA himself enjoying a Friday picnic.

"How did your visit go?" he asked, off-handedly.

"Very well. I was most impressed by everything that Karl has achieved. I'll be making you a full written report as soon as possible."

He gave me wary look, then merely said: "Come and see me in my office early tomorrow."

When I reported as bidden, he didn't mention the Schlatholt visit, but sprang a surprise. Previously, when I'd badgered him about his earlier promise of desert tours, his response had been: "I can't spare you at the moment. Too much for you to do here." Now, he took a different tack. "I'd like to get you started on a Northern Deserts tour, before Michael Crouch comes back from leave in early September. I've got some special jobs for you in mind, and want you to leave here on Monday."

Today was Friday, 30 July. Monday was only three days hence.

"This forthcoming Monday, Arthur?"

"Yes, this Monday. No time to waste. I've had problems enough persuading Pat Gray to release the HBL's Bedford 5-tonner to get you as far as Sayun by the East Road. That should take two days, after which you'll stay a night or so in Sayun, where Muhammad Al-Kharusi will meet you. He's been in charge of the Northern Deserts while Michael's been on leave. He knows the area as well as anyone, so will be your mentor and guide. I don't want you to regard this trip as a swan. I'll need a full report and a detailed route guide of your journey, to and from Mukalla, for my EAP Handbook."

It went through my mind – Why the 5-tonner? These were whopping great gas-guzzling vehicles, capable of carrying a platoon. The Duty Land Rover was in good nick and would have been a lot faster to drive the 200 miles to Sayun. And why the route guide? Both roads to the Wadi Hadhramaut were now used routinely by civilian lorries. 42 Survey Engineer Regiment had produced, five years before, a reasonably detailed 1:250,000 map covering much of my proposed route.

"What sort of information do you want me to record, Arthur?"

"Surely that speaks for itself. You've done some soldiering, and should therefore know what's needed. To spell it out, I want an accurate mileage record of distances between villages, wells and other major features, with times of departure and arrival, plus brief notes on scenery and any other matters of interest."

"What are my precise duties when I'm with Kharusi?"

"I haven't finally decided yet. However, I'll be flying up to Sayun myself before you go to discuss that. You'd better know something about Kharusi's background. His father was Shaikh Sa'id Al-Kharusi, a rich landowning Zanzibari Arab who was a friend of Ingrams. Young Muhammad came over here just before the last war to work for the Qu'aitis. Boustead then took him onto the Residency staff. Since then, he's done much good work to keep the peace in the Northern Deserts. However, I must warn you, he's got one serious weakness."

"Really?" I queried apprehensively, remembering Snell's tales of Kharusi's charming habit of chaining recalcitrant tribesmen to the roof of a fort, to cook in the sun until they saw sense. "What might that be?"

"Alcohol," the RA replied, censoriously. "I'm afraid he's picked up some very bad habits from some misguided Political Officers who should have known better."

I didn't have to guess who these might be, but managed to register mild disapproval. It then occurred to me that this might be the ideal opportunity to put a pet scheme of my own to the RA. Just over the wall of my house lay Therib, Mukalla's smelly, fly-blown caravan terminus, used by the indigo-stained cameleers who brought in charcoal and dates from the interior. Their ancient trade was now being threatened by lorries plying both the East and West Roads.

"When I've finished my tour, would be possible to join one of the camel caravans coming down to Mukalla?"

"Why on earth d'you want to do that?"

"To improve my Arabic. Get an insight into the cameleers' lives and maybe alleviate their problems. It would also provide information for your Area Handbook."

"Certainly not," he replied. "I can't possibly spare you for such boy scout adventures."

Over the next couple of days, I cleared my desk; made preparations for a journey expected to take six weeks; dispatched my cook to the suq to buy tinned food; and commissioned a local carpenter to knock up four wooden boxes for rations and equipment. In the middle of packing, I happened to glance out of my window, and saw Karl Schlatholt standing over the open bonnet of his Land Rover in the Residency compound. Only then did I remember that I hadn't yet finished writing up my Maifa'ah report. I ran downstairs to greet him.

"How did your meeting with the RA go, Karl?"

"Not so bloody vell. Ze RA and I haf a problem."

"Let's talk it over," I urged. "I'm about to leave for Hadhramaut unexpectedly, but please stay the night."

"Thank you. But no. I must get home to my Gisella."

I couldn't make him change his mind. Returning to the roof of my house, I watched his Land Rover cross the Sharaj wadi and pass the Inges' house before picking up speed along the beach until it became a mere speck. In not getting my report to Watts before his meeting, I knew I had let him down.

On the morning of my departure, the RA called me in for a final briefing.

"About this route guide. It must be entirely accurate, as I'm likely to be touring the Northern Deserts myself this autumn."

"I'll certainly do my best. Presumably I'll be staying with the Lanfears in Sayun?"

John Lanfear, a near contemporary whom I had already met in Aden, was currently acting as Senior Adviser in Hadhramaut. He had recently completed the prestigious Middle East Centre for Arabic Studies course in the Lebanon. I was looking forward to renewing our acquaintance.

"Certainly not. After all this soft living in Mukalla, you must rough it in the Government Rest House. Get you used to hard living in the desert."

After the inevitable delays, I left Mukalla that same afternoon in the HBL's one and only Bedford Model R 5-tonner, with Chief Driver Salim Bakhit at the wheel. Also on board were his assistant, my cook/bearer Mubarak, a couple of his cousins, a personal *chokrah* or cleaner, two HBL orderlies, and a bunch of leave-happy HBL soldiers cadging a free lift home. Sitting in the cabin of this mighty leviathan almost two metres off the ground, surrounded by maps, notebooks and camera equipment, I felt like a captain on the bridge of his ship. Salim fairly pounded along the coast road. He never bothered to slow down at wadi crossings, taking them like a steeplechaser, with his massive lorry bucking and shuddering. Those at the back were chucked around like dried peas.

Beyond Shihr, the road swung inland, and now the Bedford began to climb slowly upwards towards a mountain wall, by a track barely wide enough to take its width. As the afternoon drew on, dark clouds formed, the valleys pealed with thunder, and it began to rain. I felt cool for the first time in months. In the brief twilight, the encompassing hills merged into lumpy, indistinct shapes. Far down in the ravine, flashes of light betrayed the campfires of the Bedouin. Salim stopped for a short break at the village of Ma'adi, where wild-eyed urchins swarmed over the lorry like monkeys. They sold coconuts to the soldiers which they sliced open with a single stroke of the *jambiyya*, while pestering me for *bakhsheesh*. We set off again into a moonless night towards the Ma'adi Pass, grinding upwards by a spiral of hairpin bends. Some were negotiable only by hair-raising reversing which took the Bedford's rear wheels to within inches of the abyss, as Salim's barefooted assistant bawled out instructions. At 11 p.m., Salim called it a day at Karif bin 'Aqil. It had taken seven hours to climb 5,000 ft, and to cover 93 miles at an average speed of 14 mph.

Next morning, I woke up cold and stiff to a grey dawn. Without a blanket, I had dozed fitfully on the stony ground, my feet stuck into a polythene bag and an airmail copy of *The Times* wrapped round my stomach. It had rained during the night, and most of my companions were still sleeping under the Bedford, covered by their head-cloths. I looked at my watch, 2 August 1960. I had clean forgotten that this was my twenty-sixth birthday. Mubarak cooked me a special breakfast of fried fish and eggs which I ate astride a wooden ration box. I then felt ashamed that I was not sharing it with the others, as they would have done. The sun came up with an explosive force, transforming everything around to intense primary colours. Only too soon, it leached to monochrome a featureless landscape of bleached rocks and blackened stones that stretched away to a blurred horizon. Salim made a dismissive gesture towards this wasteland: "*Jol*," he muttered. "*Jol*." We were at the threshold of the grim upland plateau that, for aeons, had isolated Hadhramaut from the outside world.

An indistinct track now led up and down a succession of shallow depressions. Salim identified the odd stunted bush, or single date palm, with a place name – Khairn, Zabun, Risib, Tawilah, Qinab. I tried scribbling them down as our leviathan lurched and plunged. Throughout that day, we saw neither motor vehicle, man, camel nor any other living thing. That this ancient caravan route now ranked as a "modern" road was due chiefly to the foresight of an enlightened Hadhrami merchant, Sayyid Bubakr bin Shaikh Al-Kaf, who, in the late 1920s, had put up most of the money to build it, and commissioned a self-taught genius, 'Ubaid al-Ingliz, to be its engineer. The Bin Yemani and Hamumi tribes, who had scratched a living off caravan tolls, correctly foresaw the new road as a threat to their livelihood and so disrupted its construction. Ingrams' riposte of proscriptive RAF bombing settled an uneven match, and enabled the first motorable road between the coast and Wadi Hadhramaut to be completed in the late 1930s, thus cutting a week's journey to two days.

The East Road's high point also marked the Qu'aiti–Kathiri state boundary, indistinguishable save for two white-painted stones on either side of the track. Descending imperceptibly northwards, the *jol's* moonscape gradually softened, as bare rock gave way to a scattering of flinty fields, interspersed with clumps of *mushid* trees. In the Wadi Sah ravine, an unexpected stretch of cobbled road led to perennial waters where we stopped for lunch. The heat was so intense that I could not keep my food down. Thundering on, through dark-hued palm groves overhung by teetering limestone cliffs, I thought our journey would never end. But suddenly, like a cork from a bottle, we popped out into a wide canyon whose containing walls glowed golden in the sun. "Wadi Hadhramaut," grunted Salim, with a rare grimace. Caked in dust, we pulled up outside the Lanfear's lime-washed Sayun villa just in time for tea. The 205-mile journey from Mukalla had taken exactly 18 hours.

Gillian Lanfear invited me to stay for dinner. We ate off a polished dining-room table, adorned with intricately wrought Hadhrami silver. New company was rare and, after dinner, her normally tight-lipped husband spoke freely about Hadhramaut's future.

"After the Ingrams Peace, the wartime famines put development on hold, until HMG initiated a programme of dam reconstruction to boost agriculture. Since Indonesian and Malaysian independence, remittances have all but dried up. Unless a great deal more money is injected, or oil is discovered, I don't believe we have a long-term future here."

I was surprised by this gloomy forecast, and remonstrated: "But surely, you and Gillian don't have to worry personally. With your experience and fluent Arabic, you'll always be in demand somewhere in the Arab world."

"I don't think that's quite the point," he replied, with a brittle, self-deprecating smile, and abruptly changed the subject.

Of all my contemporaries, John Lanfear most faithfully embodied the self-denying ordinances of imperial service. Tragically, he was to die prematurely from a brain tumour.

That night, I moved into the Sayun Government Rest House. Its spacious rooms and basement bath, as large as a small swimming pool, belied Watts' idea of roughing it. At sunrise next morning, I climbed the stairs of the house to its flat roof to marvel at the panorama spread about me. Here, the Wadi Hadhramaut is several miles wide, enclosed to the north and south by 600-ft limestone walls, now tinged a faded ochre. Sayun itself, the most agreeable of Hadhramaut's great cities, resembled a green carpet of date-palm gardens with whitewashed mansions protruding from it like so many mushrooms. Rising triumphantly above them all was the Kathiri Sultan's fairy-tale palace, glittering in the sun like some enormous wedding cake.

Wadi Hadhramaut is one of Arabia's largest and most fertile valleys, running some 350 miles from its desert mouth at Al-'Abr to Saihut on the coast. Hadhramaut is mentioned in Genesis, and its great incense kingdom had already reached its apogee before the 1st century BC. By then, the newly discovered sea routes were superseding the overland caravan trade that ran from Dhofar to the entrepots of the eastern Mediterranean. Hadhramaut's cities, grown rich from caravan tolls, now declined until the advent of Islam reinvigorated its ancient civilization. Local sayyids, claiming direct descent from the Prophet, made it a centre of scholarship, virtually unknown to the West, yet famous in Arab lands. Protected by the *Jol* to the south and the Empty Quarter to the north, Hadhramaut became a land of extreme contrasts. While sultans and sayyids, grown rich from their trade and sojourn in Malaya and Java, where they had spread the word of Islam and learned the lessons of ordered government, lived luxuriously in the valley's magnificent palaces, turbulent tribesmen barely eked out a living in its surrounding barren uplands.

The first Europeans to set eyes on the Wadi were two Spanish Jesuit Fathers who had been captured off the Kuria Maria islands in 1590, and dispatched thence to San'a via Hadhramaut. The German explorer, Adolf von Wrede, disguised as a pilgrim, reached its tributary, the Wadi Du'an, after a hazardous nine-day journey from Mukalla in 1843. Another fifty years elapsed before the visit of the German Arabist and archaeologist, Leo Hirsch, coincided with that of the British husband-and-wife team, Theodore and Mabel Bent. A trickle of Western travellers followed, yet between the wars barely a dozen Europeans visited Hadhramaut. Even in 1960 visitors were discouraged, save for British government or military personnel.

To give me some insight into Hadhramaut's agricultural development, Lanfear urged me to look up Donald Guthrie, currently responsible for running the Hadhramaut Pump Scheme (HPS). Originally an aid scheme established in the aftermath of the mid-1940s famines, the HPS was formalized in 1952 by Boustead, funded largely by the two Hadhrami States, and administered under British aegis. Guthrie now had three locally trained assistants to support him. I tracked him down in the recesses of an enormous workshop filled with bulldozers, graders, generators and other mechanical devices.

"They're the best-equipped workshops in South Arabia," said a greasebegrimed Guthrie, proudly. "Wasn't always like this. Before the Hadhramis got chucked out of Indonesia, people here had got so used to eating imported rice, rather than locally grown dates and wheat, that most marginal land had been abandoned. The Pump Scheme changed all that. We've now got over 1,200 pumps working up and down the Wadi. It's my job to keep them going."

Agricultural development depended on the mechanical skills of men such as Guthrie. Unfortunately, whisky and bilharzia had already shot his health. This stunningly beautiful Wadi had an enviable winter climate, but in summer the heat was almost insupportable. That afternoon, while trying to take a siesta, I could only lie prostrate with my tear ducts dried up, and my linen pillow feeling as if a hot iron had just been run over it.

In the evening, Lanfear introduced me to Shaikh Muhammad Al-Kharusi. His powerful physique and intimidating presence betokened an African lineage. We got on famously, for he was courteous and exuded good humour, but when I asked him what my role was to be in the desert he looked blank.

"I've no idea, Mr Harding. The RA arrived here by plane this evening. No doubt he'll brief us tomorrow."

Once Kharusi had left, I asked Lanfear what he thought of him.

"I've never had to work with him directly. He's a legend in these parts, feared but respected by the Bedouin. Jim Ellis says he's done great things, but gets very violent when drunk. For all that, he's a big wheel and would be very difficult to replace."

The following morning, when I went to Lanfear's office to discuss my tour with the RA, I caught the fag end of a heated discussion between the two of them. Lanfear was arguing the case for levying a State Land Tax to support Hadhrami development. Watts would have none of it. An embarrassing deadlock was broken only when the Kathiri State Secretary arrived late, whereupon Watts switched smoothly from belligerent to joshing mode. Later, I asked Lanfear why the RA was so opposed to what seemed an eminently sensible scheme.

"I'm afraid it's all to do with personalities. Ralph Daly proposed something similar a few years ago, when he was the Assistant Adviser here and Arthur was Boustead's Deputy. Unfortunately, Ralph and Arthur never saw eye to eye. Arthur doesn't take kindly to schemes that he hasn't dreamed up himself. I should have presented this one as his own."

After lunch, I explained to Watts that I'd already met Kharusi, and again asked what specific jobs for me he had in mind. "To familiarize yourself with the area and its tribes, as I told you before," he retorted, sharply. "Pat Gray and I have gone to considerable trouble to make valuable transport available for your tour. You must rely on Shaikh Muhammad for further guidance."

Late that afternoon, two hours after Kharusi's advertised start time, the Northern Deserts group of three open Land Rovers and one Bedford pick-up assembled in Sayun's main square. It comprised a section of HBL, two Desert Guards, four drivers, my cook Mubarak, a bearer, Kharusi and myself. Some squeezed into the Land Rovers while the rest got into the back of the pick-up, already over-laden with tentage, food and ten barrels of drinking water. Just before starting, Kharusi took me aside and introduced me to a slightly built young soldier: "Mr Harding, this is your driver, 'Umar Al-Sai'ari. He is a good man, but always remember, he is a Sai'ar."

I didn't have time to question what he meant by this for, at a signal, all four drivers revved up in unison to ear-splitting pitch. We then roared out of Sayun in a dust storm, to the accompaniment of blaring horns and a staccato Bedouin war chant: "We're marching on Shibam with twenty-five rifles. We're marching on Shibam and nothing will stop us." On and away westwards, with the late afternoon sun burning our faces, the convoy snaked up the Wadi by a potholed road, past whitewashed palaces and yellow fields, where red-robed Ruths in tall straw hats reaped their native corn.

And then round a corner, Shibam appeared like a mirage. Higher, grander and more improbable than any photographic image of it can convey, the mud-brick walls of Hadhramaut's most famous sky-scraper city glowed red-gold in the late afternoon sun. Today, Shibam is a World Heritage site. In 1960, it was virtually unknown to the West. Kharusi's Land Rover juddered to a halt outside the main gate. Alighting with dignity, he came over to my vehicle: "You must now inspect the guard, Mr Harding. It is customary." A scruffy, unsuspecting Qu'aiti Tribal Guard trooped out and came raggedly to attention, just inside Shibam's great gates. I made a self-conscious inspection in dusty drill trousers and open-necked shirt. That night, we camped far up the Wadi, well beyond the last villages. After the tents had been pitched, Kharusi invited me to join him for an alfresco supper on a faded Baihani rug. Stretched out at his ease, he devoured a couple of chickens and scooped up handfuls of rice as he reminisced expansively about bygone days, joking good-humouredly about the various Political Officers he had known.

Next morning, camp was struck before dawn. The Wadi was beginning to widen out and, as its limestone walls receded, cultivated land gave way to sparse grazing, interspersed with scrub and clumps of umbrella-shaped *asher* trees. Soon, only a thin vestige of the *jol's* scarp was left to mark the northern horizon. We came to a probing tongue of sand, the Ramlat Sab'atain, a southern outlier of the Empty Quarter. Here the tyres were deflated before attempting to cross. Beyond, an indistinct track led on through gravel flats past Thukmain, a pair of dramatic Dolomite-like rock pillars. Four and a half hours after striking camp, our convoy breasted a low pass that led down to another gravelly plain, closed at its western end by four flat-topped mesas. Perched on a rocky promontory at their foot stood a Beau Geste-style fort, its whitewashed battlements gleaming in the sun. "Husn al-'Abr!" exclaimed 'Umar. We had arrived.

From the earliest times, Husn al-'Abr had guarded the Wadi Hadhramaut's western approaches. When Ingrams reconnoitered it in 1938, the old fort was a ruin with only one of its eighty wells still working. The following year, he brought in stonemasons from Tarim to dig out some of the wells and rebuild the fort. He then garrisoned it with HBL. Here, on the fringes of a sand sea as big as Western Europe, water dictated the pattern of all life. Whoever controlled the wells called the shots. At this time of year, it was so hot that even a camel could survive only a few days without water. Clustered around the wells were queues of these great beasts being watered in relays by Sai'ar tribesmen and tribeswomen. Their encampment of tattered tents and makeshift shelters littered the plain below. The whole place was in a state of continual uproar, and the stench overpowering.

Kharusi's personal quarters, in the lee of the fort, seemed to have been built as an afterthought. "Sadly, my wife is away," he explained apologetically. "I hope you don't mind sleeping in a tent, but it's the best we have. Anyway, we should all rest now. It is too hot to do anything more today." He waved me in the direction of a tiny canvas tent, occupying a corner of the enclosed courtyard, and then disappeared. I laid out my things and tried to rest, but inside was like an inferno. By midday, even the camels had gone quiet and the wells were deserted. In late afternoon, the place came to life again and, at dusk, Kharusi reappeared, inviting me join him to watch the lively scene unfolding below.

"What's our plan for tomorrow, Shaikh Muhammad?"

"We're going to drive to Thamud. After that, we go on to Sanaw and Habarut. Then we come back!"

"How long will it take to reach Habarut?"

"That all depends," he grinned. "Maybe five days; maybe more. Habarut is 700 miles away. We'll take the northern route, so I can show you something of the real desert. But we'll have to drive through the *ramlah*, the Sands, and this is not a good time of year to travel. The Sands get so hot that we should only move in the early morning or in late evening."

Small groups of soldiers had now gathered round the wells below to ogle, flirt and swap badinage with smiling, unveiled Sai'ar women, whose finely muscled arms hauled the water up in leather buckets with an effortless pull. Kharusi produced a bottle of whisky and, after offering me a nip, poured himself out a generous slug.

"Those Sai'ar women will sleep with anyone," he leered. "Marriage for them is just a marketplace. But the Sai'ar tribesmen are happy. Just listen to them singing." From below us, there swelled up a slow rhythmic chanting.

"What are they singing?" I asked him.

"Allah, give us water. Allah, give us water! At least, they'll give us no trouble while there's water here. *Inshallah*, may there always be water in these wells."

"What about these Sai'ar?" I asked him. "I've heard them called the 'Wolves of the Desert'. Didn't you warn me about my driver 'Umar?"

Kharusi seemed to find this funny. "The Sai'ar!" he laughed. "The Sai'ar. Yes, they're the big boys round here, but they're not the power they were. Their lands are worth nothing. Most of them live between the Sands and the stones of the *jol* to the north of the Wadi, where nothing grows. Don't worry about 'Umar. He'll give you no trouble. It's only his tribe that has a bad reputation. The Sai'ar say they are descended from the Kinda, warriors who ruled Hadhramaut in olden times. But they have no proper religion and neither fast nor pray."

"Why so?" I asked. "Surely prayers and fasting are two of the Five Pillars of Islam?"

"Not for the Sai'ar. They say they saved the life of the Prophet in battle, so he told them that they need not fast or pray. I don't believe it. Before Mr Ingrams came here, they did nothing but kill and raid. When he made the Peace, tribes like the 'Awamir and Manahil wanted to shoot them like dogs, but they haven't given me much trouble."

This wasn't quite the story I had heard from others, but then Kharusi had his own ways of dealing with people.

"How many Sai'ar are there?" I asked him.

"Too many! Only Allah knows, or maybe Mr Snell. Perhaps 3,000 armed men and 20,000 camels. But enough of these Badu. Tonight, Rajab will dance for us." He then rose unsteadily to his feet and bawled out: "Rajab, Rajab, where are you? Come and dance!"

Rajab was Kharusi's cook and general factotum. Like his master, he had African blood. He danced wild-eyed and rubber-limbed like some barbaric Nijinsky, mouthing incomprehensible runes as he leapt and twirled. Kharusi clapped a noisy accompaniment as he sloshed down the whisky. Tired after the long day, I quietly excused myself, and tried to get some sleep outside my tent under a full moon. Rajab's dancing went on far into the night, his crazed grotesqueries merging with my own nightmare images.

6

Desert Rumbles

THE SUN CAME UP next morning like a punch to the head, consigning the memory of Rajab's tarantellas to some dim Arabian night. Dawn's delicate hues had already become duns when the Sai'ar brought the wells back to life with relays of honking camels. There was no sign of Kharusi. I wandered round their tented encampment before breakfast, and then filled in time inspecting the Qu'aiti State's Customs House and immigration checkpoint. The latter was now being used as an open latrine. Kharusi had locked up the newly built Health Unit until the next *Hajj* season, on the principle that the Sai'ar could well look after their own.

The King of the North eventually appeared at midday, much the worse for the previous night's binge. It was the switch from whisky at supper to gin at breakfast that precipitated the fatal lunch that had left me wondering what I was doing in Arabia. Having retired to my tent, I sat on the edge of my camp bed writing up the Route Guide, and pondering on what to do next. Rajab interrupted my gloomy reverie when he poked his head round the tent flap with: "Shaikh Muhammad says we should be leaving now, Sahib. He's waiting for you outside."

The air temperature outside was approaching 50 degrees centigrade. I wondered what it would reach in the Sands. Despite Kharusi's earlier strictures about leaving too early, three Land Rovers and the Bedford pick-up were already drawn up outside the fort. Kharusi was seated in the leading vehicle, so I got into the one behind. Without another word, we roared off into the unknown. Barely six miles out, the support Land Rover's engine blew up. Kharusi sent the pick-up back to Al-'Abr for a replacement. The delay put us one and a half hours behind schedule.

At a scruffy Sai'ar encampment, Kharusi made a pit stop for tea and chat. Keeping abreast of the news, invariably about camels, wells, disputes and shootings, was not only good manners but also a vital part of the AA's job. Bedouin conversation is conducted at a painfully high decibel level. Even so, it was obvious that after half an hour of this, Kharusi had lost the plot. When he began slurring his words unintelligibly, a bearded elder kept shooting sidelong glances in my direction.

"Don't you think we should be moving on, Shaikh Muhammad," I suggested deferentially. A minute before, he had been almost comatose. At this, he came to life: "You know nothing of Bedouin ways, Mr Harding. This is my country. We'll leave when I choose to." He took another three hours to rub in his point. As a result, we camped barely 40 miles from Al-'Abr that night.

Striking camp before dawn next morning, I put the previous day down to experience. Our route to Thamud, some 300 miles away, now led north-eastwards through a maze of wadi beds, carved through the limestone outliers of the *jol*, before debouching onto the *sahra*, a level plain of firm sand interspersed with ribs of black basalt. For a hundred miles we sped along this natural highway, leaving the fading line of the *jol*'s scarp to our right, until it disappeared completely. Four hours on, we breasted a low pass where Kharusi called a halt to refill the steaming radiators. And now, for the first time, I beheld the great sand sea of Arabia, *Al-Rimal*, "The Sands". Here, at the threshold of the *Rub' al-Khali*, the Empty Quarter, a succession of golden dunes, burnished with a reddish tinge, rolled away to the farthest horizon. They looked ethereally beautiful and quite impenetrable.

Kharusi, sober now and well in command of the situation, was discussing the best way to surmount the first dune barrier with our chief guide, Tomatum bin Harbi, once a notorious raider, and now more profitably employed as a Desert Guard. This son of the desert was cupping one hand over his eyes as he stared ahead. Even the highest ocean waves seldom exceed thirty metres. Some of the dunes ahead measured more than one hundred from trough to peak. We now followed the well-tried desert travel techniques of deflating the tyres, rushing the dunes' flanks, turning them just before their crests, and then slaloming down their lee slopes. The engines could only sustain this punishment in short bursts without blowing up. Fortunately, running parallel between the dunes were flat, hard-surfaced depressions called *shaqq*s. Sometimes 400 metres wide, they became the keys to progress. By ridge hopping from one to another, we covered over hundred miles. Recent rains had set parts of the desert ablaze with colour, most prominently the yellow-flowering *zagur*.

Resting on the crest of one monster dune, Kharusi called a halt. From here I thought I saw a mirage. Far off in the golden sands, there rose, like some cathedral, a colossal drilling rig supported by two trailer platforms. Scattered around it, like discarded toys, were two giant bowsers and four house-size caravans.

"What on earth is that, Shaikh Muhammad?"

"We call it ARAMCO Camp A," he chuckled. "Some years back, those accursed Saudis told the Americans that they could come here to prospect for oil. The frontier is at least thirty miles away, so we told the Americans that they must take their drills away. When they wouldn't go, Captain Ellis came here with the HBL. The Americans fled, leaving all this behind, a million pounds of equipment. That was good for the Bedouin. They have taken everything they need."

And so they had. Not a shred of rubber was left on the giant wheel hubs. The once lavish caravan interiors had been stripped down to bare metal. "We must stop here now," continued Kharusi. "If we carry on, the engines will burst and the tyres will melt. We'll rest until 3 o'clock and then move on."

It was still only 10 a.m., but already paralysingly hot. Rajab erected an awning over Kharusi's Land Rover. His master proceeded to breakfast off a bottle of gin, and soon became incoherently drunk and abusive. This was going to be a long wait, but I hoped that he'd have slept it off by mid-afternoon. Everything went dead until midday, when an HBL wireless pick-up truck, likewise bound for Thamud, fetched up at the camp. I thought nothing more of it until my driver 'Umar, accompanied by a couple of soldiers, came across to see me.

"Their HBL lorry has almost run out of water," explained 'Umar. "We are still a day from Thamud. The soldiers say there will not be enough to drink." I said I would speak to Kharusi, and walked across to his awning. He was stretched out on the sand snoring, and only woke once I had shouted in his ear. Raising himself from the sand, he settled back heavily into his camp chair and growled: "What do you want?"

"Shouldn't we be moving on, Shaikh Muhammad?" I replied. " It's long after 3 o'clock."

He stared at me belligerently, but said nothing. I repeated the question several times. By now, several of our escort had clustered round. Kharusi's Arabic asides were unintelligible to me, but when some of the men began to snigger, I realised that my own credibility was on the line.

"Shaikh Muhammad, there's not enough water now that this other HBL truck has joined us."

"Who told you that?" he bridled. "There's plenty of water. What other truck?" Until that moment, he had not even noticed it.

Eventually, we got moving an hour later. However, yesterday's Land-Rover breakdown, and our failure to make up time over easy ground, had put us almost a day behind schedule. In my ignorance, I was also encouraging him to break a cardinal rule of desert travel. The sands take time to cool and the Land Rovers' engines, though barely started, were boiling merrily. We should have called it a day and made a pre-dawn start next morning, but events now impressed their own momentum. Fifteen minutes on, Kharusi's Land Rover stopped dead. I drove across to find him sitting on the sand, with Rajab pouring out a tumbler of gin.

"You surely can't be drinking that stuff now, Shaikh Muhammad," I remonstrated. He glared at me balefully, and tossed back the contents in one gulp. It seemed pointless to argue, so I went back to my Land Rover to await developments. Half an hour later, we were on the move again, making slow but steady progress until dusk fell. A line of mountainous dunes now barred the way. With their engines revving and roaring, our vehicles charged and recharged seemingly unscaleable inclines with everyone, except Kharusi, pushing and pulling to a rhythmic unison chanting. In this way, we ploughed on through the night. At one of many stops to refill the radiators, 'Umar came over to me with a worried-looking Tomatum.

"We can't go on like this," said 'Umar, shaking his head. "The engines are drinking water. At this rate, we won't have enough to reach Camp B."

I hadn't the slightest idea where we might be, but was now determined that we would get to Camp B that night willy-nilly. I walked across to Kharusi's Land Rover to find him stretched out on the sand. This time, shouting had no effect, so I bent over and shook him by a shoulder. It brought me up short. My open hand did not even begin to fit around it.

"Wake up, wake up, Shaikh Muhammad," I yelled in his ear.

"What in hell's the matter now?" he grunted, stirring himself.

"Are you ill?"

"No, just tired," he replied, sullenly.

"Right. Take a break and drink some water. I'll be back in fifteen minutes. We must keep going."

He fell asleep the moment I left him, but I returned as promised.

"Listen to me," I remonstrated, after shaking him awake again. "Everyone is worried about the water. We're already a day behind schedule. We've got an extra lorry load of HBL in tow, and the vehicles are drinking their radiators dry. We can't risk another day's travelling, so must reach Camp B tonight."

"There's plenty of water," he growled.

"Nobody else thinks so," I retorted.

By now, the convoy's entire entourage had gathered round, but this time there was no sniggering. Once Rajab had hauled Kharusi to his feet, the caravan moved on. Stopping and starting, retreating and reversing, pulling and pushing, it once took forty minutes to negotiate a single dune. Kharusi was now in a world of his own, driving way ahead, oblivious to what was happening behind him. Only the occasional flicker of his headlights, reflected off some distant dune, confirmed his position. Whenever we caught up, he would be asleep on the sand.

It took six and a half hours to cover those last fifty miles to Camp B. We got in after midnight, having eaten nothing all day, and promptly fell asleep on the sand. Dawn revealed another Ozymandian spectacle. ARAMCO's Camp B was a replica of Camp A. I clambered up a drilling rig, supported by two forty-metre-long trailer wagons, to get a better view of the giant bulldozer, water bowsers and caravans that had once sustained the American way of life. Kharusi was behaving as if yesterday's dramas had never been. We were only fifty miles away from Thamud, so I saw no point in having it out with him until we had got there and reported in. Shortly after striking camp, he suddenly veered off into the *sahra* to chase a herd of gazelle. Half an hour later, he rejoined us with three blood-spattered carcasses slung across the bonnet of his Land Rover. "Meat for the soldiers," he intoned. "They must have meat."

Thamud came up a lone white speck, set in a vast gravel plain. At the gates, a full guard turned out to greet us. Before I could speak to Kharusi, he and Rajab locked themselves into a cell-like chamber reserved for the Assistant Adviser, and became resolutely incommunicado. Shortly afterwards, an incandescent Julian Johnston came through on the wireless from Al-'Abr.

"Where the hell have you been, John?" he spluttered. "You're a day overdue. We were about to send out a search party."

"We've been having a little local difficulty," I explained, giving him a brief rundown of what had been happening.

"That's as may be," he shot back. "But all this bloody nonsense concerns my HBL soldiers too, not just you and Kharusi. Anyway, the Qaid here must speak to him immediately. There's been a serious incident at Sanaw which he must sort out."

Sanaw, the next fort along the line, was still ninety miles away. I went upstairs and kept banging on the door until Rajab opened it. Kharusi was stretched out on a camp bed, clutching a half-empty gin bottle.

"You're wanted urgently on the R/T, Shaikh Muhammad."

"Who the devil wants to speak to me?"

"The Arab officer commanding the HBL at Al-'Abr."

"Then kindly take his message on my behalf."

"This is none of my business. You must speak to him yourself."

"I don't take messages on the R/T. Tell them to send it me in writing."

"For God's sake, Shaikh Muhammad," I burst out. "Pull yourself together. This is a serious matter which directly concerns you as the AA responsible for this area. You must deal with it personally."

At this, his aggression suddenly evaporated.

"I'll only do it for you as a personal favour," he said, pathetically.

"This is nothing to do with personal favours," I replied. "You must speak to Al-'Abr yourself."

But nothing would budge him. I retreated downstairs to the wireless room to explain the situation to a now apoplectic Johnston. "This is quite disgraceful," he exploded. "I'm bound to report what's been happening straight back to Watts and Gray."

To get some peace from Kharusi's drunken roaring and Rajab's crazed laughter, I moved into the tiny generating station outside the fort. With nothing better to do than await instructions from Mukalla, I wrote up the Route Guide, shared the garrison's lunch of tinned tuna and rice, and inspected

Thamud's well. This was a bustling scene with several hundred camels, goats and sheep being watered in relays by tribesmen, cheeky urchins and unveiled Manahil women. Thamud had once been an important staging post on the incense route from Dhofar. Of that fabled pre-Islamic past, all that remains are an indistinct stone avenue and a well, whose mouth over millennia has been raised three metres above its surroundings from the accumulated excreta of livestock.

Early next morning, I confronted Kharusi. Disconcertingly, he was now sober, charming and affable.

"Shaikh Muhammad, you'll not be surprised to learn that I'm not coming with you to Habarut."

"Why's that, Mr Harding?" he said, looking genuinely surprised.

"Because you've been drunk and incapable for the past three days. You've disgraced your position as AAND."

"I cannot agree with you," he rallied, defiantly. "I've treated you as a friend and brother, and you've enjoyed my hospitality. Yes, everyone knows I drink – the Governor, the RA, Major Snell, Captain Ellis, Colonel Wilson. What's wrong with that? I've always done my job and loyally served the British. If you report my drunkenness to the RA, I will invoke *sharaf*."

Sharaf is an Arab's sacred honour. I now realised that my conversation with Julian Johnston might have already compromised Kharusi's. A series of "What ifs" flashed through my mind. He might be a bully, but he had faithfully served Her Britannic Majesty in a place where few Europeans could sanely last for more than a few months. Once upon a time, his huge boxer's frame might have held its drink. No longer. Julian Johnston's caustic "I expect he's drunk, they all are," came back to me. Anyway, who the hell was I to tell Kharusi that he had disgraced the Service? I was a pygmy beside him.

"I shall have to wait here for the RA's instructions," I said, stiffly.

"You must do as you please," he replied. "I must continue to Sanaw with Tomatum to deal with this trouble. I'll leave you two Land Rovers and the pick-up. Salim Baraghan will be your guide." Half an hour later, he was gone.

The previous night, I'd had ample time to consider an alternative action plan. I had decided to complete a shortened circuit of the Northern Deserts, returning to Al-'Abr by a southern route. This would take in the HBL forts at Minwakh and Zamakh. When I explained my plan to the HBL's elderly *mulazim* commanding Thamud, the old man stared at me askance. I signalled my intentions to Mukalla for approval anyway. While waiting for Watts's reply, I cast around for something positive to do. Thamud had no files, but in a corner of the "Guest Room" abandoned by Kharusi, I discovered a dusty wooden box. Inside was a tattered folder with a single directive from Colonel Boustead. It had been written in response to some long-departed Political Officer's application for overdue leave. "In the Sudan," it began, "young officers were lucky to be allowed the privilege of leave after five or even ten years, provided conditions of service allowed." It concluded with a flurry of strictures about the moral decline of a generation become too soft to undertake the great mission of Empire.

The routine of the HBL's Thamud garrison was unchanging. Exchange a bit of chat with those lithe Manahil girls drawing water at the well; keep your eye in with target practice at old tin cans; clean your rifle and strip down the Bren gun every evening; pray regularly and talk incessantly. At dawn and dusk there was a stand-to, when the fort's crenellated parapets were manned by the whole garrison. Otherwise, the day's highlight would be the evening meal, when you dug your right hand into a mess of steaming rice and goat with the best of them. Thamud's veteran *mulazim* complained bitterly about the present, but reminisced happily about the past. He held Jim Ellis and Jock Snell in particularly high esteem. I reckoned that after a few months in such company, I would be speaking reasonable Arabic.

Pat Gray kept in regular touch with me on the R/T. I had heard nothing from Arthur Watts, so assumed that he approved my revised itinerary. I left Thamud at dawn on my fourth morning with two Land Rovers, the pick-up and my own dirty dozen, guided by Salim Baraghan, bearded and wild-eyed like some Old Testament prophet. Initially, our return route followed a maze of shallow wadis, low rocky passes and sandy basins before emerging onto a vast plain of sand and shale. Here, we put up a gazelle. 'Umar gave chase and Salim, handing me his rifle, insisted that I have first shot. To hit a moving target at forty yards, with the Land Rover swerving and bucking at 30 mph, was beyond me. I handed the rifle back to Salim, who waited until we were almost on top of the wretched gazelle. He missed twice, then almost obliterated it with his third shot.

For the next three hours, we skirted the fringes of the Sands, ridge-hopping from *shaqq* to *shaqq*, before reaching Hazar. This well in the wilderness was equipped with a PCL pump supporting 300 goats, 45 camels and a group of wary-eyed Sai'ar who grudgingly offered us a bowl of camel's milk. Discouraged by their reception, I urged Salim to push on to Khashm al-Jebel, our next staging post. He replied that it was still hours away, and that the passage through this part of the Sands was so difficult that we could only cross it at dawn the next day. It was still only 8.30 a.m. and I knew that Salim's family lived conveniently nearby.

However, I had learned my lesson about pushing routes. As if to settle it, my cook Mubarak collapsed after gorging himself on half-cooked gazelle. The heat at Hazar was such as to silence even the camels. For the rest of that interminable day, all twelve of us lay prone under a canvas awning stretched out between the two Land Rovers, while a succession of dust devils twisted and twirled around our encampment.

We quit Hazar long before dawn. The pick-up truck twice got stuck in deep sand before we had even reached the Sands. As the sun lit up those burnished dunes, we braced ourselves for another epic. This second crossing was more difficult than the first, and would have been impossible an hour later. To escape the worst of it, Salim steered us in, out, through, up and over tracts of mountainous dunes, *sahra* and *shaqq* in succession. For thirty miles, I logged fifteen separate Route Guide entries. As the morning wore on, the engines began to overheat so frequently that even 'Umar began to look worried. And then, a brief glimpse of the spectacular limestone pillars of Khashm al-Jebel, breaking the southern horizon, set everyone cheering. Five and a half hours and seventy-six miles on from Hazar, we finally quit the Sands, and followed faint tracks running parallel to the outliers of the *jol.* Beneath an indigo sky, with the sun on our backs, we sped past limestone outcrops, isolated rock needles and undulating gravel flats brightened by an occasional patch of flowers. At midday, Salim doubled back up a stone-strewn wadi bed to the foot of a massive rock prow. A cube of brilliant white was perched on its summit – Husn Minwakh.

The sergeant-in-charge of the garrison killed a goat in our honour, stilling my protests with "What we have, we give". We sat out the heat of another wilting day, before heading westwards onto the *sahra* bound for Zamakh. The waning sun lent the Sands an even deeper shade of gold, and transformed the *jol*'s scarp-line into an ethereal shade of blue. Flying before the wind with 'Umar beside me, it occurred to me that this journey might be the touchstone of my Arabian experience.

Next morning, I watched the sun rise on the now-distant sands from the flat roof of Zamakh fort. Below me, the Sai'ar women were already drawing water from a 300-ft-deep pre-Islamic well in huge leather buckets by an elaborate system of ropes and pulleys. As we drove into Al-'Abr an hour later with horns blaring, I told Mubarak to buy a sheep to celebrate our safe return. Feasting with my team and some of the garrison, my Arabic was now good enough to join in the general badinage. A call to the wireless room, and Julian Johnston's crackling voice, brought me back to reality.

"Don't worry," I assured him. "We're all back in one piece. Any messages for me from the RA?"

"Nothing that has been passed to me," he replied testily.

I might have stayed on at Al-'Abr for another couple of days, but sensed that the time had come to end my desert adventure. After bidding my good companions of the past ten days farewell, I turned to 'Umar.

"I'm afraid it's back to Sayun for you and me," I said, gloomily.

"No, Mr Harding!" he replied. "I cannot come with you. My Land Rover is broken, so I must stay here until it is repaired. Salim Faraj will be your driver to Sayun."

I remonstrated, but he was adamant. Over the past two weeks, he had driven me through some of the most inhospitable country in the world. We had shared the same adventures and eaten the same food. He had been ever-courteous, and had quietly backed my decisions, right or wrong. We had forged a special bond of friendship and, now that we were parting, a small world fell about my head. As we shook hands, he clasped my shoulder lightly and said: "I will always go with you when you return." A surge of emotion overtook me. I slipped behind a tent to hide suppressed tears.

I planned to return to Sayun by a little-used route across the northern *jol*, through the Sai'ar heartland. This is the true wilderness of South Arabia, a stony desolation, devoid of vegetation and any visible sign of life. Salim Faraj took a zig-zagging line of least resistance, and as we crashed and bumped along every detail of my clash with Kharusi churned darkly through my mind. The camp just below the Rakban Pass, at over 1,000 metres, gave my coldest night to date in Arabia. At the top of the Hainin Pass, a simple plaque in Arabic recorded that Johnny Johnson, using HBL and local labour, had built the cliff-hanging road that spiralled off the *jol* into Wadi Hadhramaut.

The Wadi might have been another world. The air felt lifeless, the heat was overpowering, and the people's faces lacked the animation so carelessly worn by the men and women of the desert. Both Lanfear and his second-in-command, John Weakley, were temporarily away in Mukalla. I filled in time visiting Tarim, with its three hundred mosques, guided by Sayyid Muhammad Al-Kaf, a scion of the Hadhramaut's most illustrious merchant family. The façade of one of the Al-Kaf palaces aped that of Buckingham Palace. Its chandeliered drawing rooms and marbled bathrooms reflected a lifestyle that was shortly to disappear for ever.

Next day, I met Lanfear off the plane from Mukalla. I badly wanted to unburden myself about the Kharusi affair, but Lanfear kept his distance. Later, he sent a note to the Rest House, inviting me for a drink that evening.

"I'd be quite careful how you deal with this business," he cautioned. "The RA doesn't like any sort of trouble. If he thinks that Kharusi is indispensable, you might find yourself in a difficult position."

His warning added a disquieting new dimension to Mukalla's deafening silence. With no further instructions from Watts, I continued my Hadhramaut familiarization tour with working visits to Shibam, Al-Hawta and various agricultural projects. While inspecting an ancient dam, recently rebuilt by local masons with British aid, I let my hair down with Lanfear.

"This place has a refreshingly different working atmosphere to Mukalla. Frankly, I'm bored and frustrated doing dogsbody work. I really felt I'd come alive in the desert."

"I can understand that," he replied. "I felt much the same when I first came here. But desert life is really escapism. And whatever its frustrations, what other job offers the same satisfactions? To live and work to serve the people of this extraordinary land is a rare privilege. Give it time. However, to stay the course and keep sane, it definitely helps to be married."

After a week in Sayun, and still with no news from Mukalla, I revived my earlier plan of travelling back with the cameleers. As I made final preparations for this journey, an urgent signal summoned me back by the first available plane. My return to Riyan coincided with Amir Ghalib's official send-off to his boarding school in Egypt, so the RA kindly offered me a lift back to Mukalla. He would not be drawn on the Kharusi debacle but asked for a written report "as soon as possible". He seemed more interested in the Route Guide but then, as an aside, announced that he was appointing Julian Johnston to act as temporary Assistant Adviser Northern Deserts. I wondered where this left

Kharusi, for there was no love lost between them.

I assumed that I was done with touring, yet within a week of my return the RA instructed me to attend the Bedouin fair at Meshhed in the Wadi Du'an, accompanying David Eales, who was now acting HBL Commandant. We were to take the West Road, so that I might report back on its current state of repair. Following the line of another ancient caravan route, this spectacular road forged a precarious way up the *jol*'s 6,000-ft southern ramparts by a series of dramatic hairpin bends. Eales's long-wheelbase Land Rover was a deal more comfortable than the Bedford 5-tonner in which I had driven up the East Road, a month earlier. We stopped for a relatively comfortable night at the Qu'aiti State guest house, just below the pass of Mawla Matar, the "Lord of Rain" whose "tomb", a pre-Islamic monument twenty feet long, sited just below the pass itself, is still venerated by the local Bedouin as a memorial of the *juddud*, or grandfathers, a race of primaeval giants.

This was another, more rarefied, world. In the inaccessible gullies that seamed the *jol*'s seaward-facing scarp, grew *'ilb* (*Zizyphus spina-Christi*) and giant tamarisk trees of European proportions, spared from the depredations of goats and charcoal burners. As dusk fell, it was soon too cold to sit outside. From within, with a blanket wrapped round my shoulders and a glass of whisky to hand, I watched shifting clouds suffused with sunset hues swirl around the flanks of Kaur Saiban, the highest point of Hadhramaut, half imagining myself amongst the fells of Norway.

Next morning, the valleys below were enveloped in cloud. A chill wind was blowing as we breasted the pass and, for the next ninety miles, we bumped, lurched and juddered across the flinty surface of the *jol*. And then, without warning, our Land Rover seemed to teeter at the edge of an awesome precipice plunging four hundred metres plumb, to the bed of the Wadi al-Aisar. After crawling down the Jahi Pass, we entered the Wadi Du'an where dark-hued date plantations intermingled with bright green thickets of *'ilb*. Lining either side of this veritable canyon, the imposing, lime-washed mansions of Du'an's merchant venturers gleamed bright in the late afternoon sun.

We reached Meshhed at dusk that same evening. A sudden dust storm had tinted everything with a reddish shade. As I emerged from my tent next morning, the air was fresh and clear, and the whole place alive with noise and bustle. Knots of rifle-toting, swaggering Bedouin were drifting in from the interior, driving before them camels, sheep and goats. Tribal women beat

1. *Above:* Aden: Jebel Shamsan and Steamer Point from Al-Ittihad.

2. *Below:* Aden Port with Little Aden across the harbour. The Secretariat is the whitewashed building on the quayside to the extreme left.

3. *Above:* A stitched fishing *sanbuq* below Ras Boradli, looking across the water towards Little Aden.

4. *Below:* The dhow harbour at Ma'alla, Aden.

5. *Above:* A picnic near Kirsh, Amour, north-west of Lahej. From the left: Kenyon, Pirie-Girdon and Guillet.

6. *Below:* The "Indian Gate", Mukalla (since demolished).

7. *Above:* The Residency, Mukalla.

8. *Below:* Mukalla: Al-Bilad and harbour.

9. *Above:* Mukalla: the palace of the Qu'aiti Sultan.

10. *Below:* Mukalla: Sir William Luce's farewell visit.

11. *Above:* HH Sultan 'Awadh Al-Qu'aiti of Mukalla (left), with the Amir Ghalib.

12. *Below:* The view from the author's house, Mukalla: the camel park at Therib.

13. *Above:* Bedouin cameleers from the interior at Therib, Mukalla.

14. *Below:* Mukalla's Armed Forces assembled at Riyan. Right to left: Qu'aiti Armed Constabulary, Hadhrami Bedouin Legion, Mukalla Regular Army.

15. Residency staff at Mukalla in Col. Boustead's time. Front row, left to right: Abdullah Shawtah, Pat Booker, Jock Snell, Willie Wise, Col. Boustead, Ralph Daly, Cen Jones, George Coles. Second row, centre: Michael Crouch, with 'Isa Musallam to his right. Official Aden Government photograph.

16. *Above:* Sir Charles Johnston takes the salute outside the Residency, Mukalla.

17. *Below:* Arthur Watts with John Lanfear.

18. *Above:* Fisherman up from Fuwwa, near Mukalla.

19. *Below:* The launch of Mukalla's crayfish industry: Alec White and Ali Maas.

20. *Above:* Sayun in Wadi Hadhramaut, capital of the Kathiri State.

21. *Below:* The Kathiri Sultan's palace, Sayun.

22. *Above:* Well outside Shibam, Wadi Hadhramaut.

23. *Below:* The main square of Shibam.

24. *Above:* Husn al-'Abr, in the Northern Deserts.

25. *Below:* Camels of the Sai'ar at Al-'Abr.

26. *Above:* An elder of the Sai'ar in the Northern Deserts.

27. *Below:* At the edge of the Sands, Northern Deserts.

28. *Above:* The well at Thamud, Northern Deserts.

29. *Below:* My team for the return journey from Thamud.

30. *Above:* Salim Baraghan, Desert Guard, my driver back to Sayun from the Northern Deserts

31. *Below:* A gazelle for the pot in the Northern Deserts. 'Umar Al-Sai'ari stands to the left; Salim Baraghan holds the rifle.

drums, as gaggles of bejewelled little girls in ringlets and garish dresses raced giggling round the stalls. Cross-legged vendors sold basketwork, silver filigree and crude goatskin rugs, while fat, jolly caterers doled out fast food from steaming copper urns. Arthur Watts was holding court to a British contingent flown up the previous day from Aden with their families. Having just completed my Northern Deserts report, I was longing to get the wretched thing off my chest, so delivered it to him personally, there and then. Decidedly, the Meshhed Fair was not the right place to discuss controversial business, but I expected we would be having a full-blown *post mortem* back in Mukalla. Predictably, Watts summoned me to his office a couple of days later, yet said not a word about Kharusi. He was now preoccupied with another minor crisis.

"I want you to go back to Wadi Du'an as a matter of urgency. Julian Johnston has just signalled to say that he's pulled in a couple of gun-runners, with a cache of thirty rifles and a stack of ammunition. They're now being held at Hawra under guard. You must take delivery of the weapons and bring the captives down here for questioning. David Eales has kindly agreed to provide you with transport and an HBL escort. If you leave this afternoon, you should get to Hawra by tomorrow morning. This mission has an important political and security dimension. Johnston thinks that he's rumbled an arms-smuggling racket organised by Kharusi. Apparently, the Naib of Hawra and Qaid Salih bin Sumaida, the Mukalla Regular Army's Commandant, are included as intended recipients."

When Eales insisted that he could spare me only a Bedford 3-tonner and a pick-up, which would not be ready until 8 p.m., I knew that I could not possibly reach Hawra by the following morning. Undeterred, I set off up the West Road for the second time that week, breasting the Mawla Matar pass after midnight, and then spending the next six and a half hours grinding across the *jol*. The pick-up broke down twice before we reached the outskirts of Hawra, after twenty hours' driving. Fifty metres off the road, I spotted an HBL *mulazim* smoking a cigarette, with three soldiers stretched out on the ground beside a stack of rifles.

"Where are your prisoners, Lieutenant?"

"The prisoners are being held by the MRA at Al-Qa'udha," he replied sullenly.

"Then where is Captain Johnston?"

"Captain Johnston has gone back to Al-'Abr. There is big trouble with the

Sai'ar, a killing. He asked me to give you this *waraga*."

He handed me a dirty slip of paper with a long list of names and numbers scribbled down in Arabic. I stuffed it into my pocket, and began to make my own inventory of the rifles and ammunition. Barely had I started when a brand new MRA Land Rover slewed off the road and drove right up to us. A small, lithe Arab officer in an immaculately pressed uniform jumped out and greeted me with brisk authority.

"Peace be upon you, Mr Harding. God willing, you have had a good journey?"

I had previously met Qaid Salih bin Sumaida on ceremonial occasions. An able and ambitious soldier, he quickly got down to business.

"We must see the Naib of Hawra immediately. My men are holding the prisoners secure there. I have received a message that the RA wants you to bring them back to Mukalla without delay."

Qaid Salih seemed to know a lot more about the situation than I did, and was fast taking control. After he had ordered the HBL *mulazim* to stash the arms and ammunition into the back of the Bedford, there was little I could do but follow him to Hawra. Here the Naib, an unctuous man, greeted us. "A serious incident," he said, shaking his head solicitously, and then insisted on seeing the list of consignees. My orders from Watts had not been precise. The Naib was Governor of Hawra Province; Qaid Salih was both head of the Qu'aiti Armed Forces and responsible for the State's internal security. My authority as a cadet Assistant Adviser was peripheral. Reluctantly, I handed the Naib the list.

After both men had thanked me profusely for my co-operation, two scruffy prisoners in shackles were dragged out of the fort and bundled into the back of the Bedford. Our leave-taking was perfunctory. Watts had instructed me to report to Lanfear in Sayun. Already, I had that certain feeling that things had not gone according to plan. Now, as I arrived hours behind schedule, Lanfear's cool reception confirmed my suspicions of a bungled mission. We were offered neither refreshment nor a stopover.

In the circumstances, it was now quicker to return to Mukalla by the East Road. After a brief roadside nap, we began the long return journey across the *jol* that same night. By evening the following day, the prisoners were safely delivered to the HBL barracks Mukalla, fifteen hours after collection. I was able to report to Watts that at least that part of my 48-hour mission had been successful, sure in the knowledge that my cover had been blown from the outset. Next day, James Bridges, a Senior Intelligence Officer, flew up from Aden to interview the prisoners. Neither I nor Jock Snell, who knew more about Kharusi and the Northern Deserts than anyone, were bidden to be present or even debriefed. I never discovered the truth about either Qaid Salih's or the Naib of Hawra's alleged involvement. Qaid Salih bin Sumaida was a highly effective commander of the Qu'aiti Armed Forces and was later promoted to the substantive rank of Major-General. Unlike his successor, a Yafa'i named Ahmed Al-Yazidi, he always remained loyal to Sultan Ghalib. Watts never again referred to the *Affaire Kharusi* again, or to his alleged gun-running. Maybe Shaikh Muhammad sold the odd rifle but, at heart, he was basically loyal. In the WAP, everyone flogged arms. But, fatally for him, Kharusi was actively disliked by both Watts and Johnston. Three days later, he walked into my office.

"What can I do for you, Shaikh Muhammad?" I asked him, warily.

"I've come to get my passport in order."

"Why's that?"

"Surely you know? I've handed in my resignation, and the RA's accepted it. I've served the Qu'aiti State and the British for twenty-one years. That's longer than Ingrams, Boustead, Snell, Ellis, or anyone else for that matter. I've been accused of arms smuggling, but I deny it. I never expected this sort of treatment. I'm leaving Mukalla to take my family back to Zanzibar, where we belong. We will never return to Arabia again."

He spoke without a trace of self-pity, but would not be drawn further. Only the previous day, I had unearthed a tattered old file from the Ingrams era. It concerned the first Maifa'ah Hajar agricultural development scheme, which had been managed with conspicuous success by one Muhammad bin Said Al-Kharusi. A big man to the last, I never really forgave myself for the part I played in his demise. Nor did it cross my mind that I would ever see him again. Four years on, we were to meet in very different circumstances.

7

Loaves and Fishes

R E-ENTRY INTO MUKALLA after six weeks of adventure was predictably anti-climactic. Predictably too, the appointment of Husain Al-Minhali to take over from me as AAR had never materialized, so the slot went to an Adeni, Muhammad Naji, a mystifyingly inept political appointment. However, my upgrading to Assistant Adviser Coastal Areas (AACA) promised a fresh start, and gave me a measure of responsibility for Coastal Roads, Mukalla's Port & Water Supply, Co-operative & Marketing Agricultural Schemes, and Fisheries. These were in addition to AAR's more mundane duties.

An effective transport system was essential to the country's economic progress yet, in the EAP, only two short sections of sealed road existed in an area twice the size of England. Engineering heroics had been performed with shovels and bulldozers to fashion graded tracks across some of the world's most inhospitable terrain, but it only took one flash flood to sweep everything away. After that, the whole depressing business of reconstruction would have to start all over again.

Although my official brief was limited to coastal roads, I had become something of an expert on what Watts portentously described as the "EAP's Road Network". Having driven up and down the East and West Roads several times, and spent numbing hours recording mileages, wells, villages and landmarks for the RA's Route Guide, I was at least qualified to pronounce that the state of both these roads was "appalling". The RA took this as a personal rebuke so, after convening a Roads Committee, he commissioned Karl

Schlatholt to survey both roads. When Schlatholt confirmed that "Zee Vest Road is a bloody disgrace", Watts made a personal inspection to satisfy himself. At the next Roads Committee meeting it was he who thundered, "The West Road *is* in a terrible state. I can't possibly drive our new Governor, Sir Charles Johnston, that way until it's been repaired. Hadi Bahayan's feet won't touch the ground after this."

Bahayan, the venal Qu'aiti State's Director of Public Works, was not a man to lose his footing so easily and, in the heated discussion that followed, Julian Johnston took issue with the RA's technical assessment of why the roads were deteriorating so fast. Watts swiftly closed the meeting with: "When you have served here for sixteen years, Johnston, you'll be in a better position to question my judgement." Johnston left, spitting bile: "Watts's rockets to Bahayan are like sponges thrown against a brick wall."

Watts and he never saw eye to eye, and this proved to be Julian's last EAP tour. But there was nothing that Hadi Bahayan, or anyone else, could have done about the roads without more money, and bags of it. The RA must have been as frustrated as any of us by lack of progress, but lacked the confidence to discuss the situation candidly with his junior officers. Yet he was always loyally defensive about the Qu'aiti State's efforts to maintain its roads, and when a newly appointed Agricultural Adviser, John Jefferson, cited the EAP's appalling roads as a prime reason for its retarded agricultural development, Watts retorted that the Qu'aiti State's annual budget for road repairs was the equivalent to half the *aggregate* aid for road building received from HM Treasury over the past sixteen years. Sir Charles Johnston fully realized that no significant economic progress would be possible without a major Protectorate road-building programme. His pleas to HMG also fell on deaf ears. In the event, his planned trip up the West Road, which had raised so much heat and dust, never came off due to time pressures and Lady Johnston's fragile health.

A standard excuse for HMG parsimony was that the Protectorate's potential for profitable economic development did not justify massive expenditure. Yet one relatively modest scheme that would certainly have given a boost to the local economy was the construction of a new road to the Maifa'ah Delta. This alluvial fan, some fifty miles west of Mukalla, comprised at least 5,000 acres of rich agricultural land, and was where Schlatholt had built his dam. The Qu'aitis themselves had already raised £30,000, almost a third of HMG's annual allocation for all EAP development, to re-engineer the existing track.

Unfortunately, after a promising start, Hadi Bahayan had a blazing row with the contractors which stalled the entire project.

A more ambitious scheme, which might have transformed the entire Qu'aiti economy, was the construction of a breakwater to provide Mukalla's harbour with safe berthing. The Aden Port Trust had costed the work at £400,000. Given time and due diligence, it should have been possible to raise this sum. Yet again, negotiations snagged on the twin rocks of Hadi Bahayan's intransigence and the Sultanic Council's procrastination.

Apart from the Hadhramaut Pump Scheme, and Schlatholt's work in Maifa'ah, the EAP's agricultural development had been disappointingly sluggish. According to Colonial Office statistics, only two percent of South Arabia's land was cultivable, yet in ages past this same land had supported much larger populations, thanks to the dams and sophisticated irrigation techniques of an older civilization, long since fallen into disuse. South Arabia's soil was basically fertile, and was deficient not in mineral salts, but water. Given enough of this, properly husbanded alluvial deposits in the wadis were capable of growing a wide variety of fruit and vegetables. Even the sands of the Empty Quarter blossomed after a shower of rain.

There was no lack of expert HMG technical advice available on high-value cash crops, drainage, irrigation, soil stabilization, water exploitation and conservation. Clay samples were even dispatched to London for expert analysis to determine their dam-building qualities. A favourite Colonial Office vehicle to promote agricultural development was the market co-operative. In the Qu'aiti State, one of the few viable cash crops was Hamumi tobacco, based on Ghail Ba Wazir. The Qu'aitis had already established an experimental farm here to promote the brand, and had authorized the Ghail Ba Wazir Tobacco Growers Association, which existed solely to benefit the State Council's merchant oligarchs, to manage it. Undeterred by the Association's impenetrable internal workings, Aden's Co-operative and Marketing Department had identified this as a suitable case for treatment, and had it relabelled a co-operative society in 1956. Four years on, it still had neither a constitution nor effective external auditing, and when the demand for Hamumi tobacco suddenly collapsed, the society went bust.

However hard I might struggle to promote the Maifa'ah road, Mukalla's harbour, or the doomed Hamumi tobacco industry, an issue of more immediate concern was Mukalla's water supply. It had long been recognized that this could no longer meet the demands of the town's ever-expanding population. British engineering experts had concluded that the only long-term solution was to tap the artesian water basins at Fuwwa. However, as this was going to be expensive, the State Council was still sitting on its hands. The town's main source of drinking water was the springs at Baqarain, some five miles inland. The method of water extraction was almost identical to the Iranian *qanat* system. A mother-well would be tapped by deep underground shafts, from which feeder channels supplied an overground open conduit connected to the town. Digging and maintenance works were done by specialist artisans who descended the 40-ft well shafts with no aids save hand- and footholds cut on either side.

One bright October morning, Dr Michael Newland, the Special Duties Medical Officer, issued an SOS for a blood donor. After congratulating me on surviving an hour-long extraction process, involving pipes and syringes, he confided: "So far as I'm aware, you're the first person ever to have given blood in the EAP. Trouble is, you may not be the last. I suspect that this is a case of typhoid. If so, we're in for trouble."

Later that day, I was summoned to the RA's office, where a grim-faced Watts was conferring with Willie Wise, his newly appointed deputy, Jehan Khan, and Mukalla's three British doctors, Newland, Markham and Qaseem Khan.

"Michael has confirmed a case of typhoid in Mukalla," the RA announced, dramatically. "Apparently, there's no precedent for this, so we must activate an immediate action plan. Most likely, the town's water supply is contaminated. I want you to conduct a complete survey of the pipeline from Baqarain to Mukalla with Hadi Bahayan. Report back to me the moment you return."

Twenty years earlier, Ingrams had observed that Mukalla's water supply was "unprotected at its source and over part of its course, but there was no typhoid … . Every canon of health was flouted but merciful Providence must have kept a special eye on Mukalla." Mukalla's medical facilities had improved significantly since Ingrams' time, but Providence had at last blinked.

Starting from the Mukalla end of the five-mile conduit, in the heat of the noonday sun, my fragile relationship with Hadi Bahayan was again put to the test. As if to settle an old score, he skipped ahead of me, agile as a goat. Nothing had changed since Ingrams' day. The watercourse was exposed to every sort of contamination from goats, sheep, pye-dogs and anyone else so minded. Yet Providence still smiled for, in the event, there were mercifully few typhoid fatalities. When the scare blew over, my resolution to drink only boiled water lapsed, as did Jehan Khan's vow to get the conduit sealed.

When George Coles left Mukalla that September, I was given a couple of days to take over Military and Administrative Course Number 13. This annual event, normally the Military Adviser's responsibility, had its origins in Curzon's plan to establish a college in Aden to educate the sons of hinterland chiefs. Years later, it was Ingrams who picked up the baton and founded Aden College, intending to run it along the lines of an English public school, with an emphasis on character and physical training, particularly football. Its motto was taken from a Qur'anic text, "Verily God ordaineth justice and kindness". By the late 1950s it had become the main recruiting ground for nationalist revolutionary intellectuals. On becoming the EAP's first British Adviser, Ingrams established Mukalla's Military and Administrative Course as a watered-down version of his Aden original.

My only briefing was that this four-month course should give suitable students military instruction, and "an insight into the workings of government". For once, I imagined that this was a job for which I had some relevant experience, having spent most of my National Service training Welsh Guardsmen. It was already too late to influence the enrolment of students, mainly mature but barely literate tribesmen. However, with the assistance of my principal tutors, an MRA *Rais* and an Egyptian schoolmaster, we revised a syllabus which had previously been restricted to low-level infantry tactics, to include an element of administration. We also reduced the bloated cadre of forty lecturers to manageable proportions. My Arabic was inadequate to lecture coherently; nonetheless I made periodic inspections, set the Half-term and Final examinations, and judged the arms-drill competition at the Passing Out parade. Some of Course 13's students might possibly have benefited from the experience.

AACA's remit was proving a deal more interesting than AAR's, but my failure to make manifest progress on the development front was almost as frustrating as the absence of female company. The only unattached British girls who normally came near the place were lubricious ENSA singers, flown in from home to entertain lonely hearts at RAF Riyan. Invitations to these jokey shows shot testosterone levels off scale, as did the sight of lithe Arab girls drawing water at the well in clinging wet dresses. In Colonial Africa, local mistresses were not uncommon. In Arabia, this would have meant instant dismissal or worse. I never had the nerve to chance my luck, though, of a balmy moonlit night, the muezzin's reassuring call to prayer sometimes made me contemplate conversion as a means to an end.

Another social problem was the dearth of fellow-spirited male contemporaries. Apart from John Lanfear and John Wheatley in distant Sayun, the only other Assistant Adviser in the EAP was Michael Crouch. Time spent in the Northern Deserts had lent force to an already extravagant personality. And so, when two dust-encased horn-blaring Land Rovers, stuffed with HBL soldiers, roared into the Residency compound, I assumed that this could only be Crouch "come down from the North". A stocky, bespectacled figure, head swathed in a red and white *imama*, leapt lightly from the driver's seat and headed purposefully towards me. Clad in a multi-pocketed khaki bush jacket criss-crossed with live ammunition belts, and revolver at his hip, he covered the ground in a Groucho-Marx-style stride before seizing my hand in a Furse-like grip and pronouncing, in a penetrative baritone: "Michael Crouch. You must be Harding. I read Law at Downing. We must have been contemporaries. Funny that I didn't come across you then." I too wondered how I could possibly have missed so positive a character. During his time as my predecessor AAR, Michael had enlivened Mukalla society. His book, *An Element of Luck*, vividly describes his nine eventful years of South Arabian service.

Occasional games of tennis passed the time agreeably enough, but to get shot of the claustrophobic atmosphere of Mukalla I made occasional solo explorations into the hinterland. Once, I unwittingly disturbed a large pack of pye-dogs high on Jebel Mukalla. Normally, a raised arm or a well-aimed stone would send them packing. Salukis apart, the Arabs regard dogs as unclean, and treat them accordingly. But a big pack of pyes can make mincemeat of weaker prey, so I began a stealthy tactical retreat. Unfortunately, the gnarled leader-dog had already spotted me, and now launched itself downhill, foaming and snarling. Attack seemed my only hope of not becoming mincemeat so, armed with stones, I charged upwards towards it, yelling hysterically and hurling my missiles. Just when all seemed lost, the brute sheered off, whereupon the rest of the pack slunk away. I never went unaccompanied again.

The arrival of Stewart Hawkins changed my Mukalla life. Appointed as a temporary Assistant Adviser on sabbatical from Balliol, where he was reading Oriental Languages, Stewart's National Service in northern Nigeria had given him an easy familiarity with the Islamic world. Although sharing a house with a man who sometimes resembled a large and angry beast could be unnerving, we were always at one about the way the EAP should be run, and became bosom friends. As a Charterhouse protégé of the famous mountaineer Wilfred Noyce, Stewart was also a ready-made companion for the outdoor sallies which we shared with Eamon Conboy, newly appointed to the Eastern Bank's Mukalla branch. Boustead himself might have approved of our pioneer climbs on Mukalla's virgin cliffs, and explorations of its rugged hinterland. Here, hidden amongst a maze of multi-coloured monoliths, grew acacias, grotesque euphorbias, and the globular-trunked 'adan bush (*Adenium* spp.), with fragrant rosy flowers. Returning home like frizzled bacon at the end of such days, we competed to see who could put down most iced lager.

Jock Snell's departure on leave in early October 1960 effectively brought down the Old Guard's final curtain. His fourteen years of unbroken EAP service was rivalled by no other British officer. All the Arabs spoke of him with genuine affection and respect but, ever since Arthur Watts's arrival, Jock's personality had withered. However, a week of farewell parties restored the old soldier's morale, and his increasingly outrageous behaviour was matched only by Arthur's shrinking embarrassment. When he told me that his next posting would be Aden, I wondered how he would make out with the Secretariat's formidable file wallahs he so affected to despise. Two years later, I found that he had adapted effortlessly to this less familiar environment.

Looking after visitors and ceremonial remained my chore. It remains a disappointment that the RA never briefed me properly about one very superior person, whom I was unexpectedly detailed to accompany on her photographic tour of Mukalla. Curzon had always been a hero of mine, and Lady Alexandra ("Bubba") Metcalfe was his favourite daughter. My relationship with this grand, imperious lady might have been warmer had I only been apprised of her identity at the outset. Mukalla's most important official visitor by far was Aden's new Governor, His Excellency Sir Charles Hepburn Johnston KCMG, who had succeeded Sir William Luce in September. HE's confidential EAP programme was to include three days in Mukalla, followed by visits to Hadhramaut and the Northern Desert.

Determined to make his mark, Watts instructed me to prepare a detailed draft programme, and to fly to Aden to liaise with HE's ADC to ensure that all the appropriate Colonial Service procedures and protocol were followed to the letter. "Lady Johnston's in delicate health," explained the RA. "We've got to look after her very carefully and get exactly the right food. My wife Barbara will give you a shopping list of fresh vegetables and other things for you to bring back from Aden." When Sir William Luce had made his farewell visit ten months before, McIntosh had given me two days to get the show on the road. This time, I was allotted three weeks and also given the job of general grocer.

The 16-page programme I devised for HE's Mukalla visit nearly precipitated the RA's nervous breakdown. The final version included minute-by-minute timings for every single event, with detailed instructions for everyone, however remotely involved, to follow to the letter. It included the outward and inward journeys to and from RAF Riyan; HE's entry into Mukalla and arrival at the Residency; the Sultan's formal call at the Residency and HE's return call on the Sultan; HE's visits to the staff of the Residency, the Health Adviser's Office, the Medical Training Centre, Mukalla Hospital, the Hadhrami Bedouin Legion, the Bedouin Boys' School, the Sultan's and State Councils, and, finally, to the Qu'aiti State Secretariat.

Governor Day itself was preceded by a forty-eight hour spell during which the RA tuned himself up to breaking pitch. Having meticulously briefed the Residency's office staff, I inspected the drivers, now resplendent in their white uniforms and red turbans; the messengers in khaki jackets with polished brass buttons; and the garage boys in freshly laundered blue overalls. At Riyan airfield, an unexpected hitch arose when the official reception party processed across the tarmac to meet HE without realizing that the Sultan's uninvited sub-teenage son, the Amir 'Umar, was tagging along behind. As the Governor disembarked from the plane, detachments of the Qu'aiti Armed Constabulary, Mukalla Regular Army and Hadhrami Bedouin Legion came to attention, more or less together, to present arms. The band struck up the British and Qu'aiti National Anthems. Sir Charles, awkward and austere, proffered limp handshakes, first to the reception party, and then to each unit commander, each member of the Qu'aiti State Council, the head of every State department and, finally, to a miscellaneous collection of local notables, turned out in their best turbans, jackets and *futa*s.

Preliminaries over, the Governor's entourage was evenly distributed between the Residency's rag-bag transport fleet, with one armoured car leading the procession and another bringing up the rear. My programme had prescribed that, on arrival at the Residency, Sir Charles would be introduced to all senior staff members lining the entrance steps. However, barely had it come to a halt, the Mercedes' doors were flung open and the RA, looking neither right nor left, hustled HE up the Residency steps in a flurry. After an embarrassed pause, I meekly followed suit behind Lady Johnston, leaving the office reception committee completely bemused.

Sir Charles Johnston, the archetypal Foreign Office mandarin, was better versed in diplomatic subtleties than Colonial hurly-burly. He lacked Luce's common touch, and the following day's formal tour of the Residency office to meet the staff was a sticky affair. Thereafter, he was on more familiar ground, with the minutely detailed programme of official visits and counter-visits culminating in the traditional Palace Courtyard parade of march-pasts, speeches, sporting events, and a seemingly endless motor vehicle dismantling and reassembling competition which left Lady Johnston limp.

The RA had left it to me to determine the British community's order of precedence for all gubernatorial social events, but numbers did not quite match available dinner places. And how on earth to decide on the relative seniority of Mukalla's five medical officers? I compromised by inviting everyone to a Residency Cocktail Party, specifying white dinner jackets and black trousers for gentlemen and long dresses for ladies. The RA played Mozart as background muzak and, at the Sultan's Feast, Jaswandi Khan bashed out his usual Gilbert and Sullivan medley.

During a desultory conversation with our new Governor, he never asked me about my work, nor offered any opinion of his own. Subsequently, I was to meet him on several occasions when I worked in Aden. A Winchester and Balliol scholar, held in awe by his contemporaries, Johnston believed that the Protectorate might achieve economic self-sufficiency by developing agriculture, fisheries, light industry and tourism, underpinning this package with motorable roads. In his autobiographical *The View From Steamer Point*, published within a year of his leaving South Arabia in July 1963, Johnston records that at the time of his EAP visit, Arthur Watts was busy promoting schools, hospitals, dams, roads, and plants for fumigating dates and freezing lobster tails. This betrayed a degree of wishful thinking, if only because colonial development projects generally took several years to get off the ground. Johnston also credited Watts with promoting political consciousness in Mukalla by encouraging town councils and municipal elections, yet this flatly contradicted the RA's explicit instructions spelled out in his Secret Newsletter No. 1.

There was also more to fisheries than simply "freezing lobster tails" which, at the time of Johnston's visit, was a wholly undiscovered sideline. Fishing was by far the most important economic activity along South Arabia's 750-mile coastline, and fish as important a food source for the general population as agricultural produce. The Arabian Sea happens to be one of the world's great fishing grounds, due to the south-west monsoon and to up-welling currents from the great Southern Ocean. These carry the microscopic marine organisms that underpin the food chain, and multiply exponentially as the cold oceanic waters intermingle with the warmer coastal waters.

Prodigiously large shoals of sardine had traditionally been harvested with seine nets. These were then laid out to dry, million upon million, on the beaches of Burum, Fuwwa and Shihr, before being dispatched to the interior for food, camel feed or manure. Tuna were caught while pursuing the sardine shoals inshore. Mukalla was a traditional centre of the shark-fishing industry, where great whites, makos, leopards and hammerheads were harpooned single-handed by fishermen paddling primitive canoes. Dried shark was sold inland and also exported. Dried shark tails and fins fetched high prices in China and the Far East. The seas around also teemed with barracuda, porpoise, kingfish, horse mackerel, sea perch, rock cod, mullet and bonito, as well as moray eels and stingrays. The spectacular manta ray could take off from the water like a V-Bomber.

Russian and Japanese fishing fleets, equipped with modern refrigerated ships, were already active in the Gulf of Aden, yet the potential of Mukalla's fishing industry had not been realized. Few fishermen had vessels capable of venturing beyond sight of land. Innate conservatism militated against the introduction of new methods. The leaders of the fishermen's guilds, the *maqaddam*s, had imposed controls and limited catches in order to stabilize prices and cut out foreign competition. Traditional systems of collection, distribution and sale were archaic. Fishermen from Fuwwa might have to walk ten miles to the Mukalla fish market, staggering under the weight of fish as big as themselves, yoked on either shoulder, to sell their catch for a derisory price to the middlemen. In the 1930s, Sultan 'Umar had managed to rid Mukalla of the fearful smell of rotting fish that then permeated the town, by transferring fish-curing to Khalf, just up the coast. Since then, various well-intentioned initiatives had been launched, but neither methods nor attitudes had changed materially.

During Veevers-Carter's profligate incumbency, the confidence of both the Qu'aiti government and the local fishermen in British direction had collapsed. Initially, neither Watts nor Jehan Khan showed the enthusiasm necessary to restore it. However, in early November, the newly commissioned Aden Fisheries vessel, *Gulf Explorer*, skippered by a fiery Scots ex-trawlerman, John Watt, arrived in Mukalla with a new Fisheries Officer, Alec White. Their object was to demonstrate what could be achieved with a modern, ocean-going vessel. Unfortunately, things got off to a disastrous start, as I discovered on arriving at the quayside to welcome the *Gulf Explorer*, there to be confronted by a furious Rahman Khan.

"This ship has never asked for our customs clearance, Mr Harding. The captain is a very rude man. He hasn't allowed me on board, so I have no idea what he might be carrying. It might even be contraband. You know well what bad experiences I've had with your Fisheries Officers. I am here to do a job, and will not be obstructed."

"Of course, we can't have any of this sort of nonsense, Rahman," I replied soothingly. "Let me sort this one out with the captain."

Watt, an awkward customer, assured me that his luxuriously appointed vessel, equipped with all the latest navigational aids, echo sounders and a refrigeration unit, was only carrying fishing equipment and personal effects. I took him at his word, and reported back to Rahman Khan in good faith. Shortly afterwards, I was appalled to learn that Charles Inge had taken collection of a consignment of china, gin and wine. Not only had Watt lied to me, but if Rahman Khan had got wind of this deceit, the *Gulf Explorer* would have been banned from Mukalla, and the Aden Fisheries Department's credibility lost for ever. By sheer luck, Rahman Khan never pressed his enquiries because the *Gulf Explorer*'s engine broke down that same day. To save further embarrassment, Watt cut and ran back to Aden for repairs.

Alec White could not have been less like his predecessor. A hard-edged, incisive Kenyan, he was as much at ease discussing fisheries policy with the Chief Minister as arguing the merits of ship's engines with a maudlin-drunk Sid Morrison. Shortly after his arrival, Rahman Khan convened a board of enquiry to discover what had happened to the £18,000 (perhaps £400,000 in today's money) that the Qu'aiti State had voted Veevers-Carter to buy new fisheries equipment. Barely £215 cash was left in the kitty, and only £5,000-worth of equipment.

White and I decided that our main aim should be to restore confidence by drumming up HMG funds; persuading the Qu'aiti State Council to abolish customs dues on specified items of fishing equipment; improving liaison between the *maqaddam*s and the deeply mistrusted Council; establishing a fair marketing system; and converting the existing share scheme, which benefited the State but beggared the fishermen, into a revolving loans scheme. We would have to demonstrate how modern fishing vessels, equipment and techniques could improve catches. In turn, this should generate enough revenue to persuade the State, and local entrepreneurs, to invest in refrigeration plants, and fishing boats capable of exploiting the Arabian Sea's prolific offshore waters.

The *Gulf Explorer* should have been an ideal vehicle to achieve these aims. Unfortunately, Skipper Watt's scrape with Rahman Khan had created a bad initial impression. Moreover, the local fishermen saw this powerful new vessel as a potential threat to their livelihood. A fortnight after Sir Charles Johnston's visit, the *Gulf Explorer* unexpectedly put in at Mukalla with the Chief Fisheries Officer, Val Hinds, at the wheel. Hinds, as broad as he was tall, with a disconcertingly wild squint, had once shared rooms at Trinity College, Dublin with the hell-raising author, J. P. Donleavy, the original *Ginger Man*. Amiable enough when sober, Hinds became the quintessential Fighting Irishman when drunk. During a pub brawl in Aden, he had taken out several slightly built policemen and had decamped to Mukalla to avoid arrest. Here he caused further embarrassment by creating a disturbance in the local brothel. What with this, Watt's admission that during their extensive off-shore fishing trawl they had caught "bugger all", and a fishermen's strike precipitated by the *Gulf Explorer*'s presence in Mukalla which compelled its early return to Aden, White and I were not sorry to see the back of it and its crew.

Fortuitously, it was not long afterwards that we discovered a fisherman's Aladdin's cave off the rocky headland of Ras Burum, twenty miles down the coast. To most Arabs, crayfish were *haram*, forbidden food as being neither fish nor fowl. For this reason they were not sold in Mukalla, even though Sultan 'Alawi of Bir Ali and the barbarous Mahra were reputed to eat them. Our snorkelling recce revealed a twenty-foot high, miles-long rock shelf teeming with giant crayfish. White followed up this discovery with a more detailed coastal survey. He then brought local fishermen in on the act and, on 22 January 1961, Mukalla's first commercial crayfish consignment was despatched to Aden. The birth of this embryonic crayfish industry proved to local fishermen that good money could be earned beyond their traditional catches and markets.

As my first year in South Arabia drew to a close, the visit of the Royal Navy frigate, HMS *Meon*, to Mukalla in mid-December became the British community's main talking point. The *Meon*'s chief task had been to transport the RA to Socotra, to discuss prospective oil exploration on mainland Mahra with Sultan 'Isa. Mission completed, its crew were now free to return to Mukalla for some onshore leave. For three glorious days, a shipload of handsome, good-humoured young men transformed the British community's musty social life. My programme of picnics, lunches, teas, cocktail parties, dinners, tennis, bathing, snorkelling, duck shooting, cricket, and the inevitable football match, was a deal more fun than that devised for Sir Charles Johnston's earlier visit. Although there were no broken hearts visible at the farewell drinks and film party on the ship's quarterdeck, it was a sorrowful group of Mukallaites who gathered on the quayside, late that night, to watch the lights of HMS *Meon* fade away into the darkness.

The year ended with RAF Riyan staging a Christmas Eve carol concert, Willie Wise conducting divine service on Christmas Day, and the Dawsons throwing a traditional New Year's Eve party with some daring dancing and Auld Lang Syne. But this was not quite what I had come to Arabia for. The Northern Deserts tour had tapped springs of adventure. I had become the local expert on passports, revamped the Military and Administrative School, reorganized the Registry, and given fisheries a boost. But the Qu'aitis were still arguing about the road to Maifa'ah, nothing had been done about Mukalla's water supply, and the Hamumi tobacco industry had collapsed. I was disillusioned with the RA's leadership, and disenchanted with local obscurantism and fatalism. My Arabic had made little progress in Mukalla's English-speaking milieu, and the Kharusi business still haunted me. I needed a break to see things in perspective. And so, when Watts reluctantly agreed my application to take three weeks local leave in East Africa, I flew to Nairobi via Aden on 18 January 1961, with my sights set on Mount Kenya.

8

Land and Labour

KENYA HAD ALWAYS my *beau idéal*. My rejection of the Colonial Office's offer to serve there had always left me with an unsatisfied fringe of curiosity. After the heat and dust of Arabia, Nairobi, a clean, green, well-ordered modern city with imaginative architecture, seemed paradise enow. Mount Kenya's multi-faceted ridges and satellite spires presented a special challenge for, at that time, ascents of its magnificent twin peaks were rare, and I had not climbed seriously for more than three years. Moreover, as the scratch team I had put together was ill-assorted and largely inexperienced, we had scrapes in spades, including one 28-hour epic on the highest peak, Batian (17,058 ft), when my companion Ruth Drake became the second woman ever to reach its summit. I left Kenya with the drumbeat of Africa ringing in my ears, tinged with an element of self-reproach.

Before flying back to Mukalla, I spent a couple of nights in Aden with John Ducker, a contemporary then working in the Secretariat. On that first evening, my Mount Kenya monodrama was only checked when a messenger delivered a by-hand note: "Please come and see me in the Secretariat tomorrow at 8.30 a.m. – Robin Thorne." When I reported to Thorne, now Aden's senior Assistant Chief Secretary, he came quickly to the point: "We'd like you to do a spell in the Lands Office. It would only be a temporary appointment, but we're in a bit of a spot. Cecil Kenyon, the Commissioner of Lands, is long overdue leave, and his deputy, John Black, has gone home on emergency sick leave. There's no one currently available to fill either vacancy. This would be an interesting job for someone with legal training. If you took it on, you would effectively be running a department. Might you be interested?"

This was a bombshell. Although I knew Kenyon slightly, he had never spoken about the Lands Office, and the last thing I wanted was legal work. Yet Kenya had opened new perspectives. The achievements of direct colonial administration had contrasted strikingly with the meagre results of the advisory governance I had witnessed in the EAP. The prospect of running my own department was very tempting, so I told Thorne that I was interested in principle, but would like to know more about the work, and for how long I would be doing it.

"Cecil Kenyon will give you a full job description if you're really interested," he replied. "Arthur Watts wants you to complete your Mukalla tour, so, if you accepted, you'd start on 1 April and would have to stay on in Aden to the end of November. Think it over and give me a call this evening."

I detected several Machiavellian hands behind this unexpected offer, and also foresaw any number of downsides in extending my tour by another eight months. It would then be two years since I had left England, and I badly wanted to reconnect with the girl I had left behind me, and give my parents moral support following a marked deterioration in my younger brother's mental health. Selfishly, I had also promised myself a bumper Alpine climbing season that summer. I rang Thorne that evening politely turning down the offer, only to regret it the moment I replaced the telephone receiver. This was surely too good to pass over, so I scribbled him a note, just before catching the flight to Mukalla, requesting that he send me a fuller job description.

Watts was away in Wahidi, but Wise gave me an uncomfortably lukewarm reception, intoning the mantra that "Leave is a privilege, not an entitlement". But I had no regrets about my Kenya adventure, and had a certain feeling that my days in Mukalla might be numbered anyway. When Watts returned, I asked him direct whether my next tour might be in Hadhramaut. "We've got a good team in place there already," he replied, thickly. "Frankly, I think it unlikely." Curiously, he refused to be drawn on the Lands Office offer, though, as it happened, that same morning I had received a formal letter of offer from Thorne to say that an entirely new post of Acting Assistant Commissioner of Lands had just been created.

"Your work would be of a general administrative nature in keeping the Lands Office running, dealing with all applications from the public, working closely with the Secretariat and the Public Works Department, ensuring that revenue from land flows in steadily. I suggest that you would find the experience of value both in itself and for your future. You would, at the same time, be doing something that would be very much in the interests of Government."

Effectively, this was a Royal Command, offering promotion at a salary far in excess of what I was currently earning. I replied by return, accepting.

My last weeks in Mukalla passed in a blur. Handing over the AACA slot to Stewart Hawkins was the easy bit, for we had always thought along the same lines. But disengagement from my job as Visitors major-domo was complicated by the first official visit to Mukalla of the newly appointed head of Middle East Command, Air Marshal Sir Sam Elworthy. The unseemly flap this engendered made me recall Johnny Johnson's effortlessly laid-back reception for Elworthy's predecessor, Air Vice-Marshal Patch. That same night at the Sultan's Eid Feast, I found myself placed between two of the most unattractive members of the Sultanic Council, the sinister Chief of Police, Bin Munif, and the resolutely silent State Councillor, Shaikh Nasr Batati. It was not an enlivening occasion and, when we had finished eating, I rose stiffly from the squat, and wandered across to the balcony to listen to the rhythm of the surf beating against the sea wall of the Sultan's palace. There was no moon and, as Jaswandi Khan bashed out his well-worn repertoire, I gazed out into the black emptiness of the ocean. It came to me that this would probably be the last time I would grace this fantasy palace, with its flotsam of Victoriana. Imperceptibly, I had grown fond of Mukalla and, for several minutes, I stood there overcome by nostalgia and regret for things not done.

More than anything else, it was the failure to transform Mukalla's fishing industry that rankled. White and I had given the crayfish scheme a flyer, but we had failed to get through to the RA the wider potential of fisheries. We were not the first to have attempted to get this particular industry moving, but few of our predecessors' recommendations had been implemented, and Veevers-Carter had put the clock back by years. Over the past three months, White and I had been preparing a detailed development paper for discussion at an extraordinary Fisheries Department meeting, arranged for 26 February, to be chaired by the RA, with Hinds and Watt flying up specially from Aden. Well in advance, I had given Watts a summary of our principal recommendations. The evening before the meeting, I asked him if he needed any further amplification. "Thank you, but no. I shan't be needing any further input on fisheries policy. You should also know that I'm not prepared to spend a penny more than what I've already allocated."

I berated myself for not having followed Lanfear's sage advice by dressing the whole scheme up as the RA's own. When we foregathered next day, I knew from his expression that he was unlikely to have read either the report or the summary. Perhaps the strikes triggered by the *Gulf Explorer* had made him wary, for he dismissed the main project out of hand. At this, the fisheries team came back fighting and, after some haggling, Watts agreed to support the scheme in principle, subject to modifications. White and I reckoned that we had at last made the breakthrough. A couple of weeks later, on Hinds' initiative, two UK fishing equipment company representatives arrived at the Residency to sell their wares. Watts sent them packing with: "I don't know what the devil Hinds thinks he's up to. He must know that there's no money in the kitty for this sort of thing."

Nonetheless, I was determined to have one last shot at pushing through a modified fisheries scheme. So, on 28 March, with only two days to go before my leaving Mukalla, I convened another meeting, first routing the paper through Lanfear, now Acting DBA, for an advance steer. As White and I took our seats, the RA brandished my paper and began the meeting with a withering: "I should have been given this days ago. I can't possibly make policy on the hoof." He then proceeded to cross-examine us minutely on the feasibility of building a large ice-processing plant to store crayfish tails, for by now our innovative crayfish scheme had become a victim of its own success, with demand outstripping supply. Yet crayfish could never have been more than a sideline, whereas our aim was to transform an entire fisheries industry. Watts left no time to discuss our grand project, and when he rose to his feet with a peremptory, "I'm sorry gentlemen, I've got to leave you now to attend a State Council meeting," I assumed it was doomed.

But Alec White persevered. Within a year, he had won back the fishermen's confidence, and had converted many to using nylon nets and mechanized boats. By 1962, the revolving loans scheme was up and running, and a workshop and slipway constructed to service small, locally owned mechanized boats. A pilot cold store was built near Mukalla and another in Sayun. Progress slowed after the revolutionary nationalist regime took over in 1967, following which fishing craft and equipment were collectivized, and the fishermen organized into co-operatives. Thereafter, a sealed road to Aden opened potentially bigger markets, and inshore catches were improved by Japanese diesel engines, routinely fitted to local *sanbuq*s, though with fibreglass sadly replacing the traditional wooden variety. Later still, the main fishery concessions were granted to the Japanese and Russians, with the result that local involvement withered. The fish are still there, but the mighty Arab offshore fleet that White and I had envisaged sweeping the blue waters of the Indian Ocean remains a dream.

Stewart Hawkins threw a farewell cocktail party on the eve of my departure. The RA arrived an hour late wearing a celebratory bow tie. He forgot himself for a couple of hours, stayed on to cap everyone's stories, and then slipped off without saying goodbye. To take my formal leave of him next morning, I had to interrupt a Qu'aiti State Council meeting. After the anticipatory buzz of excitement that greeted the news of my appointment to the Lands Office had died down, Arthur proffered me his hand, with an admonitory "Now mind you don't forget our little parish", before hurriedly returning to State business.

At RAF Riyan, Hawkins, White and I had already downed more than our quota of iced "tinnies" before the Aden Airways Dakota touched down. The three of us had shared a lot together. Only when we shook hands did the realization that I was leaving Mukalla for good sink in. As the plane taxied down the runway, I peered out through my porthole window, hoping to catch a last glimpse of my chums waving goodbye from the tarmac. But their Land Rover was already on its way back to Mukalla, lost in a cloud of dust.

Aden seemed hotter, stickier and smellier than the place I remembered. Kenyon kindly met me at the airport before dropping me off at John Ducker's flat in Steamer Point. He and I spend the rest of that afternoon at the Gold Mohur Beach Club, where the unaccustomed display of near-naked female flesh created a disturbing frisson. Next morning, All Fools Day, I reported to Robin Thorne at the Secretariat. "Some good news for you, John," said Robin. "As from today, the Lands Office has been upgraded to the Lands Department. Please report to Cecil Kenyon as soon as possible."

The Department was housed, as the Lands Office always had been since its creation, in Crater. Here, where every scruffy shop displayed a portrait of the Arab hero, Gamal Abdul Nasser, thousands of transistors blared out Cairo Radio's *Voice of the Arabs* anti-British propaganda. The Anglo-Indian order and decorum of Steamer Point seemed a world away. This, the ancient Aden of Ezekiel, had been Haines's original base, when Tawahi was an uninhabited stretch of coastline. Haines had set about restoring the old city and, during the 1860s, Assistant Resident Playfair accelerated this work by repairing the historic Tawila water tanks and bringing in an army of Yemeni stonemasons and carpenters to rebuild the new town in stone.

A uniformed peon took me through to Kenyon's office, a cheerless, utilitarian room bereft of any personal photograph or memento. When staying with Cumming-Bruce, I had never got the measure of Cecil Kenyon, a pre-Second World War Colonial Service officer then aged 56. Although it was not uncommon to retire at forty-five from colonial hard stations, Kenyon was doggedly staying on to educate his children in England. Almost thirty years my senior, he was obsessively committed to his work, and a zealous disciplinarian. Although I never heard him speak a word of Arabic, he had spent most of his working life with Arabs. He had been running the Lands Office, historically an adjunct of the Public Works Department, for the past eighteen months, combining in one the roles of administrator, accountant, conveyancer, valuer and planner. He lost no time with a no-frills briefing.

"All seventy-five square miles of Aden Colony is Crown Land, most of it this department's responsibility. Developable land is at a premium. There's simply not enough to build the new schools, hospitals, houses and military installations now needed, so it's become Aden's most expensive commodity. Most land is sold by public auction. This department decides who gets the rest, at what rent, and subject to what conditions. Our business is conducted within the legal framework of the Colony's ordinances, but we're bound to take into account political and strategic considerations. Incidentally, have you any idea of the price that development land is now fetching in Ma'alla?"

"I'm afraid not," I replied.

"£400 a square foot! That's equivalent to London prices," exclaimed Kenyon triumphantly, allowing himself a wry smile. "Developers are pouring in here from all over the Arab world. Saudis and Kuwaitis with oil money but local Adenis and Yemenis as well. Aden's building bonanza has made it a honeypot. The smart boys can recoup their capital within eighteen months."

"Robin Thorne gave me an overview of the department's work, but can you be more specific about what I'll actually be doing?"

"First, you'll learn the ropes under my direction. This means dealing with all applications for land use, and drawing up the legal documentation to give good title. Much is routine, but you must watch out for the wide boys trying to buck the system. It's essentially a job for someone with legal training who can operate and negotiate within a robust administrative framework. You'll be dealing with the Services, the Munipicality and various other departments. Also, anything to do with this wretched New Town at Shaikh Othman. You'll have to pick up the detail as you go along. My job is to ensure that you're competent enough to run this department when I go on leave."

"Presumably the Department's staff is up to strength?"

"No, not really," Kenyon replied, a touch wearily. "The staff here are a mixed lot. In fact, it's a regular United Nations, reflecting Aden's multi-racial society. We've got Adeni and Protectorate Arabs, Indians, Pakistanis, Jews and Somalis, plus some stroppy British secretaries. Some are good workers, but most are pretty useless when it comes to technical work. Longer term, it's a question of finding time to train local talent, which isn't that easy. We've got one promising young conveyancing clerk, Saif Ahmed Dhala'i. He's a man to watch, so I've got plans for bringing him along. We're currently short of a Lands Inspector, an Assistant Estates Surveyor and two clerks. Normally John Black, the Estates Surveyor, looks after surveys and valuations, but he's currently on sick leave. I've no idea when he'll be back, so we've got to make do with what we've got. You'll have to get most of the technical advice from the PWD, Aden's Public Works Department. I'll introduce you to its head, Jan Deal, shortly. He'll be your overall boss while I'm on leave."

With both Kenyon and Black absent for months ahead, this list of vacancies seemed rather a lot for such a small department. At this juncture, a shambling sort of man wandered into the office, grinning apologetically. "Aah," muttered Kenyon, with an ill-concealed grimace as he introduced us. "This is John Buck, the Planning Officer. You and he may be seeing quite a lot of each other." Buck was affable, chatty, and evidently longing to discuss the planning and political ramifications of the proposed new housing development at Shaikh Othman to which Kenyon had already slightingly referred. Kenyon was having none of it. After getting rid of Buck, he grumbled: "Fine to discuss such matters over a glass of whisky after work, but not in the office."

While I wondered what subjects might be fit for office discussion, Kenyon introduced me to the Lands Department staff, lined up as for some military inspection. There were lands inspectors, rent collectors, an accountant, registrars, draughtsmen, stationery & despatch clerks, notice postermen, a conveyancer, his lady assistant and my ever-cheerful secretary, Valerie Hill. The Shaikh Othman New Town's Secretariat, headed by Mrs Cornford, had its own separate establishment of four surveyors, three draughtsmen and two typists. Kenyon made no attempt at introductions. "Can't be bothered with that lot now," he growled. "Not until they're making some useful contribution to the Department."

I was then introduced to Jan Deal, a no-nonsense engineer with an intimidating manner who had been running the PWD since 1953, and after that, to his town planners, artificers and engineers, and, later, to the Aden and Shaikh Othman Municipalities' senior staff, the Aden Port Trust and BP Refinery's lawyers, and various officers representing the Armed Forces. Everyone was friendly, but there was no hint of Mukalla's cosy camaraderie.

At first, the job was totally bewildering. In Mukalla, work was broadly what you made of it. Here, you worked to commercial deadlines. I had everything to learn and a lot to prove before Kenyon went on leave. Every morning, a flood of applications poured in from developers, institutions and individuals, all clamouring for their unfair share of Aden's barren land. There were conveyances, grants, leases, licences and permits to be drawn; site inspections to be made to delineate land and allocate quarry space; investigations to be instituted; and legal proceedings to be taken against fly-tippers, obstructionists and dumpers. There was also the issue of squatter camps. "One of our most difficult jobs to deal with effectively," Kenyon confided, with distaste. He did not elaborate, but I was to learn soon enough.

Kenyon had generously insisted that I mess with him until I was allocated my own quarters and found myself a cook. This was well intentioned, but it subjected me to his endless expositions about the Department's work with conversation seldom straying beyond the niceties of land law. Life began to look up when I was allocated my own house on Ras Marshag. This jutting headland of volcanic rock, at the eastern tip of the Aden Peninsula, overlooked Holkat Bay to the north and the featureless expanse of the Indian Ocean to the south. The view never compared with the grand sweep of shoreline, mountain and distant cape that I had enjoyed from my house in Mukalla. However, although No. 12 Clifftop was far removed from the clubs, bars and restaurants of Steamer Point, it was quiet, secluded and could be reached only by a twisting arm of road that clung to the promontory's westward face, before running out amongst a litter of PWD bungalows stranded on a hilltop like some seedy British seaside resort.

Monsoon winds might shriek around the steel stanchions that secured each bungalow to concrete moorings sunk into bed-rock, yet it was relatively cool. I also had my own stone staircase that spiralled down Ras Marshag's seaward face to a narrow rock shelf, falling ten foot plumb into translucent blue waters teaming with brilliantly coloured fish. In Mukalla I had swum daily off the beach. Off Clifftop, I did this only once, after spotting four dorsal fins moving purposefully towards me. Swimming was a touch safer in Fisherman's Bay, a sandy beach at the foot of the headland which gave safe-haven to a fleet of small *sanbuq*s. Even here, I once stepped on a stingray buried in the sand. Its whip-tailed blow sent me staggering up the hill to my house in an agonized daze. I collapsed, only to wake a couple of hours later with nothing worse than a nasty gash and an ugly bruise.

Robin Thorne had sold me the Lands Department as an administrative job with a legal element. In fact, there was much technical detail to be mastered. Kenyon set the highest standards, and I had to look well to my own. Further, as a slow starter, I had to stay on late in the office, and then take home bundles of files to work long, sticky hours into the night. And then, exactly ten days after my appointment, Kenyon slipped a disc, and had to be admitted to hospital totally incapacitated. From now on, my induction was fast-forward.

At that time, Aden's most pressing, and potentially explosive, political problem was the influx of immigrants – hinterland tribesmen, Somalis, and particularly Yemenis – drawn in by the magnet of work. During the late 19th century, when Aden's population had increased by more than 25 percent as a result of the coal-bunkering boom, the government's response to the resultant rash of shanty settlements had been to build a new town at Shaikh Othman. History was now repeating itself or, as Kenyon put it:

"Squatters and their *kutcha* settlements are posing a major problem. In Crater alone, there are probably five hundred huts tucked away behind the back streets, or hidden in the wadis coming off Shamsan. They're made of bits of wood, tin and cardboard boxes with no form of sanitation, and are breeding grounds for disease and discontent. Overall, there's probably a floating population of 20,000 homeless migrants in Aden. We can't begin to house them properly, so that's why this bungled new housing project at Shaikh Othman is so important. All we can do about the existing squatter settlements is to confine them to specific areas, leave the older ones standing, and demolish the new ones. But we can only do this after going through a gamut of formal inspections, notices to quit and court applications. And if that isn't trouble enough, we have to bring in the Police for support when we destroy the huts to ensure we don't start a riot. Enforcement's a very disagreeable business. We're fighting a losing battle, and have fallen months behind my demolition schedule."

My own introduction to the problem came soon after Kenyon went into hospital. One morning, a baying crowd of displaced prostitutes from Shaikh Othman, notorious for its brothels, invaded the office. They were carrying petitions to halt the demolition orders that had been served on their shanty houses, preparatory to clearing the way for the projected New Town. The old Shaikh Othman already housed an estimated 90,000, or 40 percent, of Aden Colony's overall population, but the proposed New Town had been conceived on such a lavish scale that the Aden Government had been obliged to apply for additional funding from the Commonwealth Development Corporation. After much vacillation, CDC had turned the application down as commercially unviable, leaving an overblown New Town secretariat to twiddle its collective thumbs. The project had become one of Kenyon's bugbears.

"The whole thing's a shambles," he grumbled. "What started as a perfectly sensible scheme, with a proper Housing Authority under the chairmanship of the Minister, has shrunk to a Small Working Committee. Without proper funding from HMG, they might as well wind the whole thing up now, and dismantle this ridiculous secretariat I've been lumbered with."

In the months ahead, I was to make a dozen visits to Shaikh Othman to monitor the new scheme's "properly aligned development". Predictably, HMG's additional funding never materialized. When I left the Department eight months later, not a single plot had been allocated.

Although Kenyon might be laid up in hospital in traction, he still exercised a tentacle-like grip on *his* Lands Department. I visited him regularly only to receive a stream of instructions on every aspect of departmental procedure and management. His powerful personality and instinct to control everything had deterred subordinates from taking any responsibility themselves, whereas I wanted to learn by my own mistakes. However, as I wrestled with unfamiliar procedures, ever-mounting piles of files, and the stream of applicants and complainants who daily choked the office corridors, the pressures of work became almost insupportable.

Kenyon was masterly at dealing with difficult customers. My fuse was much shorter. One morning, a wild-looking man, brandishing a *jambiyya*, the traditional Arabian curved tribal dagger, burst into my office shouting: "I demand your attention. You are here to serve the public." In trying to keep my head above water, I had put procedure before people. Thereafter, I inaugurated a system of visiting days when I was entirely at the public's disposal, thereby following an admirable Arab tradition.

Yet not everything in Kenyon's Lands Department was wrought seamlessly. The system of processing applications for land and registering title was bedevilled by inconsistent past policies, archaic procedures and insidious politics. To speed land allocation, it had become the established practice to issue Temporary Occupation Permits (TOPs) at a nominal rent, rather than grant formal 99-year leases at a proper commercial rent. This short-cut procedure was losing the Aden Treasury valuable revenue and begged investigation. When the Aden Trades Union Congress applied to transfer an existing TOP, originally granted to build its headquarters in Ma'alla, to another site on similar terms, I discovered that it had never paid even a nominal annual rent. Patently, their arrears had been deliberately overlooked, and when I opened this Pandora's Box it revealed another 800 TOPs with rent in arrears or conditions breached.

When a grim-faced Kenyon returned after a month in hospital, encased in a leather harness, we agreed that no more TOPs would be issued and that all existing TOPs would either be converted into leases or cancelled. The comprehensive list that I instructed be compiled had almost been completed by the time I left the Department. However, a year later, when working in the Secretariat, I asked Kenyon how the new system was working. "Far too much on for that," he snorted. "We had to shelve it. It would have been impracticable to implement those recommendations."

Just before Kenyon went on leave, John Black, the Estates Surveyor, unexpectedly returned to Aden. This enabled Kenyon to divide the Department's workload between us, allotting to me administration, land allocation, documentation, accounting and staff management, and leaving Black with technical matters. To have an unqualified new boy taking overall charge of the department must have been galling for Black, a PWD veteran of seven years' standing. Members of the Colonial Service's administrative cadre imagined themselves an elite. My spell in the Lands Department taught me that Aden's unsung heroes were the engineers and artificers of its utility departments, as the men responsible for building the Colony's houses, schools, hospitals and its infrastructure of roads, waterworks, electricity and sewers, essential to Aden's functioning as a modern city.

On his penultimate day in the office, I asked Kenyon what my priorities should be. "Concentrate on land with high commercial, political or military significance," he replied. "You'll have no trouble with the BP Refinery as their confidential agreement with the Government covers all land transactions affecting the Refinery's essential functioning. The Port of Aden's also pretty efficient, but you may have problems with the military. There's never been an overriding land-use agreement with the Armed Forces, and most of them don't know a thing about law. There's always a lot of tiresome routine stuff to deal with, particularly civilian complaints about the noise and goings-on at that wretched Forces Lido. However, anything to do with Military Reserved Areas and the new camp at Little Aden needs very delicate handling."

There was good reason for this last bit of advice. In 1960, Aden had become the Headquarters of Middle East Command on transfer from Cyprus. At that time, there was no military cantonment in the Colony big enough to accommodate its operational arm, 24 Infantry Brigade, which was mainly garrisoned in Kenya. Accordingly, the Ministry of Defence commissioned, at Little Aden, the construction of what was to become Britain's biggest, most expensive and shortest-lived military housing complex ever built. Its details were supposed to be so secret that only the Commissioner of Lands personally was supposed to know anything about them. In fact, the camp's progress was common knowledge to all the department's staff, and thus, to anyone else in the suq who might be interested.

The normally phlegmatic Kenyon was apoplectic about this particular project. "We've only just abandoned our main base in Cyprus. No doubt we'll soon be doing the same thing in Kenya, where HMG has already spent three million pounds upgrading that base. Now, it's now proposing to spend another ten million at Little Aden. I can tell you one thing for certain: we'll all be out of here before that wretched camp's finished. I weep to think what this sort of money could have done for development in the Protectorate."

Kenyon was proved correct. By the time Falaise Camp at Little Aden was finished in 1967, at a total cost of £18m, Harold Wilson's Labour Government had already served on South Arabia's rulers Britain's notice to quit. As British servicemen packed up prior to handing over the camp to a politically suborned South Arabian Army, HMG's Property Services Agency was busy making lists of chargeable dilapidations to be paid by our outgoing troops, while local Arab gangs were busy ransacking the place. Russian military units were to take over Falaise Camp during South Arabia's Marxist regime. When I revisited Aden in 1997, the entire complex had been levelled to the ground.

We gave Kenyon a rousing farewell send-off at the airport, but I was not sorry to see him go. He was an exemplary officer, but our age difference had not made for an easy working relationship. I was determined to prove that when he returned from leave, five months hence, his Lands Department would still be functioning effectively. As the new broom, I abolished what had become an infinitely elastic morning tea break, enjoyed solely by our two British lady secretaries; tightened up the Confidential Registry's security after finding a complete set of secret military cantonment plans left lying around the office; rationalized land allocation procedures; cut compliance notice times for fly-tippers, obstructionists, illegal occupants and squatters; and standardized tariffs for stone extraction from Khusaf Valley's twenty-one quarries, where acrobatic quarrymen, suspended on ropes like spiders, dangled above a Dante-esque abyss of dust and filth.

Trickier, previously undisclosed, issues now surfaced. The Aden government had always encouraged the construction of non-fee paying schools on 99-year rent-free leases, irrespective of ethnic or religious denomination. However, there was no settled policy for privately funded fee-paying schools. Accordingly, when Mr Ali Thabit applied to build the "National School Shaikh Othman" for 3,000, otherwise unprovided-for, Yemeni schoolchildren, the Chief Secretary asked me to submit a confidential viability report. This ambitious scheme promised to solve a pressing education problem in a township renowned for breeding political dissidence, so I put a battery of architects, planners and engineers on standby. Only when the PWD's site inspector pointed out that the proposed new building compromised Islamic sensibilities, by overlooking the Shaikh Othman Girls' Primary and Intermediate Schools, did its basic flaw become apparent. Mr Ali Thabit disappeared without trace.

Religious property raised more combustible issues. Until the creation of Israel in 1948, Aden had supported a flourishing Jewish community. Few Jews now remained to worship at what was left of the Taffila Moshe synagogue in

Crater. Although technically a charitable trust, the ownership of this relic had become the subject of an ugly dispute between an Arab property developer and its Jewish trustees. The principal litigants were understandably reluctant to leave Israel to contest the case, so matters had stuck fast.

In principle, there were no planning restrictions about building new mosques to accommodate Aden's fast-expanding population. However, the government's treatment of land attached to mosques was capricious. Crater's 14th-century Al-'Aidarus Mosque, the only survivor from Aden's golden age, had been rebuilt in 1859. In 1945, the then Governor, Sir Reginald Champion (who took holy orders on retirement), decreed that its site be subject to a rent-free grant in perpetuity. This ruling, taken in conjunction with one of Sir William Luce's that new shops could be built rent-free on land adjacent to Shaikh Othman's Qadi Mosque, had encouraged a rash of applications to build both shops and political clubs on mosque land. The situation was complicated by a separate Secretariat ruling that no grants would be approved unless such mosque land was first vested in an Islamic form of trust known as a *waqf*. In Aden, there was no equivalent of an overall ecclesiastical authority because each mosque was treated as an independent entity. The resulting imbroglio had created an unresolved bottleneck of twelve outstanding development applications, some of dubious religious relevance, which forced me to spend endless, abortive hours trying to trace mosque superintendents and volunteers willing to supply the requisite *waqf* deed.

I was on easier ground with commercial property, where contentious applications usually answered to negotiated settlements. Even so, Aden's municipal councillors needed convincing that they did not own Aden personally. Before it was quashed, their proposed 'Aidarus Housing Scheme, supporting free mortgages for Adenis, would have bankrupted the Colony. With the amount of money swilling around, the Lands Department's staff were obvious targets for political pressure and corruption. Hassan Bayoomi, then Minister for Labour and Local Government, and later Aden's first Chief Minister, once leaned on me to push through a pet Municipal Council scheme. Hassan Khodabux-Khan, the Municipality's Chairman, also employed special pleading to develop a blocks of flats in Ma'alla. But these were bagatelles, and I wondered whether the apparent absence of blatant corruption merely reflected my own ignorance and naivety.

One antidote to the Lands Department grind was Aden's social life which, in those halcyon days, was unclouded by the shadow of terrorism. There was no end to the cocktail parties, dinners, picnics in deserted coves, boating expeditions to offshore islands, and blue-water sailing in the Governor's ADC, Flight Lieutenant Tony Boyle's 5-ton *Chuff*, flown out from England by courtesy of the RAF. More challenging excursions were undertaken with Tony, John Ducker, Susan France and Elisabeth Fenton-Wells, when we circumnavigated Aden's wild, indented southern coastline in a day, partly by rock-hopping roped together and partly by swimming; surfed the monsoon waves in a canoe which almost capsized over a shoal of tiger sharks; bivouacked on Shamsan's summit to see the sun rise; and traversed the ancient volcano by a skein of routes on friable rock.

In this quasi-mountaineering activity, we were following an earlier tradition established by Anton Besse, Aden's most eminent merchant venturer, Evelyn Waugh's "M. LeBlanc" in *When the Going Was Good*. Besse wore nothing but shorts and *espadrilles* on his Shamsan scrambles, though he was invariably met, at the other end, by his chauffeured Rolls-Royce and a complete change of clothing. An admirer of Oxbridge and its products, he went on to found St Antony's College, Oxford. His Scottish wife did the same for Atlantic College, at St Donats in Glamorgan. Nonetheless, Aden climbing offered particular hazards, and on the crumbling rock spires of Jebel Ihsan, overlooking Little Aden's Silent Valley, we nearly came a cropper when descending from the top of one teetering needle. Without warning, the whole edifice collapsed, sending rotten slabs peeling away in clouds of dust, leaving us hanging in the balance. Boyle, who had never climbed before, seemed unfazed. I reckoned that we had been lucky to get away with it.

These diversions were amusing enough, but I realized how much I was missing the Protectorate's wider horizons when Hawkins persuaded me take delivery of a pair of gazelles from the Northern Desert, as a present for Susan and Elizabeth. "If the girls don't like them, they can always eat them." In return, after picking up the crated animals at Aden Airport, I instructed Cory Brothers to send, FOB Mukalla, twenty crates of beer for Hawkins and twenty mixed whisky and gin for White.

By the end of that August, I had survived five months of Aden's summer without a break. And so, when James Nash invited me to spend a few days at Laudar, I put in for local leave. Laudar, the mountain capital of the 'Audhali State, was only forty-five minutes flying time from Aden, but a thousand metres higher. James, the political adviser to its ruler, Sultan Salih Al-'Audhali, was waiting to meet me in his Land Rover on the airstrip.

"Welcome to Laudar, dear boy. Sadly, I've got to abandon you first thing tomorrow morning, as they've brought my leave date forward. But I've got Dennis Stewart to look after you instead. He's a Welsh Guardee who knew you from your National Service days. He'll make you quite comfortable in the APL mess."

Laudar itself was not much to look at. A mountain stronghold comprising a clutch of multi-storeyed four-square houses, built in the style of Scottish Border keeps, it occupied a strategic site atop a rocky outcrop overlooking a cultivated plain. The dominant feature was not the village, but an awesome escarpment of sheer granite, which closed the view to the north and ran to the limits of the eastern horizon.

"What a magnificent sight," I gasped. "What is that, James?"

"The 'Audhali Kaur. Impressive, isn't it? That mountain wall's over three thousand feet high and seventy miles long. At the top of it is the town of Mukairas. Dennis will be driving you up there tomorrow for luncheon with the APL."

James's house was also built in vernacular style with walls three foot thick, "rifle- if not bazooka-proof". That night, as we supped on prawns in aspic and drank champagne by the light of his silver candlesticks, he told me something about his parish.

"The 'Audhalis have probably suffered more from the Yemenis than anyone in the WAP. After the Ottomans pulled out at the end of the First World War, the Imam simply replaced the Turks with his own troops. They only left in the 1930s when the RAF threatened to bomb the hell out of them. Ever since then, the Yemenis have plagued the 'Audhalis with subversion and armed raids. The real frontier's not here in Laudar, but up on the Plateau. That's why we have to keep a sizeable APL garrison in Mukairas. Just now, it's all quiet on that front, but the whole place could blow up again at any time. Sultan Salih's father was killed in a Yemeni raid, but that's not the only reason he's a true friend of the British. He was one of the few rulers who genuinely supported Federation, though admittedly he's got more to lose than most. But it's Naib Ja'abil, his brother, who really runs this place. He brokered a peace deal with the Yemenis which is still holding up. Heaven help us if he goes bad on us."

In the years to come, I was to have much to do with Sultan Salih. I never met the legendary Ja'abil but, three years on, his shock defection to the Yemen marked a turning point in British and Federal fortunes. Ja'abil had gazed into the future and seen what lay ahead.

Early next morning, Dennis Stewart and I squeezed ourselves into an open Land Rover, with an APL escort of four, and headed straight for the 'Audhali Kaur. The new road to Mukairas, following the line of an ancient camel trade route to the Yemen, had only recently been completed by Aden's PWD engineers. There did not appear to be any sort of motorable way up the seemingly sheer wall ahead, but at the bottom of a steep spur our driver changed down into low-ratio to begin a nerve-rending ascent by a succession of hairpin bends. I soon lost count of their number, and low cloud obliterated what would otherwise have been an alarmingly stupendous view of the plain below. Even so, high adrenalin levels were maintained as grossly over-laden lorries lurched crazily towards us out of the murk, forcing halts within inches of the precipice. Tension lifted when we breasted the top of the Thira Pass, where an escort of two APL Ferret armoured cars awaited us. As we rode high above a great bank of cumulus cloud bubbling up from the plain, the sun was hot but the air thin and chill. I rolled down my sleeves and shivered as we raced across a bleak plateau, past scattered hamlets nestling in green hollows, where unveiled women scythed head-high maize in small neat fields.

Mukairas came up as a straggly village, seemingly sunk into the ground. Its tiny suq was vibrant with chattering ladies, dressed in bright colours, and stalls that overflowed with peaches, figs, grapes, apricots, plums and vegetables. This did not look like a place for dark deeds and no shouts of "Gamal Abdul Nasser" followed our convoy as we slowed to walking pace, before drawing up inside the APL garrison's walled compound. Here, a well-kept garden filled with gay flowers fronted the officers' mess tent, and an immaculate British officer emerged from within to greet us.

"Welcome to Mukairas," said Colonel Ian Waller, extending his hand. "Gather you can only stay for lunch. Pity. We could do with more of you government chaps coming up from Aden, now that Aden Airways is running a service. Lots to see and do here. Fresh air, walks along the Kaur, and bags of archaeological sites. But seriously, the Rest House badly needs civilian custom if it's to survive. No good offering bed without breakfast. A few more visitors would make all the difference."

Waller, an insouciant Black Watch regular, commanded this most isolated

APL outpost within sight of the Yemen. Apparently his garrison's main problem was boredom yet, at the same time, it had to keep itself fully prepared for anything untoward that might happen.

Heading back to the Thira Pass after lunch, the skies darkened. And then, out of nowhere, a passing cloud unleashed a bombardment of hailstones as big as marbles. Our driver slewed off the road towards a rock outcrop, under which we all scuttled for cover. The hail ricocheted off the bonnet like tracer, leaving the paintwork patterned with tiny dents. Slashing belts of icy rain pursued us all the way down the escarpment to Laudar. By next morning, the skies were clear and the world reborn. Gazing up at the cliffs of the great Kaur, now gleaming in the sunshine, I could not believe that we had really managed to drive up and down that awesome wall.

Back in Aden, the Thira Pass soaking left me in bed for a couple of days, one of the few times I was ever ill in Arabia. The prospect of the files building up in the office deterred any thought of malingering and so, only too soon, I was again drowned in a tidal wave of applications, disputes to be settled, inspections to be made, permits and vesting orders to be issued. I knew I was getting tired and stale, and even looked forward to Kenyon's return. He had written only once since he went on leave, mainly about Saif Ahmed Dhala'i, the Chief Conveyancing Clerk, who he was confident had the ability to qualify for membership of the Royal Institute of Chartered Surveyors. Saif, with his wary eyes and obsequious grin, was certainly clever, yet I could never engage with his enigmatic personality. Unbeknown to any of us, he had more pressing matters to attend to, having already established himself as a leading member of the Aden branch of the Movement of Arab Nationalists. This clandestine, rigorously structured organization later became subsumed into the National Liberation Front, the radical terrorist group whose aims were to evict the British, destroy the Federation and establish a national socialist republic. Saif later revealed his true colours as a representative of the fledgling People's Republic of South Yemen and, in 1967, made an impressive diplomatic debut in Geneva, negotiating severance terms with the British government. Subsequently, he played an important role in the early days of South Arabia's revolutionary government and became its Foreign Minister. Later, as a result of internal feuds, he was executed on the orders of his former comrades.

When Kenyon came back from leave, I had the satisfaction of handing over to him a department still in running order, and had even fulfilled an early vow of clearing the streets of Crater of the abandoned vehicles that threatened to choke its trade. My solution had been to post "Intent to Dispose" notices on all offending vehicle carcasses. After a fixed period, those still in situ were dumped unceremoniously in a disused sandpit. The day before beginning my own home leave, I said goodbye to my staff, and Kenyon thanked me for my work without a flicker of emotion. That same afternoon, Tony Boyle, John Ducker, Susan and I sailed Tony's boat *Chuff* to an uninhabited island off Little Aden. In the evening, safely moored in Sapper Bay under Ras Tarshain, a jutting promontory off Steamer Point, we drank chilled Chianti, and watched the sun disappear behind Little Aden's saw-tooth peaks.

Having completed my first South Arabian tour, I was about to sail for Piraeus for five weeks' mountaineering in Greece and Turkey, before meeting up with my family in Switzerland. Yet two clouds dimmed my horizon. One was the news from Establishments that I was likely to be posted to the Secretariat for my next tour, on the basis of a good report from Kenyon. I had already put in for a Protectorate posting, but was informed firmly that the exigencies of the Service took precedence. My other worry was more personal. Ever since I had invited Susan to stay as a guest at the Inge's to celebrate Eid at Mukalla the previous March, we had been inseparable. The prospect of not seeing her for another six months tarnished the gloss of a long home leave.

Late on 15 November 1961, I boarded the Europe Australian Line's *Bretagne* with four suitcases, two rucksacks and a load of emotional baggage. As the Aden Port Trust's launch slid away into the darkness with Tony, John and Susan standing in the bows waving goodbye, my throat developed a fair-sized lump. For an hour, I stayed transfixed at the ship's rail until the twinkling lights of Aden finally disappeared over the horizon.

9

Stuck in the Secretariat

A LEAVE RATIO OF ONE week for every four served had been one of the less idealistic reasons for my joining the Colonial Service. The voyage to Piraeus, in the company of a stunning bevy of Hardy Amies models, followed by a spell of midwinter mountaineering in Greece and Turkey, obliterated memories of the Lands Department. But the final leg of the colonial's return home by the vaunted Orient Express became farce when the train broke down in a blizzard in the middle of the Bulgarian Plain. It took a full week, from the time I left Stamboul station, to be reunited with my family at Pontresina on Boxing Day, 1961.

If South Arabia had seemed worlds away for the past six weeks, a letter from the Chief Secretary awaiting my return home swiftly brought me down to earth. It confirmed that my next posting would definitely be to the Aden Secretariat. I might more readily have squared up to another round of penpushing if the Colonial Service had promised a longer-term future. When I first joined it, I had persuaded myself that British South Arabia might buck the trend for longer than most for, despite some pessimistic mutterings, Aden's prosperity was plain to see. Moreover, the EAP was showing few obvious signs of political unrest, the Yemen frontier had gone quiet, and there were even hopes for better Anglo-Yemeni relations when the Imam definitively cut his links with Nasser's United Arab Republic in December 1961. Underpinning this edifice of false hopes was the British Government's 1962 Defence White Paper, which envisaged that Fortress Aden would remain a British base indefinitely.

Yet the speed of the Empire's unravelling in Africa, and other straws in the wind, foretold that we could not be in South Arabia that much longer. And so, when my old mentor, Alec Cumming-Bruce, now transferred to the Colonial Office, gave me luncheon at his club, I asked if he would act as my referee if I decided to change career direction. Alec was disappointed that I should have fallen out with Arthur Watts – "Definitely *not* for your own good, you know" – but nonetheless agreed. I looked around the City and, with gritted teeth, also explored the prospects of a future legal career. But even as I hedged my bets, I realized that Arabia had taken its hold. I knew that I had to go back, convincing myself that the basic cause of my discontent was lack of a wife. The rest of that leave had been little more than carefree self-indulgence, until I visited my younger brother at Cambridge. I was shocked to find him living in a world of his own and to discover that we had become strangers. And then, as optimistically as my leave had begun, it ended on another discordant note when I finally made a painful break with the girl I had almost become engaged to before leaving for Aden.

Due to staff shortages, I was recalled to Aden by BOAC plane on 29 April 1962. Stopping off in Khartoum at dawn, the sight of the sun coming up over the eastern horizon like a red cannonball brought back discomforting memories of Arabia's summer heat. My misgivings vanished when Susan and Tony Boyle met me at Aden Airport in the Government House limousine. That same evening, I was summoned to partner HE at tennis, and was informed that Trevaskis wanted me for the WAP and that Kenyon had pleaded for my return to the Lands Department. Next day, reality returned when Pat Booker confirmed that I would, after all, be posted to the Colony Branch of the Secretariat.

It was some consolation to be working for Robin Thorne, Aden's senior Assistant Chief Secretary, whom I already knew and admired. My portfolio was to include Agriculture, Fisheries, Co-operative & Marketing and Veterinary services; legal ordinances, judicial matters and the Legislative Council; the Aden Port Trust, port facilities and shipping; Communications and Electricity; Tourism, Antiquities, the British Council; Social Welfare and the United Nations report.

When I asked Robin how one person could possibly cope with so many subjects, he replied: "Don't worry. Most of this work is dealt with perfectly competently by other government departments. They're usually headed by

British officials answerable to LEGCO members in charge. The Secretariat's role is fast becoming that of a co-ordinating body to ensure that the machinery of government is working smoothly. Incidentally, you'll also be helping John Lloyd to deal with the Police, Prisons, Arms and Ammunition, Nationality, Passports, Immigration and Deportation."

Thorne had said nothing about Aden's proposed merger with the existing Federal States, the issue currently on everyone's lips, so I asked him if I was going to be involved. "You're certainly joining us at a very interesting time," he replied, guardedly. "But the federal merger is far from guaranteed, and there are still some serious obstacles to be overcome. The very concept is alien to many Adenis, and meaningless to most Protectorate tribesmen. A top-level team's working on this at the moment. However, for obvious reasons, I can't give you chapter and verse on progress but, frankly, I can't honestly see any real prospect of your being involved just now. Politically and constitutionally, Aden has reached a critical stage. Very soon, we could be riding a rollercoaster to independence. Westminster-style democracy was only introduced to Aden three years ago, and the next Legislative Council elections are barely six months away. In the meantime, we've got to settle a highly contentious franchise. The ATUC is insisting that all its Yemeni members should get the vote, but that's unthinkable. They'd simply swamp the local Adeni element. The Aden press is full of noise and thunder, but suq opinion is more influenced by Cairo Radio."

Thorne did not elaborate further, and I left his office somewhat disappointed. Even so, I reckoned that there must still be some nuggets of responsibility in my over-blown portfolio. The Secretariat was still Aden's administrative hub. Its senior posts were filled by the British administration's top brass including half the Governor's Executive Committee, which remained solely responsible for Aden's external affairs, internal security, finance and the Civil Service. A week later, I realized that the situation was exactly as Thorne had described it. My job boiled down to wading through mounds of files, and then referring any important policy decisions to my overworked boss. Occasionally, my hard-earned knowledge of passport law enabled me to frustrate what had become the common practice of certain LEGCO Members in Charge, of getting British passports for their friends, as often as not Yemenis. But this was thin gruel. My level of direct responsibility was going to be even less than it had been in Mukalla, let alone in the Lands Department.

One of the few areas that offered me a measure of personal responsibility was Tourism. Sir Charles Johnston was keen to encourage this both as a potential money-spinner and the world's window on Aden. I was invited to have dinner with Tom Oates and Robin Thorne to meet Mr Curtis, recently flown in from London to undertake a tourism survey of South Arabia. Well prepared in advance, I rattled off some banal facts and figures about Steamer Point's hotels, restaurants, and duty-free shopping, mentioning that despite its reputation, even Evelyn Waugh had found Aden full of interest.

Curtis, unsmiling in his immaculate white linen suit, looked distinctly unimpressed. "Yes, yes. I can see that the place is swarming with transit liner passengers gorging themselves on duty-free goods, but we've to look beyond that. What about local colour? I don't see much of that here in Steamer Point."

"Crater and Ma'alla have plenty of genuine Arabian sights, smells and sounds," I countered. "There are also the dhow harbours, ancient water tanks, camels pulling water-carts, fishermen casting nets and tribesmen toting *jambiyya*s, just for the cost of a taxi fare."

"I've seen all that for myself already," Curtis shot back, impatiently. "It's old hat. What we want for the modern tourist is the *Big Experience*. Aden's become a crossroads for twelve international airlines. We're already planning new airport buildings and modern facilities so that people can stop over for a few days to see the Real Arabia, not just some tired British Colony."

Curtis's "Real Arabia" had everything to make a travel agent salivate: ancient ruins, spectacular vernacular architecture, dramatic landscapes and colourful indigenous peoples, mostly unknown to the West. Unfortunately, the Protectorate was also populated by armed tribesmen who gave not a toss for tourists or tourism. I was about to tell it to him straight when Thorne coughed, and caught my eye.

"There's still a bit of a problem with transport and accommodation in the Protectorate, isn't there, John?" said Robin, brightly.

"Yes indeed," I replied, backing off. "But for an interesting day trip, Lahej is only an hour away, with authentic Sultanic palaces and exotic tropical gardens."

When Mr Curtis said he had already seen and done that, Thorne suggested Mukairas, as having regular Aden Airways flights and a new hotel. I wondered if he could ever have been there.

"Certainly, it's got some potential," I said, hesitantly. "But accommodation's pretty basic. The real problem is security. The Yemen frontier is only a few miles away."

"Tourism doesn't have to be confined to the WAP," cut in Oates. "Tell Mr Curtis something about Hadhramaut."

"It's a wonder of the world, but not yet geared up for tourism. At present, there's no suitable accommodation there, save for some pretty basic government rest houses."

"We can always build hotels," countered Mr Curtis, with a visionary glint in his eye.

At this, I pictured groups of footloose, unsuitably dressed *Nasrani*s wandering around the narrow streets of Mukalla or Shibam to taunts of "Gamal Abdul Nasser" and being showered by the odd stone salvo. I then realized that I had not painted the picture intended, so said no more. When a stony-faced Oates promised that "We will be investigating this important matter further", conversation moved on to less controversial subjects.

Clearly I had not played the right hand with Curtis. However, the Tourism slot at least offered me a genuine excuse for getting out and about. Recalling Col. Ian Waller's strictures about the British not bothering to sample the delights of Mukairas, I chose this as the first place to revisit, particularly as the Federal Ministry of National Guidance and Information was currently puffing its claims as "another attractive centre for the tourist". I booked into the recently renamed "Mukairas Hotel" with a boisterous group, which included James Nash and Tony Boyle. Its friendly manager Farook and his petite wife made us most welcome.

Mukairas was like a tonic, and the rainstorm that hit us on the edge of the 'Audhali escarpment, creating a waterfall that plunged two thousand feet plumb into the inaccessible gorges of Upper Yafa'i, was one of the most spectacular sights any of us had ever witnessed. Nearby, the Qatabanian ruins of Am Adiya might have passed as an Arabian Machu Picchu. The monumental granite blocks of its ruined citadel fitted so closely together that no razor blade could have been inserted between them. A year later, I made another visit to Mukairas, conned by an Aden Airways' puff. But by then Farook had quit, his hotel had become a shambles, and there was nowhere to go without a military escort. We took refuge in the APL mess to be royally entertained by Robert White and Johnny Rickett, seconded from the Welsh Guards, who later achieved fame by preventing an Egyptian Air Force Ilyushin from taking off from Laudar's airstrip, where it had inadvertently landed.

There had to be some better tourist destination than Mukairas so, when Donald Foster, a WAP Deputy British Agent, mentioned that he had recently been to Perim Island, I pumped him for further information. Perim was an extinct volcanic crater, 125 miles west of Aden, set in the Bab al-Mandab, the famous straits forming the southern approaches to the Red Sea. Occupied by the British in 1799 to forestall Napoleon's perceived designs on India, it was subsequently abandoned for lack of water. In 1857, it was again annexed by the British, and had since been administered from Aden once the water problem had been overcome by installing condensers. Perim's magnificent deep-water harbour could accommodate the largest ships then afloat. From the 1880s to the mid-1930s, it flourished as a coaling and cable station in fierce competition with Aden, until oil superseded coal.

When I asked Foster whether Perim had any tourist potential he replied, "Good God, no! Absolutely none – at least in the foreseeable future. Anyway, it's the very devil to get to. I had to go by coaster to inspect the lighthouse and water distillation plant. However, I don't recommend doing it by boat. It took us eighteen hours each way. You'd best travel overland, though that means having to go through Subaihi. That'll need permission from the Lahejis, and some damned good official excuse. For all that, the place is a remarkable Edwardian relic and well worth seeing. Have a word with Bob Knowles. He's the only person I know who's been there recently."

Bob Knowles, a brisk ex-Malayan Civil Service administrator serving out his time in Aden on contract, happened to be planning his second visit with his young son Andrew. Apparently we needed a reliable Land Rover and an armed FRA escort to get there overland. Jock Snell arranged both, as well as an excuse for our visit – replacement parts for the water distillation plant.

On a muggy August afternoon, our two Land Rovers set off across one of the most barren and least populated tracts of south-west Arabia. For fifty miles we slalomed across a soft, sandy plain bounded by high dunes that merged imperceptibly into a string of low, inland hills. Skirting the great lagoon of Khawr al-Umairah, the track now swung northwards, leaving to the east the jagged 2,766-ft hulk of Jebel Kharaz, the highest and most spectacular of the extinct volcanoes that run from Perim to Aden. For the next forty miles the track was guesswork, and the leading FRA Land Rover only visible as a cloud of dust. Traversing up, down and across a succession of dried-up wadi beds, we bumped, crashed and jolted towards the Lahej Federal Guard's fort at Suqayya, our landward destination. Eyelids were encrusted in sand and conversation made impossible by the din. Seven wearisome hours after leaving Champion Lines, our headlights picked out the squat shape of the fort. All that now separated us from Perim was an uncomfortable night and an 18-mile sea crossing.

Too tired to eat, we turned in immediately, cursing ourselves that we had not brought tents to escape the fort's bugs, smells and filth. I tried to sleep on the roof, but failed when it rained intermittently throughout the night. At dawn next day, the sky was a bluish-grey, and the air stale and muggy. Abandoning my dank *charpoy*, I tiptoed silently between snoring soldiers wrapped in blankets to take a look beyond the fort's parapet. Below me lay a litter-strewn wasteland and a cluster of fishermen's shacks hugging a black-sanded beach. A pack of mangy pye-dogs was scavenging a stinking rubbish dump. Thirty yards offshore, a tall-bowed *sanbuq* was riding at anchor in a gentle swell.

Gingerly avoiding the squashed remains of a couple of scorpions that the soldiery had dispatched on the stone stairway, I found a bad-tempered Bob waiting outside with young Andrew. "We'll skip breakfast," said Bob, as he shouldered the box of spare parts and strode down to the water's edge, shouting across to the *sanbuq* as he went.

"Can't see any sign of life on that bloody boat. We'll have to wade out to it." A man was sleeping in the stern with a shawl wrapped around his head. "You the *nakhoda*?" demanded Knowles, after clambering aboard and giving the man's shoulder a vigorous shake. "Why the hell didn't you come to fetch us?" The *nakhoda* clearly did not understand English, but he got the message soon enough, and started up the engine with ill grace. Soon we were sliding past the curving Subaihi shoreline that swept round a point where it joined a line of black hills dotted with forts coming down from the Yemen. Until then, I had not realized quite how close we were to hostile territory.

As the sun came up, everyone's spirits rose. The *nakhoda* smiled for the first time and broke into a low, tuneless chant. When the wind of morning ruffled the waves, he raised the sail and Knowles too came to life, got out his rod and was soon pulling in fish with every cast, to fill the bottom of the boat with shark, bonito, barracuda and the delicious *darak*, or kingfish. It was Bob, rather than Andrew, who became the schoolboy out for half term.

Perim first came into view round the headland of Al-Turbah as an indistinct, low-lying mass. The coast of Africa was now clearly visible some 20 miles beyond, across the Bab al-Mandab, the Gate of Lamentation. Three hours after leaving Suqayya, we were met on the jetty by a neatly dressed man with a world-weary smile.

"Meet Shubaili," said Knowles, pumping the little man's hand vigorously. "Perim-born and Post Master Extraordinary. He's now charged with running this place."

Mr Shubaili acknowledged this effusive greeting with a pained expression, and then escorted us to the Rest House. Here, huge punkah fans hung lifeless from high ceilings. A heavy Edwardian sideboard and corner cupboard graced the dining room. The worm-eaten cane chairs of the living room might have belonged to a Raj reconstruction film set.

"This is all that's left of the old Perim lifestyle," Mr Shubaili confided, apologetically. "In the old days, thousands of coolies lived in the lines to bunker the ships and work the lighthouses and harbour. Over a hundred European gentlemen and ladies lived here. There were race meetings, and the Perim cricket teams played visiting warships. The guesthouse you are staying in was once the residence of the Perim Coal Company's manager, Mr Davey. When the company went bankrupt in 1938, Mr Davey died of a broken heart."

Knowles, father and son, and I spent the next two days inspecting this extraordinary relic of Empire, now home to Mr Shubaili, a skeleton staff, assorted fishermen, and a detachment of Armed Police, all maintained by an £10,000 HMG annual subsidy. We wandered across blackened volcanic rocks to visit the deserted quays and coolie lines of what had once serviced the busiest harbour in the Red Sea and South Arabia. We picked up conch shells from its dazzlingly white coral beaches, and poked around the ruins of the bungalows, offices and the clubhouse that, only thirty years before, had sustained a fading imperial lifestyle. Having swum, snorkelled and fished that lazy day away, we sat out on the verandah of Davey's house after dark, watching great liners glide through the straits of Bab al-Mandab, their lights ablaze. The sight awakened the same nostalgic feelings for home as it must have done for that long-forgotten British community, who had danced their Saturday nights away on this same verandah in their black ties and cotton evening dresses, under the light of an Arabian moon.

But it was not the ghosts of the past that kept me awake on our last night on Perim. Biting sandflies and the salt-laden wind that whined round the portico made sleep impossible. I left my bed and paced up and down the verandah watching sheet lightning illuminate the storm clouds that shrouded Yemen's black mountains. Knowles too must have had a bad night, for he was up early next morning in an ill humour.

"No sign of that bloody *sanbuq*," he grunted. "Better find out from Shubaili what the devil's going on."

Shubaili was despatched to the quayside, and soon returned with a long face and two shifty-looking characters. "Very sorry, Mr Knowles, but these men say that your *nakhoda* left for the mainland last night, and won't be coming back. They've agreed to take you across instead."

"At a price, I reckon," growled Knowles. "We've already paid that other scoundrel both ways. Anyway, who are these men, Shubaili?"

"One's a *nakhoda* and the other's the owner of his ship. Naturally, they will want money for your passage."

Knowles spoke little Arabic, but made up for this with a turn of invective and negotiating skills that had made the Malayan Colonial Administration second to none. When he had finished with the *sanbuq*'s owner, the fare had been significantly reduced. On the return journey, the sea picked up a rolling swell that made fishing impossible. It also left the owner horribly sea sick, and created a surf so strong that we had to swim ashore. The wretched owner, a non-swimmer, nearly drowned.

I never reported back to Mr Curtis about Perim's tourist potential. Exotic fish abounded in its coral reefs, and the gigantic grouper into whose jaws I inadvertently peered could have swallowed a sheep whole. One day, Perim may rival Sharm al-Shaikh as a Red Sea resort but, according to a latter-day traveller, Aidan Hartley, it has now become the haunt of Somali pirates and feral cats.

During our trip, Knowles and I had discussed the recently published government White Paper Cmnd. 1814, *Accession of Aden to the Federation of South Arabia*, a blueprint for South Arabia's future. In an introductory exchange of letters between Federal and Aden Ministers and the Secretary of State for the Colonies, Duncan Sandys, the Ministers had "earnestly requested" the British Government "to give favourable consideration to the entry of Aden into the Federation". As a quid pro quo, Sandys promised Aden a £500,000 grant, payable over three years, and £190,000 to compensate some Federal states for loss of customs revenue. Annexes summarized constitutional amendments, a code of human rights, and the proposed administrative, staffing and financing arrangements.

Knowles reckoned, from his Malayan experience, that this merger was most unlikely to work. That was not the official view. Indeed, the concept of a federated South Arabia was nothing new. Various British versions had been mooted at least since the early 1930s, and the model promoted by Trevaskis had already been adopted by some WAP rulers in 1959. It had been bitterly opposed by the ATUC, Egypt and the Yemen, but had not included Aden. Belatedly perhaps, Whitehall had come to recognize that a federation without Aden could not achieve Britain's strategic objectives. Accordingly, despite the opposition of many leading Adenis, merger was being pushed through willy-nilly.

The question now exercising many expatriate HMOCS officers was how this merger, seen as a prelude to independence, would affect their future career prospects. For middle-ranking married men, whose chances of finding meaningful employment in Britain thereafter were at best uncertain, the Aden Senior Civil Servants Association offered a lifeline. Foster was the Association's chairman. On my return from Perim, he invited me to lunch and voiced his concerns about the faltering morale of Aden's British Colonial officials. To bolster this, he was about to fly to London to petition the Colonial Secretary that they be properly compensated for loss of career. As a bachelor without family responsibilities, I had never given compensation much thought, nor previously heard this sort of talk from senior officers. Foster, an ex-Indian Army officer, was to serve fourteen "barren and hungry" years in South Arabia. Despite being badly wounded by a terrorist grenade in 1963, he soldiered on, and headed various Federal ministries until his retirement in 1966.

That Aden's proposed merger had reached this advanced stage was largely due to the negotiating skills of the governor, Sir Charles Johnston. In wartime Cairo, Johnston's poetic and literary bent had blossomed in the raffish, bohemian café society that had included writers, artists, pashas, diplomats and soldiers but, above all, the fairy-tale Georgian princess, Natasha Bagration, who became his wife. Johnston's translation of Pushkin's *Eugene Onegin* is regarded as one of the best available in the English language.

As an accomplished Arabist and former ambassador to Jordan, Johnston was well qualified to take a dispassionate view of how best Britain might retain the Aden base, and safeguard its massive capital investments in the BP Refinery, Port and Airfield. His intended strategy was to unify Aden with its hinterland, create an indigenous civil service, stabilize the political situation, and promote economic self-sufficiency. He was now about to achieve the first of these aims by a diplomatic tour de force, which had involved two years of clandestine negotiations with suspicious Adeni politicians and autocratic Federal rulers.

Johnston had a formidable intellect. However, the Federal constitution he had laboured so hard to fashion was virtually unworkable. He also underestimated that peculiar Arab genius for self-destructive dissension, and assumed that once merger became a *fait accompli*, logic, self-interest and HMG's support would do the rest. In this he miscalculated. Yet Denis Healey's dismissive labelling of him as a "languid cynic" was miles off the mark. Johnston was more an idealist who sincerely believed in Britain's imperial mission. He well appreciated the inherent dilemma of achieving a fair balance between British and Arab interests. He also regarded the way in which a handful of Political Officers had brought the Protectorate under control at minimum cost and force as "an extraordinary, little-publicized achievement of disinterested British imperialism", and considered that South Arabia's best interests had been well served by an unselfish and devoted body of British public servants in Aden.

Johnston's attempt to achieve a union between a prosperous, urban and relatively sophisticated Aden and a ragbag of disparate, impoverished feudal states was backed by the British government as its only available option. Yet, given worldwide opposition and Britain's own economic weakness, Johnston's was a virtually impossible task. Paradoxically, South Arabia's later history may have vindicated the federal concept. After years of strife, a very different federation from that originally envisaged eventually emerged, manifesting itself in the creation of the unified Republic of Yemen in 1990.

When the Accession White Paper was first published, the proposed merger date, January 1963, was only five months away. This deadline should have triggered intense activity in the Secretariat. In fact, action to implement the major administrative changes envisaged was put on hold until after LEGCO had voted on the issue on 25 September. But on 19 September there occurred an event of cataclysmic importance for South Arabia's future. Just six days before the crucial LEGCO vote, Imam Ahmed, the Yemen's undisputed spiritual and temporal leader, died peacefully in his bed, having survived several assassination attempts during his lifetime.

Over the previous three years, the Yemen frontier had been relatively quiet. This was attributable to a serious famine which had forced the Imam to accept American aid; to general internal political unrest; and, most recently, to the sixty-nine-year-old tyrant's public falling out with President Nasser, who now openly supported the anti-Imamic Free Yemeni movement. On the world's stage, this signal event was overshadowed by the Cuban missile crisis. For the Yemen, it presaged the end of Imamic rule, invasion by an Egyptian army, and seven years of bloody civil war.

Imam Ahmed was succeeded by his son, Prince Muhammad al-Badr, a fervent admirer of Nasser. Within days of the old man's death, the Yemen was plunged into a civil war triggered by an Egyptian-sponsored coup led by Colonel Sallal, the son of a blacksmith, who, for years, had been chained to the wall of his prison cave by the Imam. Sallal, supposedly a friend of Prince Badr, moved quickly to reduce to rubble the royal Al-Basha'ir Palace at San'a, where Badr had taken refuge. His henchmen summarily executed key members of the Imam's administration and most of the Royal family, dumping their bodies on the streets of San'a for the dogs. Badr himself managed to escape, reputedly dressed as a woman, to fight another day.

Two days before the Yemen revolution, an apprehensive LEGCO had formally approved Aden's accession to the Federation by the narrowest majority, despite the opposition of several moderate members. The ATUC promptly called a general strike which forced the police, supported by British troops, to use tear gas to disperse rioters besieging the Legislative Council building. One was left for dead and five others wounded. News of the revolution was greeted with jubilation in the Crater suq, but took Government House, HQ Middle East Command and Al-Ittihad by surprise. A delegation of Federal ministers was despatched hot-foot to London to get Duncan Sandys's reassurance that Britain would continue to honour its treaty obligations, and take a tough line with Aden's revolutionary radicals.

Against this backdrop, Aden's accession heralded radical administrative and political changes to its system of governance. The Governor, no longer vested with supreme authority save in an emergency, was to be redesignated British High Commissioner. The Secretariat would become the Office of Aden's Chief Minister. Most Federal and Aden departments were to be converted into ministries headed by Federal rulers and based on Al-Ittihad. Only the Judiciary, Attorney-General and Speaker's departments would remain independent. Imperceptibly, the overriding power once wielded by the Secretariat was ebbing away. When the Establishments Branch moved to Crater, and the Protectorate Branch to Al-Ittihad, I asked Jock Snell what he made of it. "Damned if I know," grunted Jock. "But I tell you one thing. This place will be a sight different after merger. D'you realise that the only Brits likely to be left here will be Robin Thorne, you and me?"

It had always been official British policy that expatriate officers would be gradually replaced by Arabs. Already, 32 out of 78 designated Administrative Branch officers were indigenous. The Adenization process was being stepped up and, one morning, without prior notice, two newly appointed Adeni Assistant Secretaries arrived in the Secretariat to take over most of my portfolio. When, in exchange, the Chief Secretary offered me Approved Schools and Early Releases, the Duke of Edinburgh's Award Scheme, Ceremonies and Precedence, and Xmas Cards, I remonstrated: "I really must know how the land lies, Ken. The work with which I had first-hand experience has been allocated to people who have none. You've left me with the rubbish."

"I entirely sympathize," replied Simmonds, soothingly. "However, please appreciate that we've got to give, and be seen to give, these new boys practical experience while we're still around to guide them. Politically, I can't afford to hand over this office to the Chief Minister if it's manned by an ignorant bunch who haven't a clue what they're supposed to be doing."

Simmonds suggested that I could usefully reorganize the Secretariat's staff in readiness for the handover. I ducked the task of weeding out a ridiculously over-staffed General Office to avoid a walkout. With our British secretarial staff, the problem was more to find suitable replacements to work in a very different milieu under an Arab Chief Minister. Incredibly, the future location of the Secretariat's Secret Registry, many of whose files were marked "For British Eyes Only", had been completely overlooked. The situation was complicated by a feud between the Secret Registry's exclusively British female staff and its ultra-efficient head, Miss Cain. Morale had suffered, absenteeism was rife and poor Miss Cain went sick through worry and overwork. As a temporary replacement, I recruited the wife of an Army Intelligence officer, Tisch Klinghardt, who had fought against the British as a Romanian Air Force fighter pilot during the Second World War. Yet so fraught was the atmosphere that, with only a week to go before Accession Day, even this warrior lady threatened to resign due to "absenteeism, impossible pressures of work and general uncertainty about the future". To retain their vital services, and to preserve the integrity of ultra-sensitive files, Bernard Lewis, the Assistant Chief Secretary with special responsibility for the merger, and I decided to transfer the entire Secret Registry to the High Commission Office, without further reference to anyone.

With merger day fast approaching, both Brian Doe, the Director of Antiquities, and I were determined to preserve the Aden Government Archives, still mouldering away on Barrack Hill. Doe's recommendations, that they be transferred to a new wing of the Aden Museum, or microfilmed for a modest £1,000, were rejected by the Aden Treasury. Appalled by this abdication of responsibility, I reckoned that I might at least save several rare first editions secreted in the Secretariat Library. Thorne, normally a stickler for proprieties, agreed with me that these would be "better appreciated in the High Commission than in the Chief Minister's Office". I arranged the transfer forthwith, and like to think that at least some of those valuable books found a good home.

With only a month to go before merger, the Secretariat was barely muddling through. A duty roster, involving overnight vigils at Government House to field secret signals from London, added a frisson to the banality of normal work. My diary records: "A complete lack of leadership from above – both Governor Johnston and Chief Secretary Simmonds to blame. ... Orders are so blurred that it is difficult to know what is happening, how and why."

On one particularly fraught morning, I ran into Archie Wilson wandering aimlessly around the Secretariat. "What on earth are you doing here, Archie?" I asked him.

"Looking for Jock, if you must know. And taking a break from running that beastly little island, Kamaran," he replied.

Archie's final colonial appointment, before retiring to model for a well-known brand of gin manufacturers, had been as Commissioner of Kamaran. This former pilgrimage quarantine island, 200 miles up the Red Sea and just off the Yemen coast, was still being administered from Aden. The posting was not to Archie's taste, so he spent as much time as possible as Alastair McIntosh's guest in Aden.

"What d'you make of all this merger business, Archie? We seem to be running around like headless chickens."

"Definitely not a good show. In fact, a perfect shambles. Better discuss this over a drink, old boy – Union Club's just round the corner."

Witnessing the death throes of the Secretariat was a mournful experience. Fortunately, the year ended on a high note, when John Ducker invited Susan and me to spend Christmas in Sayun. Winter in Hadhramaut was everything that Mr Curtis might have wished for. We picnicked in the dunes of the Ramlat Sab'atain and, on Christmas Eve, ate steaks airmailed from Aden, drank champagne and danced under the stars on Alan and Heather Wren's Eastern Bank rooftop. On Christmas Day, Joanna Ellis gave dinner for twelve. Early next morning, in the spirit of Christmas, I went across to the Guest House to make my peace with Arthur Watts, up from Mukalla with his family. My call was unexpected. His unfriendly reception dashed any hopes I might have had of a future posting to Hadhramaut.

Back in the Secretariat, Jock Snell looked as if he had personally soaked up most of Aden's Christmas spirits. At a New Year's Eve party, I confided to Alastair McIntosh that I was disillusioned about having spent the best part of three years in South Arabia behind an office desk.

"I wouldn't worry about that," said Alastair. "There's not going to be that much to look forward to in 1963. You may have seen the best of your South Arabian career already."

10

Insecure in Aden

IF 1962 HAD ENDED on a high, 1963 began at rock bottom for reasons quite unconnected with Alastair's gloomy forecast. On 5 January, Susan left Aden for good, having just resigned from the Foreign Office in disillusion with what she described as "the poisoned atmosphere" in which she had been working for the past two years. "The Office has become a white elephant," she remonstrated bitterly. "The Commercial and Press Sections, and what used to be the Consular Service, still play an effective part, but the rest consists of shuffling papers from desk to desk at London's bidding."

Susan's imperial upbringing in India and Ceylon had implanted qualities admired by South Arabia's most charismatic chieftain, Sharif Husain of Baihan. The Sharif had once asked her to dinner, but as his only guest. He behaved impeccably, but his pressing invitation that she come to stay with him in Baihan "to ride across the desert together" posed a more delicate problem of protocol. Happily, *amour-propre* was satisfied when he accepted, with good grace, Susan's excuse, "I don't quite know what my mother would have to say …".

Susan was scathing about my future Colonial Service career. "Everyone with any sense knows that we only stay on in Arabia because of our base. Britain would be out in a minute, and wash her hands of the whole business if that consideration was no longer necessary." When I muttered something about "service and commitment", she snapped back: "If you're staying on in Aden for those reasons, you've got a misguided sense of loyalty. You should get out now, while you're still young enough to make the change."

I drove her to the airport before dawn to catch her plane to Nairobi. As I watched her walk across the tarmac to the waiting Comet, in the red dress I knew so well, with her long blonde hair trailing over her shoulders, memories of everything we had shared together over the past two years overwhelmed me. This was not our last goodbye, but both of us must have sensed that if ever I was going to ask her to marry me, it should have been then. Susan was a loving girl of resolute character. Not long after leaving Aden, she died of a brain tumour. Almost the last words she wrote me – "Friendships formed in Aden always turn to ashes" – became an everlasting reproach.

With Susan gone, an important part of my life vanished into limbo. More than ever before, I wanted to get shot of Aden Colony. The previous November, as the Secretariat's shutters were coming down, I had formally applied for a transfer to the Protectorate. In the New Year, I was told that I would have to soldier on in the Chief Minister's Office after Aden's accession on 18 January. Despairingly, I wrote a personal letter to Nigel Pusinelli, Director of Establishments, citing previous representations, and requesting that I be transferred to do fieldwork as an Assistant Adviser in the Federation. Pusinelli replied that he would do his best at some future date. However, in the meantime nothing could be done, as "without continuity the confusion that the changes have inevitably caused will be worse confounded".

A week before Sir Charles Johnston signed Aden's Treaty of Accession, signalling the end of 124 years of direct British rule, Ken Simmonds gave a farewell party for his Secretariat staff. He had impressed upon me that his premature retirement, after twenty-eight years of Colonial Service, should be kept secret, and that his departure should be treated as ordinary leave. His valedictory memorandum, minutely detailing the direction and method of forwarding "all mail, cards, invitations, letters, circulars, magazines, small packages, short monthly staff lists, etc" to his home address, was the last bureaucratic testament of a man who could despatch government business with mechanical efficiency, yet be so obsessed with detail that he even prescribed the precise margin widths of Secretariat memoranda. Simmonds was retiring at forty-eight as a result of ill health and overwork. Although he had been a formidable performer in LEGCO, and had done much to promote Aden's constitutional progress, his brand of colonial administration had become obsolete, and he could never have fitted into the looser federal structure. The framed photograph of Mount Kenya, which had once so inspired me, had long been packed up as "Not Needed on Voyage".

The day after merger, the Secretariat, formerly the fulcrum of British administrative order, was reduced to a shambles. As the High Commission Office and Mrs Klinghardt's Secret Registry staff moved out, over-excited peons tossed around typewriters, desks and filing cabinets as if independence had already arrived. I watched aghast as they lost control of a heavy security safe, which took off through the wooden rails of the Secretariat's first floor verandah and hit the ground so hard that it left behind a small crater. Two days later, a tropical rainstorm burst through the building's tin roof to complete the destruction. Only Robin Thorne, Jock Snell, Mrs Hillier and I were left to clean up the mess.

The old order might have quit the scene, but I contented myself with the thought that work might now take on a new dimension under the dynamic leadership of my new boss, Aden's first Chief Minister, Hassan Bayoomi. Bayoomi was a clever, self-made man and joint owner, with his brother Husain, of the Aden newspaper *Al-Kifah*. In 1960, he had come to political prominence during Sir William Luce's governorship, having courageously forced through the contentious Industrial Ordinance in the face of bitter ATUC opposition. This had earned him undying hostility both in Aden and in the wider Arab world, and prompted a campaign of intimidation, backed by death threats, against both him and his family. Without Bayoomi's unwavering support throughout the tortuous merger negotiations, it is unlikely that Aden would have joined the Federation. Yet he was no British stooge. As founder leader of the United National Party, he espoused his own brand of nationalism, advocating merger as a preliminary to Aden becoming a self-governing state within an independent South Arabian republic.

Sir Charles Johnston's faith in Bayoomi extended to the hope that he would now shoulder prime responsibility for making Aden's federal merger work. In addition, he had the equally demanding task of running the new Aden State. One of his first priorities was to speed the transition from a British-run administration to an indigenous one, yet he was canny enough to accept that it would be self-defeating to get rid of the British before there were enough local officers of sufficient calibre and training to replace them. The two callow young men who had been tasked to take over my portfolio quickly vanished.

Unfortunately, Bayoomi was a workaholic, a heavy smoker, a *qat* addict, and a diabetic who refused proper medical treatment. As Chief Minister, he was seldom seen in his office. Without him to give a lead, work took on an aimless, surreal quality. The dramatic events that unfolded every day in the Yemen seemed to pass us by completely. As an antidote to office ennui and Aden's enervating climate, I swam regularly and took up rugby again after a five-year gap, playing for Aden's BP Bureika RFC against Armed Services teams. Pitches of saline sand, overlaid with a hard crust, lacerated knees and elbows, but broken bones were rare.

One member of the Bureika Club was an ex-Welsh Guards and Cambridge contemporary, John Malcolm. He asked me to join a team consisting of Godfrey Meynell, Peter de la Billière and an itinerant architect, David Armstrong, to challenge the Royal Marines to a 2,300-yard race up Jebel Shamsan. Starting at sea level in the Gold Mohur valley, the course climbed steeply 1,740 feet to the volcano's summit. Malcolm, an Empire Games athlete, was a fitness fanatic. To me, the idea of running such a race in the heat of an Aden summer seemed absurdly masochistic.

The Scramble had been advertised for weeks in advance through posters, press and the radio. The due day, 2 May, was about as hot as it ever gets, so it was no surprise that the spectators easily outnumbered the forty-six competitors. These were drawn mainly from 45 Royal Marine Commando, the King's Own Scottish Borderers, miscellaneous locals, expatriate civilians, two ladies sensibly armed with water bottles, and one barefoot youth. When the starter's Very pistol went off, a wild mêlée of local lads took the lead. They quickly faded as we pounded up the stiflingly hot, stone-strewn reaches of Gold Mohur's upper valley. Near the top of it, with the sun still high and heat radiating off the volcanic rock, my mouth was so dry that I was tempted to drop out. Yet, at the start of the final section, involving a short rock scramble, there was only one man left in front of me, a silkily smooth-running Somali in a light blue vest, whose pace had never faltered. At the summit col there was no question that he would win easily. I was runner-up, but Lieutenant Wells-Cole, RM, pipped de la Billière for third place, so the Marines just beat us on aggregate. At the dinner we stood them that evening, it was humbling to learn that the winner, Muhammad Deria, was still a schoolboy at St Antony's College, Aden. Someone then explained that he had already represented Aden in the Commonwealth Games, and come second in the Middle East Cross Country Championships.

I still retained the Tourism slot, but had never been to Dhala', where my chum Godfrey Meynell was the resident Assistant Adviser. The Meynells' invitation to join a mixed family party and John Malcolm to stay with them over Easter could not have been more welcome. We travelled by the Dhala' Road, tucking our Land Rover in between a Federal National Guard escort. Godfrey was to join us farther up the road. Heading northwards towards the mountains, the sky soon became overcast with menacingly dark clouds. By the time we reached the Wadi al-Milah it was already raining hard. Just as the leading FNG vehicle was about to cross, the soldiers leapt out shouting "*Sayl! Sayl!*" – "Flood! Flood!" – pointing upstream and gesticulating wildly. Within minutes a dry wadi bed became an impassable torrent. Half an hour later, it stopped as abruptly as it had begun. Our convoy moved on circumspectly, until the sight of an abandoned lorry wallowing in the floodwaters of the Wadi Suhaihiyya forced a stop. After a succession of diversions leading to impasses, we returned to where we had started.

Godfrey caught up with us as night fell, whereupon the two escort Land Rovers chanced their luck and got stuck axle-deep in mud. If another heavy flood came down, both would have been lost. Fortuitously, we were now within walking distance of the Federal National Guard garrison at Thumair. Four of us linked arms to ford a rising torrent, and returned with a gang of soldiers to pull out both vehicles with ropes. Once we had regrouped on the fort at 9 p.m., I assumed that, with two toddlers in the party, we would be stopping there for the night. Godfrey had other ideas.

"I'm afraid we can't stay here. Clean yourselves up and give the children something to eat. We must then move on immediately after I've sorted out some local business."

"What's the problem?" I asked him.

"Qutaibi trouble," he replied. "My JAA, Husain Al-Bursi, looks after this corner of Radfan. Unfortunately, he's got too close to the leading Qutaibi shaikh, who's a trouble-maker, and has got himself mixed up with a bunch of no-goods who've just taken to the hills. The Bursi's a formidable character, but just for now we're better off without him. I'm going to have to tell him that I don't want him around here for the time being."

The speed of events was breathtaking. Handsome in a saturnine way, "The Bursi" looked a dangerous customer. When Godfrey gave him his marching orders, he didn't seem in the least surprised and disappeared into the night, muttering darkly. "Good riddance," said Godfrey. "But it's best we leave now." I knew nothing then of Qutaibi politics. A couple of years later, it would become a chief preoccupation.

After more heavy rain, what remained of the road to Dhala' became a deep-rutted obstacle course. As we struggled up the formidable Khuraiba Pass, one of the FNG's Land Rovers nearly went over the edge. Nine hours after leaving Aden, we reached Dhala' at midnight. Godfrey's day was not yet over. "Some wretched Arab youth's just been shot by the Marines," he groaned, as the rest of us were about to slope off to bed. "Silly idiot let off some fireworks just outside the Marine lines. He bolted after being challenged, so they winged him on the run."

At dawn next morning, I walked onto the roof of the Government Guest House to be greeted by a glorious Easter Day. Beyond scrappy fields and the neat lines of tents marking the FRA and Royal Marine fortified encampments, ridge upon ridge of blue-tinged mountains rose into a clear-washed sky. To the north-west, the 8,000-ft massif of Jebel Jihaf dominated the skyline. It was an idyllic scene, yet ever since the British had concluded a treaty of friendship with the Amir of Dhala' in 1880, Dhala' had been a trouble spot. Despite that treaty, the Turks had occupied the Dhala' Plateau for thirty years until the Resident, Major-General Maitland, complying with Curzon's forward policy, rebuilt the Khuraiba Pass for mule traffic, posted detachments of British troops along the Dhala' Road to quash the Qutaibi, and then moved up the entire Hampshire Regiment, plus the Aden Garrison and two mountain batteries, to secure the ground. A joint Turkish–British Boundary Commission was then set up to demarcate a 138-mile *de facto* boundary with the Yemen, and in 1903 Major H. F. Jacob was appointed to Dhala' as its first Political Officer. Much of his peacemaking was undone during the First World War, when Turkish troops reoccupied Dhala'. After their withdrawal, they were replaced by Yemeni irregulars who only retreated ten years later, under the threat of proscriptive RAF bombing.

The Meynells' house, built of massive stone blocks, was strategically sited on a small knoll above the plain, and surrounded by a heavily sandbagged perimeter wall. Over breakfast, Godfrey took up the Dhala' story.

"Ever since we got rid of the Yemenis there's been trouble here. Amir Haidara followed them as the area's effective ruler, but was so brutal and unpopular that we had to get rid of him. He decamped to Qataba, just across the border, and has being making an infernal nuisance of himself ever since. The current ruler of Dhala', Amir Sha'fal, has the devil's own job. His own soldiery are often in the pay of the Yemenis, while most of the Radfan tribes, who are supposed to owe him allegiance, merely pay him lip service. Violence and intrigue are endemic. It's bred in these people a xenophobia, extreme even by South Arabian standards."

The wonder was that Godfrey, his wife Honor and their baby daughter Diana should be living here at all. Dhala' was never a place for the faint-hearted, let alone a young married couple with a family. The Meynells had already stuck it out for almost two years. Dhala' had been a Political Officers' graveyard. Peter Davey, son of the Perim Coal Company's last manager, was killed in 1947 while trying to arrest a hot-headed minor shaikh, Muhammad Awas. Basil Seager, Trevaskis's predecessor as British Agent, had been stabbed and severely wounded in 1950. Charles Inge's friend, Bob Mound, had been murdered in 1955. Roy Somerset had been besieged on Jebel Jihaf in 1958. Godfrey himself had survived attempts on his life, including one as the intended victim of a tribesman who mistakenly stabbed a Federal Army colonel, Sandy Thomas, instead. Godfrey disarmed the man by wrenching the bloodied *jambiyya* from his grasp. Afterwards he visited his would-be assassin in prison, to disabuse the man of the belief that he was bent on converting Dhala' to Christianity.

Godfrey could never resist a challenge. At Eton he had never lost a boxing match. He and his school and Cambridge contemporary, John Malcolm, had harangued the comrades at a Moscow students' rally. In 1956, he had driven out to Hungary to support the uprising. To him, the "exhilarating" atmosphere of Dhala' was akin to India's North-west Frontier, where his soldier father had won a posthumous VC. He never wavered in his support of righteous causes, though this sometimes proved his undoing. Forty years on, he drove by bus to Iraq, at the start of the Second Gulf War, as part of the Human Shield. And if Godfrey was a WAP exemplar, Honor, an Ulster girl brought up in Kenya during the Mau Mau emergency, was its unflappable heroine.

Our first port of call was the Dhala' suq, around whose mean streets we wandered under the watchful eyes of our armed escort, ignoring hostile stares and the spectacle of a heavily shackled prisoner defecating in a shadowed corner. Dominating the town was a sinister fortress, perched high above on a rocky eminence. "The Amir's palace," explained Godfrey, pointing to the battlements. "That ghastly Haidara chucked his prisoners off the top, literally to the dogs."

Next we drove in convoy up a narrow, near-vertical track, past elaborately terraced fields carved out of the mountainside, for a picnic on Jebel Jihaf. Gazing northwards across a distant plain of patchwork fields, dried-up watercourses and scattered villages to a tangle of azure-tinted mountains, Godfrey seemed to relax. "That's the Qataba plain down there, and the Yemen. What a fantastic view! I really love this place, but I fear that this may be our last family picnic. Security's deteriorating, so it troubles me now to bring both my loved ones up here."

That evening, Brian Betham, the local Field Intelligence Officer, conducted the Easter Day service, with Godfrey leading some lusty, unaccompanied hymn singing. With drinks and dinner to follow, we might almost have been spending the weekend at Meynell Langley, in the heart of the Derbyshire countryside. That illusion was dispelled when our guards insisted on monitoring every stage of our undress before going to bed.

For the following day's entertainment, Godfrey insisted that the menfolk accompany him to 'Awabil to visit its Naib, Yahya Al-Khulaqi. 'Awabil was the capital of Sha'ib, and, as Godfrey explained, "It's 7,000 ft high and tucked away in one of the remotest parts of the WAP. It's only twenty miles away direct from Dhala', but it might have been two hundred until we blasted out a road last year. The Sha'ibi Shaikh prefers to live near the Yemen frontier, so can't be counted a friend. That's why I must keep in touch with the Naib, to make sure that he's not turning sour."

A pre-dawn start saw our Land-Rover convoy, escorted by a section of red-turbaned Sha'ibi Tribal Guards, grinding up into the hills by a track sometimes only discernible to the eye of faith. The Dhala' plain below was veiled by diaphanous white cloud, leaving only the odd, isolated knoll, topped by a fortified watchtower, poking through. When the track petered out over bare rock slabs angled at thirty degrees, it was faster to walk. Three joint-jolting hours after leaving Dhala', 'Awabil came up as a cluster of squat keeps huddled together on a boulder-strewn shelf. Behind it rose a huge, striated escarpment. At the door of the biggest of the keeps, a dignified man of indeterminate age awaited us. "The Naib of Sha'ib," muttered Godfrey, as he strode ahead to pump the man's hand and exchange ear-splitting greetings. Evidently the Naib had been expecting us. A ragged group of musicians, led by a wizened old man with bagpipes, accompanied by a couple of youths beating drums and clashing cymbals, appeared as if on cue. The trio broke into a discordant routine that reached its climax when the leader performed a series of prodigious goat-like leaps. After this, everyone hurried inside to eat boiled goat, rice and tinned fruit.

"Yemenis, of course," explained Godfrey, after the performers had slurped down their fill and sloped off. "Strolling players. They pop over here to do the rounds. We're less than five miles from the Yemen border. Happily, the Sha'ibis don't have such close tribal affiliations with the opposition as they do in Dhala', so security's much better. After lunch, I'll show you something of their country."

I wouldn't have minded a short siesta, but Godfrey was already on his feet, pacing the floor impatiently. After bidding the Naib goodbye, the four of us set off over hill and vale with an escort of as many soldiers. The sun was hot, but the air cool. In this harsh, treeless country only the occasional terraced field, scratched out of the rock, sustained life. At one lonely village, a scrawny elder, supervising a pair of bullocks drawing water from a well in a skin, spotted us from afar. He ran up to us, shouting "Coom 'ere lads, de anyyer know Sheffield?" Godfrey replied in Arabic, and the two settled down for a chat.

"That man used to work in a Sheffield steel mill," explained Godfrey, as we hit the trail again. "There's so little to do up here that half Sha'ib's population has to work overseas. They're sailors, mechanics and traders, and particularly like Sheffield, so many of them can speak English. We've got to encourage more of them to stay on here. I'm trying to give local agriculture a boost with loans to build dams and buy pumps. We're also experimenting with soft fruits and coffee, and have even introduced a new breed of chickens."

Driving back to Dhala', we stopped at a village to inspect a primary school. When Godfrey poked his head through the door, all lessons stopped. The schoolboys were then turned out of doors to put on an impromptu PT display. It was a spirited performance, but Godfrey was not satisfied and admonished the schoolmaster in Arabic.

"I don't like the slack way those boys stood at ease, Headmaster."

"But, ya Meylon," the man replied, "is it not difficult to instil discipline into such small boys?"

"Not at all," Godfrey shot back. "Just have them beaten. They'll soon learn!"

The Easter Party left Dhala' before dawn next day, and got back to Aden after five hours' furious driving. As I nosed my VW Beetle through the rush-hour traffic to the Chief Minister's Office, I couldn't stop thinking about the tangled hills and tortured politics of Dhala', of Godfrey's energy and enthusiasm, and of Honor's hospitality and courage. Their world was so very different from mine. Despite Godfrey's parting words – "Dhala' never fulfils the promise of its mornings" – I wanted to be part of it.

It was now four months since I had written to Pusinelli about a Protectorate posting, but I had heard nothing more. Working in the Chief Minister's Office was proving even less fulfilling than the Secretariat, largely because the Chief Minister was never there. Ten days after my return from Dhala', Robin Thorne summoned me.

"You'll probably know that Jock Snell's about to go on leave," he began. "This leaves his post vacant. I'd like you to fill it. If you accept, you'd be appointed as Aden's Acting Deputy Ministerial Secretary (Security)."

I tried to conceal my surprise. Quite what Jock's job entailed had always been something of a mystery, but this promotion was way above my seniority level.

"Of course, I'd be delighted to take it on. But what exactly is involved, Robin?"

"Primarily, to take over frontline responsibility for the internal security of Aden State and the Chief Minister's Office. This will involve close liaison with the security services and the Police and membership of various internal security committees. You will also have administrative responsibility for the Aden Police Force, immigration and deportation, arms and ammunition control and club registration. For the time being, you'll also have to soldier on with your existing Assistant Secretary schedule. Ask Jock to give you the rundown."

I knew that Jock didn't do handing-over notes. Even so, a few tips of the trade would have been helpful. He had a nose for politics and people. Unfortunately, at that time his prodigious interest in the EAP's tribes had not yet extended to devious goings-on in the back streets of Aden. I had to go back to Robin Thorne for a proper briefing.

"I couldn't get that much out of Jock, but presumably I can bone up from the files?"

"I'm afraid it's not that simple," replied Thorne. "Much of this work is not recorded on open files. However, take a look at this folder. It explains the basic framework of Aden's internal security and command structure, but don't let it out of your sight. I'll also get John Bushell to put you in the picture. Bear in mind that the Federal Constitution's a bit of a mess, so you're going to have to tread carefully when liaising with both the Adenis and Federalis. Incidentally, apart from me, you're directly answerable to the Chief Minister."

"When do I report to him? He never seems to be in the office."

Thorne grimaced. "Yes, we've got a problem there. Unfortunately, Bayoomi's a very sick man. He's currently in England undergoing medical treatment, but the prognosis is bad. If he doesn't come back, life's going to be very difficult for all of us."

I had implicit faith in Robin Thorne, one of the finest men I ever worked for. Born in India, the son of a distinguished Indian Civil Servant, he had won open scholarships to both Rugby and Oxford. On a pre-war exchange scholarship to Hamburg University, the Hitlerian hysteria had so incensed him that he had torn down swastika drapes lining the streets, and narrowly escaped something worse than imprisonment. During the war, he had fought with the King's African Rifles in Ethiopia and Madagascar and, later, in the grim Burma campaign. A gentle, modest man who never lost his cool, Robin never talked about the war, but basked in the memory of his twelve years' Colonial Service in Tanganyika with his wife Joan, where he had been the District Officer for Serengeti and Ngorongoro. Since his transfer to Aden, he had been heavily involved in the clandestine merger negotiations. In 1967, half the fingers of one hand were blown off by a terrorist letter bomb.

John Bushell, Political Adviser to the Commander-in-Chief Middle East Command, was of a different cut. A worldly-wise Wykehamist and career diplomat, he had been Susan's boss, and subsequently became British ambassador in Saigon and Pakistan. At our meeting, he rattled off some vital statistics.

"Most of Aden's security problems stem from having 85,000 mainly illegal Yemenis who represent thirty-five percent of Aden's population. That in itself has increased by 100,000 over the last eight years. Yemenis also make up most of the 25,000 members of the ATUC, an organization that has become a front for the virulently anti-British People's Socialist Party, the PSP. They were behind last November's damaging strikes which forced us to deport a hundred trouble-makers."

"What about Aden's other political parties? Do they pose an internal security threat?"

"To nothing like the same extent. Indians and Somalis still make up nearly twenty percent of Aden's population, but generally keep out of local politics. The only other Aden party of consequence is the United National Party, the UNP. It's basically moderate, reasonably pro-British, and would prefer Aden to be an independent state within the Federation as part of the Commonwealth. Trouble is, it's essentially Bayoomi's creation. Without him there's not much to it. There's also the South Arabian League, who are anti-British, anti-ruler and would like to merge with the Yemen on their own terms as part of a Pan-Arab grouping. But essentially they're a Lahej-based show, and have lost momentum ever since 1956 when their leaders were exiled, and the then Sultan of Lahej, Ali Abdul Karim, decamped to Cairo."

"And there's no one else in the field?"

"Not really," replied Bushell, glancing up at me quizzically. "There's an insignificant Communist group, and no doubt several others out there with Egyptian backers, but we don't regard them as a serious threat."

"How is Aden's internal security machine structured?"

"The Federal Supreme Council is now responsible for the Federation's internal security overall. In Aden, HE retains reserved powers, and has delegated these to his Deputy, Tom Oates."

"Then where does the Chief Minister fit in? I understand that I'm directly answerable to him for Aden's internal security."

"That's a touch more complicated," replied Bushell, wryly. "The Chief Minister's role is somewhat anomalous. Constitutionally, he's not directly responsible for Aden's internal security, so it's up to you establish the right sort of relationship with him and others concerned. To keep him in the picture, he sits on various security committees of which you'll also be a member. I gather that Robin has already given you some basic paperwork explaining the set-up."

"What about my work with the Police?"

"Ah yes, the Police," said Bushell, frowning slightly. "The Aden Police Force is seriously under strength. It has 800 men and six police stations to cover all 75 square miles of a Colony populated by close on a quarter of a million people, many of whom aren't particularly well disposed towards us. It's largely officered by a handful of British, and we must assume that most policemen on the beat are basically loyal. It needs a lot more money to make it really effective.

Nigel Morris, the Deputy-Inspector of Colonial Police, came out here last autumn after the anti-merger riots and made some important recommendations. We can only hope they get London's approval. His main internal security recommendations are also contained in the papers Thorne gave you."

Bushell now glanced at his watch, making it obvious that he had better things to do. "Look here, Harding," he said, rising to his feet as if to signal my departure, "let's get the big picture straight. Nasser's long-term objective is to get his hands on the Gulf's oil. He's already moved 30,000 troops into the Yemen. If he can control that country, he's in a strong position to get us out of South Arabia altogether. That would leave his route to the Gulf wide open. Naturally, that's not in our interests. Gulf oil apart, Aden's our most important overseas base, and the BP refinery and the Port of Aden are vitally important to world commerce. Aden's internal security is therefore crucial. That's why your job is important. I'll give you one piece of advice – make it your business to get on well with the senior officers of the Aden Police Force."

I left Bushell's office puzzled how Aden's internal security apparatus could be effective without its Chief Minister's direct involvement. Back at my own desk, I carefully reread the secret papers that Thorne had given me. It transpired that on the day of Aden's accession, 18 January 1963, Oates, the Deputy High Commissioner, had written to the Chief Minister to spell out the bizarre constitutional position that left Bayoomi with no direct responsibility for internal security in his own state. As a sop, Oates had invited him to become a member of his own Internal Security Committee, "to ensure the closest co-operation and full consultation on all aspects of internal security between myself and yourself". Bayoomi's dignified letter of acceptance – "I trust that in this way a policy on internal security may be evolved which is acceptable to Her Majesty's Government and the National Government of Aden" – was a model of self-restraint.

Hasan Bayoomi was a seasoned street fighter who had already faced down the ATUC's and nationalist opposition to merger. He probably knew more about the threats to Aden's internal security than anyone, and had once told Trevaskis that if the British wanted to prevent Aden falling under Yemeni control, they should "leave it to us Adenis". Having been intimately involved in the merger negotiations, Bayoomi must have realized what he was signing up to and, given his high standing with the Federal rulers, would probably have worked out an effective *modus operandi* with them. However, the chances of any successor reaching a comparable level of rapprochement were almost certainly doomed by the breathtaking pronouncement of Sultan Salih Al-'Audhali, the Federal Minister of Internal Security, that he did not wish "to establish any special committee for internal security of the Federation as a whole", and that if he wished to give any general direction to the Ruler of any State this would be done to the Ruler concerned. In the case of Aden he would, when necessary, "confer with the Deputy High Commissioner with or without the Chief Minister".

Aden's internal security presented the British with a difficult dilemma. While Britain's long-term objective was to give South Arabia's indigenous peoples self-government, it also had to strike a balance between safeguarding its own strategic and economic interests, while still respecting the sensibilities of the newly installed Federal government. The Federal Constitution's internal security provisions, pitched far too heavily in favour of the tribal rulers, effectively compromised both.

Nigel Morris's recommendations for Aden's internal security chain of command envisaged three separate committees. First in line was the Deputy High Commissioner's Internal Security Committee, or "ISC", briefed to direct and oversee Aden's internal security apparatus, and to ensure that all intelligence was made available to enable the Government "to formulate policy and take appropriate and timely executive action". Membership included top-ranking civil and military officers, as well as the Chief Minister. However, only one British member, Laurie Hobson, a former senior Political Officer, spoke fluent Arabic.

Second in seniority came the Chief Minister's Sub-Committee which, give or take a few, had broadly the same cast list, with a remit "to counteract any threat to Aden's security". However, before any executive action could be taken, the Chief Minister had to seek the Deputy High Commissioner's approval. Third in line was the Aden Internal Security Liaison Committee, or "AISLC", briefed to liaise with the Government, Armed Services and Police, and "to prepare all internal security operational plans ... organize IS training and combined exercises ... and ensure that the internal security machine is at all times geared for immediate action." As DMS (Security), I was a member of all three committees and secretary of the AISLC.

During my time, the Deputy High Commissioner's ISC was only convened once, and the Chief Minister's never. Bayoomi was too ill to chair his own committee and, by June, he was dead. His successor, an enigmatic thirty-two-year-old Adeni merchant, Sayyid Zain Baharoon, had been elected to the Aden's Legislative Council only six months before. Sir Charles Johnston considered him to be more "open-minded" than Bayoomi in his attitude to the ATUC and Aden's nationalist opposition. Baharoon proved this soon enough by lifting the ban on the inflammatory Egyptian newspapers, then freely available in Aden. He was unused to the administrative machinery of government, and averse to taking decisions without lengthy consultations with his own Executive Committee, a cabal of Adeni cronies. He was also reluctant to engage his British officials, save for Robin Thorne, and gave "pressure of work" as an excuse for not convening his own sub-committee. The real reason was justifiable pique about his subordinate internal security role, something he made abundantly clear at the London constitutional conference later that year, when he fell out disastrously with the Federal ministers.

The AISLC was handicapped from the start. It never received a proper steer from the Deputy High Commissioner's ISC; it was ignored by the Chief Minister; and the Federal Ministry of Internal Security made no attempt to liaise with its members. Answerable to both the High Commissioner and the Commander-in-Chief, it had, as its joint chairmen, the Garrison Security Commander and the Commissioner of Police. When on leave, the latter was replaced by a senior MI5 officer, John Lawrence, a charming if discomfortingly relaxed Australian. His opposite number, Brigadier Mike Harbottle, was a brave soldier and former commander of the Green Jackets, but above all a man of peace. True to his colours, after leaving Aden, Harbottle became a member of the messianic "Generals for Peace" movement and, ultimately, Director of the Centre for International Peace-building.

Harbottle at least strove to rationalize Aden's chaotic IS chain of command by attempting to cut down the ever-proliferating subordinate military security committees. He also tried to reactivate the lapsed Federal–Aden Joint Internal Security Committee. Unfortunately, neither he nor Lawrence had the political clout to resolve the inherent organizational problems that handicapped Aden's internal security apparatus. Their joint chairmanship, although amicable, led to divided loyalties.

The AISLC had no intelligence-gathering role of its own and, without regular access to top-level intelligence, was therefore unable to fulfil its brief of preparing "all internal security operational plans". At this time, the true nature of the terrorist threat to Aden had not been appreciated. Reliable intelligence on the Yemen was further limited after the British Legation in Ta'izz was closed down in January 1963, as a reprisal for Britain not recognizing the new revolutionary regime. Only when a former wartime hero, Lieutenant Colonel "Billy" McLean MP, undertook a personal fact-finding mission to Royalist areas, did London get first-hand information about the military situation in the Yemen. The Federal rulers had their own tribal intelligence networks, but as the Federal–Aden Joint IS committee never met, nothing from that source came AISLC's way.

In the higher echelons of the High Commission Office, I assumed that there had to be some loftier intelligence forum to which the AISLC was never privy. Socially, I often met John Bushell, Hilary Colville-Stewart, Aden's Chief Intelligence Officer, his deputy James Bridges and others in the British Security Services, but never on official business. Occasionally, the AISLC received Aden Intelligence Centre *Digests*, and the mysterious Local Intelligence Committee's *Longer Term Security Forecasts*. However, none of the gentlemen who ran either organization ever attended AISLC meetings. Intelligence was a jealously hoarded commodity, and its dissemination uncoordinated. Not until the appointment of Brigadier Cowper as Director of Intelligence in 1965 was a unified organization made responsible for Federal internal security. By then, both the Aden Police and general population had been so intimidated that locally gathered intelligence had effectively dried up.

All this lay in the future. When I first joined the AISLC in April 1963, it was still mulling over an earlier IS report entitled *Terrorism and Sabotage*. This had identified the more obvious terrorist targets as key civilian and military personnel, the British Armed Forces, and the Aden Police, particularly Special Branch. It was also known that unidentified Adenis were receiving terrorist training in Yemen, Iraq and Egypt. Nonetheless, the Local Intelligence Committee's March forecast was that, although there might be unspecified terrorist incidents towards the end of June, Aden's immediate internal security threat was low.

As the torrid summer months dragged by without serious incident, I tackled Bob Waggitt, a veteran of the Malayan and Cyprus emergencies, and currently Head of Special Branch, as to why this should be.

"I don't get it, Bob. Egypt has invaded the Yemen. Cairo and San'a Radios are both spewing out noxious anti-British and Federal propaganda every day. We've been told that cadres of revolutionaries are being trained to terrorize Aden, yet nothing seems to be happening here. We're none the wiser, and our committee seems to be sitting on its collective hands."

"I don't see it quite like that," replied Waggitt. "We had a foretaste of how external pressures can trigger internal troubles when that tiresome United Nations Committee came over from New York to investigate what they called the Aden Problem. When we refused them admission, they traipsed off to Cairo complaining to the world's press about British repression. That sparked off three days of demonstrations, and the Armed Police had to use tear gas and arrest over a hundred of the blighters."

"But surely, we're well used to ATUC demonstrations by now, and how to deal with them."

"Maybe, but don't underestimate the ATUC or its leader Al-Asnag. They've opened up offices in London, Cairo, Baghdad and San'a, and have sent missions to Middle Eastern and Soviet bloc capitals, and even to the UN, all funded by our Egyptian chums, of course."

"Okay. But what about hard-core terrorism? That troupe of Egyptian entertainers pushing anti-British propaganda at the Bilqis Cinema barely raised a ripple. Those Egyptian footballers chanting "Gamal Abdul Nasser" in the stadium would have been eaten alive at Millwall. The bomb that blew up the Shaikh Othman Youth Club was just some idiot playing with gun cotton, to celebrate the Yemen Revolution. None of this was serious stuff and seems to have lulled us into a sense of false security. Our committee seems to lack any sense of urgency. I just hope that we can move a lot faster if a real crunch comes."

"I shouldn't worry too much," said Bob, soothingly. "Most Adenis have never had it so good. They'll be getting their independence soon enough anyway. I've seen some real emergencies in my time, but we have nothing to fear here. The Adeni is temperamentally incapable of mounting a serious terrorist campaign."

Shortly afterwards, someone lobbed a Soviet-bloc grenade into the offices of the South Arabian News Agency, killing two newsmen. The British Forces Broadcasting Studios reacted immediately by installing anti-terrorist security measures. I submitted detailed recommendations to the Chief Minister as to how we might improve our own at the Government Broadcasting Studios. He never even bothered to reply.

We were living in a Fool's Paradise. Aden was still enjoying a completely free press with twenty-three newspapers, both local and Egyptian, reflecting every shade of political opinion. Yet one critically important news item barely raised an official eyebrow. This was the announcement, made by San'a in July, that a National Liberation Front (NLF) had been formed to rid South Yemen of the British by force. The NLF had never featured on the AISLC's agenda. If our own intelligence services knew anything about this organization, they never passed it on. The NLF was to play the leading role in hastening Britain's eventual withdrawal from South Arabia, yet it was outlawed only in 1965.

The NLF was originally spawned from the clandestine Arab Nationalist Movement, founded by George Habash, the son of a Greek Orthodox grain merchant, who propagated the gospel of Pan-Arabism in the aftermath of the Palestinian and Arab states' humiliating defeat by Israel in 1948. Subsequently he became the guerrilla leader of the Marxist-Palestinian faction that pioneered sky-jacking and other terrorist tactics. The NLF's ideology and tactics drew its inspiration from Marxist-Soviet models and, by the late 1950s, had identified British South Arabia as a prime revolutionary target. Whereas its rival terrorist organization, the Egyptian-backed Front for the Liberation of South Yemen (FLOSY), was basically urban and Pan-Arabist, the NLF recruited Aden's skilled and semi-skilled workforce, government servants and student radicals, as well as disaffected tribesmen, who were peddled a political line aimed at undermining tribal loyalty and fomenting discontent by attributing the hinterland's impoverishment to feudal rule and British colonialism.

The NLF was a formidable and elusive opponent. Aden's last High Commissioner, Sir Humphrey Trevelyan, records in his book, *Public and Private*, that he never once met any of its members. Given the experience of other British colonial governments in dealing effectively with terrorist campaigns in Cyprus, Malaysia and Kenya, our initial failure to identify the full measure of Aden's terrorist threat remains puzzling. Contributing factors were the breakdown in relations between the Federal rulers and Aden's ministers; the Federal Ministry of Internal Security's incomprehensible failure to liaise effectively; and the High Commission's bizarre disengagement from the AISLC. Above all, the flawed Federal constitution, later described by Trevelyan as "deplorable", created confusion at the highest level. Trevaskis, who succeeded Johnston as High Commissioner in August 1963, records that his recommendation to give the Federal rulers full control over Internal Security was rejected by Whitehall. Yet, under the Federal constitution which he had so vigorously promoted, Internal Security was specifically designated a Federal responsibility. Ultimately, it was up to the rulers and their British advisers to make it work.

Trevaskis also laid the charge that Aden's British officialdom was "remote, ignorant, superlatively complacent and untroubled by any nationalist challenge to its authority". In fact, complacency extended right up the line. When first appointed High Commissioner, Trevaskis failed to take a sufficiently firm grip on the Federal internal security apparatus until the botched attempt to assassinate him and other Federal ministers at Aden Airport in December 1963. This triggered a swift and robust response, but it was his successor, Turnbull, who first co-ordinated the Federal–Aden security apparatus in 1965. Another mystery is why the British Secret Intelligence Service, fully operational and conspicuously invisible in Aden after merger in January 1963, apparently failed to appreciate the extent of the terrorist threat until it had seized Aden firmly by the throat.

11

Port, Police and Politics

Although the AISLC never had access to the hard intelligence that might have enabled it "to ensure that the internal security machine is at all times geared for immediate action", we did have a decent stab at updating Aden's internal security operational plans. These, together with statutory emergency regulations, had been on the stocks ever since riots triggered by the creation of the State of Israel in 1947 had left more than a hundred dead in the streets. The 1962 Yemen Revolution, bringing with it the Egyptian Army's full-scale invasion, posed an altogether more serious threat to British South Arabia than anything hitherto.

The AISLC's Top Secret *Emergency Book* detailed measures to deal with counter-terrorism, riot control, deportation, individual and collective security, house searches, and the suppression of inflammatory publications. Additionally, there were various Top Secret Emergency Schemes files designed to safeguard key security points, which I happened to discover lurking overt in Jock's filing cabinet. All needed updating and, to inject some urgency into proceedings, an AISLC sub-committee was established to review each scheme and report back weekly to the main committee.

We first selected the critically important *Port Working in an Emergency* scheme as a suitable case for treatment. This prescribed measures to counter any sabotage or strike action that might otherwise cripple the Port of Aden, and thus jeopardize the Colony's economy and food supply. Although frequently deliberated upon in the past, this scheme had never been finalized because the

Aden Port Trust (APT), the Aden Government and the Armed Services could never agree on a concerted implementation policy. Although it was common ground that if local labour went on strike, the port could function only by drafting in British troops, beyond that, each party had different priorities.

The APT, primarily responsible for running the port, had to ensure that bunkering and watering facilities were maintained to prevent the world's shipping fleets otherwise bypassing Aden, probably for ever. The Government had not only to safeguard the Colony and military base, but also to take into account the potential political and legal consequences that would follow if British troops were mobilized to work the Port, and requisition essential supplies from foreign vessels. The Armed Services had to determine precise troop numbers in the light of their other military commitments. Additionally, the AISLC had to work out pooling arrangements with the international oil companies, and also discover how long the BP Refinery could continue to function with only expatriate staff. How these arrangements might fit into the Federal administrative framework was never tested.

BP responded immediately. Its expatriate staff could run the Refinery unassisted at 100 percent capacity for one month, at 75 percent capacity for a second, and at 50 percent for a third. The APT flatly refused to accept the Armed Services' estimates that between 88 and 475 troops might be needed, depending on stoppage lengths, and the number of holds and shifts to be worked. BP apart, the only statistical certainty was that Aden's essential stockpiles would last a fortnight. I then discovered that no account had been taken of the Federal States' requirements.

The workings of the Federal Government at Al-Ittihad in this particular area were a mystery. Luckily, I knew Pat Sweeney, the Federal Collector of Customs and Excise, from pre-Federation days.

"You've certainly got a problem here," said Sweeney. "No one seems to know whether this is a Federal or State responsibility. It should be that of the Controller of Civil Supplies but no one has yet been appointed. Sayyid Darwish, the Federal Minister for Commerce, has sensibly suggested to Aden that I should take on the job, but there's been no response to date, and my appointment can't be confirmed until it's been formally gazetted. Anyway, as I'm just about to go on leave, everything will grind to a halt until I return. I can knock you up some unofficial figures, though no attributions please. It's not worth my job."

Sweeney's figures tallied almost exactly with those of the APT. However, Harbottle refused to make a formal submission to his Commander-in-Chief without having the official Federal figures, backed by an Aden Government directive. This impasse could only be resolved at the highest level, so I submitted a recommendation to Oates, the Deputy High Commissioner, that a temporary Controller be appointed immediately. Procedurally, this had to be channelled through the Chief Minister personally. Weeks later, I discovered that the file had never left his desk.

An important part of my brief was to represent the Aden Civil Police. Until my first AISLC meeting, I had never met the furiously moustachioed Deputy Commissioner, "Tash" Gould, a policeman of the old school, who made no pretence of his dismay on finding that his old mucker Jock Snell's replacement should be a fresh-faced pen-pusher. After Harbottle had introduced me to each of the committee's members in turn, Gould raised his hand. "I must raise an objection, Mr Chairman. I don't know anything about Mr Harding, but I don't consider him a suitable person for this job." After an embarrassed silence, Harbottle asked Gould to explain why. "I have nothing personal against this young man, but he's altogether too inexperienced to take on this responsibility. He can't know a thing about internal security, or the Police for that matter." Harbottle contrived some soothing formula. Subsequently, Gould and I became good friends, for I had taken Bushell's advice to heart.

The Aden Police Force had originally been established in the mid-19th century on Imperial Indian principles. In 1929, it was reorganized into two separate branches: the Civil Police to maintain law and order, and the paramilitary Armed Police Force to quell riots, guard Government House, and garrison Perim and Kamaran. Special Branch was a separate, elite organization, staffed by senior British and Arab officers, mainly to undertake surveillance and the dangerous business of infiltration.

The Force's senior officers upheld the best traditions of the British Colonial Police. However, at AISLC meetings, there was a degree of wariness between the Armed Services' representatives and the policemen. The former took social precedence in the colonial pecking order. The latter considered most servicemen to be purveyors of unreliable, second-hand intelligence who knew little Arabic, and even less of what really went on in Crater and Shaikh Othman.

Just before he had gone on leave, the Commissioner of Police, Arthur

Wiltshire, gave me a frank assessment about the problems he faced as a result of Aden's merger. "Before merger, both the Civil and Armed Police were my operational responsibility, and I was directly answerable to the Governor. After merger, the Armed Police became a Federal Force under the operational control of the Federal Minister of the Interior, Sharif Husain. They're still based in Crater, and are supposed to be Aden's first line of defence. However, neither Sharif Husain nor his civil servants ever come near this place, and I now have to go through every sort of bureaucratic loop before I can use them. They're recruited from WAP tribes, and as their strongest affinities are with individual Federal Ministers, many Adenis now regard them as a quasi-military Federal Force with a mandate to control Aden at their rulers' whim. My relationship with the Chief Minister is further complicated because the constitution gives him limited powers, which can only be exercised at the High Commissioner's discretion. Operational control still remains mine."

As the newly appointed Chief Minister's man, I felt it prudent to move on to less sensitive ground.

"How d'you see the terrorist threat? Bushell seems to think that the Police are seriously understaffed."

"Certainly, we *are* seriously understaffed, though there's nothing new in that. I don't see terrorism as an immediate Aden problem, though I'm less sanguine than some. Basically, we must have more policemen of the right calibre, as Nigel Morris recommended. Unfortunately, his report seems to have got stuck somewhere along the line. The best thing you can do for us is to get it unstuck."

The Morris Report, submitted to London the previous December, envisaged a rolling police expansion programme over the three years 1963–66, including a recruitment drive and the construction of 500 new police houses. When Whitehall predictably rejected it as over-ambitious, I knew that there was scant hope of getting that sort of money from either the Federation or Aden State. Police funding was already so tight that I was having to draft parliamentary answers for the Chief Minister, in response to irate Legislative Councillors demanding to know why British policemen were decently housed when Arab police officers' houses were still without water, electricity or basic furniture. The Director of Federal Works made it quite clear that even if he had the money, there was no capacity to build houses on the scale recommended by Morris. Anyway, the allocation of building land had got hopelessly bogged down in a demarcation dispute between Kenyon and Federal officials.

I went back to Baharoon with a severely tailored police expansion scheme, suggesting that Aden State might be prepared to fund it alone. As Chief Minister, he controlled the budget, but the slight of having no operational control so rankled that he dragged his feet. As a result, we missed the closing date for the 1963–64 budget estimates. I then submitted a scaled-down version for the following year, including provision for a new patrol boat to replace three antiquated wooden *sanbuq*s, and a fire-fighting launch, essential to safeguarding the Port. I never discovered whether these proposals were accepted or, more likely, pruned to destruction. The Aden Police deserved better than this. Wiltshire always held them in high regard. Three years on, the NLF's selective assassination campaign against Special Branch left it non-operational, and its infiltration had so undermined both the Civil and Armed Police that neither force remained reliable.

Deportation taught me something about the Aden Police's operational methods, and the political pressures they laboured under. Although Aden's frontiers were porous, Westminster-style statutes had always existed to rid the Colony of vagrants, criminals and other undesirables. Deportation was always subject to a strict legal process involving hearings before a magistrate, and an appeals procedure via the Commissioner of Police, Attorney-General, Chief Minister and Deputy High Commissioner. As DMS, I might be involved at all stages of this time-consuming process.

After merger, deportation took on an altogether wider political dimension. The Federal Constitution treated it as an internal security matter and, as such, it should have fallen within the remit of the Minister for Internal Security, Sultan Salih. Paradoxically, as in the case of the Armed Police, it was allotted to the Minister of the Interior, Sharif Husain. When deportation cases touched on ministerial self-interest, special pleading followed as a matter of course. A senior policeman explained his quandary thus:

"It's becoming increasingly difficult to uphold the rule of law with all the political interference we're now having to contend with. There's this case of Ahmed Sa'id Dubai, an Adeni of Yemeni extraction, who pretends he's a cloth merchant. In reality, he runs a gang of Port pilferers, and operates as a fence, selling on stolen goods to complicit merchants. They then make bogus claims against British insurance companies. It's become such a serious racket that it's damaging the Port's trading reputation. After months of surveillance, we reckoned that we'd got him nailed. Now, we've hit a serious snag. Ahmed Sa'id's married to an Adeni girl whose father's a rich merchant, and a close friend of Baharoon's. Ever since his arrest, we've been bombarded with petitions from him and other Aden worthies, all protesting the rogue's innocence. Lack of progress is making us look like donkeys."

Before taking the matter up with Baharoon, I spent hours investigating and cross-checking the minutiae of the case. It confirmed everything the police had told me. I submitted a detailed memorandum to the Chief Minister, recommending that he support a deportation order. The file never got further than his Executive Committee.

Potentially more serious political problems arose from the Federal Constitution's ambiguities. Post-merger, Aden still retained its original colonial deportation statutes, even though the *1963 Federal Deportation Ordinance* gave the Federal Minister of the Interior overriding powers of deportation. Sharif Husain had no truck with legal niceties, and even less for Baharoon. Thus, he had no qualms about issuing deportation orders direct to the Police Commissioner over the Chief Minister's head, to the latter's impotent fury. Nonetheless, it was generally assumed that the High Commissioner, or his deputy, remained the final arbiter in the appeals process.

This was put to the test when a rabidly anti-Federalist 18-year-old Yemeni, Abdullah Al-Qirshi, personally insulted both the Federal Ministers for External Affairs and Internal Security. Everyone, even including Baharoon, supported Sharif Husain's deportation order, with one exception. This was the desperately fair-minded Deputy High Commissioner, Tom Oates, who invoked his overriding powers to reject the order, on the grounds of insufficient evidence. To resolve the impasse, I convened meetings with Donald Foster, Sharif Husain's Permanent Secretary, the Deputy Police Commissioner and the High Commission Office. Predictably, no one would budge, so I sought a formal legal opinion from the Attorney-General, Mike Maloney, as to whether Federal or Aden law prevailed. Maloney ruled that although the High Commissioner was the constitutional "Ruler" of Aden, he himself might be subject to "general directions" given by the Federal Minister of Internal Security. This confused the situation still further because the Minister of Internal Security was Sultan Salih rather than Sharif Husain. In attempting to make sense of this imbroglio, the Attorney-General concluded that it was "most undesirable that a Federal Minister should direct the Aden Police in any way …. If there is to be a harmonious and co-ordinated policy … surely it is only simple common sense that all these questions be settled by agreement."

Unfortunately, "simple common sense" was rare in such matters. I submitted yet another recommendation to the Deputy High Commissioner that this situation could only be resolved at the highest level. Inevitably, the file had to be channelled through the Chief Minister. Days before I relinquished my post as a DMS, the file mysteriously reappeared on my desk without comment. It transpired that it had never left the Chief Minister's desk. Probably, it didn't matter anyway. Police records showed that more than forty deportation orders had been made against a single individual, who simply came and went across the border, as and when he pleased.

On 5 October, Jock Snell breezed into the office after home leave to reclaim his old job.

"Well, how's it all been going, old cock? Any blow-ups, assassinations or riots to report?"

"Very little like that, Jock. Things have been pretty quiet, really. I'm doing you some handing-over notes to bring you up to speed."

"Just as I expected," grinned Jock. "But don't bother about the notes. Just fill me in lickety spit."

"The only real trouble we've had was when the ATUC staged a riot after Trevaskis sent that UN Mission from New York packing."

"Pass on that," countered Jock. "Read all about it in the British papers."

"We've also had the odd demonstration, a bomb attack on the Aden News Agency, which killed a couple of its staff, and a Soviet-made grenade scare. However, according to the LIC September assessment, no serious security threats are forecast for the next three months save for isolated terrorist acts."

"Guessed as much," grinned Jock. "That lot always hedge their bets. Then why's it all been so quiet?"

"The Police seem to have nipped trouble in the bud, and the ATUC have kept their heads down. Most ordinary Adenis seem to have lost interest in politicized protest movements. Special Branch reckon that they've got the situation under control."

"I gather that Al-Asnag was arrested for his trouble during one demonstration and put inside."

"Yes, but released soon after. He then pushed off to Cairo, where he's been twiddling his thumbs."

"Up to more than that, I reckon," grunted Jock. "He's a dangerous man. Needs watching. Then what's happened to those security committees Morris set up?"

"A bit of a disaster area, I'm afraid. The Deputy High Commissioner's only held one ISC meeting since you left, and the Chief Minister refuses either to attend or convene meetings. Only the AISLC meets regularly. We've been trying to revise the Emergency Book, but so far we've only got as far as the Port Emergency Scheme, and even that's incomplete. There's still an awful lot of work to be done."

Jock was beginning to look pensive, and changed the subject. "What happened to that Morris report on the Police? And d'you see much of Baharoon? I never had anything to do with him."

When I explained the difficulties I was having, Jock's eyes began to glaze.

"So nothing changes then, though it doesn't sound too bad overall. My sources tell me that the Gyppos are so pushed in the Yemen that they've reverted to bombing the Royalists and civilians with poison gas. We might even be winning that one. Cheer up! Let's off to the Union Club. You look as if you need a drink."

The prospect of reverting to an Assistant Secretary's stolid clay needed more than a drink. For the past five months, I felt I had been doing something really useful. Robin Thorne had written to thank me for having acted "so zealously and efficiently with the heavy, and at times frustrating, work". Now I was now back to square one. Furthermore, with only three more months to run before I was due for my next home leave, any prospect of the half-promised WAP posting had vanished.

Aden had changed noticeably over the past year. British officialdom was having to adjust to the new regime, and many familiar faces were about to leave for good. Alastair McIntosh and his pards, regrouped on Aden, were finding progressively less and less to admire in modern life. Alastair himself had retired a few days after Jock's return. He was only fifty, but alcohol abuse had taken its toll. During his Aden swansong, as Principal Adviser to the High Commissioner, he had stuck tenaciously to a daily post-work routine. Drinks at the Union Club were followed by a very late luncheon at his official residence, Lake House. Here, the menu was invariably the same. The soup's otherwise unmemorable taste was enlivened by Alastair's hot pepper sauces, brewed in two old gin bottles. One was named "Archie", after Archie Wilson, and the other "Lionel", after Lionel Folkard, a one-armed, former RAF wartime hero, now working in the WAP Office. Luncheon would occupy the rest of the afternoon. During it, Alastair might reminisce about his early days in the WAP, his explorations of Jebel Jihaf, and his hero "Ham", the Hon. R. A. B. Hamilton, Master of Belhaven. If you stayed the course, he might finish up with a poetry recital, or anecdotes of his Oxford days. And then, as the shades of evening closed, and the lights of Little Aden began to blink across the bay, you would wander off into the night pie-eyed to face the real world.

For me, Tony Boyle's departure was a particular loss. During my early Aden days, we had shared many adventures together. His father, Sir Dermot Boyle, had been Marshal of the Royal Air Force. Tony, the High Commissioner's meticulously efficient ADC, had also seemed set for a brilliant RAF career. When, at his farewell party at Government House, he told me that he was resigning from the RAF to support the clandestine guerrilla campaign being waged in the Yemen against the Egyptian Army, I began to understand why he had sometimes seemed so distant and preoccupied. Paradoxically, it was this unofficial campaign, rather than anything mounted by HQ Middle East Command in Aden, that ultimately frustrated Nasser's Yemeni ambitions.

When, in late 1962, Egyptian forces invaded the Yemen in the wake of the Yemen Revolution, Macmillan's cabinet had been divided on whether to recognize the new regime or back the Royalist resistance. While the politicians dithered, David Stirling, founder of the SAS, suggested to Colonel Jim Johnson, a Welsh Guardsman during the Second World War and former SAS officer, that he "put something together". Stirling came to Aden to stay with Sir Charles Johnston, an old friend from Cairo days who had firmly opposed HMG recognizing the Yemeni republicans. Surreptitiously, Stirling enlisted Boyle to act as Jim Johnson's liaison link and second-in-command. As the High Commissioner's ADC, Boyle had to keep a very low profile, but played a critical role organizing back-up for the handful of SAS "Advisers" spread around the loyal Yemeni tribesmen fighting an invading Egyptian army which had no compunction about using napalm, poison and gas against civilians. Tony personally flew sixteen sorties from Tel Aviv in adapted ex-USAF bombers, over-flying Jordan and then skimming down the Red Sea before turning inland at Hudaida to drop supplies and arms to Royalist positions in the Yemen. Funded largely by the Saudi Arabian government, the Royalists fought an ultimately successful war of attrition in the Yemen in which the Egyptians lost 10,000 men, and which Nasser later regarded as having been his "Vietnam". After 1967, Tony Boyle retired to farm in Shropshire. Both he and Jim Johnson unexpectedly died in 2008.

Shortly after my reversion to Assistant Secretary, the Meynells kindly invited me for a third visit to Dhala'. Three months earlier, I had joined a select tourist group to support Aden Airways' inaugural weekend at the restored Government Rest House. Advertised as "A new Rendezvous for Tourists and Photographers' Paradise, in the perfect setting for a quiet family holiday", it offered trips to the suq, camel and donkey rides, Land-Rover excursions up Jebel Jihaf, and shooting competitions "by special arrangement".

Godfrey met us at the Dhala' airstrip. The Naib's son made a speech of welcome, while a Federal Guard detachment took up defensive positions to scan the surrounding countryside for incipient trouble. Our inspection of the refurbished Dhala' Hotel was cut short when the escorting guardsmen flighted steel darts around the Recreation Room like paper pellets. Rather than risk the great indoors, we all opted for the Land-Rover trip up Jebel Jihaf. Next day, most took a longer variant of this same trip in preference to donkey rides. We survived a nerve-shredding descent down the mountain to meet Godfrey's deadline to attend a football match between the Marines and Dhala' that evening, "to give comfort to our own boys and show non-partisan support for the local lads", as he put it.

Ever since Mukalla, I'd had an aversion to football matches, but then, at least, I had been playing for the home team. Here, we were linked irredeemably with the opposition. And whereas in Mukalla firearms were banned, in Dhala' every able-bodied male shouldered a .303 Lee Enfield. Although the Commandos had the brawn, Dhala' were the more skilful team and, with only five minutes to go, scored the first goal of the match. At this, the whole place erupted. Armed spectators invaded the pitch brandishing *jambiyya*s, hurling sand into the air and yelling at the tops of their voices. One elderly man standing next to me became so excited at the prospect of victory that he smashed his thermos flask on the ground, and then swung round to face me belligerently, his eyes blazing.

After a detachment of armed police had cleared the pitch, the match continued. The referee then displayed exceptional courage by disallowing a

Dhala' goal for offside. This, incredibly, restored an uneasy calm, until the Marines were awarded a penalty for a blatant Dhala' foul in the game's dying moments. And now the atmosphere suddenly turned ugly. Gnarled fingers tightened around *jambiyya*s, rifles were unslung, and a Marine detachment hurriedly took up defensive positions. Whether by luck or good judgement, the penalty shot sailed over the bar, whereupon the referee blew the final whistle. Making our way back to the hotel under armed escort, Godfrey's considered verdict was: "A good political result." In fact, this was to be Aden Airways' one and only Dhala' tourist weekend. The night after we flew back to Aden, the Federal Army camp was attacked for the first time in months.

Three months on, Dhala' was no longer "the perfect setting for a family holiday". Godfrey met me at the airstrip clad in an Airtex shirt, shorts and gym shoes. Looking as if he meant business, he threw down the gauntlet even as we shook hands.

"Fancy a quick walk up the Jihaf?" he challenged, his chin thrust forward provocatively.

"From here, Godfrey?"

"Yes. Why not? I must inspect a couple of the forts up there to make sure that everyone's primed for action. Security's deteriorated a lot since you were last here."

The Dhala' airstrip lay at 5,000 ft, and Jihaf was nearly 3,000 ft higher. I wasn't acclimatized, I wasn't fit, and I had unwisely burdened myself with a holdall full of heavy camera equipment.

"Okay, if you really want to," I replied, apprehensively.

To Godfrey, hard physical exercise was just another excuse to mortify the flesh. When working, very briefly, at the WAP Office, he had pounded the streets of Khormaksar so hard, "to get fit for the hills", that he had impacted a disc, and for ever after had been forced to wear a Curzon-style back brace, something I only learned about years later. Without another word he shot off, leaving me and our escort trailing in his wake. Every time I tried to get near the front to photograph the column of red-capped soldiers weaving their way through fields of golden millet, Godfrey piled on the pace. By the time we had reached the fort at Sarir, I felt so weak that a kindly guardsman insisted that I eat a whole tin of peaches.

"D'you mind if we bash on?" said Godfrey, tiptoeing impatiently as if to deliver an uppercut. "I'd like to inspect that fort at Hayb. It's a particularly good viewpoint to see what's going on down in the Qataba Plain." I was beginning to know this particular view only too well, and assumed that, by now, the place must be swarming with Egyptian massed armour.

"Of course not, Godfrey," I wheezed. "But how far to go?"

"Not that far. Might add a couple of hours, provided we get a move on. You'll have plenty of scope for photography en route."

The views from Hayb were higher and wider than before, but otherwise indistinguishable. As we peered down to a familiar scattering of scratchy fields and a skein of dried-up wadi beds, Godfrey frowned and muttered: "Looks suspiciously quiet down there. Don't like that. However, now we've got this far, might as well carry on to Qarna, if you're up to it."

I wasn't really up to it, and suddenly remembered that Qarna was the same fort that our Aden Airways group had taken two hours to reach by Land Rover. However, there was no going back now. By the time we got there, it was so late that the vehicles scheduled to meet us half way down the mountain had already returned to base. At dinner that night at the Royal Marines' mess, I almost fell asleep over the soup.

Next day, Godfrey insisted that we make a lightning tour of Dhala'. A couple of men in crumpled town suits kept following us around.

"Don't worry about them. They're just Mobiloil agents," said Godfrey, after getting rid of them. "They've been looking for a bit of land on which to build a filling station. I've told them several times before that they're wasting their time. Sayyid Darwish, the Federal Minister of Commerce, already owns the land on which Shell have already built a filling station, so no one else will get a look in."

Walking back to Bait Meynell, I sensed that Godfrey was preoccupied with more than filling stations.

"What's the problem?" I asked him.

"Long story," he replied, gloomily. "I'm afraid we may be about to have trouble with the Qutaibi. You remember the Bursi? Well, one of his close chums, Shaikh Saif Hassan Ali, the premier Radfan chief, is demanding that the Federation recognize Qutaibi as an independent State. In return, he says he'll guarantee us free passage along the Dhala' road. The devil he will!"

"Not a good deal, then?"

"Absolutely not," thundered Godfrey. "It's the most outrageous bloody cheek. There are at least nine other Radfan tribes apart from the Qutaibi, and most of them can't abide Saif and his wretched tribesmen. But this bodes ill. Almost anything's better than Qutaibi UDI. It might even rupture the Federation."

"Has this trouble just blown up?"

"No, but things have recently been taking a turn for the worse. There's always potential trouble brewing with the Qutaibi, about money usually. But in this case, I suspect it's something more sinister. Traditionally, the Qutaibi extracted tolls from traffic using the Dhala' Road. We were prepared to turn a blind eye provided it wasn't excessive. However, under the Federal Customs Union scheme, tolls have been abolished, and the compensatory customs payments now go direct to the Dhala' State Treasury. Shaikh Saif's spitting mad at losing control over his main source of revenue, so is now looking Yemen-wards. In the old days, if the Qutaibi misbehaved, we could usually knock some sense into them and make it up afterwards with handouts. But direct military action is now politically unacceptable, and the Egyptians are just across the border. I particularly don't like the way that so many Radfan tribesmen have pushed off to the Yemen and then come back with funny ideas. Only a week ago, a Qutaibi called Rajih Labuza had the gall to inform me by letter that no government patrols would be allowed up the Wadi Misrah in future. That's the main Qutaibi valley in Radfan, and everyone now knows that Labuza has directly challenged the Federal Government's authority. We can't let this go by, so I'm going up there tomorrow with a company of FNG to show the flag. You're welcome to come along too, if you want to."

Combat came as naturally to Godfrey as prudence might to others. Beneath the cloak of humility there lurked a savage competitor. Unfortunately, moral certitude sometimes overruled his judgement.

I could not refuse the challenge yet, as I shaved in semi-darkness next morning, I wondered what Godfrey was letting us in for. Well before dawn, our armoured convoy stole out of Dhala'. Godfrey's Land Rover was sandwiched between a Ferret armoured car with a six-wheeled, heavy-armoured Saladin following a regulatory ten minutes behind. We rumbled down the Khuraiba Pass to rendezvous at Thumair with a company of Federal National Guardsmen, commanded by Qaid Haidar Salih Al-Habili, a dashing young cousin of Sharif Husain, who had just flown up from Aden by helicopter to lead his men into battle.

Clad in a white shirt, shorts and gym shoes, Godfrey took a cursory salute from the fort's guard. After an impromptu orders group, we bundled into three Land Rovers and set off up the Wadi Misrah, closely followed by three open Bedford 3-ton lorries packed with Federal Guardsmen yelling out tribal war cries. The early morning sun shone directly into our faces as the convoy headed south towards the dark mass of the Radfan massif, its soaring flanks still festooned with diaphanous wreaths of night cloud.

My last "Company in Attack" exercise had been eight years before, in the wet Welsh hills above Trawsfynydd. The stark rock walls of the Wadi Misrah provided a very different setting. When the going became too rough, we abandoned the vehicles, split into three columns and marched up the wadi in file. One section threaded its way through golden fields of millet in the centre. The other two hugged the low stone walls flanking either side. Godfrey, an unmistakeable target in his white shirt, went straight up the middle, sometimes astride a fine stallion. Behind him followed a rag-tag of "loyal" Qutaibis whose ranks swelled at each bend, with every newcomer proffering advice on what lay ahead.

Suddenly, a hand in front shot up. "Get down!" shouted Godfrey, as everyone scattered for cover to take up firing positions behind the stone walls. All eyes were now focused on a three-storey, fortified house dominating the top of a rocky defile. It effectively blocked further access up the narrowing wadi, and commanded an impressive field of fire. A hoarse shouting match now ensued between those inside the house and those squatting behind the wall.

"What's happening?" I asked Godfrey, after this verbal exchange had gone on for several minutes.

"The owner of that house is Fadhl Muqbil, a Qutaibi shaikh. I think that he's on our side, but can't be certain. He claims that there's some hare-brained lunatic holed up there who evidently wants to shoot me."

Godfrey went into another huddle with Haidar. Then, at a signal, a swarm of guardsmen rushed the house under covering fire. They emerged minutes later, dragging out a weedy-looking youth who, after heated exchanges, was led away under guard.

"Could have been a lot worse," said Godfrey, after the initial excitement had died down. "Reckon we must have surprised him. Just as well there weren't more of them, or we'd have been in for real trouble. We'll take this chap away for questioning. Now that we've achieved our object, Haidar wants to withdraw."

It was 11 a.m., and getting very hot. At Haidar's command, the FNG company did a smart about-turn, and began marching away down the valley, laughing and chattering. For the first time that day, Godfrey looked relaxed. Then I heard the unmistakeable sound of bullets winging overhead: crack–thump, crack–thump. Within seconds, the entire company was back behind those stone walls, blazing away at an invisible enemy somewhere up the valley.

"Can't be that many of them," said Godfrey, grimly. "But they've got the advantage of height, and may be bringing reinforcements down from the hills."

After another huddle with Haidar, it was agreed that the FNG should secure a defensive position, and then withdraw in carefully orchestrated stages. For the next two hours, wireless messages went winging to and fro between the Wadi Misrah, Thumair, Dhala' and Aden. Four hours later, the entire company was back at Thumair without a single casualty. Yet, as we drove back to Dhala' that night, Godfrey was uncharacteristically silent. The road was now alive with heavy downward traffic, and our headlights could barely penetrate the dust raised by a massive convoy of armoured cars, lorries towing 25-pounders and Bedford 3-tonners. They were transporting the rest of the FNG's Dhala' battalion to Thumair, their tribal war chants clearly audible above the din.

That night, I signalled Robin Thorne for permission to stay on for a second day's play. He wasn't having it, and ordered me to be back at my desk by Monday morning. The only way out of Dhala' now was by the Army helicopter that left at dawn. When my alarm went off at 4 a.m., I could hear Godfrey preparing himself for battle in the next-door bedroom. Puzzled by a curious grunting noise and an unpleasant feral smell that permeated my own room, I flicking on my torch. At the end of my bed was perched a large ape. The brute would only budge when Honor bribed it outside with a bunch of bananas.

Seated beside the helicopter pilot as we flew south, I picked out the whitewashed fort at Thumair, glinting in the early morning sun. What looked like a couple of darts flashed up the Wadi Misrah. "Hunters," observed the pilot. "Must be real trouble down there." Even as he spoke, Godfrey and Qaid Haidar, with the full FNG battalion and supporting armour, were about to storm up the Misrah. In the skirmish that followed, the gauntlet thrower, Rajih Ghalib Labuza, was killed by a random shell. The FNG returned to base without a single casualty. At the time the outcome seemed satisfactory enough, but Godfrey's misgivings were to be justified. This was no tribal spat, rather the opening round in the NLF's Radfan insurrection. In years to come, Labuza was hailed as a Martyr of the Revolution, and the day on which he died, 14 October 1963, celebrated thereafter as the start of the war that liberated South Yemen from the British.

Back in Aden, my world had shrunk to briefing the Chief Minister on the most appropriate terms for extending the Salim Ali Abdu Bus Company's operating licence. Few had taken on board the import of the Wadi Misrah episode. Although it triggered a spate of low-key dissident activity, it was generally assumed that the Egyptians had become too preoccupied fighting the Royalists to bother too much with the Federal States. And then, on 22 November 1963, the world held its breath on the news of President Kennedy's assassination in Dallas. Kennedy's nerve might have saved the world from nuclear catastrophe, but his Middle East foreign policy of supporting Egypt to counter Russia's growing influence, and recognizing the Yemen revolutionaries in the face of British opposition, had undermined Britain's position in South Arabia. It also strengthened the resolve of the emerging terrorist organisations to destroy the Federation. Recently back in Aden after his spell in Cairo cosying up to Nasser, Abdullah Al-Asnag was busy devising a strategy which would, or so he hoped with Egyptian connivance, enable him eventually to inherit the mantle of British authority.

A month before, the British Minister of Defence, Peter Thorneycroft, had come to Aden to try to resolve the serious differences that had arisen between Aden and the other Federal states. It was agreed to follow up this attempt at mediation with a constitutional conference in London that December. As the South Arabian delegation, led by the High Commissioner, Sir Kennedy Trevaskis, assembled at Aden Airport on 10 December, a grenade was thrown in their midst. Trevaskis was the prime target, but George Henderson, the WAP's Deputy British Agent, threw himself forward to deflect the blast. The High Commissioner escaped with only minor injuries. Henderson died in hospital two weeks later from grenade splinters. He was posthumously awarded a bar to the George Medal he had won a few years earlier, when routing single-handed a gang of dissident 'Aulaqi tribesmen.

The airport grenade killed two people and wounded another 51. Trevaskis immediately declared a State of Emergency, deported 280 Yemenis and interned 57 prominent members of the ATUC–PSP including Al-Asnag. One of them, Khalifa Abdullah Hassan Al-Khalifa, was arrested and charged with Henderson's murder. The case against him fell apart when the prosecution's main witness disappeared. The following April, he was released from prison at Anthony Greenwood's request, following his election to LEGCO.

Trevaskis's prompt measures created a hysterical reaction throughout the Arab world, the United Nations and in Soviet satellite countries. Condemnations poured forth from Cairo and San'a Radios. At the PSP's invitation, Britain's Labour Opposition despatched a Parliamentary Delegation to Aden. This criticized Trevaskis personally, and the Federal rulers collectively, for adopting firm measures. In fact, it was these that helped ensure that there were no terrorist deaths in Aden for the next ten months, save for one British officer injured by a landmine.

Immediately after the bomb outrage, Sharif Husain closed the Yemen border. A new Federal statute was rushed through to provide that any alien not registered before 31 January 1964 would be liable to fines, imprisonment or deportation. I was given a week to devise a scheme to register Aden's estimated 100,000 aliens. For this to have had the faintest chance of success, effective liaison between the Federal authorities and the Aden Government was essential. Yet even in so dire a situation this proved impossible. Sharif Husain would not appoint an Aliens Registration Officer so, when no name was forthcoming, I took it upon myself to suggest that the Deputy Commandant of the Federal Guard be appointed, and then got on with the job myself.

Theoretically, the only way to have made such a registration scheme work would have been to corral all aliens at designated registration stations, and then issue them with finger-printed registration cards. But even assuming that 100,000 mainly illiterate and unco-operative Yemenis and Somalis would take the blindest notice of government edicts, it would have needed an additional battalion of Armed Police to prevent intimidation, riots and strikes. In addition, 280 clerical staff, working a three-hour, five-day week over and above their normal office hours, plus translators, messengers and menials, would be required to administer the scheme. Even on the most optimistic estimate, it would have taken a minimum of six months to implement, so I told Donald Foster, the Sharif's Ministerial Secretary, that the 31 January 1964 deadline was patently ridiculous. Nonetheless, I went through the motions, and submitted my Report on 18 December 1963, adding a caveat that I could not see how it could possibly work within the allotted time. Three days later, I caught a plane to Nairobi to begin my second home leave, with an uneasy feeling that I might be deserting a sinking ship.

12

Lahej *Mon Amour*

TEN DAYS BEFORE I flew out of Aden, John Malcolm organized his second, and last, Shamsan Scramble. This time, the Royal Marines were determined to live up to their hard-man reputation, and although Muhammad Deria was again the easy winner, the Commandos packed most of the top places. Absurdly, the Scramble was given as much prominence on the front page of the Aden Forces newspaper, *The Dhow*, as the airport bomb outrage that heralded the advent of terrorism in Aden. While the realization of what this blatant attack might hold for the future shocked Aden's civilian population, British expatriates were equally dismayed at the British Labour Opposition's condemnation of Trevaskis's State of Emergency.

With a whiff of betrayal in the air, and no further assurance of a WAP posting, I was again looking to the hills to refocus my own perspectives. The lure of adventure that had originally drawn me to Arabia had largely been unrealized, and so, to kick-start this leave, I was planning to go another round with Mount Kenya, followed by an expedition to Ruwenzori, the fabled Mountains of the Moon. When I flew into Nairobi, that certain end-of-empire feeling was heightened by the rash of Uhuru flags that bedecked the town. Kenya had been granted its independence only eight days before.

Six weeks of thrills and spills in East Africa temporarily obliterated all thoughts about the future. On Mount Kenya, we caught the fag-end of the rainy season, which left the mountain encased in ice and involved us in a series of escapades. One nearly ended in disaster when a detached slab of rock almost swept both me and my companion off a new route on the south face of Nelion. Our fortunes changed in the Ruwenzori, where we climbed every major summit in the space of twelve virtually cloud-free days, accompanied by the cry of the rock hyrax by day and the cough of the leopard by night.

Returning to a particularly dismal British winter, I faced up to reality. The fragility of Britain's position in South Arabia made it virtually certain that independence would be granted by 1968 at the latest. Robin Thorne had written that it might be a lot earlier, because "the British Government is desperately anxious to shed sovereignty at the earliest possible moment". Now approaching the defining age of thirty, I was impatient to set a longer-term career course. I reinvestigated openings in the Law and the City, though still unclear idea as to where I really wanted to go. When I spotted a Vocational Guidance Association advertisement offering "to find holes for square pegs and anyone else standing at the crossroads", I enrolled for a series of tests. The results merely confused the issue. My ratings for literary and artistic aptitude were high, and for Law better than average. However, for administration, the very activity I thought I had been engaged in for the past four years, I scored near zero.

Imagining that my six months' involvement with internal security might open arcane doors, I approached a nameless Foreign Office department for an interview. After an ambivalent chat with two urbane gentlemen, I was bidden to attend a two-day Civil Service Selection Board at Savile Row. I never quite recovered my equilibrium on discovering that my old chum, James Nash, was a competitor candidate. James's robust and incisive performance was altogether more convincing than mine, so it was no surprise to receive the anodyne brush-off: "We are looking for a rather mixed cocktail of qualities and it is no reflection on your good qualities that we have not been able to accept you."

With leave fast running out, and with still no news about a WAP posting, my *angst* at the prospect of another desk job in Aden reached a bizarre climax in the Chanrion Hut. Set high in the Alps, this marks the half-way mark in the High Level ski-mountaineering route linking Zermatt to Chamonix. With a blizzard blowing outside, and the hut deserted save for my companion and our guide, I penned a letter of resignation to the Director of Establishments. The following day, when the weather forced us to retreat to the valley, I had the letter stamped at the post office at Orsières. Some instinct held me back from posting it, and I only came across it forty-five years later, still unopened.

Three days before I sailed for Aden on 2 June 1964 aboard the P&O's *Arcadia*, I had an exploratory chat about the solicitor's profession with Francis Tufton, a senior partner in a leading City law firm. At the end of it, Tufton unexpectedly offered me Articles of Clerkship, to commence at the end of my forthcoming tour, subject only to his partners' written confirmation, which would be telegrammed to Aden.

The day before I sailed, I also received a letter from Ralph Daly, the WAP Office's Senior Adviser East. "You are coming to us in the WAP," wrote Ralph. "Leave behind your moral scruples and suchlike, don your suit of mail, and get ready for adventure of the sort I think you find on mountains, working with a team of crazy but likeable individuals on a job which, every now and then, is rewarding and is, after all, well paid."

Dear Ralph. I never received better advice or a more accurate description of what my life was to become. Had I only received his letter a few days earlier, I would probably have cancelled my meeting with Tufton. Fatefully, his telegram awaited my arrival in Aden, confirming his firm's offer. Having already agonized overlong about the future, it seemed crazy to let this opportunity pass by. I immediately informed Oates, Thorne and my new boss, Ian Baillie, the WAP's British Agent, that I intended to resign at the end of this tour. Ian took it with his customary *sang froid*, but it could hardly have been a worse way to start my WAP career.

Much had happened in South Arabia since I went on leave almost six months before. Trevaskis's Emergency Regulations might have deferred serious terrorist activity in Aden Colony, but the Wadi Misrah episode had proved the curtain-raiser for the Radfan insurrection. This had escalated into a full-scale Federal and British Armed Forces operation, occupying the first half of 1964. Radfan was eventually subjugated, but at a cost disproportionate to the end result. The intensity of the fighting also put a new complexion on what might be expected in future. Belatedly, London was beginning to realize that we were up against a well-trained, politically motivated guerrilla force backed by Egyptian money and expertise. To counter this, Whitehall had authorized the WAP Office to undertake overt and covert counter-operations, including subversion and black propaganda, cross-border raids, mine-laying and retaliatory sabotage, particularly against Egyptian bases.

Many of the WAP's Assistant Advisers in the field were actively involved in such operations. This lent to the High Commission Office, Al-Ittihad (effectively the old WAP Office, and known as such) a very different atmosphere to Aden. Some form of WAP Office equivalent had existed since 1854, when Hormuzd Rassam, a Chaldean Christian from Mosul, was appointed to Aden's "Arabic Department". Rassam became the hinterland's first Political Officer in all but name and, by the 1860s, the Arabic Department had its own separate office in Crater, with a sufficiently large staff and guesthouse to stage lavish entertainments for visiting tribal leaders. Rassam was succeeded by another outstanding Arab political officer, Salih Jaffar, who effectively directed Aden's hinterland policy for thirty years.

Although Captain Haines had recognized that the key to Aden's security and survival as a British base was through peaceful rapprochement with its hinterland tribes, successive British governments had adopted a policy of minimum involvement, at the least possible cost. From time to time, so-called "forward policies", involving direct British military intervention and administration, had been advocated by the likes of Lord Curzon, but costly pacification campaigns against warlike tribes were generally viewed with horror in Delhi, Bombay and London. As a result, Aden's hinterland had been left to moulder, at least until the Colonial Office was given political responsibility in 1926. Thereafter, belated attempts were made to impose peace and introduce the rudiments of modern agriculture, health and education.

The Political Officers originally entrusted with this task in the WAP – Lake, Champion, Hamilton and Seager – all possessed both the military backgrounds and the political skills necessary to undertake the pacification operations to staunch what Hamilton once described as "the devastating tide race of blood feuds". Hamilton, later Lord Belhaven, had been a regular soldier before transferring to the Aden Protectorate Levies in 1931. Three years later, he accompanied Sir Bernard Reilly on his mission to San'a as ADC. Transferring thereafter to the Colonial Service, he was given the near-impossible task of pacifying 50,000 square miles of wilderness, inhabited by tribes who had known little but tyranny, banditry and blood feud. The swashbuckling Hamilton wrote like a poet but, unlike many who become addicted to all things Arabian, he remained ambivalent and maintained that there was an "unbridgeable gap" between Europeans and Arabs.

Certainly, to qualify as one of Ralph Daly's "crazy individuals" required unusual character traits. The Colonial Service prided itself on running well-ordered, law-based administrations. Outside Lahej, the WAP was anything but.

Up to 1943, only Lahej and Dhalaʻ had schools of any kind. Despite the post-war influx of ex-servicemen into the Colonial Service, the WAP Office always struggled to find recruits. Even in 1947, its establishment barely exceeded that of the mid-19th-century Arabic Department. Trevaskis records that during his eight-year spell as British Agent, 17 out of the 20 new Political Officers appointed had moved on within two years.

There were several turn-offs to service in the WAP. Where every tribesman, since puberty, had a *jambiyya* stuck inside his belt and a rifle slung over his shoulder, life was cheap, and this was definitely not the sort of place that most men would chose to bring a wife, let alone children. Paucity of funds for development, and the absence of direct administrative responsibility, made for job frustration. The degree of advice that any ruler was prepared to accept from his adviser depended solely on whether or not he liked you. This alone put a premium on personality, which tended to develop exponentially in those who stayed the course.

Unlike the EAP, the WAP Office had a quasi-military role and, like Gaul, was divided into three parts. At Headquarters, Ian Baillie was assisted by Willie Wise, Roy Somerset, Lionel Folkard and Hugh Walker. Area East's boss, Ralph Daly, was assisted by Peter Hinchliffe (shortly to take over as acting Senior Adviser for that area); and Bill Heber-Percy, ex-Welsh Guards and APL, held the particularly demanding post of AA Baihan, Sharif Husain's frontline fiefdom and a conduit for Yemeni Royalist arms and support. Area West, to which I was about to be posted, was headed by Robin Young, assisted (temporarily) in Al-Ittihad by Godfrey Meynell, with James Nash in Dhalaʻ, Stephen Day handling both the Fadhlis and the ʻAudhalis, Brian Somerfield in Radfan and Rex Smith in Jaʻar. The task of this tiny cadre of field officers was to advise most of the sultans, amirs, sharifs and shaikhs who, by their various lights, ruled the sixteen different states of the WAP, and guide them into the paths of good governance.

My overall boss, Ian Baillie, was a highly principled Scot who broke the more traditional WAP warrior mould. Intelligent, calm and balanced, Ian had previously served in the Gold Coast, and had been Aden's Protectorate Secretary prior to his present appointment. I sometimes wondered what he really thought of HMG's South Arabian policy. It was also his unenviable fate to have succeeded, as British Agent, the most charismatic of South Arabia's post-war British leaders, Kennedy Trevaskis.

Trevaskis had succeeded Johnston as Aden's High Commissioner in August 1963, yet his ghost still stalked the WAP Office. A clergyman's son, educated at Marlborough and King's College, Cambridge, he had soldiered with distinction during the Second World War in Eritrea. After post-war Colonial Service in Northern Rhodesia, he had transferred to Aden in 1951. Four years later, he succeeded the legendary Basil Seager as the WAP's British Agent. This was a time of rampant Yemeni aggression. Starved of funds for development, Trevaskis developed his own brand of political chicanery to keep a form of peace. Yet his quip, "He's either a knave or a fool", masked a subtle and perceptive mind. As its principal architect, Trevaskis saw the Federation as Britain's only hope for maintaining a long-term connection with South Arabia, and he remained the main influence on British government thinking until Labour's election in October 1964. But the years of strife and frustration, which only strengthened an immoveable resolution, affected his judgement. He staunchly championed the traditional tribal chiefs yet was unable, if indeed it were possible, to make them fully accept the responsibilities of government. Fatally, perhaps, he had little time for most urban Adenis, or indeed, Aden's British administrators. Respectfully known to his trusties as "Uncle", he was in every sense a big man who inspired devotion and loyalty in his junior officers.

My immediate boss, Robin Young, was Trevaskis's most unquestioning disciple and, with his pipe and avuncular manner, even bore a curious physical resemblance to his master. Robin had previously served in the elite Sudan Political Service before transfer to Aden in 1956. Generous and hospitable, he was generally supportive and sympathetic to the needs of his Assistant Advisers. However, having already given in my notice, I could not have expected much cordiality when I first reported to him for instructions.

"We're sending you to Lahej," announced Robin, gruffly. "There's been no resident Assistant Adviser there for years. It's a cushy introduction to the WAP. After a short spell there, you'll go on to Zinjibar to get stuck into development work."

I knew little about Lahej, so asked him what my work was likely to involve.

"Before I answer that question, I'll tell you something about the place. Lahej is the premier state in the WAP. It's also the richest and, in many ways, unique. The 'Abdali ruling family have their own Shari'a, tribal and agricultural courts. Their administrative districts and local councils are run by *naib*s and *'aqil*s, local governors and shaikhs. They've had a constitution since 1951, a Council of Directors, a Legislative Council, a supposedly independent Judiciary, and internally audited State accounts. Administratively, this puts them way ahead of any other WAP state. There's also some talk about a human rights charter, though I've yet to see any evidence of that."

"Then where do I come in? It sounds as if Lahej scarcely needs a new boy with little political experience."

"The short answer is, you don't. You'll have no executive authority whatsoever. Moreover, the 'Abdalis don't like *Political* Officers who poke their noses into their affairs. Nonetheless, Lahej is very important to us politically. The fact that you've never served in the WAP before is probably an advantage. Your main job is to get on with the Amir, Abdullah bin Ali, the Sultan's brother and the State's Chief Minister. You must feel your way very carefully as it's he, not the Sultan, who runs Lahej. If you hit it off, you could be useful. If not, you'll be wasting everyone's time."

"Might I have a more detailed briefing from whoever I'm replacing?"

"No hope there," chuckled Robin. "Michael Crouch was the last person to actually live in Al-Hauta – incidentally, that's the proper name of the state capital, not Lahej. But he was basically doing my job running Area West rather than advising the Amir. Anyway, he's now gone back to the calmer waters of the EAP. Robin Bidwell was also there for a short spell, and before him there was only Arthur Watts, who won't be much use to you now he's Protectorate Secretary," Young added, somewhat sourly.

"What about my staff. Is there anyone with whom I can discuss day-to-day matters?"

"Yes, you've got an excellent Junior Assistant Adviser in Sayyid Husain Al-Wazir. He knows all the ropes, but he also carries a load of baggage. You must remember that he's from a collateral branch of the former Yemeni royal family. His father, Abdullah, staged the coup in 1948 against Imam Yahya. Yahya was killed, but his son Ahmed, the last Imam, led a successful counter-coup. He then beheaded most of the Al-Wazir family, and had Abdullah garrotted as he said his prayers. Most of what was left of the Al-Wazirs fled to Aden for sanctuary. Although this made us very unpopular with Imam Ahmed, it puts Husain firmly on our side, at least for now. Husain's intelligent but proud and prickly. Most importantly, he has the ear of Amir Abdullah, and also plays a key role in intelligence gathering, so you must make allowances for this. He's here today to meet you, but brush up your Arabic. He doesn't speak a word of English."

It was another week before I moved to Lahej and ate my first supper – fried sausages and chips from a tin. My house was really a palace. It stood on a corner of the town's tree-lined *Maidan*, looking across the square to the grander establishments of Sultan Fadhl and the Amir Abdullah. I never got round to viewing all its forty rooms. The airy top floor alone was big enough for a badminton court. In its walled garden, tended by an ancient gardener, there were fruit bats with 18-inch wingspans, and a pride of peacocks who nested in a clump of giant *'ilb* trees and made enough noise at dawn to dispense with reveille. At the back of the garden lay the wreck of a cage that had once housed a mangy lion. This creature had been kept as a pet by the palace's last ruling occupant, Sultan Fadhl bin Abdul Karim. When young, Sultan Fadhl had been shot in the head by a former member of his entourage, leaving him blind in one eye and mentally deranged. His increasingly erratic behaviour was exacerbated by drink. On one crazed night, he had three of his close relations tied to stakes in the back garden and summarily executed for treason. He then fled to the Yemen with retainers, concubines and a bagpipe band, never to set foot in Lahej again.

My halting Arabic made initial exchanges with Sayyid Husain embarrassingly stilted. Courteous but aloof, his title of Junior Assistant Adviser, or "JAA", was misleading. Not only was he incomparably more experienced and knowledgeable than I but, as a member of a family which claimed descent from the Prophet and had held the Imamate of the Yemen in the late 19th century, he was my superior in every respect. The rest of my establishment consisted of a young clerk, Othman Nasser, who spoke faltering English, a messenger, a gardener, a sweeper, and two armed guards who did sentry go under the faux-marble, pillared portico that over-arched my front gates. Both Husain and Othman supported large families in the nether regions of the palace's labyrinth.

Having inspected my own quarters, I despatched my cook, Abdu, on a cockroach hunt around the kitchen. I then undertook a routine audit of the furniture, stores and office equipment. Most had gone missing, so I wrote to my predecessor, Michael Crouch, for a lead. His dusty reply, "Fancy people actually making inventories and things in the WAP – not in *my* day", put me firmly in my place. The "AA's Office" had also been the Crouch sitting-room, so I moved down to the large ground-floor room, shared by Sayyid Husain and Othman, to be nearer the action. Othman remonstrated that this might be "dangerous", though for no particular reason, except perhaps to avert my getting too close to Sayyid Husain's clandestine Yemeni intelligence contacts, shifty-looking types who occasionally drifted in and out of the office to whisper conspiratorially in a dark corner which Husain reserved for himself.

When I asked Othman if I might see the office files, he replied, "No files here, Sir", vigorously shaking his head. Sayyid Husain then produced a key, and gestured to a battered safe. Inside, was a dog-eared card index on local personalities compiled by Robin Bidwell; a couple of files about Dhala' matters; and a sheaf of outdated intelligence reports. Later, when I asked Robin Young what had happened to the Lahej files, he replied: "They don't exist. This isn't like Aden, you know." I was on a fast learning curve, without a script. Both of my predecessors, Watts and Bidwell, were formidable Arabists. If inexperience was my only asset, this was going to be a rough ride.

The 'Abdali Sultans of Lahej were descended from a line of despotic Yemeni governors who had declared themselves independent of the Imam in 1728. They alone, in the hierarchy of Federal rulers, were entitled to the dignity of being addressed as "Your Highness", and accorded an eleven-gun salute. They still regarded themselves as the rightful Sultans of Aden for it was from their predecessor, Sultan Muhsin, that Captain Haines had seized Aden in 1839. Lahej's wealth, and its geographical proximity to Aden, had ensured that its rulers remained principal players throughout Britain's time in South Arabia.

The British–'Abdali relationship tended to seesaw with each Sultan's personality. Sultan Muhsin became Haines's lifelong adversary, whereas his son, Sultan Fadhl, once advised the Political Resident, Major-General Tremenheere, that if 500 British troops were ordered into the interior, the whole country would submit to British rule. Sultan Fadhl's son, Ahmed, was an able and ambitious ruler whom Curzon invited to attend the 1901 Delhi Durbar, and subsequently had knighted. His son, Ali bin Ahmed, was also accounted a friend, until British troops mistook him for a Turk during the Ottoman invasion of Lahej in 1915 and accidentally shot him dead. His successor, Sultan Abdul Karim, impressed Ingrams as a "Ruler who rules". Hamilton, on the other hand, shortly to become the 12th Baron Belhaven, thought him a selfish despot whose "exaggerated airs of dignity, which he assumed on all occasions, were unbecoming in an Arabian chief."

Before they came to know the aristocratic tribal rulers of the hinterland better, Aden's British administrators had found it easier to relate to the 'Abdalis' princeling-style of rule than the anarchy that passed for government elsewhere. However, when a thoroughly modern Sultan, Ali bin Abdul Karim, succeeded the deranged Sultan Fadhl to the throne in the early 1950s, they were presented with a dilemma. As an educated, Westernized Arab who admired Gamal Abdul Nasser, imported Egyptian teachers to raise the Sultanate's education standards, supported the pro-Egyptian Lahej-based South Arabian League and drove fast cars, Sultan Ali was a new phenomenon amongst South Arabia's rulers. The British were at a loss to know how to handle him.

Ali's republican ideals and mixed blood (his mother had been an African slave) also made him unpopular with 'Abdali traditionalists. However, to June Knox-Mawer, the young wife of Aden Colony's Chief Magistrate from 1952 to 1958, this black-turbaned young man, "dressed in an immaculate dinner suit" with his "high prominent cheek bones and square jawline and a face to delight a sculptor", not only quickened her pulses, but represented the future. Sultan Ali became a close friend of the Knox-Mawers, but kept his distance from the WAP Office and Aden's establishment. He was also the last major ruler to sign an advisory treaty with the British.

Lahej's affluence and settled government had created a political class with a taste for radicalism. By 1958, it had become a hotbed of revolutionary disaffection. When the iconic Sayyid Muhammad Al-Jiffri, a driving force behind the South Arabian League, openly advocated union with Nasser's United Arab Republic, the British were forced to act. Al-Jiffri fled to the Yemen while Sultan Ali flew to London, effectively into exile. After the British formally withdrew recognition, Ali was deposed as Sultan by a Lahej electoral college. He was succeeded by Fadhl bin Ali bin Ahmed, the present Sultan and Minister of Defence. With hindsight, Sultan Ali can be judged more a moderate nationalist than a revolutionary. Had he been allowed to remain a leading player in South Arabia, its latter-day history might well have been different.

The effective ruler of Lahej was Sultan Fadhl's brother, Amir Abdullah bin Ali, a man hated by some and feared by many, including, it was said, the Sultan himself. Before being granted an audience with the Amir, I had to get on terms with Sayyid Husain. This was no easy task with Husain speaking no English and my Arabic suffering from four and a half years' under-usage. One evening,

32. *Above:* The fair at Meshhed, Wadi Hadhramaut.

33. *Below:* Camel loaded with fodder at the fair at Meshhed.

34. *Above:* Women and livestock at the fair at Meshhed.

35. *Below:* Laudar, capital of the 'Audhali State, Western Aden Protectorate.

36. *Above:* The Dhala' Plateau in the Amiri State, Western Aden Protectorate. The Assistant Adviser's house stands left of centre, with British Army lines to the rear.

37. *Below:* The summit of Jebel Jihaf, looking over the Qataba plain below.

38. *Above:* En route to Sha'ib, Dhala': Godfrey Meynell in white shirt; John Malcolm seated.

39. *Below:* 'Awabil, capital of Sha'ib.

40. *Above:* A Saladin descending the Khuraiba Pass.

41. *Below:* Thumair Fort, Radfan: British Ferret and Saladin armour.

42. *Above:* Qaid Haidar Al-Habili, Federal Guard Commander, during the Wadi Misrah operation, Radfan.

43. *Below:* Godfrey Meynell goes to war, Wadi Misrah, Radfan.

44. *Above:* Advance up the Wadi Misrah, Radfan.

45. *Below:* Sultanic palaces in Lahej.

46. *Above:* Subaihi: village poverty with backdrop of Yemen mountains.

47. *Below:* Group at Tor al-Baha. Back row, left to right: Ahmed Bindari, Sayyid Husain Al-Wazir, Husain Al-Habshi, Tom Heaton, with Lahej escort and local *'aqil*s.

48. *Above:* Subaihi: Jebel Kharaz.

49. *Below:* Orders group, Dhala' Road, with James Nash in white shirt.

50. *Above:* Convoy on the Dhala' Road.

51. *Below:* The British base at Habilain, Radfan.

52. *Above:* Bryan Somerfield and escort, Radfan.

53. *Below:* British Army Scout helicopter, Radfan.

54. *Above:* A fortified house and terracing, Radfan.

55. *Below:* Sultan Salih Al-'Audhali, at the Radfan Tribal Conference.

56. *Above:* Amir Sha'fal (right), at the Radfan Tribal Conference.

57. *Below:* Tribesmen at the Radfan Tribal Conference, Habilain Fort at rear.

58. *Above:* On patrol with the Coldstream Guards, Radfan.

59. *Below:* A mining incident at Badubain, Radfan.

60. Radfan Tribal Guards.

61. The author as POL Habilain, in front of his roll-barred Land Rover at Dhala'.

he announced that the Amir wanted to meet me next day, to discuss "matters of importance". At the appointed hour, he and I walked across Al-Hauta's dusty *Maidan* to the Amir's palace. Elbowing our way through a long corridor packed with a noisy, good-humoured crowd, we respectfully presented ourselves before Lahej's Chief Minister.

More powerfully built than most Arabs, with a hint of African blood, the Amir was seated on a dais at the end of a large reception room. His manner was unaffected but his authority effortless. It was his custom to dispatch routine business every day at a levee. By tradition, this could be attended by any petitioner, on the excellent Arab principle that even a sweeper may solicit his Sultan. Having motioned us to be seated below him, he continued to deal with the morning's business with impressive dispatch. Some petitioners he heard sympathetically. Others he dismissed out of hand, screwing up their paper submissions into tiny balls that he chucked out of a nearby window with practised accuracy. And then, with a wave of his hand, proceedings were abruptly brought to a close. Guards cleared the room and, within minutes, hubbub was replaced by calm. Now, at last, the great man deigned to give us his attention.

Formal greetings over, the Amir directed a torrent of incomprehensible Arabic at Husain, occasionally glancing at me as if to give his deliveries extra emphasis. Although the Amir and Husain clearly enjoyed a special relationship, Husain added little to the conversation. When the Amir eventually stopped talking, an enormous black servant swept into the room with a trayful of ginger-flavoured coffee, served in dainty cups. "*Tafaddal*," said the Amir, inviting me to take a cup. Coffee drunk, Husain rose. Nothing more was said. Our audience was over. When we got back to the office, I went through what, for several weeks to come, became the familiar routine of unravelling what the Amir might or might not have said. The gist of an early session might have gone something like this.

"The Amir seemed very agitated this morning, Sayyid Husain."

"Yes, he was," replied Husain. "He is angry about British soldiers throwing empty Coca-Cola tins into the coffee shop at Al-Hauta. But that is not important. His concern is about the compensation that Lahej is long overdue from the Federal Government."

"What compensation?" I asked, thumbing frantically through my dictionary for the right words.

"The compensation that the 'Abdali State is due for losing its customs revenue. You must speak to Mr Young about this. The Amir is also very worried about the Federal Agriculture Department. They want to set up an agricultural loan scheme to help the farmers of Lahej and Subaihi."

"But surely, that is a good thing?"

"No. It is a very bad thing. The Federal Department only interferes and makes trouble. The Amir wants this money to be given to the Lahej State Treasury. He can then organize his own loan scheme for Lahej's farmers through the State's own Agriculture Department."

"But the Lahej farmers are rich. What about the poor farmers in Subaihi? Surely it is they who most need Federal help?"

"Subaihi?" mused Husain, frowning slightly. "Subaihi is Bedouin country. We can do little for them. The Amir says they eat money."

I soon learned that anything to do with either Lahej agriculture or Subaihi had to be approached with extreme delicacy. Lahej's agricultural development was way ahead of any other WAP state except the Fadhli Sultanate with its Abyan development. Al-Hauta itself was set in a lush delta of rich alluvial soil watered by the Wadi Tiban, with massive artesian water resources just beneath the surface. Its ancient forests had long been replaced by extensive groves of limes, oranges, bananas, coconuts, quince, mangos and dates which now supplied the suqs of Al-Hauta and Aden with fresh fruit and vegetables. In its luxuriant gardens grew rambler roses, bougainvillea, jasmine and magnolia. Exceptionally, Lahej also had its own Agriculture Department with a permanent staff of fifty. The Amir had formerly been its Director. As the 'Abdali ruling family owned most of the best land, they effectively controlled Lahej's economy.

For all this, the 'Abdalis remained deeply envious of the success of the Fadhli Sultanate's Abyan Scheme, which had benefited from generous British funding. It was also the Amir's constant complaint that Lahej was denied Federal support. Yet he refused to take Federal agricultural advice except *in extremis*, and even then would only do so without strings attached. Ray Sturge, the hapless Commissioner for Co-operative Development & Marketing, had unwisely failed to do his homework before parachuting into Lahej a callow protégé, Ali Abdul Qawi, to promote a co-operative and marketing scheme. Not only had he failed to consult the Amir in advance but, worse still, Ali Abdul Qawi's father had already incurred the Amir's wrath by disputing title to the ownership of Lahej's only cinema, which the Amir naturally claimed as his own.

When Sturge got no response through official Federal channels, he insisted that I arrange a personal audience with the Amir. Imprudently, he then pressed his case so hard that the Amir summarily dismissed him. "Who is this Sturgeon, Mr Harding?" roared the Amir, after his guards had seen Sturge off the premises. "Please *never* bring him here to see me again. I will not be told how to run agriculture in my own state." Lahej agriculture was strictly off bounds. Likewise the Lahej Cotton Board which, unlike Abyan's joint Arab-European Cotton Board, never admitted outside members. Its organization and accounts remained a mystery, but it was common knowledge that its profits were remitted direct to a Swiss bank.

In economic terms, Subaihi was to Lahej what the Protectorate was to Aden. Ever since my first trip to Perim, this wild tract of sand, stone and mountain, stretching 140 miles from east to west, had gripped my imagination. Historically, it had always been disputed territory, inhabited by a mishmash of segmented tribes, sections and families with no single shaikh powerful enough to form a single confederation. Not a state in the normal sense, Subaihi had been subsumed into the 'Abdali Sultanate only in 1898, by Sultan Ahmed bin Fadhl. Only a few years before that, the British and Ottoman governments had delineated a theoretical frontier across the rough-hewn mountains that Subaihi's tribes shared with their Yemeni kinsmen. It was during this survey that Captain Warneford became the first Political Officer to be murdered in South Arabia. His patience had snapped at the end of a tiring day, and in exasperation, he lightly struck one of his escort, an unpardonable and, in this case, fatal insult.

The Aden government had actively supported Sultan Ahmed bin Fadhl's Subaihi take-over as a means of combating the lucrative gun-running trade through that area that then supplied South Arabia with the deadly Martini Henry rifle. Sultan Ahmed had been a strong ruler, but after his death order was replaced by chaos, arms trafficking and highway robbery. Not until the mid-1930s, when Hamilton undertook military operations against the Subaihi tribes to secure the Aden–Ta'izz trade route, was a measure of peace restored. Thereafter, and up to 1947, Subaihi was administered jointly by the British and the 'Abdalis, yet neither spent a penny on it. The presence of a 30,000-strong Egyptian Army, now operating on the Yemeni side of Subaihi's undefended 180-km border, was at last forcing both to take notice of this long-neglected corner of the WAP.

I was determined to promote Subaihi's development, so suggested to Sayyid Husain that we should visit the area together to assess its needs. He gave every sort of excuse for not going. "It's the wrong season and too hot to travel. The people are ungrateful, unfriendly and dangerous. Subaihi is a hopeless case, and anyway the Amir doesn't want us to go." In fact, and although reluctant to admit it, the Amir had become increasingly worried about dissident activity along the Subaihi frontier, ever since the NLF had given notice of launching their armed struggle the previous July.

Subaihi presented the Amir with a dilemma. Reluctant in principle to get either the British or Federal Government involved in Lahej's internal affairs, he was equally aware that he might need their military support if something serious blew up. Still fresh in his mind was last year's fiasco when a British military "adventure training" party of servicemen and women had inadvertently strayed across the border at Tor al-Baha. They had come under fire from Yemeni tribesmen and, in the ensuing shoot-out, some British were killed, some fatally wounded and others captured. Only after Michael Crouch's skilful negotiation and American diplomatic intervention were the captives released from Egyptian custody. The Amir did not want a repeat performance.

Nonetheless and despite misgivings, he agreed that Husain and I should do a short familiarization tour with a Federal Guard escort. Husain was right about the weather. The heat of the coastal plain was withering. However, as we climbed up into the hills, the air became cool and the monotonous sand scrub of the littoral gave way to scattered cultivation and date groves. The fort at Tor al-Baha, perched on a rocky knoll, gave a bird's-eye view of the mountains of Yemen. Below it, in a bright green wadi, a perennial stream watered groves of banana, pawpaw, citrus fruits and grapevines, zealously husbanded within tight, stone-walled gardens. Clearly visible beyond was the burned-out hulk of the British Army's "adventure training" lorry, serving as a reminder that the frontier was only a few hundred yards away.

"What does your village need?" I asked the village's grizzled headman. "Pumps," he replied. "Pumps. The government talks of help but gives us nothing."

I suggested to Husain that we should inspect the village health unit and school. Both looked in urgent need of repair, though the school was well attended. Outside it was parked a smart Land Rover, guarded by a Lahej FNG escort. As I wondered to whom this might belong, a lithe figure jumped out.

"What on earth are you doing here, Tom?" I asked him.

"Just part of the job, and part of my beat, actually."

I wasn't that surprised. Tom Heaton, the Federal Chief Inspector of Schools, was like no one else I ever met in Arabia. We'd become close friends during my first tour in Aden. Tom's early life was a mystery; by his own account, his Persian mother had been sold by her German husband for a horse. After National Service in the British Army, he had taken a First in Arabic and Persian at the School of Oriental and African Studies before joining the Colonial Education Service. With the possible exception of Arthur Watts, Tom was the most accomplished British Arabist then serving in South Arabia. In addition, he had an instinctive empathy with all races and creeds, irrespective of gender, which enabled him to integrate into any culture he cared to adopt. His love life was tempestuous. His first wife had been Iranian, his second English, and his current live-in girlfriend was his Somali servant, a married woman with her own marital problems.

Tom's work as an education officer masked his other role as a lynchpin in the British Secret Intelligence Service's network. Articulate, contentious and forever battling with personal demons and a search for identity, Tom's lifestyle was always leading him down dangerous byways. Professionally, he set the highest standards and was deeply committed to improving South Arabia's education. He both mistrusted and misunderstood the Establishment, yet remained a courageous patriot who shouldered immense personal risks without diplomatic protection. He became one of the most marked men in South Arabia, yet emerged at the end unscathed. The twists of his subsequent career led him to East Africa where he retraced the steps of the Hungarian explorer, Count Teleki, around Lake Rudolph. He died in Entebbe in 2004, aged 76, in the arms of his Ugandan wife.

Accompanying Tom were Sayyid Husain Al-Habshi and Abdul Qadir Bindari. Our seemingly chance encounter in this remote hill village was not accidental. A key figure in Tom's clandestine world was Husain Al-Wazir, the main conduit of reliable Yemeni intelligence. It was the Amir Abdullah, Husain's protector, who had lent Tom his personal Land Rover and provided the armed escort. No other Federal officer would have been given such favoured treatment. After lunch, the Arab contingent settled down to a *qat* session, while Tom polished off half a bottle of whisky. When we shared the Amir's Land Rover on the way home, I asked him about his companions.

"Bindari's an Egyptian. Came over to Lahej eighteen years ago and has been its Schools Supervisor ever since. He does what he's told by the Amir, though he's a republican at heart like his former master Sultan Ali Abdul Karim. I like him personally, but I don't trust him. He's probably running an Egyptian spy ring in Lahej, abetted by his chum Husain Al-Habshi. That's the Indonesian-looking one who's half-Hadhrami and is one of twenty brothers. One of them is Shaikhan Al-Habshi, that smart lawyer who represented the South Arabian League when Trevaskis and Shaikh Muhammad Farid went over to New York last year to put the Federal case before the United Nations. They got nowhere of course. Since then, Trevaskis has done his best to get Shaikhan out of South Arabia, better dead than alive. If he's got any sense, he'll pack Husain off with him, along with that other sly devil of a brother who's working as a translator in the WAP Office. It never ceases to amaze me how we employ such subversive people in these sensitive posts!"

"Where else d'you get to in Subaihi, Tom?"

"Just about anywhere that suits the Amir. The other day, I went to Turbah. No funny business, of course, just to visit a school. It's about as remote as anywhere you'll find in the WAP, tucked away at the top of the Wadi Haqaran, in the far north-west corner of Subaihi. Tribes like the Kaluli and Aghbari have never seen a European, and wouldn't recognize a frontier if they saw one. They live in the most beautiful mountain country you can imagine. Get the Amir to let you go there sometime to slake your thirst for mountains. I doubt that anyone from the WAP Office has ever seen the place."

We stopped off for a break at Am Farajah, another frontier village guarded by a fort. A group of giggling, pretty unveiled girls in brightly coloured clothes were drawing water at a well.

"Good lookers, these Subaihi girls," I remarked. "Nice change after those black-cowled crows you see in Lahej."

"Oh yes," Tom leered back, "and easy to sleep with, too. But strictly for Arabs only, so keep your hands off. But to talk shop, now you've seen something of Subaihi and the state of its schools, you'll realize how much has to be done here. Lahej is relatively well advanced educationally, thanks largely to Ali Abdul Karim's recruitment of Egyptian schoolmasters during the early 1950s. But Bindari's views on Subaihi education are really those of the Amir

– 'Let them stew!' I'm trying to change all that."

When I next visited Al-Ittihad, I asked the Federal Director of Rural Education about Bindari. He complained that the Egyptian was undermining his Ministry's efforts to liaise with the 'Abdalis. I thought it more likely that the Amir, ever resentful of Federal interference, was responsible for putting up the barriers. In time, I got to know Bindari personally, and couldn't help liking this fat, jolly man with his Egyptian courtesy and charm. Adjoining his tiny house was a chaotic courtyard, crammed with sheep, goats, dogs, cats, turkeys and rabbits, all living together in domestic harmony with his twelve children. He was a generous host who entertained his guests royally with whole roast sheep.

Tom's enthusiasm to improve Subaihi education spurred me to launch my own development scheme. But first I had to gain the Amir's confidence. Some intimation that I might be on track came when he invited me to dine at his palace in Crater. Having foregathered in a heavily scented rose garden, his guests were ushered through a succession of high-vaulted anterooms carpeted with dramatic Bakhtiari kilims. These gave way to an enormous reception room, where six superb Persian carpets, each measuring 20 by 15 feet, covered the floor. After introducing me formally to Sultan Fadhl and each of the Lahej State Councillors, the Amir beckoned to me to sit next to him for a gargantuan Indo-Arab spread served European-style. Conversation was stilted, but our relationship had begun.

As confidence developed, the Amir gave me permission to visit Amour, an impoverished mountain area to the north-west of Lahej which had particular political and strategic significance as forming a geographical salient into the Yemen. "I want you to meet the Naib of Kirsh, Ali bin Ahmed," instructed the Amir. "He will tell you about the problems we face from trouble-makers in his area."

Many of these "problems" were self-inflicted. They stemmed largely from late 19th-century conflicts, when the 'Abdalis had seized Amour from the neighbouring Haushabi Sultanate. Since then, boundary disputes and mutual loathing had characterized 'Abdali–Haushabi relations. In the days of the Imamate, the 'Abdalis had generally found a complicit ally in the Imam. Since the Yemen revolution, that cosy relationship had been upset. Quick fixes could no longer be guaranteed.

Kirsh, to which I had been before, was little more than a scruffy village. But as a nodal point through which any motorized invasion from the north would have to pass, it was important strategically and heavily garrisoned. Just as we were about to leave Lahej, the Amir threatened to cancel the visit on account of one Herr Schmidt, a German TV man, who had arrived in Lahej unexpectedly on Godfrey Meynell's unsolicited invitation. Overweight and perspiring profusely, Herr Schmidt arrived outside my house at dawn, armed with six large stainless-steel boxes of camera equipment and an Arriflex cine camera. He was precisely the sort of visitor likely to reveal those aspects of the 'Abdali State that the Amir was most anxious to conceal. After much huffing and puffing, he allowed Herr Schmidt to join me, but with the strict injunction that I was not to stop or allow him to film or take photographs. Being midsummer, the mountains were obscured by haze anyway. On arrival in Kirsh, Naib Ali immediately put Herr Schmidt under house arrest, while I went through the usual motions of inspecting the frontier guard and the run-down health unit. As if on cue, the Naib gave me a bellyful of complaints about the frontier troubles he was having, compounded by the Federal government's shortcomings.

With two preliminary visits under my belt, the Amir now agreed that Husain and I could make a full-scale tour of Subaihi to assess its development potential. As part of the package, I was urged to become better acquainted with the State's security problems by inspecting the 'Abdali National Guard's Subaihi forts, strung along a 350-kilometre circular arc from Lahej to Suqayya and then back along the frontier. Husain insisted on bringing along his two sons, Ibrahim (11) and Abdul Rahman (10), both proudly wearing Boy Scout uniforms.

The 170-km drive to Suqayya in the Amir's Land Rover, with full escort, proved even more uncomfortable than when I had done it with Knowles. The monsoon blew so strong that we had to make an unscheduled stop at the National Guard fort overlooking the 8-km-wide lagoon of Khawr al-'Umairah. Here, in 1940, Brian Hartley, Aden's pioneer Agricultural Officer, happened to be encamped with a Bedouin Camel Corps patrol when, unexpectedly, the *Galileo Galilei*, flagship of Mussolini's Red Sea submarine fleet, surfaced. Hartley's signal to Aden, by a bicycle-powered transmitter, alerted the British ship *Moonstone* to attack and fatally damage the submarine.

Suqayya's fort was even nastier than I remembered. As we drove up to it through a huddle of squalid shacks, a half-clothed guardsman emerged to make a charade of saluting. Its detachment of *qat*-befuddled soldiers cleared a space on the earthen floor to share with us, and several hundred cockroaches, a mess of tinned tuna and rice cooked over a charcoal fire sited next to a stinking, scorpion-infested latrine. The intense heat forced us to rest up here during the hottest part of the day. Thereafter, we thankfully set a new course directly inland, along a switchback of dried-up watercourses, into the face of an eye-melting offshore wind.

We reached Am Shatt late that evening. The fort lived up to its name, with latrines more disgusting and cockroaches even bigger than those at Suqayya. Vicious bugs were active throughout the evening's political parley, mainly conducted between Sayyid Husain and a scowling Naib who eyed me suspiciously throughout. After I had taken refuge on the fort's roof to avoid the stench and heat, the wind grew so strong that by midnight it shifted the stones anchoring my bedding. I retreated downstairs to the foul-smelling common room in which the entire garrison was snoring raucously. Sayyid Husain's tubercular expectorations, directed against the wall next to my head, soon drove me up to the roof again for a sleepless night.

At dawn next day, a dry, sand-bearing wind left my eyes feeling as if they'd been rubbed by sandpaper. Abandoning Am Shatt without ceremony or breakfast, we now headed NNW through scrub and tamarisk country reminiscent of East Africa. Climbing upwards towards a jagged line of blue mountains, we came to the Subaihi Shangri-La that Tom Heaton had so enthused about. Turbah's fort commanded fine views over the surrounding countryside and the tousled hills of Yemen, marching away to the north, ridge upon serried ridge.

Husain and I spent most of that day in conclave with local *mansab*s, *naib*s and farmers, inspecting their fields and water courses, discussing wells, water and money, and listening to a catalogue of woes. By late evening, we were long tired with talking, so set our course for home, reaching Al-Hauta in the early hours of the following morning. Never once did I hear the merest whinge from Husain's two boys.

I had now seen enough of Amour and Subaihi to make my own assessment of what was needed to stabilize these potentially explosive areas. The solution was to bolster agriculture and build more schools and health units. Canvassing an outline development scheme with the Federal Ministry of Commerce, I came away with a raspberry. I then belatedly realized that my only hope of getting anywhere would be through the Amir Abdullah. When Husain and I formally reported back to him about our trip, he insisted that Tom Heaton came along too, raising not a murmur when Tom complained about Tor al-Baha's unsatisfactory teacher/pupil ratio, the dilapidated state of its school buildings, and the absence of textbooks. However, when I suggested that agricultural development, rather than increased military spending, would be the more effective way of keeping the peace, he reacted angrily.

"It's all very well *you* saying that, Mr Harding. You know nothing about these people. They understand only force. Have you not heard about these disloyal Subaihi *'aqil*s who are now seeking asylum in Aden, and are using Bayoomi's *Al-Kifah* newspaper to spread their poison about Subaihi?"

I shook my head. "What is this poison, O Amir?"

"Surely, you have heard about it by now! These are the same rascals who complain about lack of schools and health units, and then form their own subversive political party, The Subaihi Sons Association. They do nothing but spread bile. You've now seen for yourself the forts we have built with Lahej money to protect our state. Where does the money for this development you talk about come from? I provide it for Lahej, but will you British provide it for Subaihi? We can achieve nothing without security. So what are you British doing about these dissidents who make such trouble along our frontiers?"

I backed off. At this stage, my Arabic was not up to arguing the toss with the Amir. I also needed Husain's active support for my scheme. Unfortunately, development came low on his list of priorities. His first was to maintain a close relationship with the Amir, to whose patronage he owed so much. His second was the covert intelligence work he undertook for the British Secret Service. Before the Yemen revolution, this particular role was readily explained by the hatred he bore the Imamic family who had executed his father. Thereafter his rationale was less clear for, by now, he was effectively supporting the scions of that same family against the Egyptian invader. Moreover, the links with Yemeni Shiite Zaidis that this covert work demanded made him deeply unpopular with Lahej's mainly Sunni commonalty. Time spent with his British controllers was at the expense of his administrative work, and also marked him as a prime terrorist target. I greatly respected Husain, but we did not always see eye to eye. When he unexpectedly went on sick leave for TB treatment, I said to him, "Now you are leaving, Husain, my right hand goes with you," to which he replied, pointing to my clerk Othman and driver Ahmed, "But now you have two right hands!"

It was not quite like that and, initially, Husain's departure left me treading water. However, his absence helped cement my relationship with the Amir and, when the latter invited me to the sumptuous wedding feast he threw for three male members of his family at the Sultan's Al-Rawdah Palace, I was the only European present. His 500 guests were seated in long rows under an enormous awning covering the entire palace garden. On a raised dais set in the middle, the three bridegrooms sat huddled together, looking anything but ecstatic at the prospect of matrimonial bliss. Before the wedding feast began, I was parcelled around to meet the 'Abdali ruling family, resplendent in their Hyderabadi-style headdresses and elegant buttoned-up frock coats. I ate in somewhat lowlier company, squatting cross-legged between Shaikh Mahmoud, the much-despised ruler of the vassal 'Aqrabi State, and Shaikh Ali Bazara, a portly Hadhrami merchant who ran the Arab Navigation Company and who wolfed down great fistfuls of mutton without so much as a word. After coffee was served and *qat* distributed, I found myself next to Abdullah Salim Basendwah, Aden's Minister of Finance, a pleasant, moderate ex-Bayoomi man and one of the few Aden ministers who got on well with the Federal rulers. Abdullah confided that he saw Federation as a vital stepping-stone to eventual independence.

Much encouraged, when next the Amir summoned me I took the opportunity of resurrecting the Subaihi aid scheme.

"Yes, yes, yes, Mr Harding. But I must ask you again: where does the money come from? We are not rich, and must look to you British to help us. My brother tells me that your government has given Al-Ittihad £500,000 for development. Can we not get some of this money to develop Subaihi?"

When I spoke to Young, I got a very different story.

"Don't get over-excited. Yes, we've at last squeezed something out of HM Treasury, but it's now been cut by half, and is wrapped up in Commonwealth Development & Welfare Scheme red tape, so it'll be months before we can get our hands on it."

"The Amir seems to think that £500,000 has been allocated and might be available for Subaihi."

"Then he's got it all wrong. That £500,000 represents the whole of the Federal development allocation for the WAP for the next couple of years. You'll be lucky to get £35,000. Even then, you'll have to make a damned strong case for it. You'd better put him right straightway."

When I explained the situation to the Amir, he took it philosophically, and agreed to support my aid scheme in principle, subject to his final approval on detail. The devil now lay in getting the co-operation of the Federal Ministries of Agriculture and Education, both mired in inter-departmental jealousy. Tom Heaton's close links with the Amir had apparently offended his own Director's *amour-propre*. My personal dealings with a blatantly unhelpful Acting Director of Agriculture prompted a diary entry: "Working in this place is like disgorging one's own blood into some vast, sandy desert." Nevertheless, after weeks of discussion, I finally produced my Subaihi and Amour Aid Scheme. Of the £35,000 promised, half would provide cheap loans for farmers to dig or deepen 150 wells and install pumps, and buy one bulldozer and two tractors for leasing out from the Lahej Agriculture Department. The balance would be used to repair health units and rebuild the primary schools at Huwairib and Malbiyya. The *mansab*s of both villages were so keen to get started that they hired stonemasons without waiting for the money to come through.

If I thought I was home and dry, I had underestimated Colonial Office bureaucracy. My scheme had first to be submitted to London, supported by detailed cash breakdowns. It would then have to be referred back to Young's Co-ordinating Development Committee for Federal approval. Only after passing muster would the money be allocated, and then, not direct to the Lahej State Treasury, but to me personally. Thereafter, all expenditure and revenue had to be accounted for in the State estimates, with written receipts required for each individual payment.

When, I tried to explain this convoluted procedure to the Amir, he exploded.

"First you promise me £500,000. Then, you offer me a pittance for which I am required to account to you like some miserable clerk. You British treat us like suq beggars."

"I never promised you £500,000," I protested. "I know it's far too little, but I've done my best to get even this. If you have any better ideas about raising the money, you must speak direct to Mr Young or the Federal Minister of Agriculture."

I had never dared speak to the Amir like this before, but he found my outburst hugely amusing. We were on the same side.

My Subaihi scheme was ready for submission to London by early September, the first of its kind since the Radfan campaign had spurred HMG into belated action. But then the Amir insisted that he wanted more time to consider whether the money allocated to dig surface wells might better be spent on expensive tube wells to tap the Lahej Delta's artesian water. I could see the economic logic in this, but argued that the variation would chiefly benefit Laheji rather than Subaihi farmers. The Amir took another six months to make up his mind, and then insisted on tube wells. I spent my last days in Lahej frantically recasting the original scheme and despairing for Subaihi.

Disillusioning though this might have been, in the wider scheme of things it was more important that I maintain good relations with the Amir Abdullah, the eyes and ears of the Sultanate. My almost daily audiences with him were usually unilateral exercises in which he would unleash a barrage of rhetorical salvos at me, and then provide the answers himself. His favourite targets were Federal bungling and interference, Haushabi criminality, British policy failures and, increasingly, the Subaihi frontier. "Dissidents, dissidents everywhere on our borders, Mr Harding. What do you British propose to do about them? You won the war in Radfan, so why don't you back the Saudis properly and give arms to the Royalists to get rid of these Egyptian scoundrels?"

He must have known that we were already giving clandestine military support to the Royalists, channelled through Baihan, but these thunderous denunciations masked an underlying uncertainty about British motives. It was a fear shared by other Federal rulers, and encapsulated in Sharif Husain's bitter aphorism: "It is better to be an enemy of the British than a friend. For as an enemy there is the possibility of being bought, but as a friend the certainty of being sold." The Amir espoused his own form of patriotism, following a time-honoured 'Abdali tradition of maintaining Lahej's predominant position amongst the WAP states by what Haines had once described as "sinuous subtleties, duplicities and deceptions". In a rapidly changing world, it required fast footwork to achieve this, so the Amir stuck to that other abiding 'Abdali principle of keeping sweet with the Yemen, whatever that country's political complexion. With chill winds blowing from the north, the Amir now pressed for the abrogation of the British advisory treaty that Sultan Ali bin Abdul Karim had been so reluctant to sign, "to free our hands and enable us to face an uncertain future", as he realistically put it.

It was not for me to debate such weighty constitutional issues, but the Amir liked to use me as a sounding board, knowing that I would be reporting everything back to Young. This hedging of bets also explained why he sometimes blew hot and cold. One day, he might erupt with feigned fury about the hated Haushabis rustling a few miserable cows, demanding immediate Federal action. On another, he might huff and puff about British "weakness", having already adopted his own effective remedies. With the fragmented Subaihi tribes, he would play one lot against the other, usually with bribes or other inducements. This was often with tacit Yemeni complicity, given that Ta'izz was finding it quite as difficult to maintain order on its own side of the frontier. When some hooligans, banished from Ta'izz, shot one of the Naib of Kirsh's cows, the Amir wrote to his opposite number in Ta'izz: "Please remove these people from our borders and keep the security situation under control, and let us be good neighbours according to our agreement." Such agreements were no longer as watertight as they had been in the Imam's day. Nonetheless, 'Abdali–Yemeni liaison was still maintained at the highest level.

One morning, the Amir summoned me and, after brandishing a crumpled signal in my face, thundered: "Do you know what this is all about, Mr Harding?"

"I'm afraid I have no idea, O Amir."

"Then, by God, I shall tell you. This is a personal signal from the Sultan to President Sallal in San'a. The Sultan is very angry. He has decided to address this message not to the British High Commissioner, but to the President of the Yemen himself to get satisfaction."

"What does it say?" I asked, awestruck.

"It gives details of our plan to assassinate that accursed Amour dissident, Muhammad Sa'id Humaidi. That vermin wants to reclaim his so-called 'lost lands' by invoking some ancient blood feud. If he's allowed a free hand to do this, all the good work we have done to keep the frontier at peace all these years will be destroyed. The Sultan is asking President Sallal to agree our plan. What do you say, Mr Harding? Do you British support us?"

I wasn't in the assassination business, but hastily agreed that Humaidi should not be allowed to upset the peace, and promised to discuss the situation immediately with Young for him to take it up with the Federal Minister of the Interior. Actually, this was not what the Amir really wanted. In the past, he might have got rid of Muhammad Sa'id as he might swat a fly. Now, the Egyptian invasion was forcing him to take into account uncertain new factors. Publicizing Lahej's frontier problems with other Federal rulers was not a preferred option as it would only underline 'Abdali impotence. Yet, if anything serious were to come of this Humaidi business, what better scapegoat than the British, for failing to take appropriate action?

At least as pertinent a reason for the Amir raising frontier issues at this time was to extract additional arms and ammunition from the WAP Office. Such handouts had been the traditional method of giving rulers material support when nothing else was available. The practice had its origins in the 19th century, when precision rifles, smuggled in from French Djibouti through Subaihi, had supplanted the sword, dagger and matchlock, thus speeding the destruction of South Arabia's fragile social cohesion, and becoming as commonly accepted currency as the Maria Theresa silver dollar. After the First World War, the Aden government could obtain unlimited supplies of Lee Enfield .303 rifles at cost, and made free use of the facility.

Although both the Sultan and the Amir were given generous personal allocations over and above the 'Abdali State's standard quota, this was never enough. Shortly after the Humaidi episode, the Amir summoned me. "What has happened to my allocation of rifles and ammunition, Mr Harding? I have just given Shaikh Hamid Mushwali Ten and Ten to teach those dissidents a lesson. Now, I have nothing left in my armoury."

"Ten and Ten" was shorthand for ten rifles and ten boxes of ammunition. Once, I had harboured a naïve objection to issuing rifles, but had come to realize that they were one of the few useful tools at our disposal. Even so, as supplies were not inexhaustible, and had to be used with discretion, I had established with the WAP Office that the 'Abdali State had recently received 1,000 rifles, the Sultan 150 and the Amir 30. There was also a reserve stockpile of 412 rifles, apparently still undrawn.

When I pointed this out to the Amir he was incandescent. "You ask *my* support for *your* Subaihi scheme. Did you not know that Shaikh Hamid is the same loyal man who has already pledged his support to build your new school in Malbiyya? Do you now deny him British protection? But leave that aside. My complaint is that we have received none of the rifles due to be delivered by your Crown Agents. And do you know why?"

I shook my head dumbly, expecting some scandalous exposé.

"It is because your Crown Agents want us to pay them in advance! I will never agree to this. Indeed, I will only pay on delivery to ensure that my State Treasury loses no interest."

I recalled hazily that the Qur'an had something to say about usury, but backed away from citing precedent.

"But can you not use the 412 rifles that are stockpiled in the State Armoury until the Crown Agent's consignment arrives?"

"By God, Mr Harding," the Amir spluttered. "You must know very well that in peaceful times I would sell my own rifles to help the farmers. But surely even you can see that everything is different now. Ammunition is too expensive to buy in the Aden suq. Anyway, I will only use official government sources. I must have 5,000 rounds immediately to stop the situation in Kirsh getting any worse."

"I will ask Mr Young for 1,000."

"Please be serious," he snorted. "That's not enough ammunition for one rifle. And don't *you* tell me how to protect my borders. The enemy grow stronger every day. Unless the British and the Federation show strength, and give me weapons to support my loyal chiefs, Subaihi will become another Radfan!"

How often had I heard this plea! Nonetheless, I scuttled off to find Young in an uncharacteristically shaky mood. Apparently, several soldiers had been killed during a skirmish at 'Awabil only the previous day. "What the devil's the man talking about!" exploded Robin. "We gave those bloody Lahejis an extra 300,000 rounds only last month. Find out what on earth's happened to them. Anyway, why the hell doesn't he get on to his brother, the Minister of Defence? I've got far too much on my plate to worry about gripes from Lahej. You must sort this one out yourself."

Actually, this was not that easy to sort out. A cooling-off period was clearly in order, so I avoided seeing the Amir for the next couple of days. The obvious course should have been for him to go direct to his brother. Yet nothing to do with the 'Abdali ruling family was ever straightforward. Sultan Fadhl and Amir Abdullah might be brothers, but their characters were very different and their relationship enigmatic. Although I was Adviser to the Sultanate and saw the Amir almost every day, I seldom encountered the Sultan himself, who spent most of his time either at Al-Ittihad or at his Crater palace.

It so happened that to mark the Sultan's return from the London Constitutional Conference in early July, I was invited to attend a formal audience at his Rawdah Palace in Al-Hauta, after meeting him off the plane with Young. The Sultanic guard came raggedly to attention as I walked through the palace gates. I was then ushered into a long audience chamber filled with

Lahej's dignitaries. The Amir Abdullah, disarmingly affable, signalled me to take my place next to him. After fresh lime had been served, all present were bidden to take up positions on either side of the avenue that led from the main gate to the palace steps. The Amir Abdullah was first in line. Next to him stood the elderly Amir Ahmed bin Ali, a charming old boy, who exchanged pleasantries in English. Then came me. Outside in the *Maidan,* the band played a Mukalla-style medley as latecomers scurried in. Some kissed the Amir's hand deferentially, some exchanged formal greetings, and others pointedly ignored him. The Sultan arrived outside the palace gates half an hour late. At this, the band struck up the Lahej National Anthem. Muted applause from outside the palace compound was soon drowned by noisy ululations from the harem within. His Highness took the salute and inspected the guard, after which the bandsmen switched smoothly to a bagpipe lament before marching off in quick time to the *British Grenadiers.*

The staged effect of the Sultan's grand entrance into his palace was spoiled by the appearance of a scruffy beggar, who had somehow managed to force his way through the heavily guarded gates at the same time as his ruler. Sweeping the man aside, His Highness Sultan Fadhl bin Ali bin Ahmed bin Ali bin Muhsin Al-'Abdali cut an impressive figure in his silken Indo-Arab frock coat and white-crested turban. Gracious and poised, he did a round of the entire line-up, with the Amir in close attendance and me tagging along behind. At the reception inside the palace, I was placed between the Amir and Qaid Ali bin Ahmed, the Sultan's Sandhurst-trained cousin, who was both Commandant of the Lahej Federal National Guard and Chief of Police. After adulatory speeches of welcome from both the Amir and Abdul Qadir Bindari, the Schools Supervisor, the Sultan rose to his feet. He spoke with urbane authority, but his handsome, imperious face was marred by a weak, loosely hanging lower lip. He also looked completely washed out.

Celebrating my own 30th birthday in Aden that same evening, I remarked on the Sultan's jaded appearance to Tom Heaton. "Nothing to do with the stresses of the London Conference, though that was a complete flop," he said. "Just put it down to sexual excesses in London, Rome and Beirut."

Sir Charles Johnston admired the political dexterity of Sultan Fadhl who, in Lahej at least, was marginally more popular than his brother. Sayyid Husain would never criticize the 'Abdali ruling family, but my clerk Othman Nasser, a subversive source of suq gossip, once took me into his dubious confidences.

After inviting me to his wedding in Shaikh Othman, where he graciously received his guests on a dais, smartly stuffing their monetary offerings into an old pillow case as a green-shirted band bashed out Egyptian pop music, he let slip the depth of his republican sympathies and his intense hatred of the 'Abdalis.

Othman was not alone in his views. I got some inkling of the popular undercurrents that lay beneath the surface of Lahej's murky waters when the Amir asked me to investigate the source of some seditious leaflets freely circulating around the suq. Describing the Federal rulers as "the agents, stooges and bandits of imperialism", they portrayed the Amir as a greedy tyrant who bought blocks of flats in Ma'alla with profits from the Lahej Cotton Board, bought off the police, rigged the Shari'a courts and tortured political prisoners. The Sultan was castigated as "the lover of the depraved harlot Hala – the Satan of Lahej"; the latter being a Jordanian lady who happened to be his wife. Five men were later arrested for distributing these leaflets and held in custody in Aden. When the Amir demanded that I have them deported to Lahej for trial, I had to explain that the laws of Aden did not sanction extradition for purely political offences. A quiet word in the ear of Sharif Husain should have done the trick, without the Amir having to importune me. However, he wanted this particular extradition to be both covert and have a veneer of British acquiescence.

The Sultan's wife should have been above suspicion. However, as Robin Young's "eyes and ears" in Lahej, it was my job to keep my political antennae attuned and provide the WAP Office with local intelligence. Some weeks after the leaflets episode, I received a Special Branch secret report on an attempted assassination plot which allegedly implicated both the Sultan and his wife, Hala. Apparently, when Hala had been a pupil at the Aden Girls Secondary School, disciplinary proceedings had been taken against her for exceptionally bad behaviour. Another Jordanian girl, Subhiyya, had sided with the School's headmistress, Mrs Petrie, thereby earning Hala's bitter hatred. Shortly after leaving school, Hala had been introduced to Sultan Fadhl, who married her in 1963. Subhiyya, meanwhile, had married a Jordanian bank clerk, Sidqi Kattee. To pursue her vendetta, it was alleged that Hala persuaded the Sultan to pay a longstanding palace servant, Abdullah Khamis, to kill Kattee, fire his car and steal Subhiyya's jewellery. The assassination attempt failed, but Khamis was later arrested by the Aden Police in the act of planting a bomb in Kattee's house. Under interrogation, he confessed to an Aden police superintendent and two inspectors that the Sultan had personally given him the bomb, but at his trial this evidence was treated as inadmissible and he was sentenced to only one year's imprisonment.

When both Jock Snell and a senior British police officer corroborated these unedifying facts, I tackled Robin Young. "Can't we do something about this? The whole business stinks."

"Of course it does," replied Robin. "But the case has already been tried by an Aden court, Khamis was found guilty and put in jug. His confession may or may not be true, but if he ever gave evidence which implicated the Sultan he'd be a dead duck. More to the point, we'd have a political crisis on our hands, which we can best do without. Let's get on with things that really matter."

Fortunately, the Kattees were sensible enough to pack their bags and return to Jordan.

As my immediate boss, Robin was almost as much a part of my everyday life as the Amir Abdullah. He came over as an unemotional if boisterous member of the "Biff 'em and bash 'em" school, and never showed the slightest surprise about anything I reported back to him about Lahej. Maybe he knew it all. Robin was adept at *realpolitik*, and whenever we argued the toss on policy matters touching on moral principle, was unswervingly pragmatic. Yet he was true to his own values, and could not have been more considerate when, at a most inconvenient time for all concerned, I went through a shattering personal crisis. His father had served with distinction in the Sudan Political Service, and Robin must have found the disintegration of Britain's last imperial outpost in the Arab World a profoundly depressing experience.

In so far as any one day in my Lahej life was typical, part of it might involve an early morning visit to Robin. Making a pre-dawn start, I would drive the twenty-five miles to Al-Ittihad by a road that crossed what was then desert. He and I would then discuss business over a hearty breakfast on the verandah of his house. That done, I might either have meetings at a Federal ministry about development, or drop in to the WAP Office's "Morning Prayers" for a security update. Here, gathered round a long table, would be the WAP's Senior Advisers, along with Security and Armed Services representatives, tasked to assess Federal political and military intelligence.

Long before the meeting was called to order, the meticulous Ralph Daly would have skimmed through and already digested a fistful of signals from his Assistants in Area East. Reports would then be read out about dissident activities, NLF "fronts", arms smuggling, murders, miscellaneous shootings, and counter-terrorist operations, to an audience which reacted with mixed levels of attention and interest. Few conclusions were ever drawn, but at the end of each month secret intelligence digests were circulated to thirty-one named recipients ranging from the Commander-in-Chief Middle East to AA Lahej, though not, inexplicably, to DMS (Security) Aden. The occasional exhortation, such as "any sign of weakness by the Federal Government at this stage would encourage the tribes to revolt beyond Radfan", did nothing to allay my conviction that our intelligence apparatus still lacked direction and co-ordination.

A minor episode illustrating this came my way when a Yemeni Army sergeant and two private soldiers gave themselves up at Suqayya to seek political asylum. The Amir had them slung into Lahej's barbaric prison. A month later, he asked me what I thought we should do about them.

"Are we sure that they are bona fide political refugees?" I ventured.

"Of course they are!" the Amir shot back, grimly. "No doubts about that after what they've been through with us over the past month. We now know more about these men than their mothers ever did."

"Then why not release them?"

The Amir threw up his hands in mock horror. "Oh no, Mr Harding – never, never! Propaganda, propaganda, Mr Harding. We must learn from Cairo Radio. Now these birds have enjoyed our hospitality, they will sing as sweetly as we want them to over Aden Radio. We must not lose such an opportunity. Please take them down to Aden immediately, and pass them on to Mr Hobson. He'll know exactly what to do with them."

Laurie Hobson's assistant at the High Commission knew nothing of his boss's whereabouts, and disclaimed any knowledge about Yemeni political refugees. I took the three men over to the Aden Broadcasting Services offices, only to find that its Chief Officer, Husain Safi, was unobtainable. Eventually, I cobbled together an impromptu interview team. That evening, Aden Radio's airwaves crackled with messages to the Arab World about the trio's brave bid "to cast off the shackles of Egyptian tyranny to help restore Imam Badr". After the three had done their bidding, I asked Hobson's assistant what he proposed doing with them.

"You realize that they're virtually dead meat for going on air," I told him. "We must at least find them some sort of government employment."

"Nothing to do with me," he replied. "I've had no instructions about them whatsoever. I can't possibly keep them here, so you'd better take them back to Lahej."

I did so, but when I asked the Amir if he could find them work, he washed his hands of the whole business, declaring that it was now a Federal matter. For the next month, the Yemeni Three were forever hanging around my office, begging for special passes to get work in Aden. After exploding at one Morning Prayers meeting about our lack of policy or principle, I lobbied everyone from Arthur Watts to Sharif Husain himself, embarrassingly interrupting a private meeting he was having with Sultan Fadhl, to get satisfaction. The Sharif said that he would find the sergeant a job as a sweeper. The other two would have to fend for themselves.

Life was never dull in Lahej. However, as in Mukalla, AA Lahej acted as a general dogsbody, fielding everyone's complaints. The Lahej Police complained about the misbehaviour of Radfan-bound British convoys; Lahej contractors about the British Army's rates of pay; Lahej farmers about money they were owed by the 'Abdalis; 'Aqrabis about bad water, sewage, unemployment and 'Abdali exploitation. Even the odd Haushabi would pop in to whinge about 'Abdali oppression and wrongdoing. When an RAF Belvedere helicopter crashed just outside Al-Hauta, killing the two brave airmen who had managed to steer it away from the town, I helped conduct the board of enquiry. Then, on any day, with or without warning, visitors private and public, official and unofficial might fetch up from Aden to see something of the "real Arabia" and then stay on for a drink, a meal, a game of badminton, or maybe a bed.

Early on, Arthur Watts had been helpful in lobbying various Federal ministries to support my Subaihi Scheme. To return past hospitality, I invited Arthur and Barbara to dinner at Lahej. Another guest was Qaid Ali bin Ahmed. I had assumed that Arthur might be interested to learn that the Amir had just given me virtual *carte blanche* to press ahead with the Subaihi Scheme, forgetting that, as the first Assistant Adviser to be appointed to Lahej, he still regarded this as *his* parish. Having made his point and re-established the pecking order, I let him do all the talking. He kept us all in fits with his description of Sir Tom Hickinbotham's 1954 British mission to Ta'izz which, he maintained, had set back relations with the Imam for years. Warming to his audience, he then went wildly over the top by claiming that the banished Sultan Ali bin Abdul Karim had not only been his protégé, but had also been an altogether more effective ruler than the present Sultan. Ali bin Ahmed, Sultan Fadhl's cousin, sat stony-faced and silent.

This was not Arthur's last visit, and I like to think that our past disagreements had long been forgotten. He could be quite charming when the mood took him, and his knowledge of Arabic and of South Arabia and its personalities was exceptional. His early retirement, at a time when his special talents might most usefully have been employed, remains a mystery. After leaving Arabia, he devoted much of his life to training people to teach music in schools. He died unexpectedly in December 1972, aged only fifty-six. As a memorial to his work, the East Sussex Music School established a fund to provide musical instruments for disadvantaged children of high musical aptitude. I shall never forget that evening we spent together in Mukalla, following the score of the Bach violin study.

13

Roads to Radfan

WHEN THE MOOD TOOK him, the Amir Abdullah would happily discuss world events, and might even seek my views on British politics, after airing his usual beefs about the Yemen frontier and Federal interference with Lahej's internal affairs. When, at Young's behest, I raised the hoary issue of the Federal Army's five-year-stale application to build a new military camp at Naubat Dukaim, a nodal point 17 miles north-west of Lahej up the Wadi Tiban, his response was always the same: "You must take this up with Mr Young. I can get no sense out of the Ministry of Defence." The Minister of Defence was, of course, the Amir's brother, the Sultan. I came to realize that any Federal military installation that got too close to the frontier was likely to upset the 'Abdali game of keeping sweet with the Yemen. Predictably, the camp at Naubat Dukaim was never built.

The Amir's criteria of suitability were quite different when it came to military projects nearer home, as in the case of Makhnuq. The RAF wanted to use this deserted stretch of the Subaihi coast for a bombing range. The Aden Civil Aviation Authority's objections that this presented a hazard to overflying civilian aircraft were easily brushed aside by HQ Middle East Command, on the grounds that the Armed Services' requirements were paramount. Even so, the RAF were puzzled that their application had got nowhere with the Federal authorities, failing to appreciate that Makhnuq was in 'Abdali territory, and that the Amir had no truck with Federal officialdom. When I explained the airmen's problem to him, he agreed to their request without demur. "What does Makhnuq matter? It's just a miserable fishing village. Let them have their bombing range, but of course, we must charge them a proper commercial rent."

By now, the Amir was positively encouraging me to get personally involved in Lahej's internal security, even to the extent of instructing me to accompany Qaid Ali bin Ahmed to assess the political situation at Tor al-Baha. Apparently, the despicable Muhammad Sa'id Humaidi, the Amir's one-time intended assassination target, was still in the area stirring up trouble. Sandhurst-trained Qaid Ali, a tall, handsome man in his early thirties, was very close to his uncle the Amir, and when we left Lahej together at dawn with an armed escort, the Amir paid us the unusual compliment of personally seeing us off from his palace gates. We drove north-westwards towards the mountains through acre upon acre of fertile land, irrigated by artesian wells and an elaborate system of water channels. Qaid Ali proudly pointed out that these rolling acres belonged to his uncle. Until then, I had not appreciated the full extent of the Lahej Delta, nor that much of its soil comprised accumulated silt more than four metres deep.

It took four hours of hard driving to cover the 73 miles to Tor al-Baha. The Naib, Yeslam Rassoul, forewarned of our visit, had laid on a traditional ginger coffee break before convening a meeting to which, inexplicably, he had invited two minor local shaikhs, Ali Shukri and Ali Ruwaihi. Having earlier described these two as "dangerous malcontents", he was soon out-talked by this voluble pair who vociferously denied any involvement in the recent troubles, which they darkly attributed to "fear on the part of the people". Qaid Ali whispered to me that they were lying and that, as the Amir's Adviser, I was now expected to lay down the law. My anodyne warning, that "any recurrence of this sort of trouble will be severely dealt with by the government", was made without the slightest idea how it might be enforced. Inadvertently, it had the effect of peremptorily ending the meeting, whereupon the two malcontents slunk off, muttering darkly between themselves.

Driving back to Lahej, Qaid Ali confided: "That Naib is a weak man. I don't trust him any more than those other two rogues, but the Amir wanted you to see for yourself the sort of people we are having to deal with. Frankly, I'm not too worried about our military preparedness at Tor al-Baha for the time being, as our garrison is strong enough to defend itself, but the political situation is giving the Amir concern."

It was not long before the Amir was proved only too right.

The 'Abdali Sultanate might be the Federation's premier state, but not even ingrained 'Abdali hostility to Federal military projects could overrule the Federal Supreme Council's grand design to rebuild the Dhala' road. During the First World War, Britain's hold on South Arabia had been roughly shaken by the Turks, who occupied Lahej until after the Armistice. After it, Qutaibi tribesmen, sensing British weakness, had effectively closed this ancient caravan route to regular traffic. When the 1934 Anglo-Yemeni Treaty of San'a encouraged the Colonial Office to adopt a more robust approach, Hamilton forcibly reopened this "river of trade". Thirty years on, the Radfan Operation had proved conclusively that the old Dhala' road was quite unsuitable for transporting tanks and heavy artillery.

In early July, Young gave me the news over breakfast: "It has at last been decided to build an all-weather road to Radfan, and ultimately Dhala', to give the military proper access to its forward bases. The first and longest section to Thumair will go through your parish, so it's going to be your job to sell the scheme to the Amir as, without his co-operation, it's virtually a non-starter. The Sappers and Federal PWD will be responsible for the new road's construction, but they'll need local Laheji labour, so you'll have to liaise with all concerned, and help sort out security requirements."

"Where's the money coming from, Robin?"

"We've squeezed £120,000 out of HMG. The Federalis will somehow have to find the rest."

I knew nothing about road building, but I was certain that a mere £120,000 to build an 80-km road over some of the most rugged and dangerous terrain in the WAP simply didn't add up.

"Surely, that's not nearly enough?"

"Of course it's not," Young retorted. "But we've got to make a start pretty damn quick. I'm coming under enormous pressure from on high to get this thing moving. Money's not your problem. We can always ask for more once the road's got under way."

To my surprise, the Amir readily agreed the scheme in principle, despite his being given only three days' notice that the Royal Engineers wanted to site their headquarters construction camp at Al-Anad, twelve miles north-west of Lahej and just short of Naubat Dukaim. His only proviso was that he must be responsible for contracting all local labour. After flurries of preparatory activity, the inaugural meeting of the "Thumair Road Committee" was held on 10 August. From then on, the Dhala' Road became my foremost preoccupation. PWD engineers and a succession of Royal Engineer supremos came and went. But the man on the spot, who kept the whole thing moving forward, was Major Bob Anderson, commanding 6 Field Unit Royal Engineers.

To make an initial technical assessment of the most likely route, Anderson and I joined a team of road engineers, unwittingly choosing one of the hottest days of the year to traipse up and over, round and about eroding wadi banks, boulder fields, bare rock and shifting sands. After taking copious notes and photographs en route, the engineers confessed at the end of a very long day that this was indeed the first professional survey of the road yet undertaken, and that the earlier estimated timescale and costs had been grossly underestimated. Nonetheless, the project went into overdrive forthwith, though just before construction work was officially due to begin, the Amir summoned me to drop a bombshell.

"I want to have nothing more to do with the hire of labour for this road, Mr Harding – nothing!"

"I'm very sorry to hear that, O Amir. What is the problem?"

"So far as I'm concerned, there is no problem. But you British must take full responsibility for the security of my Lahej workmen. You realize, of course, that part of your route goes through Haushabi, territory over which I have no control. By God! I can promise that you will have trouble there. From now on, you must hire all local labour yourself."

For the Amir to pull out at this late stage was potentially disastrous. The alignment of the route had only been settled after further back-up surveys and endless technical discussions. It could not now be changed without putting the project back by months. Moreover, I was not confident I could handle the inevitable wage-bargaining sessions and industrial disputes without the Amir's official support. I well knew that he loathed the Haushabi Sultan, but suspected that it was as likely the unwelcome prospect of Federal involvement that had raised his hackles. I let matters lie for a day or so, hoping that this would give him time to appreciate that labour contracting gave him the perfect excuse to squeeze more money out of the British Army.

Soon enough, he summoned me. "I have now decided that I *do* wish to be involved in providing labour for this road. However, I won't have those Federal people bringing in their roguish Adeni contractors who will only take the bread from my people's mouths. I shall appoint local contractors, but must leave it to you to recruit the unskilled labour – men from Lahej only, of course."

Before he could change his mind, I got Sayyid Husain to put the word round the suq that road hands were needed. Long before dawn on the oft-postponed start day, 1 September, more than a hundred men turned up outside the gates of Al-Anad to fill the thirty slots available. A separate group of four elbowed their way to the front of the queue, each claiming to have been appointed as contractor-foreman by the Amir. Selecting the unskilled labour was easy enough, but by the end of that long, hot morning I had also appointed a Laheji as the main contractor, the Naib of Naubat Dukaim as overall supervisor, and two local *'aqils* as foremen. Our twenty-eight labourers readily agreed to work an eight-hour day, seven days a week. No restrictive union rules here, but the pay was well above average.

For the next six months, several days every week, I would slip out of Lahej at dawn to drive the 15 miles to Al-Anad for meetings with Anderson to sort out recurrent labour and security problems. Arabia was always at its best in the early morning. To head northwards up Lahej's tree-lined avenue was to witness another world at work. Strings of camel caravans trundled in from the interior. Farmers astride game little donkeys, their feet dragging along the ground, rode in to the suq. Women in gaily-coloured dresses would already be active in the fields on either side of the road, cutting ten-foot-high *gasab* with sickles. Later in the day they would return home, carrying their precious cereal in reed baskets balanced on their heads, swinging their hips to an innate rhythm. After the floods, the dun fields would be transformed to a brilliant green and, once cleared, clouds of white egrets would descend upon them to feed upon myriad insects. So began nature's cycle anew, an idyllic picture of rural harmony. And always ahead, adding its own high drama, rose the spiky mass of Jebel Manif and, beyond it, the hazy blue heights of Radfan. That view forever remains in my mind's eye, a vision of eternal morning.

Three weeks after construction work had begun, Anderson and I made our first full trial run right through to Thumair. The Sappers' camp at Al-Anad, once a haphazard dump of stores and equipment, had become a typical British Army base, complete with neat, tented lines and whitewashed marker stones. The whole, now ringed by a high barbed-wire perimeter fence, had been implausibly described by San'a Radio as one "which their puppets and stooges claim to be no more than a site for chemical and agricultural research".

We left at sunrise. Although I had deliberately not told my driver Ahmed where we were bound, it seemed that everyone at Al-Anad knew already. Leading Bob's convoy was an armour-plated Bedford 3-tonner. Another Bedford 5-tonner, packed with soldiers, brought up the rear with our two Land Rovers sandwiched in between. As we roared out of the camp in billowing clouds of dust, an RAF Hunter screamed up the valley above. "We'll soon be travelling through Injun Country," said Bob, glancing up at the fast-retreating warplane. "I'm taking no chances. We Sappers have already lost fifteen vehicles and suffered eighteen casualties from mines over the past three months. That Haushabi stretch alone has been responsible for three separate mining incidents. Until the road's sealed, it's too damn easy to lay mines."

Not far up the road, tyre fragments and the wreck of an upturned Land Rover told their own story. At the entrance to the Wadi Milah, two British Army 3-tonners blocked the way. A Ferret armoured car stood guard, with its heavy machine gun trained on two stationary civilian lorries. Their drivers and passengers squatted resignedly in the shade of a thorn bush, with a single British soldier sitting opposite, cocked rifle resting casually across his knees. His comrades were busy chucking out the lorries' contents with deliberate abandon. Many of the wooden crates had split open, spewing their merchandise about the stony ground.

My immediate instinct was to remonstrate with their officer that this treatment might be counter-productive. I then remembered the wrecked Land Rover, and the British soldiers who had been killed or maimed along the way, so merely asked what he was looking for. "Guns and grenades," he replied. "These buggers are Yemenis. They tried to drive off the road immediately they spotted us, but we nabbed them. When we brought them in, two of them threatened our interpreter."

We left the soldiers to their business and drove on into the heart of Qutaibi country. Here, in the sweltering trough of a wild wadi, an enormous bulldozer, driven by a bronzed young Sapper stripped to the waist, was shifting house-sized boulders. In his wake came a gang of the very Lahejis I had recruited, chanting merrily as they cleared away the rubble. Manning the heights above, FNG picquets scanned the surrounding countryside for trouble.

Thumair was unrecognizable from the isolated little fort from which I had marched up the Wadi Misrah with Godfrey Meynell the previous autumn. Since the Radfan Campaign, it had become the biggest British military base in the Middle East outside Aden, and now supported a British infantry battalion, artillery, armour and a Royal Engineer squadron. As we arrived, a giant Beverley transport landed on the extended airstrip to create a miniature dust storm. At the battalion mess, I bumped into two of my brother Assistant Advisers, James Nash and Bryan Somerfield. James, previously responsible for the political direction of the Radfan campaign, and currently based on Dhala', cut a very different figure from the pin-stripe-suited gent I had last seen at the Civil Service Commission Board at Savile Row. Now sporting Arab headdress, rifle, revolver, ammunition bandolier and portable wireless, he was dressed for the part, save for a bulky briefcase.

"What on earth's that for, James?"

"Papers dear boy, just papers. But please don't touch my briefcase. It's set to blow your hand off if you don't know the lock settings."

"What are you up to now, in Dhala'?"

"Playing the opposition at their own game. They mine us, so we mine them. Tit for tat. I'm usually more successful, as I pay my team more than theirs, at 250 quid a shot."

I had not previously met Bryan Somerfield, who had taken over from James as the Assistant Adviser for Radfan, based on Thumair. An ex-RAF officer and experienced Arabist, he was less gung-ho and older than most of the WAP's new generation of Assistant Advisers, entrusted with the daunting task of putting Radfan back on its feet. I asked him about its future prospects.

"Most people in Whitehall, Aden, and even Al-Ittihad, don't begin to realize what's happened here as a result of the campaign. Okay, before the fighting really started, we dropped the usual leaflets warning people to get out, or else. But many of the old men, women and children couldn't possibly leave just like that. So they got thumped indiscriminately and much harder than the bad boys, who either fought us or scarpered. Campaign instructions were to attack anyone still left in the vicinity, burn their fodder, destroy crops and kill all livestock. All that was done only too effectively, leaving behind nothing but swathes of devastated land and a legacy of bitterness."

"But wasn't that inevitable? Surely we had to win the war?"

"Yes, of course we had to. And it was well done," replied Bryan. "But now we've got to win the peace. The cost of this campaign has been stupendous. Most of the younger tribesmen have pushed off to the Yemen to lick their wounds. But they'll be back in their own time, thirsting for revenge. This place is in a frightful mess. Since the campaign ended, the only significant rehabilitation work has been done by the British Army, digging out a few wells and drilling the odd bore hole. No one at the top seems to have thought this thing through. We've got to prove that we're here to help these people get back to normal, and I've only been given peanuts to do it."

"But surely you'll be getting most of the £500,000 that has been earmarked for WAP development aid? Robin's already promised me £35,000 for Subaihi."

"Really?" replied Bryan, with a grimace. "And pigs might fly. No one's told *me* what I'll be getting. Anyway, even half a million's a spit in the bucket for what needs to be done up here. My spies tell me that those High Commission boobies have only just referred the WAP development package back to London for approval, yet it's now over three months since the campaign ended."

In the aftermath of the Radfan campaign, the Federal Supreme Council had asked Whitehall for £8 million to fund hinterland development, spread over 1964–66. Trevaskis, as High Commissioner, had personally pleaded for an emergency £3 million aid package. HMG was unmoved. The military budget was maintained, but £500,000 was all the WAP was ever going to get for development. Our host at lunch, Brigadier Blair, the officer commanding the Thumair Brigade, was as gloomy as Somerfield about the future.

"I can't see that there is a long-term military solution for Radfan, and no one has yet come up with a political one."

As we drove back to Lahej in the heat of the afternoon, the mountains had become obscured by haze, and the road was barely visible for the dust kicked up by the lorry in front of us. As we bumped along, I pondered on whether the cost of this military operation would have been necessary had only a fraction of the money been spent on pumps, wells, schools and health units long before it started.

When I reported back to the Amir on the progress of the Dhala' Road, he was suffering from uncharacteristic nerve failure.

"You know, of course, that our Lahej drivers are threatening strike action?" he remonstrated aggressively. "What do you intend doing about it?"

This was news to me, so I asked him the reason.

"The reason is the British Army's downright meanness," he retorted. "They are not paying our drivers enough money for the dangerous work they do. This is purely a money issue. You must sort it out with the Army immediately if you want these men back at work."

Sayyid Husain reckoned that ATUC agitators had instigated the trouble. I summoned all the strikers together and made a big show of collecting their names, with the threat that these would be referred back to the Minister of the Interior for further investigation. Next day, I called another meeting, this time attended by the Amir in person. After another sultry morning's argy-bargy, most of the men agreed to return to work, provided that their terms and conditions were formally incorporated into a written agreement, personally sealed by the Amir.

With honour thus satisfied, we had very little labour trouble along the Dhala' Road until we reached Haushabi. This minor sultanate, bordering the Yemen, was one of the WAP's most impoverished states, containing some of its wildest mountain country. Hyena, lynx and even leopard, a mangy specimen of which I had seen hanging from a tree outside the Sultan's palace at his capital, Musaimir, still survived. Its administration was shambolic and its Sultan, Faisal bin Sarur, a sly, venal character whom the Amir Abdullah had once described to me as: "That anti-federation absentee. That active supporter of republican Yemen. That debauchee. You British must get rid of this man, Mr Harding!"

When Haushabi had first joined the Federation, Sultan Faisal had been given the sinecure of Minister of Posts and Telegraphs. He never attempted to fulfil his ministerial functions, so was awarded the booby prize of Minister without Portfolio. The Amir Abdullah was not alone in his views. The previous year, Michael Crouch had rumbled Sultan Faisal for flogging his standard WAP Office arms and ammunition issue to Yemeni dissidents. For this there was no official reprimand. Sir Richard Turnbull probably had the likes of Faisal in mind when making his valedictory judgement that most Federal rulers were "futile, useless, self-serving puppets".

Although the Dhala' Road only barely touched on Haushabi, I had made a fatal mistake in not taking to heart the Amir Abdullah's earlier warnings about Faisal. Naively, I had also assumed that Al-Ittihad would have sought his formal permission to allow the new road to pass through his territory. On the day that work on the short Haushabi section was due to begin, Anderson and I inspected the impressive collection of bulldozers, house-high American-made Michigan road-lifters and the 10-ton dumper trucks that were assembled, ready to roll. As there was nothing more for me to do on site, I then returned to my Lahej office. Here, I was confronted by a tall, scowling man pacing up and down the floor. When he turned on me with a ferocious "What are the British Army doing in Haushabi territory, Mr Harding? Who gave them permission to do this?" I realized at once that I'd met this character before – Husain Nasr Al-Bursi.

Godfrey Meynell once described his former JAA Thumair as "energetic, charming and formidable, but unpredictable". The WAP Office must have decided that Al-Bursi was either too valuable an ally or too dangerous an enemy to ditch, so had moved him sideways to become Haushabi's JAA. I had strayed into his manor uninvited, and he wasn't having it. After I had offered him larded apologies, he calmed down, indulged in some lofty talk about mutual co-operation, and then came to the point.

"Your 'Abdali workmen are taking the bread from the mouths of my Haushabis. They too must be given road work."

Fair enough. I promised him that the Army would suspend operations until we had agreed an equitable distribution of work. I also suggested that he and I have an on-site meeting with the Royal Engineers. To make his point, Al-Bursi didn't bother to turn up. Eventually, we reached a *modus operandi* after I had co-opted one of his former comrades-in-arms, the Waqil Qaid stationed al-Milah, to act as an intermediary.

With Al-Bursi ostensibly on side, I imagined that the Dhala' Road could now go full-steam ahead. In this I was mistaken. Within a week of our entering Haushabi, Al-Anad suffered its first dissident attack. When I complained to the Amir that the camp's Lahej Guard had made no attempt to return enemy fire, he first reproached me for not having taken his earlier warnings about Haushabi more seriously. He then promised to provide a mobile patrol, and would also ask his brother to review Al-Anad's security at Federal level. We got the Lahej mobile patrol soon enough, but that was the last I heard about Federal support. Autumn was a close season, when both the Sultan and the Amir repaired to Beirut for their annual night-clubbing binge. It was left to Qaid Ali bin Ahmed's deputy, 6 Field Squadron's excellent Regimental Sergeant-Major and myself to devise an effective defensive strategy to protect the camp.

In fact, these early attacks were little more than irritants. The success of the Radfan campaign had temporarily stabilized much of the hinterland. In Aden too, Trevaskis's State of Emergency had significantly reduced terrorist incidents. However, the forthcoming Aden Legislative Council elections, scheduled for 16 October, after an eighteen-month postponement to allow post-merger consolidation, were seen as posing a significant internal security threat. Trevaskis's rejection of Zain Baharoon's sensible proposal to extend the 1959 franchise to a 20-year residential qualification (to include women), meant that the Aden electorate remained at 8,000 out of an estimated population of 250,000. The PSP's response was to order an election boycott. Explosions set the scene for demonstrations, intimidation and violence. One scurrilous suq rumour, relayed to me by Tom Heaton, was that when Trevaskis heard that one of his clerks was proposing to stand, he offered him 100 rifles and 100 boxes of ammunition to desist.

Aden's election day was bizarrely timed to coincide within a day with the 1964 British general election. On the preceding afternoon, I was summoned from Lahej to attend an emergency meeting at the Aden Police Headquarters. Here a glum, disgruntled group of senior British government officials, including several ministerial heads of department, were already assembled. Jock Snell brought this restive meeting to order, and then launched into a rambling exposition of why the elections posed a security threat, concluding with a lame plea that all present should volunteer to help supervise Aden's polling stations.

Unfortunately, this was not Jock's scene. While he might happily parley for days on end with wily Bedouin, he was hopelessly out of his depth with a bunch of jittery British bureaucrats, whose main concern was their own personal safety. Flustered by hostile interjections, he was flummoxed when someone asked whether contract officers were automatically eligible for compensation from injury. With this question left hanging in the air, Robin Thorne had to drive to Government House to get clarification from the High Commissioner personally. Meanwhile, the curdling cream of expatriate officialdom sat around in conspiratorial huddles, muttering amongst themselves. When Thorne returned with a vague assurance that anyone with conscientious objections would be absolved from polling station duty, a senior Establishment Department official stalked out, and was swiftly followed by most of those present. Jimmy Lloyd, Brian Doe, Hugh Walker, myself and a few others stayed put, and were rewarded with the offer of choosing our own polling stations.

Hugh Walker, recently arrived from Kenya's rugged Northern Frontier

District, was already thoroughly disenchanted with Britain's South Arabia policy. He baulked at HMG's unqualified support for its reactionary rulers, and objected both to the WAP Office's counter-terrorist tactics and the arms and ammunition handouts. This pre-election day collapse of morale added to his disillusionment and so depressed us both that, at Robin Young's Westminster Election Night party that same evening, we only stayed on to hear the opening results. Robin stayed up all night and, when Harold Wilson's Labour Party narrowly won, he correctly prophesied that this change of government effectively marked the end of Britain's role in South Arabia. Denis Healey, the new Defence Secretary, lost little time in giving notice that although Britain would be retaining the Aden base, it had no intention of preserving the powers of "the feudal sultans".

Early next morning, I drove in from Lahej to report for duty at the Government Primary School, Saila Road. Crater was stiff with armed police, and the streets eerily quiet. There was little activity at my polling station, and half way through the morning Jock arrived in a police Land Rover. "No fuss, no worries," he announced, beaming. "Everything's under control, so I'm standing all volunteers down. You can go back to Lahej."

The Aden election passed off smoothly enough, with a 76 percent turnout. As expected, Zain Baharoon was returned as Chief Minister. But of the fifteen members elected, the PSP claimed that seven, including Khalifa Abdullah Al-Khalifa, who was still in detention as the prime suspect for the Aden Airport bomb, were party sympathizers. Each of us volunteers received personal letters expressing the High Commissioner's gratitude "for your willingness to come forward and help on this occasion".

Aden's election results, announced on 17 October, triggered well-rehearsed student demonstrations in both Aden and Al-Ittihad. Three days later, there were similar demonstrations in Lahej. When the Lahej police failed to disperse the mob, Amir Abdullah courageously confronted it in person making an appeal for calm. When he was pelted with stones, the Lahej Federal Guard were summoned with orders to open fire if necessary. Although this temporarily dispersed the mob, it regrouped next day outside the Amir's palace, waving UAR and Yemen Arab Republic flags, and chanting "Long Live Gamal Abdul Nasser!" In the mêlée that ensued, sixty shots were fired and ten soldiers and policemen injured before the rioters scattered. The trouble quickly spread to Tor al-Baha, where demonstrations lasted for two days.

I lunched in Aden soon afterwards with Tom Heaton, who reckoned that the student protests had been encouraged by militant infiltration, and forecast more serious trouble ahead. That same afternoon while in Steamer Point, I happened to notice Arthur Charles, Aden's Speaker and Public Service Commissioner, taking an evening constitutional with his wife. I recorded in my diary "the evocative sight of an old-school colonial servant following a well-worn path". A year later, Charles would be gunned down by an NLF assassin after a game of tennis on one of Crater's public courts, another of his regular pursuits.

Driving back to Lahej that night with John Ducker, who happened to be staying with me before his home leave, we were stopped at the Dar Sa'ad frontier post by armed police. "There have been bombs in Aden and Lahej," explained the officer-in-charge. "I have orders to ask you to report to Mr Young at Al-Ittihad immediately."

I drove back the way we had just come to find the High Commission Office deserted, so telephoned Robin at home. "Your house and the Sultan's palace have been attacked by bazookas. Get back to Lahej immediately to see what's been happening," was all he said. We reached the house to find that the lighting system had packed up. Most of the windows on one side were blown in, and my long-drop lavatory, a carbuncle-like structure protruding from an outside wall, completely obliterated. An agitated guardsman explained that Sayyid Husain and Othman had decamped to Shaikh Othman with their families, after Othman's wife had gone into hysterics. Next morning, closer inspection revealed two ragged, four-foot-diameter holes blown through the perimeter wall at the rear of my house. The Amir came across in person to inspect the damage, and was as good as his promise to have it repaired that same day. When a very strained-looking Husain reappeared that afternoon, his only comment was: "This is the first time the Amir has ever visited us. It must be a good sign."

The attack on my house made the front page of *The Daily Telegraph*, but the Amir made quite sure that there was no publicity about the more serious damage done to the Sultan's palace. A week later, someone lobbed a grenade into the Lahej Police Station. When Qaid Ali bin Ahmed identified the culprit as a well-known Shaikh Othman merchant, I telephoned Aden's Special Branch immediately. Predictably, by the time an officer had raced out to help search the suspect's two houses, both their owner and any incriminating evidence had disappeared.

The heat was getting ever closer to Lahej, yet it was its mean and despised vassal state of 'Aqrabi that now posed the more serious threat to Aden's internal security. 'Aqrabi would scarcely have merited inclusion in the Federation had it not occupied a strip of sand conveniently equidistant between Aden and Little Aden. In 1958, the Federated States had commandeered a chunk of this to build the new capital, Al-Ittihad. In return, its ruler, Shaikh Mahmoud, was granted one of the Federal Council's 85 seats plus a modest rental. 'Aqrabi's "capital", Bir Ahmed, was a scattering of squalid houses grouped around a single street which boasted a five-shack suq and one fly-blown coffee shop. Its open sewers and mosquito-infested pools were an affront to any administration. Yet it need not have been thus. Although the rapacious 'Abdalis had siphoned off most of the Wadi Tiban's surface flood water before it even reached 'Aqrabi, it was 'Aqrabi inertia that had allowed its own irrigation system to collapse. Savvy outsiders, such as Shaikh Muhammad Farid, the Minister for External Affairs, entrepreneurial Lahejis, Aden merchants and grasping federal officials had all tumbled to the potential of the massive subterranean outflow beneath 'Aqrabi's sands. But while they had successfully invested in tube wells and farming operations, a bitterly envious Shaikh Mahmoud and his batty, one-toothed "Director of Agriculture", Shaikh Haidara, merely complained about the iniquity of it all.

On his return, in very poor shape, from an extended jolly on the back of that summer's London Constitutional Conference, Shaikh Mahmoud invited me to lunch along with his entire state council. They proceeded to bombard me with endless gripes about British failings to remedy 'Aqrabi's unemployment, lack of clean water, non-existent schools and health facilities. When I inspected Bir Ahmed for myself, with Shaikh Mahmoud and a train of his councillors in tow, it became clear that 'Aqrabi's parlous state was due largely to Shaikh Mahmoud's apathy and greed. His Cattle Farm Project had soon gone bust because the cattle had been neither watered nor pastured. While his own and his officials' salaries had increased fifteen-fold over the past four years, agricultural expenditure had remained static.

In an attempt to get 'Aqrabi moving, I extracted a British Government Commonwealth Development & Welfare grant of EAS 120,000/-, and another EAS 50,000/- as a loan from National & Grindlays Bank, to fund an 'Aqrabi pump scheme to be managed by a newly established co-operative and marketing company. Shaikh Mahmoud flatly refused to contribute to the venture, as in no way could he get his hands into this particular till. Casting around, he had looked elsewhere to supplement his income.

The day after the grenade was lobbed into the Lahej police station, I happened to be discussing the 'Aqrabi estimates with Mahmoud, trying to persuade him that 'Aqrabi's economy could be transformed if only he would match his Federal grant from his own pocket. The only concessions I could wring out of him were promises to improve the town's water supply and repair the roof of the mosque. Just as I was leaving, he demanded "Two and Two [200 rifles and 200 boxes of ammunition] to replenish my exchequer". I told him bluntly what he could do with it.

That same afternoon, Robin Young summoned me urgently to Al-Ittihad. "We've just received reliable reports that arms and ammunition are being cached at Bir Ahmed. The place is being used as a transit station for terrorist weapons being smuggled into Aden. I'm having it searched by the Federal Guard tomorrow, and I want you and Husain Al-Wazir to be there too to confront Shaikh Mahmoud personally. See Sultan Salih first to get Federal clearance. Otherwise, don't mention this to a soul. The last thing we want is for that ghastly little Mahmoud to know that we're about to rumble him."

"But this is quite ridiculous, Robin," I remonstrated. "I've just spent the entire morning with that man discussing 'Aqrabi estimates and getting nowhere. When he had the gall to ask me for Two and Two, I told him politely to get stuffed. Now you tell me that he's gunrunning. Why the hell can't we just go in and arrest him."

"Keep your shirt on, John," said Robin. "We've got no hard evidence as yet. That's why you're going in tomorrow. Let's just get to the bottom of this business. We'll worry about 'Aqrabi's estimates later."

The prospect of catching Shaikh Mahmoud red-handed had an element of *schadenfreude*. After reporting to Sultan Salih, Sayyid Husain and I arrived at Bir Ahmed at 10 a.m. with a company of 120 Federal National II Guardsmen. The soldiers cordoned off the entire village with all the appearance of efficiency, at which point Shaikh Mahmoud, who normally spent his nights carousing and his days in bed, put in an appearance. He looked so spent and fraught that I almost felt sorry for him. I then wondered how, as his Adviser, I was going to handle the situation if arms were actually found. Put him under close arrest, or what?

Providence then came to Shaikh Mahmoud's rescue when a sand storm suddenly blew up from nowhere. It enveloped Bir Ahmed in a swirling shroud that made it impossible to see what was happening. When it subsided half an hour later, the officer commanding the company insisted on conducting the house-to-house search personally, refusing point-blank that Husain and I should accompany him, on the pretext that this was strictly a Federal military matter. Only the previous day, it had taken a trained Special Branch officer and myself more than two hours to search two empty houses in Shaikh Othman. This FNG lieutenant took less than an hour to clear the whole of Bir Ahmed. When he reported to me that he could find nothing, I knew that the trap had already been sprung.

I went back to Robin spitting blood. "We didn't find a thing, of course. I reckon that Mahmoud knew we were coming, and no doubt had the stuff shifted either before or during the sand storm. That *mulazim* probably did the rest. A right stitch-up. I simply can't understand why we're handling this corrupt little man with kid gloves when he's up to his neck in a terrorist arms-smuggling racket."

"You're almost certainly right," replied Robin, with a shrug. "But without hard evidence, we can't nail him. The *mulazim*'s collusion is more serious. I'll have to take that up with Sultan Salih."

Sensing that we had exhausted that particular line of enquiry, I doggedly reverted to the 'Aqrabi estimates. "I'd really like to close this charade, Robin. I've raised enough money from outside sources to fund a scheme that will tap Bir Ahmed's underground water, yet Mahmoud refuses to co-operate. He could have funded that whole thing himself, if he hadn't already blown half this year's state income on booze and tarts in London."

"Perks of feudal rulership, I'm afraid," sighed Robin.

"But why can't we put the screws on him? 'Aqrabi's a monument to our own neglect. Surely, we should be taking a much tougher line?"

"Right again," replied Robin, wearily. "But we can't force these people to do anything they don't want to. 'Aqrabi's no longer a British protected state but part of the Federation. Anyway, you should have seen the place before 1958!"

Ultimately, neither gunrunning nor cosying up to the revolutionaries did Shaikh Mahmoud any good. By September 1967, when most Federal rulers had fled the country, he was still hanging in there, but had already outlived his usefulness. Soon after, the NLF arrested him and his family, thus condemning them to certain doom.

"Now let's stop bothering about 'Aqrabi and think positive," said Robin, brightly. "You've finished your Subaihi aid scheme and the Dhala' Road is coming on nicely, so I want you to help out in Radfan. Bryan Somerfield's got more than enough on his plate up there. We need someone to take a fresh, hard look at what's needed. I'd like you to prepare the same sort of scheme for Radfan as you did for Subaihi."

If I had imagined that I already had enough on my plate in Lahej, I had miscalculated. However, the prospect of taking on Radfan was an irresistible challenge. The Radfan War, effectively begun and ended during the first half of 1964, had been a seminal event in British South Arabia's latter-day history. Following the Wadi Misrah operation, the Federal Regular Army had secured key lowland areas in the face of fierce resistance but, lacking the necessary manpower and resources to occupy the mountains, had eventually been forced to withdraw to Thumair. A newly constituted "Radforce", combining British and FRA units with RAF support, was then assembled to clear Radfan of dissidents. As a preliminary to controlling the high ground, an SAS troop of nine was dropped on the Bakri Ridge at night by helicopter to establish a landing site for a much larger force. Disastrously, the SAS men were spotted lying up during the day, came under heavy fire and, despite repeated strafings by Hunter fighters, four of them, including their commander Captain Robin Edwards, were severely wounded or killed. The remaining five made a daring escape under cover of darkness. The mutilated bodies of Captain Edwards and Sapper Warburton were taken back to Qataba, and their severed heads stuck on poles for public display.

Radforce was brought up to full brigade strength in May. The Thumair airstrip was extended, and Wessex helicopters from HMS *Centaur* brought in for support. A two-pronged, parallel advance was made into the Radfan heartland up the Wadi Misrah and via the Bakri Ridge. After bitter fighting against dogged resistance, British and Federal units, supported by artillery and Hunter rocket strikes, converged on Jebel Hurriyya, the highest point of the Radfan, which was finally was captured by the Royal Anglians and the FRA on 10 June 1964.

On the face of it, the Radfan campaign had been a military success. But what had originally been planned as a single-battalion task lasting three weeks had taken a brigade group nearer six months to achieve. Without helicopter support, the outcome might have been less certain. The cost, involving 600 air sorties, 2,500 rockets, 200,000 cannon rounds and 20,000 artillery shells, to defeat resilient but lightly armed tribesmen seemed disproportionate. The operation did little to halt the passage of arms and ammunition smuggled into the WAP, and not only encouraged dissident activity elsewhere, but also facilitated the NLF's political infiltration of the tribes. Cairo and San'a radios claimed Radfan as an Arab military victory, casting Britain as the imperialist aggressor, while the UN, Communist bloc and Third World now gave voluble support to the NLF as a revolutionary, liberating force. The guerrillas might have got a bloody nose, but most had melted away to fight another day. By the end of the year, the NLF would switch their main operations to an altogether softer target – Aden.

Young had echoed Somerfield's concerns about the lack of meaningful HMG funding, but it did seem extraordinary that no contingency scheme yet existed for Radfan's post-campaign reconstruction. On 19 October, I flew up to Thumair to collate information for the proposed aid scheme. From the cockpit of a four-seater Army Air Corps Beaver, piloted by David Swan, Lahej appeared as a tiny green triangle set in a vast yellow desert. Jebel Manif, the mountain I had so often gazed up to when driving to Al-Anad, now took the form of a complex massif of steep ridges and inaccessible wadis radiating from its summit. "Still stuffed with dissidents, I reckon," was Swan's laconic comment.

Bryan Somerfield met me at the Thumair airstrip and drove his heavily armour-plated Land Rover to the four-square building that served him as both house and office. During the campaign, his bathroom had been used as a common latrine. Five months of rough living had taken its toll.

"I don't know what sort of brief Robin gave you," began Bryan, wearily. "I can only repeat that we've got an almighty problem here. We really need two Political Officers to cope: one to deal with security and the military side of things; the other to restore this place to some semblance of normality. The upland economy was always fragile, but large areas are now devastated. Anyway, what sort of money are we talking about? Any advance on the pittance you mentioned when you were last here?"

"Sorry, Bryan. There's still only £35,000 in the kitty."

"That's ridiculous, of course," he snorted. "The Army were shooting off more than that in half an hour. If we can't be more generous with these people, there's no hope for peace in future."

Bryan then introduced me to Major David Forrow, the GSO2 Brigade HQ. "David's a genuine Arabist," explained Brian. "He's done the full MECAS course, and has become the Army's Radfan guru. Unfortunately, as a Sapper, he's also a nuclear defence expert, so just when he's most needed here, they're sending him back to England in a few days' time. Bloody typical. Best pick his brains while he's still with us."

When I explained my mission to Forrow, he gave me a sharp look.

"Really? And about time too. Since the campaign officially ended, precious little's been done from your end to put this place straight. Frankly, I don't begin to understand what the Federal government's priorities are. Bryan's been doing a fantastic job with damn-all back up. Thumair's stuffed with high-ranking military types, yet he's running the entire political and administrative show on his own."

Forrow seemed to be the only person around with detailed written records. I scribbled down everything I could before going to bed. Next morning, just as he and Somerfield were about to show me round Radfan by helicopter, we ran into a confused-looking Brian Doe, the Federal Director of Antiquities, who was hanging around the airstrip.

"What on earth are you doing here, Brian?" I asked him.

"Just dropped in from Aden, actually. I've heard reports about a cave complex in this area with prehistoric wall paintings and fifteen-metre high sphinx-like statues. If that's correct, it'll put a completely new complexion on South Arabia's archaeological history."

Doe achieved much in his field, but I, too, pondered on Federal priorities as our helicopter swung over Jebel Subaha, otherwise Arnold's Spur, after its heroic capture by the Parachute Regiment under CSM "Nobby" Arnold. Next, we landed on the 1,802m-high redoubt of Jebel Widna, which held out long after the campaign had officially ended. It gave grandstand views of the 400-square-mile Radfan massif, with its ragged peaks and dizzying ravines, patterned by thousand-metre slopes of elaborate stone terracing. When I offered some prosaic comment to Bryan on this being a testament to man's ingenuity, he replied: "You're lucky to be seeing this place in its pristine state. Before the campaign, no European had ever set foot here. Radfan's gradually been deteriorating from years of neglect and blood feud. Given peace, money and encouragement those terraced fields could grow almost anything. Sadly they're now mainly given over to *qat*. It's become a cash crop, like heroin."

The following day, we flew up to Jebel Hurriyya, scene of the Radfan tribes' last stand. Gazing down into the grim depths of the Wadi Dhubsan, into which the Paras had made a daring abseil to get a footing onto the Bakri Ridge, I could just about pick out some patches of cultivation, and a scattering of houses, at the bottom.

"Anyone still living down there?" I asked Bryan.

"Almost certainly, and probably foemen. But it's far too difficult to investigate and, once they saw us coming, the bad boys would scarper."

From Jebel Hurriyya we walked through Mas'udi country to inspect war damage to wells, small reservoirs, known as *birkah*s, terracing and houses. Seemingly out of nowhere, a group of aged tribesmen appeared and insisted on accompanying us. When they pointed proudly to the largest *birkah*, whose cupped interiors were lined with a smooth lime and gravel mixture, I asked who had built them. "The *juddud*," they replied, a reference to the "Grandfathers", or giants, to whom such constructions, and the more elaborate terracing, were freely attributed.

Although only 15 out of the 150 Mas'udi houses we inspected had been seriously damaged, the energy of the Grandfathers had been replaced by resigned apathy. One old man beckoned us over to a low, stone-built house. Here, in a tiny whitewashed room only five foot high, with walls artistically patterned with black-and-white designs and its earthen floor furnished with rugs, an attractive, unveiled young woman was lying prone on a heap of cushions.

"She got hit by a shell splinter during a bombing raid," explained Bryan. "Her thigh's badly damaged. We flew her down to Lahej for an emergency operation. Unfortunately, it hasn't worked. She's now partly paralysed, so I'm arranging for the Army to casevac her to Aden to get her treated properly at the Queen Elizabeth Hospital."

On the way back to our helicopter, we met the girl's father. He appeared to bear us no ill will, and was more concerned about his own eye troubles. When I got back to Lahej a few days later, the same Mas'udi woman fetched up at my office. The Army had flown her down to Aden, but she had been refused admission to the Queen Elizabeth Hospital. Incensed, I drove her there myself to confront a duty doctor. He insisted that he was bound to stick to the prescribed admission hours. I got her admitted nonetheless. That same morning, Philip Fazil, the Adjutant of the 2nd Battalion Coldstream Guards and cousin of King Farook, lost a leg from a mine planted near

Little Aden's Baboon Bay.

While we sat it out on a bare mountaintop waiting for our helicopter to drop us back at Thumair, Bryan again unburdened himself about the country which had become his entire world. "It's these upland areas that are most in need of aid. The lower valleys can soon be brought back into cultivation, but up here life is much harder. Before the Operation, we hardly knew that tribes like the Bakri and Mas'udi existed. Most of their young have gone to the Yemen, but they'll be back in time, whether we go or stay. In the meantime, we've got to prove that the Federal government is doing something positive by digging more wells, repairing their *birkah*s and terracing, and rebuilding their houses. And even if we ever get the money, I'm somewhat at loggerheads with Young and Baillie about how best to spend it. They think we should keep the Qutaibi sweet because they live nearest the Dhala' Road. I don't agree, and I don't trust that lot. It's here that the need is greatest."

On my last day in Radfan, Somerfield, Forrow and I, along with Maj. Mike Stevenson and Lt. Mike Bourne of the Royal Anglians, flew up to their forward camp at Khalla, on the Bakri Ridge, to make another war damage survey. This was virgin ground, even for Bryan, so he had arranged for the newly appointed Bakri chief, Shaikh Ghanim bin Ahmed, to be our guide. At first, this lithe mountaineer looked dubious when Bryan explained that he wanted to travel on foot. He then joined in the spirit of the thing, and for the next seven hours we walked a great loop from Am Giblah to the Wadi Musuk, taking in some of the remotest and most spectacular country in Radfan.

Up and down a succession of stairways cut out of the living rock, the merest suspicion of a path inched along perilous walkways girdling the cliffs of a colossal amphitheatre. In this harsh land, where soil had to be scoured out from between rock, thorn and tough succulents to make the terraced fields, only the hardiest survived. Every stone-blocked house was its own fortress, some up to four storeys high, with mere slits for windows. The only entrance was at ground-floor level by a door hewn from two-inch-thick *'ilb* wood. Inside, there was stabling for livestock, and a spiral staircase that wound upwards to living quarters into which the light of day barely penetrated.

Approaching the village of Na'man, through a sisal thicket still being harvested by local rope-makers, we wove in and out of a maze of interconnecting walls, the equivalent of slit trenches, built to avoid sniper fire. But none could have withstood bombardment from RAF Hunters. This former stronghold of the dissident leader, Shaikh Ahmed Muhammad Shirani, lay in ruins. We pressed on to Urgub, Shaikh Ghanim's own village. Strafed and battered as it was, he had every reason to be bitter for only one habitable room was left of his once imposing keep. Yet he treated us as honoured guests, laying on a feast of roast goat, stew and rice, seasoned with the hot, white radish, Radfan's most common vegetable.

While waiting for the helicopter, Bryan and I sat in the doorway of the Shaikh's ruined house, watching the late afternoon sun play on the blue-shadowed flanks of Jebel Halmain.

"We've never penetrated those Halmaini mountains, and now I doubt we ever will," mused Bryan. "Most Radfanis are sick and tired of warfare, and all the tribes, bar two, surrendered months ago. But we've failed to follow up whatever the Army gained, and formal negotiations to close this whole miserable chapter are still held up somewhere along the line. I only hope that your development scheme will get things moving. Otherwise, we're going to reap the whirlwind."

For a second night running, we had almost resigned ourselves to an uncomfortable bivouac, but eventually our helicopter turned up. Back at Thumair, in the Brigade Mess, we argued long into the night about the cost of the Radfan Operation, and why we had got involved in the first place. In retrospect, it was easy to pass judgement. However, once Egypt had invaded the Yemen and become directly involved in anti-Federal operations, Britain and the Federation had effectively been fighting a proxy war. Radfan had been the touchstone, so military victory became essential if confidence in the Federation was to be maintained. Generous and timely British development aid might have improved the situation, but more probably our moment in South Arabia had already passed, and only fundamental social and political changes from within would transform this fossilized economy and tribal attitudes for so long poisoned by obscurantism and blood feud.

Brushing such musings aside, I wrote up my Radfan Scheme, attempting to balance upland and lowland needs. I allocated two-thirds of my £35,000 to fund long-term loans to farmers, mainly to hire tractors and heavy well-drilling equipment, but also to buy disc ploughs, rakes, seed drills, and wire-netted gabions for wadi bank protection. This money would be paid into the Dhala' State Treasury, with AA Thumair responsible for overall supervision. The remaining £10,000 would be distributed at AA Thumair's discretion to upland tribesmen, either by way of direct payments, or as loans to sink wells, rebuild terracing, *birkah*s and houses, and to buy grain seed and cement. Somerfield, writing from home, generously approved the scheme as "very good indeed". The sums involved were ludicrously inadequate, but at least we would have control over expenditure.

Scarcely had I completed the Radfan Scheme when Robin asked me to do the same for Dhala', giving me two days to pick the brains of Federal Ministries for suitable projects. When I discovered that the Ministry of Agriculture had already been allocated £130,000 to make an exploratory survey next year of groundwater resources in Dhala', I decided that education and public works should take priority. The news soon got round and I was pressurized by Shaikh Hassan Freijun, the ambitious Federal Director of Rural Education, to improve existing school buildings in Dhala' and build much-needed accommodation for teaching staff. The Federal PWD's Ken Hardaker also lost no time in impressing upon me that unless the Dhala' water supply was upgraded, the town would not only run out of water, but also be faced with a typhoid epidemic.

To resolve these conflicting demands, I flew to Dhala' on 17 November for my fifth visit. The feelings of wonder once evoked by the magical sight of early morning mists floating above its mountain-girt plain were now tempered by wariness. As James Nash drove me back to his house along a road which had become a prime target for mining, I pondered whether the *nawbat*s, or watchtowers that guarded the green fields of *qat,* were manned by friend or foe. The Amirate of Dhala' had always been a populous but troubled area, with an estimated 35,000 inhabitants, maybe 65,000 if Radfan and Halmain were included, to give it one of the highest population densities in the Federation. Most of the country was mountainous, but the fertile Dhala' Plateau, covering an area of more than a hundred square miles, was the natural strategic, trade and communications centre, not only for the Amirate but also for the adjacent Yemeni plain of Qataba, with whose peoples the Dhala'is had ancient ties of kith and kin. At an altitude of over 1,300 metres, the Plateau's climate was relatively temperate. It also enjoyed higher than average, if sporadic, rainfall, although the farmers wasted their best land growing *qat*. Jebel Jihaf's terraced slopes supported a complementary range of cereal crops, vegetables and fruit.

Dhala' unquestionably had potential, but poor husbandry, proximity to the

Yemen and the temper of its people, the Amiri, had retarded its development. It was indeed a tortured land with a sullen, dangerous, treacherous atmosphere, its people twisted and ever-resentful. These underlying neuroses could, in part, be attributed to oppressive Ottoman and Yemeni occupations, exacerbated by the cruel and tyrannical rule of Amir Haidara, who liked to dispose of imprisoned opponents by tying them to a plank, which had dynamite underneath, and then lighting the fuse himself. Beyond the confines of the Plateau lived a fragmented tribal society scattered over wild, mountainous country, where brute strength had always been the traditional form of governance.

The unsettling atmosphere of Dhala' again impressed itself forcibly when James drove up to his fortress-like house, now surrounded by a metre-wide, two-metre-high stone barricade, or *sangar*, with another built just beyond it. The walls were pocked with bullet marks, and work was in progress to repair bigger holes drilled by bazookas. Inside the threshold, a gang of unsavoury characters hung about like hyenas.

"Just some of my heavies," grinned James, as he led me through the heavily reinforced front door. "I've got sixty of these characters on the payroll. The money's good and most have a grudge to settle. I'm working on an Uncle principle, 'If you can't squash 'em, square 'em'."

"What d'you use them for?" I asked.

"General bodyguard, but mainly for raids across the border. The opposition are Egyptian-trained, based on Qataba, and come over here almost nightly to shoot up the Amir's palace, the FRA camp and, not least, this place. Now you're here, let me give you one tip. *Don't* on any account go outside on your own. You need an escort of three, even in the immediate vicinity. Beyond it, you'll need at least a section and, once outside Dhala' itself, a company."

In the Meynells' time, the AA's house had resounded with children's laughter, with toys littering a floor that was now cluttered with rifles, machine guns, bazookas, mortars and mines.

"Can't be that much fun living here now, James."

"No, it's not, dear boy. It's Cowboys and Indians at one level, but death or glory at another. To square the opposition we're having to work on the two-for-one principle."

"What's that?"

"Simple. For every border raid they make, or for every mine planted or grenade thrown, we respond in double kind."

I spent part of that afternoon helping James load Bren gun magazines, and in the evening found him instructing his toughs how to use live hand grenades in his ground-floor office. An old friend, Robert White, now Field Intelligence Officer in Dhala', came over for the evening. James prepared a Lebanese *tahina*, crushed sesame seed mixed with garlic, lemon and water, to go with our drinks, and then produced paté, *ratatouille* and cheese for dinner. Afterwards the three of us played backgammon, before adjourning to the roof to watch "the nightly fireworks display". The British and Federal Armies would loose off Bren Gun tracer, mortars, and a particularly noisy anti-armour weapon, on fixed lines of fire in the general direction of Qataba, with James blazing away with his own Bren-Gun. The enemy replied in kind. After an hour or so, everyone got bored and went to bed. Robert stayed for the night. Anyone moving about after dark was fair game for either side.

James Nash managed to combine martial savagery with a rare aesthetic and culinary refinement mixed with poetic sensibility, like some latter-day Richard Burton, "Ruffian Dick". Yet, even for him, life in Dhala' was dangerous, uncomfortable and ultimately rather pointless. His counter-terrorist role made him a target, not only for enemy guerrillas but also, on one occasion, for an over-zealous company of Royal Marines, whose misdirected fire onto his house wounded eight guards and sparked a short-lived mutiny. Shortly to resign from the Colonial Service and transfer to the Foreign Office, James subsequently moved on to qualify as a chartered surveyor, practising in both Egypt and London. He never lost his taste for adventure and, in later years, rode the Crusader route to Jerusalem solo with horse and cart to raise money for the Knights of St John Eye Hospital. Until very recently, he was still riding his horse and cart around the leafy lanes of Somerset.

Lack of security made it impossible for me to travel outside Dhala' without an unjustifiably large military escort. I had already seen something of the country so, for background information, scoured the old files, handing-over notes, reports and the handbooks that had been compiled, over the past twenty years, by the dozen or more Political Officers who had served here. Their names read like a historic WAP rollcall. Bell, Davey, Groom (the only living survivor from the immediate post-Second World War intake), McIntosh, Wise, Inge, Young, Lloyd, Folkard, Somerset, Henderson, Meynell, Crouch, Hinchliffe, Somerfield and Nash. Meynell had stuck it for two years, while only eight months covered the last four. They, in turn, were later followed by Walker, Hinchliffe (for a second time) and, finally, Paxton. On literary merit, the accounts of Groom, McIntosh and Meynell topped my list.

The recent upsurge in dissident activity had prompted Robin Young to be in Dhala' at the same time, as part of a delegation led by Sultan Salih to review the security situation. Robin made it clear that agricultural development would have to take a back seat until things settled down, though I had already decided that public works, health, and education would give most give immediate benefit to the local population, and kudos to Amir Sha'fal. I allocated half the scheme's £35,000 to improve the town's water supply, backed by the Royal Engineers' assurance that they would use their specialist equipment to drill the wells. £5,000 would build a house for a doctor and hostels for male and female nurses. £6,000 would go towards upgrading primary schools. £4,000 would build accommodation for the headmaster and deputy of the new intermediate school in Dhala'.

This still left £10,000 to support upland farmers, mostly to buy heavy mechanical equipment to hire out for well deepening and strengthening reservoirs, culverts and terraces. The balance would fund small individual loans under the supervision of AA Dhala' and the Agricultural Officer. When I discussed this aspect with James, he said: "Now that this is effectively a military zone, I suppose you know that it's become virtually impossible to recruit civilian staff? But don't worry," he added, "I've got a little surprise for you." With that he yelled out "Muhammad", and in walked Shaikh Muhammad Al-Kharusi.

I was dumbfounded. Never in my life did I expect to see Kharusi again. But here he was, four years on, larger than life, though sadder and greyer. We pumped hands like long-lost brothers.

"I bear you no grudge, Mr Harding. But life has not been easy for me since I left Mukalla."

"What happened to you, Shaikh Muhammad? I thought you'd retired to farm in Zanzibar."

"Indeed, I did. With my wife and children. As you know, my family were big landowners there, and much respected. But after Zanzibar became independent there was a revolution, and people like me were regarded as enemies. We had to flee the country of my fathers, with only £40 and the clothes I stood up in. We went back to Mukalla, but everything has changed, and there was no work for me to do."

"But why come here, to Dhala'?"

"Why, indeed? This is a harsh land, and the people are unfriendly. Yet I must work to keep my family alive. I've been appointed Assistant Agricultural Adviser here because no one else will take the job on. But I owe you one thing, Mr Harding. I have stopped drinking."

As 1964 drew to a close, I took stock of my tour to date. As AA Lahej I had become engrossed in my work as never before. I had gained the Amir Abdullah's confidence, been the author of four separate development schemes, and played my part in rebuilding the Dhala' Road. Of an evening, I might sit out on the roof of my palace overlooking the *Maidan* for a moment of reflection. To the north, beyond the ornate royal palaces and the lush gardens and date groves of the Delta, the brooding massifs of Jebel Manif and Radfan were ever a challenge to adventure. To the south, the air was sometimes so clear that the black silhouettes of Aden and Little Aden seemed to be within touching distance. Westwards, the great volcanic plug of Jebel Kharaz was clearly visible, 55 miles away. This should have been the happiest of times, but for two unresolved problems.

One was the question of my resignation. Life had been so hectic that I had pushed this inconvenient subject to the back of my mind. When Robin Young raised it in November, I temporized by offering to extend my tour to the end of May the following year. However, the question of whether I really wanted to quit Arabia was further complicated by a devastating personal dilemma. Earlier that year, I had asked Fay to marry me. She worked for the Security Services in Aden, and we had known each other for eighteen months. When she left for England on leave in mid-September, we had agreed to get married in Aden four months hence. During her absence, I had a crisis of confidence about our forthcoming marriage and, after returning from Dhala' in early December, had asked Young if I might take compassionate home leave to resolve the impasse.

This could hardly have come at a worse time. We were desperately short-staffed, with Subaihi about to blow up. Robin was not the marrying kind, but sympathetic to my dilemma. He agreed that I should take four days' leave, with the parting words, "If in doubt, don't". My return to England, on 5 December, did nothing to resolve the situation, so I suggested to Fay that we should postpone the wedding until I had sorted myself out. She flew to Aden anyway, two days after my own return. The wedding was cancelled but, with nowhere for Fay to stay, we lived together in Lahej. It was an impossible predicament, which caused great social and political embarrassment, and gave immense pain to all involved.

14

"POL Habilain"

IN THE WIDER UNIVERSE of things, December 1964 marked an irreversible turning point in the history of British South Arabia. After barely eighteen months as High Commissioner, Sir Kennedy Trevaskis, the principal architect of the Federation, was sacked by the new Labour government. Trevaskis, the quintessential "Rulers' Man", was seen as an impediment to the socialist-nationalist brand of constitutional progress favoured by Labour. His departure was mourned by most Federal rulers, though not by many Adenis. For all his vision, courage and commitment, some thought that his appointment as High Commissioner, after eleven continuous years' service in the WAP, made him the wrong man for the time in this particular job.

Trevaskis's replacement, Sir Richard Turnbull, was an unusual choice. Since his first appointment in 1931, as a District Officer in Kenya's North-west Frontier Province, he had spent all his colonial service in East Africa. An admirer of warrior tribesmen, and much admired by those who had served under him, Turnbull was fluent in Swahili but spoke no Arabic. He had proved himself an outstanding colonial administrator of the old school when, as Kenya's Minister of Internal Security and Defence from 1954 to 1958, he had been largely instrumental in the suppression of Mau Mau. He had also been an effective Chief Secretary and Leader of Kenya's Legislative Council. But what particularly impressed his Labour government sponsors was his achievement, as Tanganyika's last governor, in reaching a rapport with Julius Nyerere and, thereafter, in steering that country to independence in 1961.

Harold Wilson assumed that Turnbull would find more common ground with Adeni nationalist aspirations, and adopt a more balanced approach to solving the Federal–Aden conundrum, than had Trevaskis. On this account, he was not a popular choice with the Federal rulers, who saw him as anti-Federalist. For less obvious reasons, he was actively disliked by Robin Young, Trevaskis's most faithful disciple, who was to lead a clandestine group of diehards to oppose Turnbull's policies, misguidedly imagining that in this way they might salvage what they saw as an otherwise doomed Federation.

In fact, by this stage, Turnbull had the near-impossible task of bringing order out of a chaotic Federal–Aden mismatch. Once in office, he followed a somewhat different line to that which the Labour government had anticipated. Having tried, unsuccessfully, to reconcile the disparate interests of the Federal and Hadhrami rulers with those of the Adeni politicians, he realized that the only hope for the Federation's survival lay in securing Saudi Arabia's active support. This initiative was never energetically pursued by a British government which, by now, wanted out of Aden. Turnbull argued vehemently against Denis Healey's 1966 Defence White Paper, which effectively absolved Britain from any further responsibility for the Federation's defence. Thereafter, his days were numbered. In 1967, he was sacked, after only seventeen months as High Commissioner, having falling foul of George Brown. Turnbull naturally found this disgraceful treatment painfully humiliating.

Turnbull's valedictory views on the South Arabian situation were not dissimilar to those of his successor, Sir Humphrey Trevelyan. He regarded the Federation as "a ramshackle contrivance", and although he judged some Federal rulers as "brave, handsome and charming", most, in his view, were "a futile, useless bunch of self-seeking puppets who had been jockeyed into positions they were wholly unfitted to occupy". While he sympathized with the Adenis' pride in their democratic institutions, he considered most of them "smug grocers".

Shortly after Turnbull's arrival in Aden, I was detailed to accompany him up Jebel Shamsan, tailed closely by his British Army bodyguard. Courteous and approachable, we talked of little but mountains, though he let slip the comment that the greatest mistake an in-comer could make was to rely over-much on the advice of old hands steeped in their own prejudices. By this time, security throughout the Federal States had markedly deteriorated, and most particularly in Aden which, during the last two months of 1964, suffered thirty-nine casualties. Most outrageous was the grenade attack on a children's Christmas Eve party in Khormaksar which killed the 16-year-old daughter of Air Commodore Sidey. Turnbull, who had been the "Hammer of Mau Mau", took a firm line on internal security, and was the first High Commissioner to appoint an overall Director of Intelligence to pull the whole rag-bag apparatus together.

Dissident activity was also beginning to affect Lahej. When I returned from London on 9 December, Amir Abdullah, well aware that the wedding to which he had been invited had been cancelled, left Fay and I alone to lick our wounds. But when, on a lonely Christmas Day, shots were fired over Lahej, he could contain himself no longer and summoned me to the palace.

"Are you aware of what's been happening on our frontiers while you have been away?" he demanded.

For some time, Lahej's frontier problems could not have been further from my mind, and my expression must have shown it.

"Obviously not," he snorted. "So now I will tell you. The whole place is alive with dissidents. They've been bringing in arms, bazookas, mines and grenades from Yemen. That dog of a troublemaker, Muhammad Al-Tali, has occupied Dar Qutaim, a village on Jebel Suqmi, with 150 dissidents. They are poised to attack our forts at Mizja, Mudharriba, Masharig, Am Farsha and Tor al-Baha. So what are you going to do about it?"

I couldn't begin to think what I could possibly do about it, so weakly deflected his question with: "But who are these people, O Amir?"

"Muhammad Al-Humaidi, Salim Zain Al-Wahti, Muhammad Al-Duqm, etc., etc. ...," he thundered back, reeling off a string of names which meant nothing to me. My obvious ignorance only incensed him. He rose to his feet, lips quivering and mouth working, before shouting at the top of his voice: "I am looking to *you* to do something about these people, Mr Harding. I get no help from your High Commission Office. I get no help from the Ministry of Defence. Unless firm action is taken *now,* Subaihi will become another Radfan!"

I had never seen him so agitated. Normally, he enjoyed letting off steam at British expense, but this time he was deadly serious. I drove to Al-Ittihad post-haste to discuss the situation with Young, who instructed me to submit an immediate written appreciation, as a preliminary to military action. Back in Lahej, I attended a meeting with the Amir, Qaid Ali bin Ahmed and Ali Muhsin, a shaikh from the Jebel Suqmi area. Ali Muhsin confirmed that dissidents had indeed occupied a frontier village, but was unable to give details about the group's strength and armaments. This lack of precision incensed the Amir, so Shaikh Ali was completely ignored thereafter. The only positive that emerged from this excitable meeting was that Dar Qutaim had been a rebel redoubt even in Seager's time; yet no one present could positively identify it on a map.

When I reported back to Young, he gave approval for a limited military operation, codenamed "Seid", subject to my liaising with the military and 'Abdalis on a joint course of action. Predictably, this guaranteed a confused command structure, though momentum was restored when Brigadier Viner, the FRA's British commander, confirmed from his own sources that a dissident HQ had definitely been established on the frontier. Various military options were now considered including tribal action only; an FRA and Lahej National Guard joint ground operation; selective RAF bombing; and, as a last resort, a combination of all three, backed by a full-scale RAF strike. A junior officer's sensible objection, that bombing might have serious international repercussions, was brushed aside on the grounds that Dar Qutaim was so inaccessible that no meaningful Egyptian force would willingly commit itself to retaliatory action. Fortunately, the dubious logic of this argument was not pursued because Dar Qutaim's exact location remained unresolved. To remedy this lacuna, it was agreed that Qaid Ali bin Ahmed and I should make an aerial inspection of the area to take photographs for expert interpretation. Just in case we were shot down, I was issued with a revolver, but not with either a parachute or a camera. "You're a keen photographer aren't you? Your own should do the job perfectly well," said Young.

We took off from Khormaksar airfield at 8 a.m. on 2 January in a Beaver light aircraft, and headed in a north-westerly direction. When the pilot, Squadron Leader Jock Kennedy, asked me if I knew where we were going, I had to admit that I hadn't a clue. Half an hour later, we began circling over what Qaid Ali estimated must be the approximate site of Dar Qutaim. We could see absolutely nothing below, as the mountains were blanketed in cloud, so returned to base none the wiser. Two days later, the stakes were raised when I was instructed to have tactical discussions with the RAF's Strike Wing. Fortunately, higher authority now belatedly stepped in to prevent the full-scale air strike against an unidentified target on the Yemen border that would have precipitated an international incident.

And then, just as rapidly as "Operation Seid" had risen to the top of the Amir's agenda, it came off again. Dissident activity in other parts of the Sultanate was making him doubly cautious about committing his limited Laheji forces against an enemy of unknown strength without full Federal backing, particularly when the FRA announced that it was too stretched in other theatres to undertake a major operation in Subaihi anyway.

Yet one thing was for certain. Lahej was no longer a "cushy number". Almost daily, the Amir confronted me with reports of incidents that I must "do something about". Mines were regularly being planted along the unfinished 'Abdali stretch of the Dhala' Road. The fort at Tor al-Baha had been hit by bazookas. Three Yemeni Army lorries, stuffed with soldiers, had been spotted near Suqayya fort. There was trouble at Mahariq, and there had been an all-day shootout at Fatwan. When a deserting Egyptian parachutist was picked up in Subaihi, the Amir's outraged response was: "Parachutists dropping all over our Sultanate, Mr Harding. What next?"

Far more worrying from the Amir's perspective was the raid on a Yemen-bound convoy of four vehicles, near Kirsh, by a hundred armed men. Two drivers had been killed, and the Ta'izz Lorry Drivers Association had closed the road in protest. "This is quite disgraceful," he spluttered. "It will disrupt the *qat* trade, and make us deeply unpopular in the suq."

At the time, the only good bit of local news was the surrender in Lahej of a dissident leader, Salih Al-Dhuwad Humaidi, a kinsman of that other Humaidi the Amir so loved to hate. This particular coup almost ended in tears when the gang's cache of hair-trigger plastic explosives threatened to demolish the Lahej Police Station. Disaster was only averted by the prompt action of a Royal Engineers bomb disposal squad. Young suggested to the Amir that Salih Humaidi should be rewarded with "20 & 20". The Amir refused point-blank, demanding the reward for himself.

As the pace quickened, even Aden Intelligence began to show some interest in Subaihi. Joint meetings were held to determine the size of the rewards that might be appropriate for information received or weapons discovered, and even how best Yemeni deserters might be used for propaganda purposes. The Amir hinted that he might soon need permanent Federal military assistance on tap, darkly observing that "time is running out"; though, invariably, this came with the caveat: "Ultimately, the Sultan must decide." I knew, by now, that the Minister of Defence would never commit Federal forces to Subaihi if he could possibly avoid it.

By the time Dar Qutaim had been positively identified, the Amir's proven mixture of intrigue, bribery and secret deals with Yemeni tribal leaders and officials had enabled him to hold that particular front firm until Ramadan, when both sides automatically suspended hostilities. After the month of fasting had ended, most dissidents went home to celebrate the Eid. The Amir then gave the local shaikh, Sa'id Mulait, sufficient inducement to persuade him that it was no longer worth his while to co-operate with the gang leader, Muhammad Al-Tali, who, in turn, was bribed to go away. With the coast clear, the Amir swiftly despatched a strong force of Lahej Federal and Special Guardsmen to occupy Dar Qutaim without a shot being fired.

The Dar Qutaim saga did not quite end there, however. When Al-Tali's money ran out, he came back to stir up more mischief. However, by now the Yemenis were as fed up with his antics as were the 'Abdalis. So, when the Amir instructed me to obtain a set of updated British aerial maps to resolve, once and for all, whether Dar Qutaim was in 'Abdali or Yemeni territory, I sensed that the end might be in sight. After a mutually satisfactory meeting with the Yemeni Naib of Ta'izz, Al-Tali vanished off the screen for ever. Much dust had been raised, but if only the Amir had been left to sort things out in his own way from the outset, the incident might never have become a crisis.

In the midst of this imbroglio, Young informed me that he had decided not to post me to Zinjibar, as originally intended, but to Radfan. My domestic affairs were in chaos. Living with Fay without being married was an affront to both British and Arab behavioural codes. Robin broke the ring of confusion, Fay flew home, and we never got married. The past month had been a profoundly traumatic experience for both of us, and the scars never quite healed.

Radfan offered a completely fresh start. In the following weeks, I was too busy tidying up outstanding Lahej and 'Aqrabi business to dwell on what had been a paralysing personal crisis. I spent yet more futile hours cajoling Shaikh Mahmoud to modify the 'Aqrabi estimates, and passed a poisoned chalice to Val Hinds to take over a projected Subaihi fisheries scheme dreamed up by the Amir in my last days. To bone up on Radfan, I flew up to Thumair for meetings with Somerfield, and picked the brains of Federal officials on ways and means to implement my Radfan Aid Scheme.

Almost my last formal Lahej responsibility was to organize an official visit for the new High Commissioner, Sir Richard Turnbull. Sultan Fadhl wanted no frills so, after the Amir had graciously received Sir Richard and Lady Turnbull at the city gates with a guard of honour and band, the programme was restricted to a brief meeting with the Council of Directors, a school visit, and another to my house to meet the staff. After luncheon at the palace, we inspected Lahej's more impressive agricultural projects, and thus closed what was probably Sir Richard's last relaxed Arabian outing. As terrorism took hold, he was generally confined within the perimeter walls of Government House, except when moving around by helicopter. It was a miserable imposition for such a courageous man.

My imminent Radfan posting brought to a head that other issue I had long managed to duck. The trauma of the cancelled wedding had utterly confused my thoughts about leaving the Colonial Service. Yet, I felt that in fairness to everyone, I could defer this decision no longer. Accordingly, the day before I left Lahej, I wrote a formal letter of resignation to Pusinelli, the Director of Establishments, and took this down to Al-Ittihad with the intention of discussing the situation anew with Robin Young, half hoping that he would change my mind with a clarion call to duty. But fate decreed that Robin was not available that day, so I dispatched the letter anyway, having no idea of what new horizons were about to open. No one ever replaced me as AA Lahej. Although Robin had it in mind to install the energetic Peter Hinchliffe there as his base from which to run Area West, the 'Abdalis had by then decided that a British presence was no longer required.

I took leave of my staff with real sadness, but particularly of Sayyid Husain, a brave and honourable man. Unfortunately, his arrogance and sharp tongue had made him enemies, and in that world of uncertain loyalties I feared for his future. Barely a year on, his family's past, and South Arabia's bloody present, caught up with him when an assassin riddled his body with bullets and left him to die in the grubby backstreets of Shaikh Othman. Aged only 36, he died intestate, leaving a young wife and six small children. Many years later, when I was practising as a City Solicitor, Dick Holmes QC, formerly the Federation's Advocate General and a convert to Islam, asked my advice on how Husain's family, still living in Aden, might obtain Letters of Administration in order to release a substantial deposit account held in Husain's name by prominent London bankers. In the chaos that had followed the NLF's takeover of South Arabia in 1967, the lawyer who had been dealing with the case had vanished.

The bank refused to release the deposit without recognized legal documentation, but under Aden's new regime this was proving impossible to obtain. Before the matter could be resolved, Dick Holmes died suddenly. I attended his funeral in a Whitechapel mosque, adjacent to a synagogue, where his body and embalmed waxen face were displayed in an open coffin according to the rites of his faith. With Dick's death, the trail went dead.

Having devoted so much time to help build the Dhala' Road, it was only appropriate that I should drive to Thumair to take up my new appointment on 21 February. Five and a half hours later, I was greeted by an anxious Bryan Somerfield. "Thank God you've got here in one piece. Just up the road this morning, two civilian lorries and an FNG truck carrying 100,000 rounds were ambushed and attacked by bazookas. Some of our soldiers were seriously injured. Another inside job, I'm afraid. If the same thing had happened to you, I would have had to cancel my leave."

Somerfield looked even more exhausted than when I had last seen him. He and I had previously discussed Radfan often enough, but though I thought I knew broadly what I was taking on, there had been no time for a detailed briefing from Young, so I asked Bryan to fill me in.

"I don't pretend this is an easy job," he said, whisking me round the draughty, unfurnished rooms of the three-storey block-house that was to be my home for the next four months. "For all that, I've found the work hugely satisfying. At least your brief is clear. You're officially the Adviser to Amir Sha'fal in Dhala', but effectively you run your own show. It's a mixture of political and military work. You're ultimately responsible to the High Commissioner, via the WAP Office, for putting Radfan back on its feet. You're also the political adviser to the Commander of Area West and the British armed forces based here in Habilain. For signals and other purposes you're "POL Habilain". The Federal government is supposed to come into this somewhere, but to date their ministries have shown damn-all interest in what's happening. By the way, did Robin tell you about the meeting?"

"What meeting?"

"Why, the Radfan tribal meeting that's to be held here in three days time. Sultan Salih's coming up from Aden to chair it with Robin, plus a full-blown Federal VIP delegation. Amir Sha'fal will be flying down from Dhala'."

"But what's it all about? Robin never mentioned it to me."

"Really? Well, he certainly should have done. It's critical for Radfan's future.

Sultan Salih is going to explain to Radfan's tribal leaders that they're to be given a new administration here in Habilain. You're in the hot seat now as the chap who's going to set it up and run it. Tell you what, although I'm officially on leave with effect from tomorrow, I'll come back again for the day to give you moral support. Incidentally, you'd better check up on the hospitality side of things. I've no idea how many people will be coming, so haven't had time to make arrangements for any sort of party. The Army will lend you a tent if you ask them nicely. You can discuss other details with Bubakr Salih, your JAA. I'll introduce you to him later."

If I was nonplussed, I tried not to show it. The prospect of taking over Radfan from Somerfield, one of the WAP's unsung heroes, was daunting enough without my having to stage manage a full-blown tribal meeting with no advance warning, let alone establish a brand new Radfan administration. The Radfan military operation might have hit British newspaper headlines, but the bulk of this wild mountain tract had remained both *terra incognita* and off-bounds to British colonial officials, and just about everyone else, until battle had commenced in 1964. Indeed, though barely 60 miles inland from Aden and clearly visible on a winter's day, Radfan had known no recognizable form of governance since the disintegration of the pre-Islamic incense kingdoms. From time to time, strong rulers had made their imprint by a combination of force and fear, achieving transitory power by the sort of bloodletting that had paralysed this fragmented society for generations.

The only recent political event that had nudged any part of Radfan towards the 20th century was the decision of the Amir of Dhala' to join the Federation in 1960. In theory, at least, the anarchic Radfan tribes owed the Amir a form of allegiance. Accordingly, it was decided to establish an embryonic administration at Thumair, an undistinguished but strategically sited upland village which also happened to be a stronghold of the Qutaibi, the biggest Radfan tribe. The Qutaibi were a querulous, unruly lot, but they were one of the few Radfan tribes with whom the British had previously had any meaningful contact, largely on account of the trouble they had habitually caused along that part of the Dhala' Road traversing their territory. Unfortunately, in a world where tribal feuding had acquired the refinements of an art form, the Qutaibi were universally hated by all other Radfan tribes. Thus, Thumair as a location was irredeemably tarred with the Qutaibi brush, but as both the British and FNG forces were already firmly based there, the headquarters of the proposed Radfan administration had to be sited in the same general vicinity. To get over this difficulty, the British military base and the AA's house were renamed Habilain after a nearby hill, to distinguish it from Qutaibi Thumair, even though their juxtaposition made Habilain's unpopularity with other Radfan tribes inevitable.

And it was here, at Habilain, that the first All-Radfan Tribal Conference was scheduled to be held on 24 February. On that fateful morning, I waited apprehensively on the airstrip with Colonel Kettles, the Commander of Area West, to greet a high-powered Federal delegation flown up from Aden comprising Sultan Salih, the Federal Minister of Internal Security, Robin Young, Don McCarthy, the High Commissioner's newly appointed Political Adviser, Bryan Somerfield, various Federal officials, and a lone Swiss Red Cross representative. Amir Sha'fal and his kinsman Amir 'Umar arrived separately from Dhala'. Having foregathered at my house, we wandered across to a patch of level ground, some hundred yards away, to where a large British Army tent had just been erected. After the delegates had solemnly taken their seats, there followed an embarrassing hiatus, for Radfan's tribal leaders were nowhere to be seen. And then, at 10.30 a.m. precisely, a rising cloud of dust from the direction of Thumair signalled their approach. From out of it emerged a mêlée of tribesmen who stalked across the no-man's-land separating Thumair from Habilain in eerie silence. Without a word, they squatted down within a couple of yards of the marquee's open entrance to confront the seated delegation with solemn, hostile faces. I noted with relief that none seemed to be bearing firearms.

Many of these hawk-faced, beturbaned men were sworn enemies who had never previously met each other. Some gave sour, surreptitious sideways glances, while others stared stonily ahead. A low expectant hum greeted Sultan Salih as he rose to address the gathering, though most would never have set eyes on him before. Wearing a white cotton jacket over his *futah*, with a delicate, silk *mushadda* bound tightly above his oval, unlined face, the Minister for Internal Security now held the stage.

"O Ye Tribesmen of Radfan, I, Sultan Salih bin Husain Al-'Audhali, greet you on behalf of the Federal Supreme Council. For a thousand years, Radfan has had no stable government, but from today, you will have your own administration. The Amir of Dhala', Sha'fal bin Ali Shaif Al-Amiri, has come here with me to reassert his ancient paramountcy as Ruler of Radfan. His kinsman, the Amir 'Umar, has agreed to be based in Habilain to deal with all your problems."

At this, Sultan Salih made an expansive gesture towards Amir 'Umar, a small, insignificant man who looked like a frightened rabbit.

"Habilain will be your new capital," Sultan Salih continued. "A council chamber will be built here to house a Radfan Committee and Court. Its members will be drawn from your leaders. Stipends will be paid to all Shaikhs and 'Aqils. Your lands will be restored. Grain for sowing your fields and cement for rebuilding your houses will be distributed, and the Federal Government will provide drills to dig wells, and lend you money to hire modern agricultural equipment. On this, I give you my word."

This rosy picture left most of Sultan Salih's audience determinedly unmoved, and there was no applause when he sat down. The Sultan was a decent, honourable man, yet I wondered why he had been chosen to deliver this homily rather than the Federation's senior ruler, the Sultan of Lahej, whose borders ran with Radfan, and whose interests were more closely intertwined with its peoples. Some might have taken Sultan Salih's message on trust. Others would not have believed a word of it.

Amir Sha'fal followed. Slightly built and unassuming, with a couple of fountain pens incongruously sticking out of his breast pocket, he did not cut much of a figure. Yet he spoke with quiet dignity, without affectation. Robin Young rounded off the speeches looking uncharacteristically ill at ease. His muffled, gravelly voice soon became inaudible above the low hubbub that now swelled from an increasingly restive audience, more concerned to discuss the worth of Sultan Salih's promises than Robin's unfamiliar platitudes.

Almost immediately after the ceremony had ended, hoary antagonisms bubbled to the surface. The tribesmen quickly split themselves into self-contained groups muttering, "Where is this money that the Sultan promises us?"... "Why are our houses left in ruin?"... "This is just a Qutaibi plot" ... and so on. All around me, I heard a litany of complaint. The *'aqils* of the Hujaili, Dhanbari and Muzahim tribes pointedly refused to accept the generous "expenses" that Young had instructed I dish out, insisting that Dhala' should have been chosen as the seat of this new Radfan administration, rather than "Qutaibi Habilain".

It was a bad sign, and my attempts to break the ice by personally handing round Pepsis and Fantas got few takers. When the last of the tribal leaders had drifted away, a subdued VIP delegation made its way back to my house. The meeting's premature breakup, and an unexpectedly large influx of hangers-on, threw my domestic arrangements. There were insufficient chairs to go round, barely room to stand, and lunch had to be served with the mutton half-cooked. The only happy face was that of the Swiss Red Cross representative for whom I had arranged a helicopter flight round Radfan, and who came back bubbling over with excitement. Just before the Twin Pioneer arrived to take a morose delegation back to Aden, Robin Young took me aside. "Not a bad outcome really. Some glum faces, but that's to be expected. Anyway, no real bust-ups, and no one drew a knife. And at least they've seen what you look like. It's now up to you to get on with it."

Far from getting on with it, I didn't really know where to begin. The prospect of setting up an administration from scratch with a bunch of warring tribesmen whose villages had been destroyed, whose fields had been ravaged, and to whom concepts of governance meant nothing, was daunting. The Tribal Conference had revealed the underlying depths of suspicion and hostility felt towards a Federal government that had done nothing since the end of the war, eight months previously. Along the Bakri Ridge alone, 50 percent of the houses were in ruins. Reconstruction was going to take years, as building work was traditionally done by specialist outside masons. Damage to terracing was potentially more serious, for unless repairs were made before the onset of the next rainy season, spates coming off the mountainside could smash through one terrace bank after another, sweeping away in minutes the work of generations. Up to 25 percent of Radfan's livestock had been destroyed, and few farmers had been able to sow seed after the last summer rains, making the threat of famine a reality. Most serious of all was the shortage of manpower. In the Wadi Taym alone, the post-operation population was a third of what it had been before, as most of its young men had decamped to the Yemen.

I decided that I must, at least, operate from a firm and relatively comfortable base, so indented for a bath, flush lavatory, sink and basic furniture. Somerfield had got by with only a camp bed and a few chairs. My next priority was staff. Both Somerfield and I had argued with Young that it needed more than one AA to run Radfan, yet after the first Tribal Conference I never set eyes on Amir 'Umar again. During my first two months, my sole assistant was my JAA, Bubakr Salih, a tribesman from distant 'Aulaqi, a state with no obvious connection with Radfan. Nonetheless, he was popular with the locals, and proved an invaluable buffer to winnow through the petitioners who daily besieged what passed for my office. Early on, an Adeni Arab clerk reported for duty, but after two days went permanently AWOL. A British RASC clerk stuck it for a month, but after being granted a week's leave never appeared again. Without Jean Randall at the WAP Office to decipher and type my execrable scrawl, Robin Young might never have known what was happening in Habilain.

I could get by without a clerk, but it would have been impossible to function without my Messenger, Salih Fara Risha, who was ever-willing to accompany me as factotum on forays into Radfan. Above all, my very life depended on my two FNG bodyguards, Ahmed and Muhammad, who at dawn every morning would spend an hour meticulously probing the unsurfaced track that led up to my house to search for buried mines. These deadly weapons alone accounted for thirty-seven casualties during my time in Habilain. Both men might have been paid-up members of the NLF, yet I never doubted their personal loyalty.

In the middle of April, welcome relief arrived in the form of Michael Tamblyn, then an undergraduate at Durham University reading Arabic. With him came Robin Young's explicit instructions that although "young Mike was not to be wrapped up in cotton wool", I was to take every precaution to ensure his safety, or face dire consequences. Neither of us need have worried. Mike was immensely keen, energetic, and oblivious to danger. He also had mechanical skills that I lacked, and did sterling work directing well-drilling operations in the Wadi Taym and assisting with other development projects.

My immediate task was to tackle the mountain that was Radfan's new administration. I already knew something about the country and its problems, but all too little about its detailed tribal structure. This was essential if I was to design an administrative framework that would give each tribe fair representation on the proposed Radfan Committee and Court. But where to start? Politically and economically there was no such entity as Radfan. Rather, it was a geographical area, which took its name from the rugged massif from which radiated a complex of narrow ridges, sheer escarpments, steep-sided wadis and gorges. To the north, these debouched into the fertile wadis of the Taym, Rabwa and Danaba. To the south, they disappeared into the wastes of the desert littoral.

The Radfan tribes, known in the British Army as the "Red Wolves", had for convenience been lumped together as a confederation. In fact, it was only their mutual response to the military operation and NLF infiltration that had drawn them together. Although some professed allegiance to the Amir of Dhala', their primary loyalties were to their own tribal leaders, and for most purposes their only common bonds were race, geographical location and a similar way of life. The two main tribes, the Qutaibi and Ibdali, were traditionally deadly enemies. The Qutaibi, essentially lowlanders, had age-old feuds with three of the principal upland tribes, the Bakri, Dhanbari and Hujaili. In turn, the Hujaili perpetuated their own feuds with the Ibdali, Bakri and Mahla'i. And so it went on, and on.

To devise a fair system of representation, I needed reasonably accurate population figures, a task complicated by there being ten main tribes, with countless variations in their internal structure. Thus, although the Ibdali and the Qutaibi each mustered some 1,400 fighting men, the Ibdali had one single ruler and 25 sections, whereas the Qutaibi had 11 sections, each with its own ruler, and no less than 36 sub-sections, many of whom cordially loathed each other. The remaining eight Radfan tribes mustered at least another 24 sub-tribes between them.

It was settled government policy that any one tribe's hostile involvement in the Radfan campaign should not in itself become a bar to aid or representation. Nonetheless, it would have been imprudent not to recognize professed friends as distinct from manifest enemies. Some denied that they had had anything to do with the fighting. Others, such as the Bakri, Ibdali, Hujaili, and some sections of the Qutaibi, were unashamedly proud to have taken on British and Federal forces. By now, all save the Mahla'i and Dairi had formally surrendered, and given hostages as guarantees. What was not accurately known was how many fighting men had taken refuge in the Yemen, and to what extent those tribesmen who remained were now supporting the NLF.

Averaging out Somerfield's figures, Army Intelligence tribal lists, official surrender documents and word of mouth, and taking into account that tribal leaders invariably exaggerated their tribal strength, I decided that the Radfan Committee should consist of twenty tribal representatives. The Qutaibi and Ibdali would each get four seats; the Dhanbari, Hujaili, Bakri and Da'ar al-Harath, two each; and the other four tribes, one each. Twenty was probably too large a body to constitute an effective administrative forum, but I could not see how we could go below this figure without putting noses out of joint. That settled, I could now allocate salaries to individual chiefs, leaving it to them to decide what to pay their own *'aqils*.

With the building blocks of the new Radfan administration in place, I now had the more difficult task of choosing the Qutaibi's four Radfan Committee members. This dysfunctional tribe had no paramount chief, yet between its eleven separate sections it had contrived to elect thirteen different sub-chiefs. It was effectively leaderless because both Shaikh Saif Hassan, the prime advocate of an independent Qutaibi "state", and his brother, Naib Mahmoud Hassan, were currently in prison for having played leading dissident roles during the Radfan campaign. Although temporarily out of contention, Shaikh Saif still mustered a strong local following, particularly from his own shaikhly house of Ahl Lahram, to whom he had freely distributed what remained of the customs compensation monies, after liberally helping himself. Somerfield had recommended that Shaikh Saif be exiled to Socotra. Unfortunately, this sensible solution had been rejected by the High Commissioner as unlikely to recommend itself to the Colonial Secretary, Anthony Greenwood. Saif's imprisonment had never been announced officially because Al-Ittihad was still undecided how best to deal with him, so he was still being paid a generous government salary *in absentia*.

I would have preferred not to become involved with Shaikh Saif's financial affairs, but the existence of this Federal salary was a lure to any successor. A complicating factor was that Shaikh Saif owed EAS 150,000/- (a considerable sum by South Arabian standards) to a number of important creditors, including the Amir of Dhala', Sultan Salih himself, A. Besse, Aden's most important trading company, and a local building contractor, Muhsin Muhammad Qutaibi. In consequence, there was stiff resistance in high places to sacking Shaikh Saif, for so long as the Federal government continued to pay him a salary, his creditors had some prospect of repayment themselves.

Initially I took the view that Shaikh Saif's debts were his creditors' worry. They became mine when I learned their identities, and that Muhsin Muhammad had already been awarded the main contract to build the new Radfan Secretariat, even though he had previously been imprisoned for actively supporting Qutaibi dissidence, and had intrigued against Amir Sha'fal. Confident of his creditors' support, Shaikh Saif showered me with tendentious petitions, always concluding with the spurious claim that he was speaking on behalf of all Radfan's tribes, and accusing his rivals of "personal gain, greed and self-interest".

The only other serious contender for the Qutaibi Shaikhdom was another Ahl Lahram family member, Fadhl Muqbil. This was the very man who owned the house in Radfan's Wadi Misrah from which fire had been directed at Godfrey Meynell. Fadhl Muqbil had subsequently revealed himself as a leading dissident but, perversely, Somerfield had put him in charge of the Qutaibi administration on the principle that he was "a bad boy trying to make good". Cunning rather than clever, he initially tried to treat my office as his own, quickly reverting to ingratiation when I gave him a flea in his ear. As I got to know him better, it became clear that he was actively aiding and abetting the enemy. Yet, as I was never able to confront him with proof positive, I worked reluctantly with the devil I knew.

Temperamentally, my natural inclination was to play a straight political hand, yet it was impossible not to become drawn into *keeny meeny*. The Amir Abdullah had been a master of this art, ever working the interlinking circles of tribal and personal politics to his advantage. Lesser players might be content to balance the conflicting interests of one tribal leader against another. As a Qutaibi, Fadhl Muqbil had many enemies, including the Bakri Shaikh, Ghanim bin Ahmed, who had so gamely shown Somerfield and me round his battered land the previous November. I much liked this rugged mountaineer, though his loathing of the Qutaibi sometimes made constructive conversation difficult.

"Why do I always have to come to see you in Habilain," he would complain. "This is Qutaibi country, whereas I owe my allegiance to Amir Sha'fal in Dhala'. This so-called Radfan administration in Habilain is just a trick for the Qutaibi to take over. And when is the government going to rebuild our houses, dig us new wells and give me the money that Sultan Salih promised us, so that I can pay my loyal *'aqil*s who work so hard to keep the peace? I have four hundred fighting Bakri, and shoulder a heavy burden keeping them sweet. Yet, as sole leader of my tribe, you give me less to live on than that criminal Fadhl Muqbil, a wicked man who is not even a proper shaikh! I warn you to be wary of him."

Shortly after one such outburst, the simmering Bakri–Qutaibi feud burst to the surface. A member of a remote Qutaibi sub-section, Salih Haidar, had built a new house overlooking Bakri territory. The Bakri claimed that this threatened their security, but rather than refer the dispute to the new Habilain administration (effectively me, as the proposed Radfan Court was as yet non-existent), both sides agreed that a wise Ibdali *sayyid* should adjudicate. Sayyid Haidara's ruling, that Salih's house should stand on condition that neither side opened fire on the other, accorded with traditional tribal custom, and, if both parties had accepted it, the matter should have rested there.

Unfortunately, Shaikh Ghanim was having none of it, and complained to me bitterly that this was yet another example of Qutaibi perfidy. I reckoned that if it became common knowledge that land disputes were still being settled on terms that even hinted at a resort to arms, the fragile Radfan Peace would become a mockery. Accordingly I summoned the various parties to Habilain; upheld the kernel of Sayyid Haidara's judgement; and issued a warning that any further talk of shootings would prompt harsh sanctions. Unfortunately, this smack of firm government hit the wrong target. Shaikh Ghanim stalked out of the meeting, leaving Fadhl Muqbil triumphant. I would always have preferred to have that stalwart hillman on my side in a scrap, yet it was essential to remain impartial. In Sayyid Haidara I had found an excellent Ibdali candidate for the Radfan Committee, but I had probably lost Shaikh Ghanim as a valued ally and friend.

Having settled the basic structure of the new Radfan administration by early March, I now addressed the issue of Radfan's reconstruction. Although the campaign had finished months ago, virtually nothing had moved on the ground. What, I wondered, had happened to my Radfan Aid Scheme? And where was the ready cash that the WAP Office had produced after the campaign, to fund anything from widows and orphans relief to outright skulduggery? Digging around, I discovered a covert Rifle Fund whose very existence contravened a post-campaign edict that no tribesman should bear arms, except with POL Habilain's express permission. Apparently my JAA, Bubakr, had been using this to dish out arms and ammunition to his chums. Another fund, originally established to compensate Radfan tribesmen serving with government forces for loss of family property, had become the equivalent of a free-for-all, small-claims court. I consolidated these, and other spare cash, to support future development projects, and to compensate families for accidents caused by unexploded ammunition, as when three Ibdali children were tragically killed when playing with a shell. Claims for such accidents were formally channelled through the appropriate military authority, but these could take months to settle, so prompt payment was preferable.

During the campaign, normal accounting procedures had gone by the board. When I imprudently suggested to Young that Radfan's finances should be put onto a regular basis, he hoist me with my own petard. "Fine," said Robin. "You do just that, and while you're about it, you might as well prepare proper estimates for Radfan, Qutaibi and 'Alawi." This had not been my intention, but it achieved a useful object, for after lumping together the various political funds, my £35,000 Radfan Aid Scheme moneys, a £14,500 "pot" to buy grain for upland farmers, and a hitherto closet £21,000 Reserve Grant to sink three tube wells in the Wadi Taym, I reckoned that I had well over £70,000 (perhaps £1.5 million in today's money) for reconstruction and development.

But what I had not taken on board were the not-so-simple mechanics of translating paper proposals into the real thing. Wondering what had happened to the well-drilling equipment, pumps and other items which I assumed had been ordered months before for my Radfan Aid Scheme, I flew down to Aden to confront Wilson-Jones, the Ministry of Agriculture's Director. "Nothing like that will have been ordered, unless you gave us precise details of the terrain to be drilled, and the location and depth of existing wells," he confessed. "Without that information, we couldn't possibly have given the Crown Agents the necessary specifications to ship the stuff out here."

"But did no one in the WAP Office raise this with you?" I protested. "Radfan's rehabilitation is one of the Federation's most urgent priorities."

Wilson-Jones shook his head. It was that all-too-familiar story of a communications breakdown.

In Radfan's case, we were not even leaning against an open door. When not otherwise feuding and fighting, the Radfanis were settled farmers, not Bedouin, who practised a relatively sophisticated agricultural economy. Although much of the best land was now being used to grow *qat*, mainly for the Thumair suq, millet, wheat, barley and more staple crops were also easily grown, as well as, given enough water, tobacco, sisal, bananas, limes, melons, pawpaw, onions, chives, radishes, tomatoes, olives, almonds and walnuts. Coffee sometimes found its way to Aden, and in the rich alluvial lowland basins of the Taym and Danaba, good-quality cotton was marketed through, though mainly for the sole profit of, the Lahej Cotton Board. Radfan's basic problem was lack of water. Rainfall, scanty and confined to the summer months, usually came in cloudbursts which could indiscriminately sweep away soil, stones and vegetation down the steep, narrow wadis in violent spates, stripping the land bare. Run-offs were partially conserved by *birkah*s, but these tended to dry up in summer, and the underlying solid rock made it difficult to tap subsurface water. The keys to Radfan's agricultural development were wells and pumps.

The Director and I worked out the details of a structured loan scheme, how best to harness local well-digging expertise, and provide a spares back-up service. We agreed that I should make a preliminary inspection of selected lowland areas to collate general information about spate flows, existing well locations and irrigated acreages. Wilson-Jones and his experts would make their professional assessment later in the month. To avoid another equipment hiatus, he agreed to order ten standard Petter diesel pumps, two tractors and basic well-digging equipment immediately. Later that day, I got Robin Young to transfer the necessary funds into the Dhala' Amirate account.

The two lowland areas offering the best prospects for profitable agricultural development were the Danaba Basin and the Wadi Taym. I chose the Danaba for my first recce, though with some misgivings. The main tribe in this area were the Hujaili, the third largest in Radfan, with an estimated 600 fighting men. They had been amongst the first to engage British forces, had stubbornly defended the Rabwa Pass, and had only surrendered last October. Their territory was still so contentious that a British infantry company was permanently stationed at a forward base known as Monk's Field. This could only be reached safely by helicopter because of mining. However, restrictions now imposed on Area West meant that only two Scout helicopter flights per week, not exceeding three hours' duration, were available, so advance booking was essential.

One sunny morning, I flipped over the mountains, and twenty minutes later touched down at the Monk's Field airstrip. The Danaba Basin, overlooked by redoubts known to British Forces as Coca Cola, Gin Sling and Cap Badge, had a hostile, sullen atmosphere, quite unlike anything I had experienced in upland Radfan. Next morning, after an uneventful night with the resident Coldstream Guards company, I set off on foot with a comfortingly large escort of guardsmen to inspect the ground and make personal contact with the Hujaili and Daibani chiefs. Neither had attended the Tribal Conference, and the Hujaili had a particular axe to grind as both their campaign leaders, Shaikh Muhammad Thabit and his son, Fadhl, had been killed in the fighting. Their deaths had not only created great resentment, but had also triggered a bitter internal squabble over succession. The new Hujaili Shaikh, Muhammad Othman, had refused to meet me in Habilain, so I had given him advance warning of this visit. When we reached his village, it was deserted save for a few old men. Shaikh Muhammad had left a message that my presence was not welcome, a snub that confounded traditional tribal hospitality, and boded ill.

As we moved on into Daibani territory, I advised my escort commander to maintain high alert. The overtly friendly reception by the Daibani shaikh, Ali Mana, reflected the lowly status of his tribe's hundred men-at-arms. Even so, the Daibani were reputed to be good workers. As we drank tea together, Shaikh Ali, an unprepossessing, shifty type, strenuously denied any involvement with the fighting, and swore undying loyalty to Amir Sha'fal. Having made this declaration, he demanded generous aid to rebuild his country.

I knew that he was lying on both counts. His complaint – "My young men have all gone away" – and the fact that twelve houses as well as the mosque in his village, Nagaffah, had been severely damaged, said it all.

Nonetheless, I promised to give his farmers loans to sink new wells, and threw in a pump for his personal use. He showed neither pleasure nor displeasure. But why should he have done? We had destroyed 65 percent of his building stock, and scattered his young men to the winds. Just as I was leaving, he pressed a scruffy envelope into my hand. "Please take this to Mr Young. It is a letter from Amir Sha'fal. He has recommended that I be given one rifle and a box of ammunition as a reward for my loyalty." Arms were officially proscribed in Radfan. Also, I knew perfectly well that Amir Sha'fal deeply mistrusted Shaikh Ali. I sent the letter to Young anyway, for by such means was South Arabia still governed.

The last tribal area on my visiting list was that of the Dairi. As one of two tribes which had not yet formally surrendered, they had been forbidden to return to their lands. Their leader had absconded to the Yemen, leaving one Ali Nasser and his family as the tribe's only representatives *in situ*. They had been allowed to stay, only on the basis of Ali Nasser's claim to have assisted the British Army during the operation. On the strength of this, some units had employed him as an unofficial intelligence agent. The Coldstream had formed a less favourable opinion. Within a week of their arrival at Monk's Field, two guardsmen had been killed when a guerrilla mortar scored a direct hit. The unit had become doubly wary after discovering that, during this and a subsequent night attack, Ali Nasser had conveniently absented himself to Thumair.

I went to Ali Nasser's house to question him about these incidents. Predictably he denied all knowledge but, as we were about to leave, my escort discovered three men skulking around at the back of the house.

"Who are these men, Ali Nasser?" I demanded. "They are not members of your family, so have no right to be here."

"I had never seen them before, until they came to my house last night," he replied. "Is it not customary to give shelter to strangers?"

After rigorous questioning, he eventually admitted that one of the men was the brother of Fadhl Muhsin Mahla'i, a member of the other Radfan tribe that had not yet surrendered, and a prime suspect for the recent attacks on Monk's Field.

"So, you are harbouring terrorists, Ali Nasser?"

He denied this hotly, but I did not know how much further I could usefully pursue this line of interrogation, so ordered the three men to leave the area immediately. Minutes after they had slunk off, I realized that I should have had them arrested on the spot. Angry with myself, I warned Ali Nasser that if there were any further security incidents in Dairi territory, he and his family would be banished. Inevitably, there were. But I was reluctant to act. The war had not been of his choosing. In its aftermath, all Radfanis shared a common cause. Our job was to put the pieces back.

Wilson-Jones and his team came, saw and went. He remained enthusiastic about the Danaba's potential, but having tested the water for myself I knew that this scheme was doomed. The Hujaili remained hostile; the Dairi had not surrendered; and NLF guerrilla groups were based in Jebel Halmain, only a few miles to the north. The approaches up the Wadi Rabwa were only too easily mined; the cost of lifting in heavy equipment by air was beyond contemplation; and no well-drilling team would have lasted long in the Danaba without massive military protection. The whole scheme was unviable. I blamed myself for having picked the wrong place at the wrong time.

If the Danaba had proved a damp squib, I was determined to make a success of the Wadi Taym. This was an equally fertile wadi to the north and east of the main Radfan massif, and had once been its most densely populated area. Its principal tribe, the Ibdali, along with scattered sections of the Hujaili, mustered between them 2,000 fighting men, almost 40 percent of Radfan's male population. All had fought bravely against the British, so it was critically important to keep them on side. Control of the Taym had always been a prime military objective as it bestrode the ancient caravan route to dissident strongholds in Upper Yafa'i to the north-east. In consequence, much time and treasure had been expended building an all-weather road into it. After his tribe's surrender, the Ibdali Shaikh had willingly co-operated, whereas the Hujaili Shaikh remained stubbornly hostile. Nonetheless, Young had approved Somerfield's earlier recommendation that we should buy three very expensive International tractors to get things moving. Two had been presented to the Ibdali Shaikh, and the other to the Hujaili Shaikh on the basis of "gentlemen's loans", to be repaid by instalments over two years. The very concept was risible. When I wrote to the Ibdali Shaikh to remind him that his first instalment was long overdue, he expressed outrage that his tractors should be regarded as anything but outright gifts, and that my demand impugned his honour. The Hujaili Shaikh never bothered to reply.

I knew only too well that neither "loan" would ever be repaid, but was more concerned that this short-term fix threw away our one political ace, a reputation for even-handedness. Favouritism to one tribe only aroused hatred, envy and malice. In any event, it was pointless to dish out expensive equipment to people who had no idea how to handle it. The British Army was ever-generous in giving basic training to drivers, but it was impossible to conjure up competent local mechanics capable of maintaining unfamiliar and sophisticated equipment. Sure enough, all three tractors were soon run into the ground, and then abandoned. This process would repeat itself indefinitely, unless we gave the farmers proper training, and built maintenance workshops.

But I wasn't going to give up on the Taym, not just for the loss of three tractors. A hydrological survey, made at the beginning of the year by Professor Moseley of Birmingham University, had confirmed that this alluvial basin held huge reserves of underground water. On his evidence, the WAP Office had already allocated £21,000 to sink three tube wells, and, having already earmarked two-thirds of my Radfan Aid Scheme for well drilling generally, we had enough money in the kitty to begin operations. And when Lt.-Col. Holmes, commanding 24 Field Squadron Royal Engineers, agreed in principle to lend us full Sapper support, we had the necessary expertise also.

But then, for reasons never explained, the promised Royal Engineers assistance was deferred. Although, as a stopgap, 24 Field Squadron's admirable SQMS Wells agreed to deploy his small Habilain team to repair and dig surface wells, impetus had been lost. Even greater frustration followed when the

Ministry of Agriculture informed me that the ten diesel pumps, that I assumed Wilson-Jones had ordered, could not be delivered without still further detailed information on well and water depths, earth composition, proposed usage and population densities.

After an initial emotional explosion, I blamed myself for not having kept up the pressure on Al-Ittihad at every turn. When I had collected myself, the prospect of this scheme slipping away triggered a frenzy of activity. For several days, I rushed around the Wadi Taym frantically collating the necessary information, and by the end of April had submitted a detailed report and equipment order, this time direct through Robin Young, for immediate delivery. Only then, did I discover that the Royal Engineers had already made a comprehensive Radfan well-location report, and that the Army Intelligence Corps had also compiled a land utilization map the previous year. This lack of liaison, allied to the Federal bureaucracy's failure to deliver the cement so badly needed to repair Radfan's reservoirs, wells and houses, almost led me to despair. Morale was restored by a direct appeal for help to the Commander-in-Chief, General Sir Charles Harington. Then, as if by magic, a couple of British Army lorries brought the stuff up by road within a couple of days.

If the business of getting Radfan's reconstruction off the ground was proving frustrating, my experience the tiny 'Alawi Shaikhdom went some way to compensate. 'Alawi, admitted to the Federation only that March, occupied a sixty-mile-square pocket of land squeezed in between Qutaibi and Haushabi territory. Its 3,000 independent-minded, hard-working farmers lived in harmony with the soil, and had little love for their disputatious neighbours. If their ruler, Shaikh Salih bin Sayil, was to be believed, they had taken no part in the recent fighting. As a token, Young had promised the Shaikh generous aid, and presented him with 50 rifles, "to give benefit to your tribesmen who remained loyal to Government". I had no reason to doubt the Shaikh's loyalty, but took the liberty of asking him if he would kindly send me, at his convenience, a list of all those who had benefited from this largesse.

Shaikh Salih took no offence and, the next time I visited him, I brought along Wilson-Jones with me to assess 'Alawi's agricultural potential. The 'Alawi plain, watered by spates coming off the Radfan mountains, was divided into ten separate agricultural areas which grew wheat, maize, millet, sesame, limes, pawpaw, citrus fruits and cotton. The soil was fertile but rainfall irregular, so only one annual crop was normally possible. Wilson-Jones was convinced that if 'Alawi's underground water reservoirs could only be tapped by tube wells, its subsistence economy could be transformed. Transport and marketing should pose no problems, for once the Dhala' Road had been completed, Aden would only be one and a half hours away.

Shaikh Salih had none of the hang-ups and chips that hallmarked many Radfan tribal leaders. Further, while most Federal rulers rode the wheel of fate, Shaikh Salih was a self-starter. He had already built a rudimentary secretariat and school; raised a bank loan to purchase a bulldozer and sink three wells; and had also persuaded the Royal Engineers to clean out and recement old wells, install gabions and help train local masons. Impressed by his initiative, the WAP Office had approved a £5,000 CD&W scheme to dig and deepen surface wells, buy pumps, and make small grants to selected farmers.

Determined not to repeat previous mistakes, I went over this proposed scheme with Wilson-Jones and a toothcomb. We concluded that the business of prospecting for surface wells without a preliminary survey was likely to be abortive, so recast the original scheme to include a programme of test drills to establish the depth of the water table, and only then sink tube wells. I found a Lahej contractor willing to do the job at a fixed price, warning him that if anything went awry, Amir Abdullah would put the screws on him. The only snag was the significantly increased cost. When I explained this to Shaikh Salih, he asked me to review his state estimates to see how we might raise the extra money. At our closing meeting with Young at Al-Ittihad, Shaikh Salih formally approved the new £16,500 tube well scheme funded by the CD&W scheme's £5,000, the whole of his Federal grant, a tranche of 'Alawi State funds, and his own generous personal contribution. I thought back ruefully on all the past battles I had fought to get development schemes off the ground. No ruler I ever met in South Arabia was as enlightened as Shaikh Salih bin Sayil.

15

Arabian Exit

N O ADMINISTRATIVE, POLITICAL, economic or agricultural progress was ever going to be achieved in South Arabia without peace. In Radfan, this had been frustrated by tribal warfare and anarchy for more than a thousand years. To pacify this turbulent land, Britain had fought a campaign at a cost vastly in excess of anything it had spent on Aden's hinterland over the previous 125 years. Although condemned by Britain's enemies as "imperialist oppression", and criticized by others as a political blunder, the Radfan Operation had indisputably brought a measure of peace, at least for the time being.

The British Army was still holding the ring. As POL Habilain, my job was not only to consolidate administratively what had been achieved on the battlefield, but also to give guidance to the military on political issues. It was never easy to draw hard and fast lines between these two aspects of the work, but to be of any use it was essential to establish a good working relationship with both the British and Arab military commanders. Radfan's security and the defence of the Habilain base were the responsibility of three separate military arms: the British Armed Forces, the Federal National Guard, and the Radfan Tribal Levies. When I first took over, there was uncertainty about the precise roles of the Arab forces, and although all three arms were eventually brought under the overall command of Area West's Commander, Colonel Kettles, effective integration was never achieved.

Overwhelmingly the most important security force was the British infantry battalion, backed up by British artillery and armoured units. The business of getting on with its officers and men, and understanding their role, was immeasurably helped by the fact that almost every Assistant Adviser serving in the WAP had previous military service. He also knew the language, the area and its people, and his tours of duty generally lasted at least six months. By comparison, British battalions usually changed round every four to six weeks.

Many of Radfan's continuing military problems stemmed from external factors. At both the highest and local operational levels, there were basic policy differences, and a marked lack of liaison between the British Government, the Chiefs of Staff, the High Commission, Middle East Command, and the Federal rulers. As a result, civilian and military objectives were not always consonant. There was also some confusion about the true nature of the enemy and how best to deal with him. The threat posed by NLF gangs, still referred to in some quarters as "dissidents" or "local malcontents" rather than well-trained guerrillas, directed and led by battle-hardened commanders, was either over- or underestimated. The Labour Government's lukewarm attitude to the Federation and its sensitivity to world opinion was reflected in a Ministry of Defence directive, issued that January, which ordained that, in future, the British forces' role was to be defensive rather than offensive. Although the Radfan operation was officially over, sporadic guerrilla activity had never ceased, and in a theatre where unforeseen exigencies were the norm and improvised tactics essential, aggressive patrolling and swift retaliatory action, rather than reluctant acquiescence, should have been the military's imperatives.

At local level, British battalion commanders sometimes adopted a different tactical approach to that of Area West. Individual regiments had disparate views on the reliability of local forces, and the cultural gulf between British soldiers and the local population offered scope for misunderstanding. The average British soldier had a healthy respect both for the tribesmen who had fought so bravely against him, and for the stoical older generation who were left behind to till their war-torn lands. This attitude was markedly different to that of the cigar-chomping US Army delegation of hard-bitten Vietnam veterans to whom I made one Area Presentation, and who made no pretence of being underwhelmed by our failure to inflict heavier casualties on "the enemy". Even so, when British soldiers, undertaking what was supposed to be a peace-keeping operation, were mortared, shot up and mined, their sympathies could soon turn sour. And however much the Radfanis might yearn for peace after philosophically accepting the war's legacy of ruined houses, wasted crops and slaughtered cattle, few could have harboured warm feelings towards a Christian army of occupation, or the near-invisible Federal Government that did so little to help them.

This underlying local hostility, and our failure to appreciate the extent of NLF subversion, also made it difficult to assess the value of tribal intelligence, on which the military's tactical appreciations had to be based. POL Habilain generally had access to more reliable intelligence sources than his military counterpart, the Battalion Field Intelligence Officer, who tended to be a bird of passage. Yet, as over-devotion to intelligence gathering would have left me little time for anything else, I took the view that the quality of intelligence received was most likely to reflect our progress in reconstructing Radfan.

An effective working relationship with the resident British battalion required a degree of diplomacy, if only because its commanding officer would normally be a seasoned veteran, several years older than the civilian Assistant Adviser. During my time, three British battalions were successively based in Habilain: 45 Royal Marine Commando, 2nd Battalion Coldstream Guards, and 4th Royal Anglians. The Royal Marines had more experience of South Arabian operations than any other serving British unit, having first arrived in Little Aden in 1960. Both they and the Royal Anglians had fought with distinction in Radfan. The Marines had been posted back to Habilain the previous December, under their newly appointed commanding officer, Lt.-Col. Robin McGarel-Groves. Colonel Robin came over as more the soldier-scholar than the gung-ho mountaineering types of my previous acquaintance. Dining at the Marine mess, I was surprised by its unusually restrained atmosphere, and that some subjects of normal conversation were apparently taboo. Half way through my first dinner, a volley of shots sent everyone diving for cover. Order was quickly restored when the attackers were silenced by a formidable artillery weapon, the Mowbat.

Next day, I inspected the nearby ridge at which the Mowbat had directed its fire. From the heap of enemy bullet cases left inside a stone sangar, some way from the shell impacts, the Mowbat had clearly been off-target, so I passed this on at the Area West evening conference. That night, the Marine section commander stationed on the roof of my house asked my permission to bring down the Mowbat's defensive fire on this same sangar, should there be another attack. I assumed this to be a mere formality, so when we came under a barrage of small-arms fire later that night, the Mowbat responded automatically with three mighty rounds. Within minutes, an equally loud blast came down the telephone from McGarel-Groves.

"May I ask who gave permission to fire that weapon?" he demanded icily. "Don't you know that those rounds cost £60 a piece?"

I was more at home with the 2nd Battalion Coldstream Guards, who took over on 15 March under the command of the bluff, no-nonsense Lt.-Col. Iain Jardine. I had served with many of this battalion's young officers at the Guards Training Battalion and, with the furiously red-haired Andrew Napier, now a company commander, had embarked on my first madcap sailing adventure. The success of the Radfan operation had deterred the enemy from engaging the British Army in open warfare, so it had switched to selective guerrilla attacks against the British military camp and my house. Our standard defensive ploy was to respond with heavy artillery and mortar fire, automatically targeting the most frequently used enemy positions, with an NCO stationed on my roof relaying grid references by wireless. This did little to halt the frequency of attacks, and more positive results would have been achieved by adopting that British infantryman's traditional stand-by, the night patrol. Unfortunately, aggressive night patrolling by British units had been proscribed, so I suggested to Colonel Kettles that the Federal National Guard (FNG) might fill the gap.

Originally raised as the Tribal Guards, the FNG's original role had been that of an armed gendarmerie. It had since been upgraded into a frontline defence force. However, unlike the Federal Regular Army, which began as the British- and Indian-officered Aden Protectorate Levies organized and trained on Indian Army principles, the FNG was altogether less structured. Apart from its British commander, it was exclusively Arab-officered, and although some, like Qaid Haidar Al-Habili who had conducted the Wadi Misrah operation, were of excellent quality, others fell somewhat short. Another inherent weakness was that the FNG was divided into two separate forces, FNG I and FNG II, which were never properly integrated. And whereas the former was directly controlled from their Champion Lines HQ, the latter generally operated as disparate state forces, primarily answerable to their respective rulers.

Secure in its stone-built fort, Habilain's FNG I garrison's ostensible role was to act as the base's second line of defence. However, with a garrison strength that fluctuated between 30 and 65, depending on whether or not its

Area Commander was likely to pay a visit, reliability could not be guaranteed. Few British commanders were satisfied with its performance in the field and, being wary that a mere *mulazim,* or lieutenant, should be the FNG's officer-in-charge, all were adamant that he should not attend Area West's confidential evening liaison meetings. This presented me with a potentially embarrassing political situation and so, to keep the FNG on side, I always arranged for a short routine meeting with the *mulazim* before the main one took place. I also persuaded the FNG's Area Commander that his Habilain force should serve directly under the British commander of Area West.

Colonel Kettles supported my suggestion that the FNG should undertake night patrolling three times a week, but when I put this to the *mulazim* he looked dubious. "I will, of course, prepare my men for this task," he said without enthusiasm. "But this is difficult and dangerous work, and we lack proper training." A few days later, he came back to say that the undertaking was impossible, due to lack of manpower. Lack of training was one thing, but this excuse didn't wash. The FNG was currently up to strength, and night patrols were usually undertaken by not more than a dozen men. I could have gone over the *mulazim*'s head, but this would have blackened his face, with unforeseeable consequences. More significantly, this episode confirmed suspicions that the FNG might already have been penetrated by the NLF.

Radfan's third military arm, the Radfan Tribal Levies, was a body of 100 tribesmen, principally Halmainis, but leavened with Ibdalis, Hujailis, Muzahimis and Daibanis. The perceived wisdom was that such a force, if sufficiently well rewarded, might play a useful role patrolling and policing selected areas. The contrary view, held by most British units, was that this tribal ragbag was wholly unreliable. On balance, I reckoned that it was better to retain than disband it, if only to give employment to some, and put more money into circulation.

That the Halmainis were not strictly a Radfan tribe probably explained why they gave the impression of being our most effective Levy unit, even though few of their commanders had formal military training. They had been given only the vaguest terms of reference, but had the important job of guarding the northern approaches to the Danaba Basin and Wadi Taym. The rugged mountains of Halmain had never been penetrated by the British, and their premier shaikh, Fadhl Muhsin, swore blind that his tribesmen had never been involved in the Radfan fighting. I found this difficult to believe because any enemy guerrilla group coming in from the north must inevitably have traversed his country. Nonetheless, given his importance as a putative ally, I agreed that Halmain should get a special development aid package on condition that the Halmain Levies' section leaders reported to me personally in Habilain at the end of each month to collect their men's pay; accounted fully for all ammunition expended; and submitted written reports on any security incident. After a relatively successful trial period, Young agreed my recommendations that the Halmain and Ibdali Tribal Guards should form the nucleus of a new Radfan Security Force. This was eventually incorporated into the Radfan Federal Guard, and added to the regular Federal payroll.

If reconstituting the Radfan Tribal Levies was a minor success, the Qutaibi Tribal Guards (QTG) experiment was a disaster. Somerfield had originally proposed that the QTG be established as a local Habilain defence force, consisting of 30 men, each armed with a rifle and 260 rounds of ammunition. Although Young had instructed that this force be recruited by early February, it was still in limbo when I took over. Given the Qutaibis' past record, I insisted that before it was formally raised, its terms of reference and operational area must first be agreed with both Col. Kettles, Commander of Area West, and the British battalion commander; also, that no rifles or ammunition be issued until then. Meanwhile, groups of surly Qutaibi tribesmen mooched around the Thumair suq, complaining bitterly that they had nothing to do and were not even being paid for it.

Another compelling reason for delaying the QTG's formation was the unresolved question of who should command it. Fadhl Muqbil, effectively my sole, if unreliable, guide on Qutaibi matters, strongly pressed the suit of his nephew, Ali Saif Muqbil. I realized that to appoint this slovenly man was inherently risky, for not only was he the son of the imprisoned Shaikh Saif Hasan, but he was also a former enemy combatant who had returned from the Yemen barely three months before. Having cast around for an alternative, I realized that this was yet another case of Hobson's Choice, so appointed him commander on the principle that the poacher might turn gamekeeper. On 18 March, I formally raised the Qutaibi Tribal Guard and incorporated it into the Habilain Defence Force, though reducing its strength from 30 to 25, and its ammunition issue to 50 rounds per man.

We had already established that most of the night attacks on Habilain were the work of guerrilla groups of between 15 and 25 men. They usually took up positions on the nearby Jebel Hamra, some 200 metres to the south-west of my house, from where they would blaze away for half an hour or so before melting away into the night. As the FNG had refused the challenge, I offered the QTG a chance to prove their mettle by mounting nightly patrols to cover this area. Four days after their formation, Ali Saif reported triumphantly that twelve QTG had successfully taken on a much larger enemy patrol. After congratulating him, I asked who these people were and where they came from. "I have no idea," he replied. "There were too many of them to count. We had to fight for our lives."

I smelled a rat and, after probing him for further details, got him to admit that he had not been present himself during the engagement; but he insisted that his men had expended at least 350 rounds, so urgently needed replenishment. When I asked the Coldstream piquet, operating in the same area, to corroborate this story, I was assured that this "action" had been nothing more than a brief exchange of fire involving less than a dozen rounds. When I told Ali Saif that his claim was preposterous, he replied that unless he was given the ammunition, the QTG would be unable to discharge any further duties. I relieved him of his command on the spot, and instructed Fadhl Muqbil to find another leader forthwith.

Next day, a self-styled *mulazim*, Ali Thabit, came to see me claiming to represent the QTG, and demanding that each of *his* men be given 250 rounds. I gave him a chit for 25 and, after sending him on his way, summoned Fadhl Muqbil.

"Who is this Ali Thabit? Did you appoint him leader?" I challenged.

"No," he shot back. "Ali Saif was their leader, and you dismissed him. The men have appointed Ali Thabit."

"Ali Saif lied to me about the ammunition and was insubordinate. Ali Thabit has also lied to me. I want a leader I can trust. I also want the QTG to patrol the Wadi Rabwa tomorrow to stop the Army's telephone line being cut. Would you kindly find such a man by this evening."

Fadhl Muqbil glared at me, turned on his heal, but returned later that afternoon. "The Qutaibi Levies will do nothing more until they are given their ammunition. Your refusal blackens their face."

"Let us be quite clear about this, Fadhl Muqbil," I told him. "I want no more talk about ammunition, and unless you can find a reliable leader, I will disband the Qutaibi Tribal Guard altogether. I will give you until tomorrow morning to think things over."

Next morning, he returned to say that there was no other leader available. With that, I told him to summon the QTG. After they had fallen in, I formally disbanded them, and ordered that they hand in their rifles and ammunition that same day. Most of them did so with bad grace. Nine went missing. Eventually, I got all twenty-five back.

I had probably overstepped the mark, and to have lost the QTG within a week of their formation was more than careless. It might also have earned me a bullet in the back. However, subsequent events made me doubt that their presence would have made a jot of difference to Habilain's security, and indeed, on the following night, my house suffered a tit-for-tat attack. My handling of the situation did not go down well with Young, who complained that I had blackened Fadhl Muqbil's face, with all that this might entail. I felt I had done the right thing, but insisted that we must at least keep our word and pay the QTG for their miserably short service.

This episode shook what remaining faith I had in Fadhl Muqbil. Shortly afterwards, my house was subjected to a more serious and sustained barrage from automatic rifles and light machine guns. Apart from peppering the outside walls, setting some furniture alight and puncturing my favourite Thermos flask, little damage was done. A characteristically rapid response from a Coldstream patrol surprised and wounded at least one of the attackers. The following day, my informants gave me the names of seven members of this gang. One was Ali Saif Muqbil, who was currently living with his uncle, Fadhl Muqbil, in Thumair, with other members also billeted there in local safe-houses. That evening, I cordoned off the entire village with three armoured cars, supported by Coldstream and Federal guardsmen. I also dispatched the Coldstream Field Intelligence Officer with a platoon to conduct a similar operation at the nearby village of Shedada. Thorough searches were made of several houses, but we found nothing. The trap had been sprung.

By now, I had no doubt that Fadhl Muqbil was an NLF collaborator, and that both he and his nephew, Ali Saif, should be arrested and put inside. But without firm corroborative evidence, I was wary about taking precipitate action without Young's clearance. I signalled him the facts, and asked whether suspicion of dissidence was an arrestable Federal offence. It was a silly question, to which I never got an answer.

The guerrilla attacks on Habilain had nuisance value, but caused few casualties. We gave better than we got, and if only the British infantryman had been allowed off the leash, the enemy would have suffered more than a bloody nose. We knew that these gangs operated out of NLF bases in Yemen, from which they would filter down remote Haushabi wadis unopposed, picking up local sympathizers on the way. They would then attack either Habilain or the Royal Engineers road construction camp at Al-Milah. Unfortunately, Haushabi lay outside the operational ambit of Area West, so our crack regiments had to sit tight and get shot at, rather than hit back with aggressive search and destroy tactics. Even so, both the Coldstream and the equally bold Royal Anglians occasionally stretched their remit.

Compared with Habilain, Al-Milah was a soft target because the Haushabi Sultan gave free passage to NLF guerrillas. It beggared belief that the Federal government would do nothing about it. The Bursi had since been replaced by an altogether less dynamic JAA, Abdullah Shaqqa, who, from fear of being mined en route, had refused to attend the weekly liaison meetings with the Royal Engineers which had been set up to provide advance intelligence about prospective guerrilla attacks. I had to fill this gap, help devise counter-guerrilla measures, and adjudicate on a messy and convoluted demarcation dispute that had developed between the Haushabis, Qutaibis and 'Alawis about the ownership of Al-Milah, and the consequent legal entitlement to British Army rent.

The Lahej–Habilain section of the Dhala' Road was still within my remit. Completion date had slipped six months, and the original estimate of £120,000 had risen to £400,000. Yet it had to be finished, for closure would have been of immense propaganda value to the enemy. On the remaining unsealed sections, mining constituted the most serious threat. Many of these cheap and deadly weapons were of British manufacture, left over from the Suez base. The British Army's heavily guarded, strictly disciplined convoys were winning through, and I insisted that our British Agency vehicles must always join such convoys. But it was difficult to make civilian users to do the same, for any travel restrictions were unpopular as bad for trade, and also tarnished the Federal Government's credibility. Anti-mining measures were primarily a military responsibility, yet POL Habilain was expected to provide advance intelligence about those responsible for laying the mines, a virtually impossible task. I employed mine wardens from neighbouring villages to guard designated stretches of the road, with the tried system of sticks and carrots, but it never worked entirely satisfactorily.

A more intractable problem was the mining of unsealed tracks, particularly those linking Habilain to the British Army's forward posts in the Wadi Taym and Danaba. Heavy armour plating, sandbags and roller-bars gave Land Rovers a limited measure of protection except from a direct hit. The Tribal Levy patrols provided some deterrent to mine laying by day, but not by night. I also warned villages along the route that if any mine exploded, or was found in their general vicinity, they would be collectively fined for the first offence, and thereafter imprisoned and evacuated from the area.

A fortnight after issuing this draconian edict, I was travelling up the Rabwa with an armoured patrol of the Inniskilling Dragoon Guards. At Badubain, a tumbledown house with four outbuildings, a mine exploded under the leading Ferret armoured car immediately in front of me. The Ferret was blown bodily off the track. As the dust cleared, its dazed driver eased himself out from the turret unscathed, but one of his crew was seriously injured. I instituted an immediate search of Badubain, now occupied by Khalid Saif Absari and family. In an outhouse we discovered a box of Cordex explosive wire and some plastic explosive. Khalid denied all knowledge of it. The box was dust-covered, so there was no prima facie evidence to link him with this particular mine. However, as this was the fourth incident to have occurred in his area over the past fortnight, I had him arrested and imprisoned and his family banished. Soon afterwards, my house suffered another night attack and, after investigation, I happened to learn the names of those who had planted the Badubain mine. Khalid's was not amongst them. Rough justice, without the panacea of reconstruction, merely exacerbated a growing sense of resentment.

Militarily, the daylight battle had long been won. On patrol, the Coldstream lived up to their regimental motto, "Second to None", despite the cumbersome equipment that put even the fleetest-footed guardsman at a disadvantage against lightly armed, splay-toed, bare-footed tribesmen who covered the roughest ground like chamois. Yet peace was an illusion, as exemplified by our niggling failure to maintain effective land-line communication between HQ Habilain and the Army's forward posts in the Danaba and Wadi Taym. Mobile telephones and satellite links did not then exist, and wireless was so unreliable that day-to-day communication depended on a single telephone line. This was an easy target for the line cutting which became the bugbear of every British battalion commander, and something that POL Habilain was expected to remedy forthwith.

Fadhl Muqbil, of all people, had suggested that I imprison selected villagers for these line-cutting incidents, knowing full well that no one was going to split on the real culprits, and that such measures would only cause resentment. My penalties for line cutting were never as severe as those for mining, and, as with the Dhala' Road, I made each village responsible for guarding a specific stretch, backed by threats of suspension of their *'aqils'* stipends, closure of the Rabwa Pass to the highly suspect camel traffic that came in from Yafa', and ultimately the imposition of a blanket proscription, though it never came to that.

There now emerged a serious external threat to Radfan's security, engendered by a growing suspicion that Whitehall and the Chiefs of Staff no longer considered Radfan worth the candle. Evidence of this came in the form of the Federal Regular Army's unexpected withdrawal from Jebel Hurriyya, the most strategic forward position in Radfan. It was also rumoured that the equally dominant Jebel Sabaha post would soon be abandoned; and, even more alarmingly, that the British forward units at Monk's and Paddy's Field would be pulled back altogether, and that Habilain's British garrison was to be significantly reduced. For the Army, the operational problems caused by overstretch and strict helicopter rationing were exacerbated by the frustrations of official confinement to a strictly demarcated defensive perimeter, and its resources were already being strained to the limit just to maintain the road into the Wadi Taym. If the British Army did pull out, NLF guerrillas would quickly take over, and Radfan's infant administration would be stillborn.

I argued that any further troop withdrawals, before Radfan's administration was firmly established with its own security force, would be disastrous. Fortuitously, a chance card strengthened a weak hand. It was agreed government policy that the British Army's commitment to Radfan could not be reduced until the Dairi and Mahla'i tribes had formally surrendered, as the propaganda value of a British withdrawal without achieving this would have been immense. The Dairi were scattered to the winds, but although the former Mahla'i shaikh had long departed, one of his putative successors was running a shop in Thumair, with another stationed in Habilain as an FNG *mulazim*. Both men assured me that the Mahla'i refusal to surrender had nothing to do with pride or principle, but was simply because no one could agree on the shaikhly succession. The twists and turns of this dynastic dispute were so complex that I could see no way of disentangling them. However, for so long as the Mahla'i were left to argue the toss amongst themselves, no formal surrender was ever likely, so I made no effort to intervene. British and Federal troops were to stay firmly put in Radfan for another two years.

My tour as POL Habilain ended on 25 May 1965. In Lahej, I had been at the Amir Abdullah's beck and call, with Robin Young looking over my shoulder. Here, I had been my own boss, left to my own decisions, and had had to make do with the best and the worst of those "crazy individuals" that Ralph Daly had so accurately predicted would cross my path. The job would have been impossible without the unfailing support of the British Armed Forces, not only for acting as a shield, helping me deal with all manner of alarums and excursions, and providing armed support and helicopters for visits and inspections, but also for laying on transport maintenance, water supplies and other essential services. Combined defence measures, convoy planning, anti-mine and wire-cutting measures added spice to the adventure that had become my daily fare as POL Habilain.

I had realized early on that *keeny meeny*, meat and drink to some of my brother political officers, was never really my thing. On the other hand, I had few scruples about adopting a tough line when fining villages, imprisoning suspects or, perhaps misguidedly, disbanding the Qutaibi Tribal Guard. Arabians are a subtle, finely tuned people, yet they respect strength, and it was important to prove that the government meant business in keeping the peace and enforcing the rule of law. I might have handled Fadhl Muqbil better, but both he and Ali Saif had other loyalties, so our respective objectives could never be consonant. Given more time, I would have recast the Qutaibi budget, effectively set in stone ever since Shaikh Saif had created a hundred-strong civil list chiefly to benefit his chums. At least I had had the small satisfaction of reducing the Ahl Lahram's stipends.

After all the time I had spent preparing the Radfan, Dhala' and 'Alawi aid schemes, as often as not involving fruitless discussions with Federal officials, and all the time spent carrying out mapping, population and agricultural surveys, inspecting innumerable drilling sites, wells, and reservoirs, adjudicating on administrative boundaries, supervising agricultural loans, and raised merry hell just to get hold of grain and cement, it was disappointing that Radfan's agricultural reconstruction had made such slow progress by the time I left.

If I had achieved anything, it was to have laid the foundations of the new

'Alawi and Radfan administrations and to have marshalled the funds for future development. My 1965/66 Radfan budget, approved by Amir Sha'fal as a result of protracted discussions in Dhala' and the invaluable support of Hugh Walker, increased the previous year's £2,000 revenue to £115,850. Of my proposed £100,000 expenditure, 75% would go towards agricultural development. The balance would fund officials' stipends, the Radfan Committee's expenses, the new Radfan Secretariat, Habilain's new fruit and vegetable market, and the crucially important mechanical workshops. These sums were pathetically small, and even at today's depressed values would have bought no more than a half-decent house in London. Yet the healthy surplus of revenue over expenditure might even have justified Ian Baillie's advice, given me five and a half years earlier, that I should "get stuck in to sound administrative procedure".

I did not really believe that I was leaving Habilain until the Commander-in-Chief, General Sir Charles Harington, paid Area West a visit a week before my departure. After inspecting the FNG Guard, he generously allowed himself thirty-five minutes for lunch at my house. I flew up to Dhala' and down to Lahej to make sorrowful farewells to Amir Sha'fal and the Amir Abdullah. Godfrey Meynell arrived soon after to take over as POL Habilain. At dawn the following morning, he was making an indelible mark on the roof by frenetically running on the spot. I scribbled down an account of the Miscellaneous Political Services Fund on a sheet of flimsy and, by way of handover, presented Godfrey with the Radfan, Qutaibi and 'Alawi account cheque books and safe keys. I gave my Arab and Army friends a farewell lunch, and on the eve of my departure was honoured to dine with 45 Royal Marine Commando as their guest.

I had hoped to sail from Aden a couple of days later, first-class on board the Italian Adriatica Line's *Bernina*, with the intention of disembarking at Izmir to join a mountaineering expedition to Turkish Kurdistan. The trunk sent sea-freight from England containing all my climbing equipment went missing and so, after spending five fruitless days searching for it amongst the godowns of the Ma'alla Wharf, I missed the boat. Weeks later, having caught up with my climbing friends, I took lessons in hands-on administration from the Turkish Governor of Hakkiari Province in remotest Kurdistan. I watched in awe as he took the wheel of an enormous bulldozer, which he then drove unflinchingly up the hair-raisingly steep tracks of mountain country even more spectacular than Radfan's. Back in Istanbul, I got news that my brother had gone missing. I dropped everything, and took the first available means of transport to get home.

Just before leaving Aden, I had unburdened myself to Sir Richard Turnbull about my still unresolved career dilemma. Although my South Arabian experiences had left me disillusioned with the British government's muddled policies, which even then seemed doomed to disaster, this last tour had been a revelation. I felt deeply unhappy about resigning at this difficult time, and this was reinforced on reading a letter from Turnbull that awaited my return home. In it, he thanked me for my "years of devoted service in South Arabia. ... The way in which you tackled the numerous problems of Radfan and, at the same time, laid the foundations for an administration in what has been hitherto an uncontrolled area, won the admiration of us all." His closing words, "Should you wish to return to South Arabia at any time, then I am sure that your colleagues will be delighted to welcome you back", threw me into confusion. He suggested that I was missing my vocation, and I knew he might be right.

Not long after my return, they found my brother's body. He had taken his life, aged twenty-seven. His death broke my parents' hearts, and made me reassess my own priorities. I could have gone back to South Arabia even then, but reckoned I had reached the end of that uneven road. A new career awaited me, and I was needed elsewhere. Yet it was difficult to excise that extraordinary place and its remarkable peoples from my mind and, as the situation in Aden deteriorated, I bitterly regretted my decision to resign. A couple of years later, we pulled out anyway, leaving our enemies to triumph and our friends to fend for themselves. All who served in that barren land will have vivid memories of those times. For myself, I came to realize that the romance of Far Arabia was nothing more than a dissolving dream, yet unforgettable nonetheless.

Envoi

THE DOLEFUL CLOSING years of Britain's time in South Arabia have been well chronicled by many authors, and of those cited in the Select Bibliography, several were participants. Even so, this book would not be complete without a summary of those troubled times, and a brief analysis of what went wrong. Harold Wilson's incoming 1964 Labour administration provides a convenient starting point, for this marked the moment when the Federal concept, so assiduously promoted by Trevaskis, was first questioned and then scuppered.

Initially, and notwithstanding the Labour Party's doctrinal objections to imperialism and feudal rule, Wilson pledged support for the Federation on the assumption that this would create a single, independent state, with Britain retaining the Aden base yet still, somehow, maintaining cordial relations with the Arab world. But over the next three years, Britain was confronted by a series of economic crises, culminating in the 1967 sterling devaluation. The US President, Lyndon Johnson, had originally urged Wilson to maintain Britain's overseas military commitments, in return for what amounted to a financial bail-out. Denis Healey's 1965 Defence White Paper affirmed Britain's intention to retain the Aden base, but by then Wilson was beginning to realize that this had become an unsustainable and unaffordable albatross; also, that Johnson's proposed deal would effectively make Britain a client state of the US.

Trevaskis failed to persuade Anthony Greenwood, Labour's Foreign Secretary, to support his policy of maintaining a strong Federation under

British protection, and so, in January 1965, he was sacked and replaced by Turnbull. Greenwood then proposed a wider-based constitutional conference to include Abdullah Al-Asnag, the Egyptian-backed PSP leader, but neither the Federal nor the Hadhrami rulers would agree to participate. By now, Egyptian-backed terrorism was beginning to strangle Aden, and in April Turnbull outlawed the NLF, which had joined a loose political grouping with the PSP and a reinvigorated South Arabian League. As relations between Aden's politicians, the Federal rulers and the High Commissioner deteriorated, Baharoon proffered his resignation, which Turnbull, perhaps unwisely, accepted. Baharoon's successor, Abdul Qawi Meccawi, promptly sided with the revolutionary factions and, having declined to condemn the murder of the Speaker, Arthur Charles, was summarily dismissed by Turnbull, who then reimposed direct British rule.

In November 1965 Lord Beswick, a junior Minister for the Colonies, was dispatched to Aden to reassure the Federal rulers that Britain would honour its treaty commitments. Healey, as Minister of Defence, publicly affirmed this but, within three months, Beswick announced that although the Federal states would be granted independence by 1968, there would be no protective British defence agreement. Healey's February 1966 Defence White Paper confirmed this cynical *volte face*, and signalled Britain's effective abandonment of South Arabia. President Nasser promptly declared that his 70,000-strong Egyptian Army would now remain in the Yemen until Britain had quit both Aden and the Gulf States.

With the ground now cut from under the Federal rulers' feet, security deteriorated throughout the Federation. During 1966 the NLF's infiltration of the tribes quickly spread to the Arab armed forces and the Aden police. A belated British initiative to constitute a unitary state was aborted by events, and the despairing Federal rulers now sought, unsuccessfully, to reach some rapprochement with the revolutionaries, and to enlist Saudi support. In April 1967, an avowedly anti-British United Nations delegation arrived in Aden to recommend means of implementing the UN's pro-nationalist resolutions. However, having refused to deal with the Federal government, it was rebuffed in turn by both by FLOSY and the NLF. In May, Turnbull, having fallen foul of both Lord Shackleton, Labour's Minister without Portfolio, and George Brown, the Foreign Secretary, was sacked, and replaced by Sir Humphrey Trevelyan, whose brief was to organize an ordered British withdrawal and, if possible, leave behind an independent Arab government.

By now, Federal morale and any semblance of Federal government had collapsed. The Egyptian-backed FLOSY openly engaged in ferocious internecine warfare with its hard-left rival, the NLF. In June, the Six Day War humiliated Nasser, so undermining the Egyptian threat to South-West Arabia, but Arab bitterness at this Egyptian defeat only exacerbated anti-British sentiment within Aden and the Federation. The Federal Army mutinied, British forces withdrew from the hinterland, and the NLF progressively took over most states. During July, British civilian and service families were successfully evacuated from Aden, and by September most Federal rulers, having refused to accept Trevelyan's proposals for a reconstituted form of government, fled, only to be pilloried by the Foreign Office for "deserting their posts". Trevelyan was forced to acknowledge the *de facto* rule of the revolutionary forces even though, by October, the Egyptian Army had withdrawn from Yemen. This event, coupled with the Federal Army's declaring for the NLF, destroyed any lingering FLOSY hopes of victory. On 2 November, George Brown announced that South-West Arabia no longer required British protection. On 28 November 1967, Trevelyan, who had personally witnessed most stages in the demise of empire since joining the Indian Civil Service thirty-eight years earlier, boarded an RAF plane bound for England, while the Royal Marine's band struck up *Fings Ain't Wot They Used To Be*. At midnight the following day, the last British troops left Aden aboard HMS *Albion*. Qahtan Al-Shabi, the Lahej-born, Aden College-educated leader of the NLF, returned in triumph to form the People's Republic of South Yemen (PRSY) as its first President.

Rejoicing was short-lived, and those who were to suffer most were the local population. British service deaths in the hinterland over the previous five years had been some 200, with another 1,500 wounded. These casualty figures were roughly comparable with those of the 1982 Falklands campaign, though fractionally more than the 179 British service deaths suffered in Iraq over the six years up to 1 April 2009, the date on which Britain's military command of southern Iraq was ceded to US forces in controversial circumstances. During the 1964–67 insurgency, there were more than 2,000 casualties in Aden State alone, 800 of them British servicemen and civilians and the rest local nationals. But this was nothing compared to the loss of Arab life that occurred during the next twenty-seven years of bloody revolutionary rule. In the immediate aftermath of Britain's withdrawal, the families, friends and supporters of the former rulers who had not already fled, were rounded up, imprisoned and routinely executed. Factional and tribal fighting followed with a spate of executions, revenge murders and wanton killings. In later years, political purges and internecine warfare exacted an even heavier toll.

More damaging was Aden's economic collapse. The closure of the Suez Canal after the Six Day War reduced its trade by 80 percent. Many thousands previously employed at the British base, and by foreign commercial concerns, became jobless overnight. Indians and Somalis left Aden in droves, and the town's population shrank by 100,000. In 1969, a vicious power struggle resulted in the execution of most of the original revolutionaries by their more radical comrades. All banks, insurance companies and trading houses were nationalized, land was redistributed, and commercial agriculture collapsed. After a Marxist coup in 1970, the country was renamed the People's Democratic Republic of Yemen (PDRY), and became the first, and only, Arab communist state. Soviet advisers poured in to make Aden a Russian submarine base, and a launch pad to support the Marxist regime in Ethiopia. In 1978, President Abdul Fatah Isma'il signed a 20-year treaty of friendship with Soviet President Brezhnev, confirming the PDRY's status as a Soviet client state. It had also become a training ground for extreme revolutionary terrorist groups operating in Europe, Japan and Palestine. But by 1986, the regime's harsh, repressive measures had fuelled such factional jealousies and tribal unrest that a violent, though barely reported, civil war had broken out, resulting in many thousand more deaths. The Soviet Union's disintegration in the early 1990s precipitated the PDRY's economic collapse, and between 1990 and 1994 North Yemen forcibly brought into being the unified Republic of Yemen, a federation in all but name. In 1997, the year in which the Royal Yacht *Britannia* visited both Aden and Jeddah, President Ali Abdullah Salih's application to join the British Commonwealth was summarily rejected.

Many Arabs were mystified, and some dismayed, by Britain's precipitate retreat from South Arabia. Disengagement was inevitable and, for several years, 1968 had been the official projected target date. Yet our callous abandonment fell dismally short of the standards achieved during the ten years prior to 1967, when Britain had granted independence to twenty-four of its former colonial territories, generally leaving behind soundly based administrations, stability, law and order. In South Arabia, our legacy was chaos and confusion. Only Palestine offers a comparably disastrous example.

Some reasons for our failure have been advanced in this book. One is also tempted to indulge in historical speculation. For example, what if ex-Sultan Ali Abdul Karim had been reinstated as a Federal figurehead? What if Whitehall had accepted Luce's plan for devolution and independence by 1962? What if Hassan Bayoomi had survived his illness? What if the Conservative government had backed Abdullah Al-Asnag before he became radicalized? What if Labour had lost the 1964 British General Election? What if the Foreign Office had made a more focused effort to enlist Saudi Arabian and American support? And what if a more determined political and military effort had been made to hold the Federation together after Egypt's defeat in the Six Day War?

At the time, many took the view that the Federation might have survived if only the gulf between Aden's prosperity and the Protectorate's poverty had been bridged earlier by more generous British aid. But this was probably unrealistic. The British Empire was founded on mercantilism. Aden prospered because it was strategically important in maintaining trade with India and the Far East. By contrast, its hinterland was bereft of natural resources, so pacification and development would always have been immensely expensive. After the Second World War, when Britain was almost bankrupt, a remarkable and largely successful effort was made to pacify the Protectorate, and a measure of development was also achieved. However, by the 1960s HM Treasury was determinedly averse to sinking any more British taxpayers' money into Arabia's shifting sands than it could possibly help.

Even so, it should still have been possible to achieve a better end-result, particularly as the political challenge came from Arab nationalism rather than Islamic fundamentalism. Unfortunately, the Federal Constitution, skewed in favour of feudal rulers who were generally unfitted for modern government, was fatally flawed, and the rulers themselves undermined by Labour's doctrinaire antipathy towards them. British and Federal intelligence initially failed to identify the nature and extent of terrorist infiltration, but effective counter-terrorist measures were then handicapped by the Labour government's determination to appease Arab and Third World opinion. Likewise, its irresolute and inconsistent military policies effectively tied the British Army's hands, when resolute action against FLOSY and NLF terrorists in Aden, and enemy guerrilla bases in the Yemen, might have changed both the Federal Army's and popular perceptions about the final outcome. Ultimately, economic realities exacerbated a failure of British political will. Healey's 1966 Defence White Paper, a flagrant betrayal of trust, dealt a hammer blow to the Federation.

Comparisons can fairly be drawn between South Arabia and the Gulf. In both areas, Britain's original strategic and commercial objectives were broadly similar and were achieved by securing special relationships with backward, feudal rulers; pursuing policies of non-interference with their internal affairs; making little effort to push democratic reforms (save in Aden); and providing the minimum of development aid. But whereas in the Gulf States a measure of shaikhly authority could generally be imposed and upheld, anarchy was endemic in the WAP. The Gulf's rulers might have had periodic border disputes with their powerful neighbour, Saudi Arabia, but for the British in Aden the Yemen frontier was a scene of almost constant unrest. Again, the Yemen Revolution, and the Egyptian invasion in September 1962, had no parallel in the Gulf, while the 1967 Six Day War comprehensively terminated Egypt's wider territorial ambitions.

Personalities too played an important part. In South Arabia, Trevaskis long dominated the scene; but apart from Hassan Bayoomi, Aden produced no local politician of stature, and no Federal ruler seemed either willing or capable of leading his peers. The Gulf States had rulers of authority, and were particularly fortunate in having Sir William Luce as Political Resident for the five critical years 1961 to 1966. Mindful of the problems that beset the South Arabian Federation, Luce promoted an altogether looser concept of Peninsula solidarity under the leadership of Saudi Arabia. Although his scheme was initially rejected by HMG, it prepared the ground, and when, in 1970, Luce was recalled to duty to negotiate Britain's formal withdrawal with the Gulf States, Saudi Arabia and Iran, he not only achieved this object, but also laid the foundations of the United Arab Emirates. Ultimately the most critical factor was the impact of oil, to Arabs, "the gift of God". By 1964, the Gulf was already producing 31 percent of the non-communist world's production, while South Arabia had none. Oil was to transform the Gulf's economy and the life of its peoples, who have prospered mightily and who, for better or worse, are still governed by their traditional rulers.

Aden was by no means Britain's concluding engagement with the Arab World, but our withdrawal from Iraq on 30 April 2009, after a six-year US-led peace keeping operation, might prove to have been the last. This ill-considered venture, based on a false prospectus, cost the lives of an estimated 600,000 Iraqis; left the British taxpayer with a £7 billion bill; and has bequeathed to Iraq, despite its oil, a very uncertain future. Britain's disengagements from both Aden and Iraq were largely impelled by economic crises and military over-stretch. Both served to re-emphasize our dramatic fall from being the Middle East's predominant post-Second World War foreign power, when our governing writ had extended from Egypt, the Sudan, Palestine, Jordan and Iraq, to Aden and the Gulf, to our current status as a pliant American subordinate.

Glossary

'aqil	Leader of a tribal section
atfaddal	"Please", lit. "be preferred"
'ayb	Shame, stigma
bakhsheesh	Alms
bir	Well
birkah	Cistern; small reservoir
charpoy	Wooden bed frame with stringed base
dar	Dwelling, fortified tower house
futah	A garment of cloth worn round the waist
gasab	A cereal crop
ghayl	Spring-fed perennial water
hajj	Pilgrimage
haram	Forbidden; sacred. A sanctuary
huri	Dug-out canoe
husn	A fort, or fortified tower house
'ilb	*Zizyphus spina-Christi*, the Wild Jujube, a common tree of the wadis providing fine timber
imama	Headcloth
inshallah	God willing
jambiyya	The curve-bladed Arab dagger
jol	Barren plateau (EAP)
kassar sharaf	Insult, shaming action, or remark that offends a person's dignity or respect
kawr	Plateau; also used to describe the spectacular 'Audhali escarpment
keeny meeny	Political intrigue, or manoeuvring

kutcha	Shanty dwelling
maidan	Square, or public open space
mansab	Local tribal leader, or dignitary
muezzin	Mosque official who calls the faithful to prayer
mulazim	Army lieutenant
maqaddam	Leader of a fishermen's guild
mushadda	Turban head cloth
nakhoda	Ship's captain
nasrani	Non-believer; lit. "a Nazarene".
naib	Deputy local governor
nawbat	Fortified tower, or lookout
qadi	Judge of *Shari'a* law
qaid	Lieutenant-Colonel
qat	Narcotic leaves of the *Catha edulis* bush, chewed as a stimulant
ramlah	Sand. In the plural, *Ar-Rimal*, "The Sands", i.e. the Rub' al-Khali, or Empty Quarter
rais	Army captain
sahrah	Level sand plain
sanbuq	Type of dhow, fishing boat
sangar	Stone wall fortification
sayyid, pl. *sada*	A descendant of the Prophet
sayl	A flash flood
Shari'a	Islamic Law
sharif, pl. *ashraf*	A descendant of the Prophet; head of certain Arabian ruling families
shaqq	Depression between sand dunes
suq	Market
waraga	Document, paper
waqf	A religious trust or charitable endowment
ziyara	A fair; lit. "visit" to a shrine, often associated with a fair

Select Bibliography

Aithie, Patricia, *The Burning Ashes of Time: From Steamer Point to Tiger Bay.* Bridgend: Seren, 2005

Allfree, P. S., *Hawks of the Hadhramaut.* London: Robert Hale, 1967

Anon., *Welcome to Aden.* Nairobi: Guides & Handbooks of Africa Publishing, 1961

Balfour-Paul, Glencairn, *The End of Empire in the Middle East.* Cambridge: Cambridge University Press, 1991

Belhaven, Lord (The Hon. R. A. B. Hamilton), *The Kingdom of Melchior.* London: John Murray, 1949

—— *The Uneven Road.* London: John Murray, 1955

Botting, Douglas, *Island of the Dragon's Blood.* London: Hodder & Stoughton, 1958

Boustead, Sir Hugh, *The Wind of Morning.* London: Chatto & Windus, 1971

Brent, Peter, *Far Arabia: Explorers of the Myth.* London: Weidenfeld & Nicolson, 1977

Bury, G. Wyman ("Abdullah Mansur"), *The Land of Uz.* London: Macmillan, 1911. Reprinted Reading, UK: Garnet, 1998.

Crouch, Michael, *An Element of Luck: To South Arabia and Beyond.* London: Radcliffe Press, 1992

Fielding, Xan, *One Man in His Time: The Life of Lieutenant-Colonel N.L.D. ("Billy") McLean.* London: Macmillan, 1990

Foster, Donald, *Landscape With Arabs: Travels in Aden and South Arabia.* Brighton: Clifton Books, 1969

Furse, Sir Ralph, *Aucuparius: Recollections of a Recruiting Officer*. Oxford: Oxford University Press, 1962

Gavin, R. J., *Aden under British Rule, 1839–1967*. London: Hurst & Co, 1975

Great Britain, Admiralty, *Western Arabia and the Red Sea*. London: Naval Intelligence Division, Geographical Handbook Series, 1946

Groom, Nigel, *Sheba Revealed: A Posting to Bayhan in the Yemen*. London: London Centre of Arab Studies, 2002

Hartley, Aidan, *The Zanzibar Chest: A Memoir of Love and War*. London: HarperCollins, 2003

Hinchliffe, Peter, John T. Ducker and Maria Holt, *Without Glory in Arabia: The British Retreat from Aden*. London: I.B. Tauris, 2006

Hickinbotham, Sir Tom, *Aden*. London: Constable, 1958

Holden, David, *Farewell to Arabia*. London: Faber & Faber, 1966

Ingrams, Harold, *Arabia and the Isles*. London: John Murray, 1942

Ingrams, Doreen, *A Time in Arabia*. London: John Murray, 1970

Johnston, Sir Charles, *The View from Steamer Point: Being an Account of Three Years in Aden*. London: Collins, 1964

Knox-Mawer, June, *The Sultans Came to Tea*. London: John Murray, 1961

Kour, Z. H., *The History of Aden, 1839–1872*. London: Frank Cass, 1981

Ledger, David, *Shifting Sands*. PLACE: Peninsula Publishing, 1983

Little, Tom, *South Arabia: Arena of Conflict*. London: Pall Mall Press, 1968

Longhurst, Henry, *Adventure in Oil: The Story of British Petroleum*. London: Sidgwick & Jackson, 1959

Lord, Cliff, and David Birtles, *The Armed Forces of Aden, 1839–1967*. Solihull: Helion, 2000

Macintosh-Smith, Tim, *Yemen: Travels in Dictionary Land*. London: John Murray, 1997

Morris, James, *Farewell the Trumpets: An Imperial Retreat*. London: Faber & Faber, 1978

Naumkin, Vitaly, *Red Wolves of Yemen: The Struggle for Independence*. Cambridge: Oleander Press, 2004

O'Kelly, Sebastian, *Amedeo: A True Story of Love and War in Abyssinia*. London: HarperCollins, 2002

Paget, Julian, *Last Post: Aden 1964–1967*. London: Faber & Faber, 1969

Ponting, Clive, *Breach of Promise: Labour in Power, 1964–1970*. London: Hamish Hamilton, 1989

Reilly, Sir Bernard, *Aden and the Yemen*. London: HMSO, 1960

Phillips, Wendell, *Qataban and Sheba: Exploring the Ancient Kingdoms on the Biblical Spice Routes of Arabia*. London: Victor Gollancz, 1955

Scott, Hugh, *In the High Yemen*. London: John Murray, 1942

Stark, Freya, *The Southern Gates of Arabia: A Journey in the Hadhramaut*. London: John Murray, 1936

—— *A Winter in Arabia*. London John Murray, 1940

—— *The Coast of Incense: Autobiography 1933–1939*. London: John Murray, 1953

Thesiger, Wilfred, *Arabian Sands*. London: Longmans, Green & Co., 1959

Trevaskis, Sir Kennedy, *Shades of Amber: A South Arabian Episode*. London: Hutchinson, 1968

Trevelyan, Sir Humphrey, *The Middle East in Revolution*. London: Macmillan, 1970

—— (1980) *Public and Private*. London: Hamish Hamilton, 1980

Villiers, Alan, *Sons of Sindbad: An Account of Sailing with the Arabs in their Dhows*. London: Arabian Publishing, 2006

Walker, Jonathan, *Aden Insurgency: The Savage War in South Arabia 1962–1967*. Staplehurst: Spellmount, 2005

Waterfield, Gordon, *Sultans of Aden*. London: John Murray, 1968

Waugh, Evelyn, *When The Going Was Good*. Middlesex: Penguin Books, 1951

Index

NOTE: In alphabetizing, Al- is ignored. Where the family name is known, members are indexed under it.